BRING 'EM BACK ALIVE SID

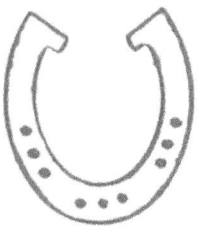

THE LIFE AND TIMES OF SHERIFF WILLIAMS

DON R. WILLIAMS

Table of Contents

Dedication...7

Forward 7

Acknowledgments 9

About the Author...9

Introduction and Summary 10

PART 1 - DAD'S PREDECESSORS 11

C.P. Williams and Martha Campbell 13

Getting a Civil War Pension 16

Captain Billy Williams & Robert Williams 36

The Early Williams Families 45

Paleolithic Ancestors..45

PART II - DAD'S ENTREPRENEURIAL PURSUITS 49

Preemptions, Homesteads, and Ranching in Nebraska, South Dakota & Wyoming.... 53

The Preemption Homestead 53

Other Enterprises & The Indian Scarc of 1890-91............................58

Sid As A Cowhand..58

Foremen of the Circle Bar (0-) Ranch 59

The Lost Six Shooter...60

A Bad Injury 60

The Battle of Lightning Creek-Last Indian-White Skirmish on the High Plains 60

Ranches and Other Properties 64

Ardmore Ranch 64

Webberville Property, Michigan 64

Bourret Ranch 64

Woodruff Ranch 65

The Dryer Ranch 65

The Wyoming Ranch 65

Marriages 67

Cattle and Horse Drives 71

The Agricultural Depression of the 1920's and '30's 72

Disposal of the Ranches 78

PART III - YOUR GRANDDAD'S SPORTING CAREER 79

Racing Thoroughbred Horses 81

The Early Years 81

Racing During the Depression 85

The Ak-Sar-Ben Fire 85

Donald W. Wins 86

Donald W. Sets South Dakota Track Record 86

Sid's Last Big Win. 90

The Last Horses 91

Racing in Canada 91

Media Attention 91

Other Williams Family Members in Racing 95

4 Generations of WILLIAMS FAMILY In Nebraska Horse Racing 93

    Rob Williams - Nebraska Veteran Williams Gets Ride In Breeders' Cup 96

    Nebraska Native John Nerud Will Not Boycott
    Race Awards Party This Time 97

    Maintaining A Sharp Edge 98

Sid's Baseball Team 99

PART IV - SID'S OTHER ACTIVITIES 101

Sid Williams-Cattle Buyer, Dealer & Brand Inspector 103

PART V - SID'S LAW ENFORCEMENT CAREER 107

Early Law Enforcement Events 109

    The Doc Middleton Affair 109

    The Killing of Harry Williams 110

    More On Middleton 110

    The Bob Wallace Incident 113

    The Stolen Car 113

    The Foiled Robbery 114

The Noble Experiment That Failed 114

Sheriff Sid Williams Liquor Law Enforcement Policy 115

Harrison Sun News Items 117

Chasing a Horse Thief and Catching a Bride 122

Liquor Law Raid & Arrests 126

The Dan Jordan Raid 131

The Jordan and Williams Family Relationships 131

More on the Jordans 134

Large Still Captured 138

Stills Destroyed 139

A Most Persistant Moonshiner 152

PART VI - OTHER LAW ENFORCEMENT ACTIVITIES 165

"BRING 'EM BACK ALIVE SID"- Earning The Title 169

Charles Zimmerman Ambushed And Shot By A Neighbor 172

Frank & John Parsons Arrested For Cattle Stealing 179

The Mexican Murder Case 181

Russell – "I'll Never Be Taken Alive" 202

Fire & Death Threat Used To Extort Money From Rancher 221

Lone Bandit Killed Following Holdup Of Bank 238

Sheriff Williams Picks Up Two-Gun Man Wednesday 251

Your Granddad's Final Illness & Death 255

PART VII - OTHER EVENTS AND INCIDENTS 259

A Skeleton In Our Closet 261

The Liver, Ear, Mudhole and Other Incidents 266

CONCLUSIONS REGARDING
THE LIFE OF YOUR GRANDDAD, SID 268

APPENDIX

Appendix A: C.S. Williams Additional Homestead Documents 271

Appendix B: Martha Williams Additional Affidavits For Civil War Pension 285

Appendix C: Charles M. Russell Additional Legal Documents Arrest #1 1931 297

Appendix D: Charles M. Russell Arrest #2 1932 303

Appendix E: Charles M. Russell Arrest #3 1937 313

INDEX 323

BIBLIOGRAPHY 337

Dedication

This book is written to and for the benefit of my children, Sidney, Steven, Judy, Jeffrey and Donald, and it is dedicated to all the lesser known pioneers, homesteaders, cowboys, cattlemen, law enforcement officers and others who contributed so much to the development of the west and this country.

Forward

Your mother and I have watched with intense interest, satisfaction and enjoyment in seeing the five of you grow up and develop into first class professional citizens, contributing to your communities, and nation, and guiding the development of your own families.

I think you should know about the trials, tribulations and sacrifices your predecessors went through to bring us to this point in time of unprecedented personal freedom and prosperity.

Fortunately, you kids knew three of your grandparents and something of their life histories. I know how important it is for a child to have an association with their grandparents. This comes from my own experience. I knew only one of my grandparents, Adaline (Rogers) Sturdivant, and I had a close relationship with her. She told me many stories of the early days of cowboys, Indians, storms, homesteading hardships, the Johnson County, Wyoming cattle war between the small cattlemen and the cattle barons, etc., and I soaked up every bit of it.

However, I always felt a deep void because I never knew my other three grandparents and I often wondered what wonderful stories they could have told. It is for this reason that I decided to record on paper everything I know about my dad and your granddad, Charles Sidney Williams Sr., the grandparent you never knew.

My dad was a great story teller, but being not yet nine years old when he was called away, a great deal of what he said has been forgotten or lost. However, I was able to gather quite a few facts from my half-brothers, Sid Jr., Floyd (Stuffy) Williams and my half-sister, Ethel Downey, and from others that were acquainted with dad. Some published information was made available to me in 2002. I am the only one with some of this knowledge and if I don't set it down on paper it will be lost when I am gone. Therefore, that is one of the reasons for this biography.

Some of the incidents and stories provided by others are vague as to time, place, and other details, but I have no reason to doubt the information and voracity of the informers and I will tell it as it was told to me. And although dad had many admirable qualities, I will not shirk

7

from describing his few faults and will describe his personality and character to the best of my ability.

A secondary reason for doing this project is to prove or disprove a wild and implausible story that I have heard from a few individuals during the past 50+ years. The story goes that your granddad set out to arrest Charley Russell, a Sioux County rancher, that had served time in the penitentiary for an alleged murder and who had a proclivity for feuding with his neighbors. Russell said that he would never again spend time in jail and that he never intended to be taken alive.

The story goes that your granddad, county sheriff, went to the Russell Ranch to make the arrest on complaint of assault with firearms. As Sid approached the ranch entryway a dynamite blast blew up a fence gate post. Russell hollered out a warning that the next blast was for the sheriff. Thereby, Russell thwarted arrest. My plan was to research the courthouse records and newspapers of the time in question to the extent possible. My suspicion was that the story was a figment of Russell's imagination and that the story was propogated by those sympathetic to Russell and by those resenting law enforcement authority. Dad was never known to back down from anyone. My conclusion, based on the results of this research, is discussed in a later section.

Thus, with limited literary and journalistic ability I have undertaken this very difficult project. I have compiled the newspaper and magazine articles, courthouse arrest warrants and other legal documents; stories as told by relatives, old timers, other individuals and my own recollections.

Acknowledgments

Acknowledgment is made to the staff members of the Harrison Nebraska Museum, the Sioux County Historical Society, namely Meredith Bixler, Doris Wickersham, and others who provided assistance to me while assembling the data for this book. Also, thanks goes to Virginia Coffee and other Sioux County residents who provided encouragement in this endeavor.

Thanks is also due to the County Clerk's office staff that helped me find some of the information; the late Sioux County Sheriff Deputy, Rick Mounts that made the jail house records available.

A special thanks is due to my daughter, Judy Hoos who typed the manuscript and facilitated it through the various processes in the final publication of this book.

About the Author

Don Williams (Master of Science Degree, University of Illinois), retired petroleum geologist, enjoyed a forty year career in the industry as an oil and gas exploration geologist, working primarily for Monsanto Company and Kerr McGee Corporation. Later in his career, in addition to subsurface work, he was responsible for the training of newly graduated and hired geologists in the art and science of subsurface exploration. Also, in his latter working years he was an independent geologist as well as a consultant for Devon Energy Corporation. Currently he raises Brangus cattle on their ranch in Okfuskee County, Oklahoma.

INTRODUCTION AND SUMMARY

Sid Williams, Sr. (born Sept. 22, 1869-died May 6, 1938) was well known and was identified with the early development of the area south of the Black Hills, around the towns of Ardmore, Fall River County, South Dakota, and Harrison, Sioux County, Nebraska. He was a homesteader, cowboy, rancher and lawman in those areas 1886-1938.

Dad could be described as a "Transition Lawman" as he served as an occasional Special Marshall during the early days of Ardmore, South Dakota and later as Sioux County, Nebraska Sheriff in the relatively modern times of the 1920's and 30's. He was absolutely fearless and was truly one of the last "**bold** lawmen". He arrested murderers and outlaws who swore they would never be taken alive and earned the title: **"BRING 'EM BACK ALIVE, SID"**. Dad disarmed and arrested the notorious Doc Middleton, Bob Wallace, and C.M. Russell, all convicted or alleged killers.(1)

Your granddad was a friend to the Sioux Indians and allowed small hunting parties from the Pine Ridge Indian Reservation to hunt antelope on his ranch near Ardmore at the turn of the century. He sometimes gave them an old cow in the event of poor hunting.

Also, he and his brother Bernie Williams operated the famous Circle Bar (0-) ranch along the Nebraska-South Dakota border for a time during the early years. The ranch was owned by David Anderson.

Dad was also a great sportsman. He once imported a bunch of college baseball players from Wisconsin, filed them on homesteads and furnished each with a wagon and team of horses. His only requirement was that they play baseball for him.

He also had a stable of race horses and he raced them throughout the Midwest and set at least one track record.

His one great fault was that he could not resist the charms of beautiful women. He was married five times and my sister, Ila Mae and I are the results of the last marriage. He was a strict teetotaler and never smoked.

(1) This Charley M. Russell was not related to the famous western artist by the same name.

PART 1
DAD'S PREDECESSORS

The American Civil War, 1861-1865, was the most costly war in terms of casualties of any war in our history. Over 600,000 Union and Confederate soldiers were killed or died of disease. These casualties exceeded the total United States casualties of both World Wars. The Civil War occurred at a time when the U.S. population was only 30 million, compared to about 120 million in 1945 and 300 million in the year 2006. A similar ratio of casualties today would be about 6.0 million.

Almost every American family was adversely affected by the Civil War and the Williams family was no exception, and as a matter of fact the war impacted our family for decades afterward. Your grandfather, Charles Sidney Williams Sr. was born Sept. 22, 1869 into a society, country, and family still reeling from the effects of the war. His birthplace was a farm near St. Charles, Minnesota.

Before we go any farther into your grandfather's life we will discuss his parents and other more distant ancestors.

C.P. Williams and Martha Campbell

Dad's father was called "C.P." and sometimes Perry. He was born in 1824 in Crawford County, Greenwood Township, Pennsylvania. We don't know much about his life and no picture of him is known to exist. His parents were William ("Captain Billy") and Sarah Seely. The William Williams family was part of a large colony of Welsh settlers who had settled in northwestern Pennsylvania in the late 1700's.

Martha Campbell was Dad's mother and she was also born in Crawford County, Pennsylvania in 1829. I am uncertain about her parents, but a Mark Campbell's home was the place of her marriage to Perry. Mark was probably her father. Present, also at the February 3, 1848 marriage was a brother, Alexander Campbell, named after her grandfather, believed to be Alex Campbell, but conclusive evidence is lacking.

Census data indicates Alex was a mariner. This fits in with the information furnished by Uncle Bern and Aunt Eva Williams. I, when a young man of about 17-18 years of age, late 1940's, visited them at their home in Edgemont, South Dakota. Bernie (b. 1872-d.1953) was Dad's youngest brother. Eva told me that Martha's grandfather, Alexander fought on Lake Erie against the British in the War of 1812 when they "cleaned out the English", as she put it.

Eva said Martha's mother's maiden name was Custer (maybe Custiss) and that she was a cousin of General Armstrong Custer of Civil War and the "Battle of the Little Bighorn" fame against the Sioux in 1876.

Aunt Eva also told me that grandmother Martha talked a lot about the Sioux War of 1862 in Minnesota and that the massacred soldiers of one battle were placed in a row on the board walk in town. The leader of the slain soldiers was a Captain Chauncey Williams. Martha and Perry named one of their thirteen children Chauncey, born July 1, 1861. Was the slain Captain Chauncey Williams a relative that the baby was named after or is this a coincidence?

Aunt Eva said that Perry was an Evangelistic preacher during a large portion of his life and that he traveled from place to place on horseback to do his preaching. He would come home long enough to get his wife Martha pregnant and then take off on another preaching tour, leaving the boys behind to take care of the farm.

13

There were a lot of preachers in the Williams family. One, Oliver Emmett Williams, (b. 1878-d.1974) great grandson of Captain Billy, was a famous preacher and the first to have regular radio broadcasts. The Reverend Billy Graham is said to have modeled his preaching style after that of Reverend Williams.

Perry Williams was mustered into the Union Army with the rank of Private, August, 1862 for a term of 3 years. His unit was Company A, 83rd Infantry Regiment, Illinois Volunteers. He was described as 37 years of age, 5'8", blue eyes, light hair and complexion. According to the Illinois State Archives his residence was Roseville, Warren County, Illinois.

The 83rd Illinois Infantry Regiment, including Perry's Company A, was active in the wilderness campaign in Kentucky and Tennessee. Dad said his father was severely wounded during the Civil War and was in poor health as a result of his wounds for the rest of his life. The National Services Administration, National Archives & Records Service list Perry as being present in the Company A Muster Roll of Nov. 5th, 1862, but in the hospital at Paducah, Ky. also in Nov. of that year. A muster roll of March and April, 1863 list him as absent without leave at home, Warren County, Illinois since March 1863. Deserted at Clarksville, Tennessee. See the military documents on pages 21 to 27.

The Illinois Adjutant General's Report of Regimental and Unit Histories containing reports for the years 1861-1866 states that the 83rd Regiment moved to Ft. Donelson, Tennessee Sept. 3, 1862. The report, in part also reports the following quotations: "The Regiment had heavy guard duty to perform and as the whole country, especially the banks of the Tennessee and Cumberland Rivers were infested with the guerrillas. We had daily skirmishes with the enemy. Some of them were quite severe as at Waverly, Tennessee, and at Garrotsburg, Kentucky". Colonel W.W. Lowe, Fifth Iowa Cavalry, commanding Brigade.

So, according to the above report I believe Perry was severely wounded in action against the guerrillas later in November, 1862.

These documents show that Perry deserted the army after only seven (7) months service of a 3-year enlistment period. The documents also show that he spent several of the seven (7) months in the hospital at Paducah, Kentucky.

Before we judge him too harshly for deserting, consider that according to family tradition he was severely wounded in some sort of military action. Apparently, he felt he could no longer fulfill his military obligations and he left for home. His health was ruined, he no longer could do much farm work and he died relatively young at 56, on November 3, 1880. He died at home from pneumonia. The one mistake he made was not waiting to get an official medical discharge. Years later this caused his widow great difficulty in getting a government Civil War pension. She had to get it based on her son Lewis' service.

Aunt Eva told me that the weather at the time of Perry's death was extremely cold and the ground was deeply frozen. The family had to store the body in a shed for several weeks until weather conditions improved permitting burial. Burial was at Wynot, Cedar County, Northeastern Nebraska.

Also, Perry's eldest son, Lewis (my uncle) died of typhoid fever while serving in Company H, First Minnesota Volunteers. The National Archives lists his death as occurring on June 28th, 1865, after Lee's surrender April 9, 1865 at Appomattox Court House. Lee's surrender led to the rapid winding down of the Civil War.

Lewis, determined to get into the fight ran away from home at age 16 and joined the Union Army, March 31, 1865.

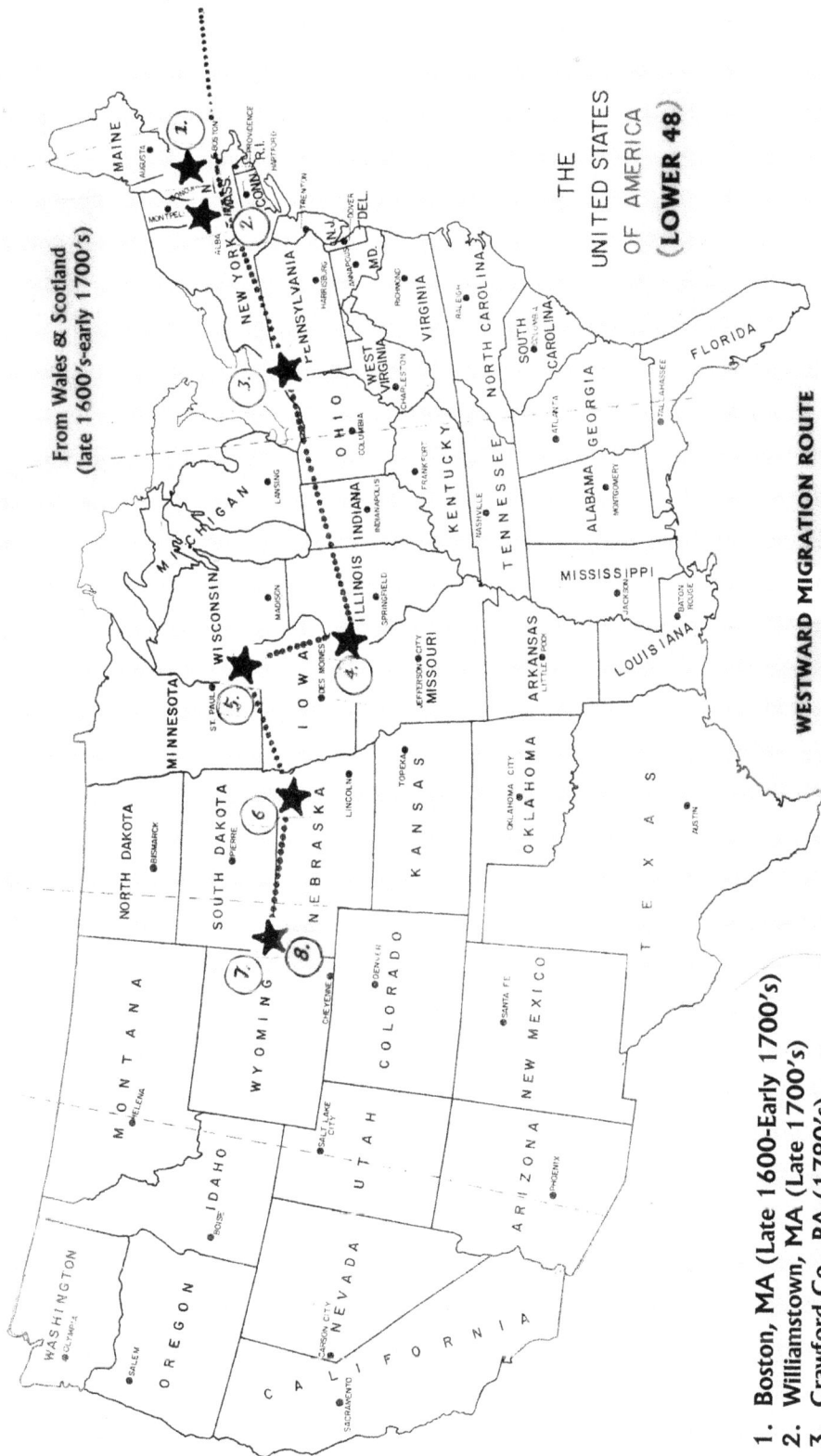

THE
UNITED STATES
OF AMERICA
(LOWER 48)

From Wales & Scotland
(late 1600's-early 1700's)

WESTWARD MIGRATION ROUTE
OUR WILLIAMS FAMILY

1. Boston, MA (Late 1600-Early 1700's)
2. Williamstown, MA (Late 1700's)
3. Crawford Co., PA (1790's)
4. Warren Co., IL (1860's)
5. St. Charles, MN (1865-1875)
6. Cedar Co., NE (1875-1885)
7. Fall River Co., SD (1886)
8. Sioux Co., NE (1886)

*Locations 7 & 8 Are Adjacent Stops

15

Getting a Civil War Pension

Martha tried for many years to get a Civil War pension. After Perry and Lewis' death the family was poverty stricken and she had to take in work from the neighbors to make ends meet.

Listed on page 32 are the 13 children of Perry and Martha. An examination of the data indicates that the family made several moves during their married years, from Pennsylvania to Illinois, to Minnesota. They moved to Cedar County, northeastern Nebraska sometime after 1874 when their youngest child, Nellie, was born.(2) In 1886 Martha and sons Sid and Bernie moved to Chadron, Nebraska, then the western terminus of the railroad under construction. They joined her ninth child, Russell, who was already in the area. At Chadron Martha operated a boarding house. After a short time in Chadron Martha moved to Ardmore, South Dakota to be near her sons.

Eleven affidavits were obtained from the National Archives, Washington, D.C. indicating Grandmother Williams' attempts to get a pension on the basis of being a dependent mother. Two affidavits follow and the others can be found in Appendix B.

She finally got one, initially for about $12.00/month. The affidavits provide some idea of her difficulties. Grandmother Williams died, age 93, November 2, 1922 at Dad's ranch (the old Woodruff Place), Sioux County, Nebraska. During her last years she was blind (cataracts) and senile.

Dad's application for reimbursement of burial expenses, legal for all military pensioners, indicate the details of her death and the costs of a burial in 1922.

These documents show that your granddad applied for reimbursement of burial expenses for his mother. I believe the amount was $255.00. This is the same amount that is now paid toward the burial of Social Security recipients. Some other valuable information is provided in the documents.

(2) Nellie was born when Martha was 45 years old and was mentally and physically deficient, probably because of Down's Syndrome.

Charles Sidney Williams Sr., 1874, about age 5, photo was taken from a tin-type, near St. Charles, Minnesota (two years before Custer's defeat on the Little Bighorn River, Montana)

Charles Williams Sr., about 1898, 29 years old

Charles Williams Sr., Ardmore, S. Dakota, approximately 1904,
about 35 years old

Sid Williams Sr., Ardmore, S. Dakota, about 1905

PAUL POWELL
SECRETARY OF STATE AND STATE ARCHIVIST

THEODORE J. CASSADY
ASSISTANT STATE ARCHIVIST

The records of the Adjutant General's Office, now in the State Archives, show the following Civil War service record on:

Name: Williams, Perry   Rank: Private

Unit: Company A Eighty-third Infanry, Illinois Volunteers

Age: 37   Height: 5'8"   Hair: Light

Eyes: Blue   Complexion: Light

Marital Status: Married   Occupation: Farmer

Nativity: Town --   County: Crawford   State: Pennsylvania

Joined for Service and Enrolled.   When: August 4, 1862 Term: Three years

Where: Monmouth   By Whom: Captain Reed

Mustered into Service.   When: August 21, 1862

Where: Monmouth   By Whom: Captain Christopher

Residence: Town Roseville   County: Warren   State: Illinois

Mustered Out.   When: --

Where: --   By Whom: --

Remarks: Deserted on September 30, 1863.

THEODORE J. CASSADY
Assistant State Archivist

A RM-16

Documents obtained from the National Archives, Washington D.C.

W | 83 | Ill.

Perry Williams

Pvt. , Co. A. , 83 Reg't Illinois Infantry.

Appears on

Company Muster Roll

for ____ Sept & Oct 5, 1862

Present or absent ____ Present

Stoppage, $ ____ 100 for

Due Gov't, $ ____ 100 for

Remarks:

Book mark: ____

W | 83 | Ill.

Perry Williams

Pvt. , Co. A. , 83 Reg't Illinois Infantry.

Appears on

Company Muster Roll

for ____ Sept & Aug 31, 1862

Present or absent ____ Present

Stoppage, $ ____ 100 for

Due Gov't, $ ____ 100 for

Remarks:

Book mark: ____

W | 83 | Ill.

Perry Williams

Pvt. , Capt. Reed's Co., 83 Reg't Ill. Inf.

Age 3 years.

Appears on

Company Muster-in Roll

of the organization named above. Roll dated

Monmouth Ill. Aug 21, 1862

Mustered in to date ____ Aug 21, 1862

Joined for duty and enrolled:

When ____ Aug 11, 186

Where ____ Monmouth

Period ____ 3 years.

Bounty paid $ ____ 100; due $ ____ 100

Remarks: ____

Book mark: ____

The organization subsequently became Co. A 83 Reg't Ill. Inf.

Card 1 (right)

α | 83 | Ill.

Perry Williams
Sgt ....., Co. A, 83 Reg't Illinois Infantry.

Appears on
Company Muster Roll

for _____ Sept. 1863.

Present or absent _____ absent

Stoppage, $ _____ 100 for _____

Due Gov't, $ _____ 100 for _____

Remarks: Absent sick .... at Paducah Ca Ill ....
Sent '63

Book mark: _____

_____ Sergeant

Card 2

α | 83 | Ill.

Perry Williams
Sgt., Co. A, 83 Reg't Illinois Infantry.

Appears on
Special Muster Roll

for _____ April 17 1865.

Present or absent _____ absent

Stoppage, $ _____ 100 for _____

Due Gov't, $ _____ 100 for _____

Remarks: Absent without leave ....
at in Warren Co Ill

Supposed to be Special Muster
for April 10, 1865.

Book mark: _____

_____ Sergeant

(160.)

Card 3

α | 83 | Ill.

Perry Williams
Sgt., Co. A, 83 Reg't Illinois Infantry.

Appears on
Company Muster Roll

for _____ Jan. Feb. 1863.

Present or absent _____ absent

Stoppage, $ _____ 100 for _____

Due Gov't, $ _____ 100 for _____

Remarks: Sent to Hospt. at Paducah ....

Book mark: _____

_____ Sergeant

Card 4 (left)

α | 83 | Ill.

Perry Williams
Sgt., Co. A, 83 Reg't Illinois Infantry.

Appears on
Company Muster Roll

for _____ Nov. Dec. 1862.

Present or absent _____ absent

Stoppage, $ _____ 100 for _____

Due Gov't, $ _____ 100 for _____

Remarks: Sent to Hospt. at Paducah ....

Book mark: _____

_____ Sergeant

23

Card 1

N | 83 | Ill.

Perry Williams

Pvt. , Co. A , 83 Reg't Illinois Inf.

Age 98 years.

Appears on Co. Muster-out Roll,

dated Nashville, Tenn., June 6, 1865.

Muster-out to date _____ 186_

Last paid to _____ 186_

Clothing account:

Last settled _____ 186_ ; drawn since $_____

Due soldier $_____ 100 ; due U. S. $_____ 100

Am't for cloth'g in kind or money adv'd $_____ 100

Due U. S. for arms, equipments, &c., $_____

Bounty paid $_____ 100 ; due $_____ 100

Remarks: Nashville Sept. 30/63.

Book mark: _____

(861)

Card 2

N | 83 | Ill.

Perry Williams

Sgt. , Co. A, 83 Reg't Illinois Infantry.

Appears on

Company Muster Roll

for Sept. & Oct. , 1863.

Present or absent _____

Stoppage, $_____ 100 for _____

Due Gov't, $_____ 100 for _____

Remarks: Reported absent without leave since
Oct. 1863. Dropped
from the Roll + Oct.
Sept. 30, 1863.

As on Roll

Book mark: _____

Chandler , Captain.

Card 3

N | 83 | Ill.

Perry Williams

Pvt. , Co. A, 83 Reg't Illinois Infantry.

Appears on

Company Muster Roll

for July & Aug. , 1863.

Present or absent Absent

Stoppage, $_____ 100 for _____

Due Gov't, $_____ 100 for _____

Remarks: _____

Book mark: _____

Chandler , Captain.

Card 4

N | 83 | Ill.

Perry Williams

Pvt. , Co. A, 83 Reg't Illinois Infantry.

Appears on

Company Muster Roll

for May & June , 1863.

Present or absent Absent

Stoppage, $_____ 100 for _____

Due Gov't, $_____ 100 for _____

Remarks: Absent without
leave at Mound Co. Ill.

Book mark: _____

Chandler , Captain.

24

W | 83 | **111.**

Perry Williams

Pvt. , Co. A, 83 Reg't Illinois Infantry.

Appears on

Descriptive List of Deserters

dated _____ Oct 2 _____, 186 3.

Age 38 years; height, 5 feet 8 inches.

Complexion light; eyes blue; hair light

Where born Crawford Co, Penn.

Occupation _____ Farmer

When enlisted _____ Aug 4, 1862

Where enlisted Monmouth, Ills.

When mustered in _____ Aug 11 1862

Where mustered in Monmouth, Ills

For what period mustered in, 3 years.

When deserted _____ Sept 30, 186 3.

Where deserted Clarksville, Tenn.

When apprehended _____, 186 .

Where apprehended _____

Remarks : _____
He was reported absent
without leave since Mar.
1863 and is dropped from
the rolls as a deserter this
30th day of Sept. 1863

Book mark : _____

Austin

(353) Copyist

RECORD OF DEATH AND INTERMENT.

Name and number of person interred.

Number and locality of the grave . .

Hospital number of the deceased . .

Regiment, rank, and company . . .

Residence before enlistment . . .

Conjugal condition, (and if married,
the residence of the widow) . .

Lewis E Williams

Private Co H 1st Min Vols

Single

Fever

Pens Case 284.570 closed Mch 10-83

30

Unknown

Date of death and burial . . . . *June 28th* , 186*5.*

[A duplicate of this Record has been forwarded to the Sexton, and another remains at this Hospital.]

To

Sir:

It becomes my duty to inform you that the person above described died at this Hospital as herein stated; and that it is desired his remains should be interred with the usual military honors.

Respectfully,

Fred. W. Hughes

1st & N.Y. Vols. Surgeon U. S. Army.

in chg Field Hospital 2 Div 2 C

MILITARY HOSPITAL,

This copy of Record is to be transmitted to the Adjutant General at Washington immediately after the place of burial and the number of the grave have been ascertained and registered.   The above notification is to remain attached.

Inventory of the effects of _Lewis E Williams_ late a _Private_ of Captain _Lt K W Holden_ Company _A_ of the _First_ Regiment of _Minnesota_ Volunteers, who was enrolled as a _Private_ at _Rochester_ in the State of _Minnesota_ on the _31st_ day of _March_ 186_3_, and mustered into the service of the United States as a _Private_ on the _31st_ day of _March_ 186_3_, at _Rochester_ in Company _A_, _First_ Regiment of _Minnesota_ Volunteers, to serve _One_ years or during the war; he was born in _____ in the State of _Pennsylvania_; he was _17_ years of age, _5_ feet _6_ inches high, _Dark_ complexion, _Grey_ eyes, _Brown_ hair, and by occupation, when enrolled, a _Farmer_; he died in _____, at _____ on the _28_ day of _June_ 186_3_, by reason of _____

INVENTORY.

ARTICLES.	No.	ARTICLES.	No.	ARTICLES.	No.
Hats		Pairs trowsers		Knapsacks	
Caps		Pairs flannel drawers			
Forage caps		Pairs cotton drawers			
Great coats		Flannel shirts			
Uniform coats		Cotton shirts			
Uniform jackets		Pairs boots			
Flannel sack coats		Pairs shoes			
Blouses		Pairs socks		MONEY. Specie	$
Stable frocks		Blankets		Notes	$
Fatigue overalls		Haversacks,			

I CERTIFY, ON HONOR, that the above inventory comprises all the effects of _____ _Lewis E Williams_ _____, deceased, and that the effects are in the hands of _____ at _____ _____ to be disposed of by a Council of Administration.

(DUPLICATES.)

W J Holden
1st Lieut
Commanding the Company.

STATION: _Jeffersonville Ind_

DATE: _July 15"/63_

A. G. O., No. 104.]

27

DECLARATION FOR AN ORIGINAL PENSION OF A MOTHER
STATE OF NEBRASKA COUNTY OF CEDAR

July 9, 1881

On this 9 day of July, A.D. one thousand eight hundred and eighty one personally appeared before me, the undersigned B. Jolsten, Clerk of the District Court, the same being a court of record within and for the county and State aforesaid, MARTHA WILLIAMS, a resident of Smithland, County of Cedar in the State of Nebraska, aged 51 years, who, being duly sworn according to law makes the following declaration in order to obtain the Pension by Acts of Congress granting pensions to dependent Mothers. That she is the widow of P.C. Williams, and Mother of Lewis Williams who enlisted under the name of Lewis C. Williams at Minnesota on the 28th day of March A.D. 1865 in Co. H. of the 1st Regiment, Minnesota Volunteers in the war of 1861 who, died near Washington D.C. of chronic diarrhea on the 28 day of June, A.D. 1865; that said son Lewis C. Williams left neither widow nor child under sixteen years of age surviving, that she was greatly dependent upon said son for support; that her husband, the aforesaid P.C. Williams, aged 58 years, died November 3, 1880 at Wancapona, Nebraska that there were surviving at date of son's death his brothers and sisters, who were under sixteen years of age, as follows:

Alex Williams, born July 27, 1850

Frank Williams, born November 28, 1855

Mark Williams, born March 3, 1856

Harry Williams, born November 28, 1858

Lizzie Williams, born February 1, 1859

Chauncey Williams, born July 1, 1861

Russell Williams, born April 24, 1864

That she has not heretofore received or applied for a pension; that she has not aided or abetted the rebellion; that she hereby appoints E.D. Gelston & Co. of Washington, D.C. her Attorneys to prosecute the above claim; that her residence is at the post office Smithland County of Cedar, State of Nebraska and that her Post Office address is the same.

Signatures:

Meark Mesamed

Martha Campbell,

Claimant

N.J. Aberey

Two attesting witnesses who

can write their names

GENERAL AFFIDAVIT

AUGUST 28, 1888

State of Minnesota, County of Winona, SS.

In the matter of Claim by Martha Williams for pension.

ON THIS 28th day of August A.D. 1888, personally appeared before me, a Notary Public in and for the aforesaid County, duly authorized to administer oaths, Lester Becker age 63 and Shanah Becker, age 52 years, residents of Saratoga in the County of Winona and State of Minnesota well known to me to be reputable and entitled to credit, and who, being duly sworn, declares in relation to aforesaid case as follows:

That they were near neighbors and well acquainted with the Claimant, Martha Williams and her husband Perry C. Williams from 1863 to 1873. That during all of that time the said Perry C. Williams was a very feeble man and unable to support his family by his labor. They had no income and no property and wholly dependent on their son, Lewis C. Williams for support. That the said Lewis C. Williams enlisted late in the war of the rebellion and they believe in the year 1865 and died within a few months thereafter. That neither of his parents had any property or income from 1863 to 1873 except what was derived from the labor of said son as they (sp) believe. That said soldier was never married to the best of their knowledge and belief. And that he was the son of the claimant and that he left no widow or children. That the said Perry C. Williams appeared to be about 45 years of age at the time the soldier died. They know these facts above stated by being a near neighbor and intimate with the parties during all the time from 1863 to 1873. Their Post Office address is Troy, Winona County, Minnesota. They further declare that they have no interest in said case and not concerned in its prosecution.

Signatures: Lester Becker

Shanah Becker

(affiant)

APPLICATION FOR REIMBURSEMENT.

(This application, when properly executed before some officer having authority to administer oaths for general purposes, should be forwarded, together with the pension certificate and itemized bills of all expenses, to the Commissioner of Pensions, Washington, D. C.)

State of ......South Dakota......
County of ......Fall River......

On this ......9th...... day of ......December......, A. D. one thousand nine hundred and ...twenty-two... personally appeared before me, a ......Notary Public...... within and for the County and State aforesaid, ...Charles S. Williams...... aged ......53...... years, a resident of ......Post Office, Ardmore, S.D.,...... resident of County of ......Sioux......, State of ......Nebraska......, who, being duly sworn according to law, makes the following declaration in order to obtain reimbursement from the accrued pension for expenses paid (or obligation incurred) in the last sickness and burial of ......Martha Williams......, who was a pensioner of the United States by certificate No. ...255718..., on account of the service of ......Lewis C. Williams...... in ......Private Co. H. 1st Battallion, Minn. Volunteer Inf....... That pension was last paid to ...Oct. 1st,..., 19 22

That the answers to questions propounded below are full, complete, and truthful to the best of my knowledge, information, and belief, and that no evidence necessary to a proper adjustment of all claims against the accrued pension is suppressed or withheld.

1. What was the full name of the deceased pensioner? ......Martha Williams......

2. In what capacity was decedent pensioned? (As invalid soldier or sailor, or as a widow, minor child, dependent relative, etc.) ......mother, dependent relative......

3. If decedent was pensioned as an invalid soldier or sailor—
   (a) Was he ever married? (Answer yes or no.) ......
   (b) How many times, and to whom? ......
   (c) If married, did his wife survive him? (Answer yes or no.) ......
   (d) If so, is she still living? (Answer yes or no.) ......
   (e) If not living, give full names and dates of death of all wives ......
   (f) Was he ever divorced? (Answer yes or no.) ......
   (g) If so, is the divorced wife still living? (Answer yes or no.) ...... (If living, a copy of the decree of divorce must be filed.)
   (h) If not living, give her full name and the date of her death ......

4. Did pensioner leave a child under 16 years of age? (Answer yes or no.) ......No

5. Is any such child still living? (Answer yes or no.) ......No

6. Were any sick or death benefits paid on pensioner's account? If so, give name of society and amount paid ......None

7. Was there insurance (life, accident, or health) in force on life of pensioner at time of death? (Answer yes or no.) ...No

8. If so, give the name of each company in which a policy was carried and the amount in which each policy was written ......

9. Who was the beneficiary named in each policy? ......

10. What was the relation of each beneficiary to the pensioner? ......

11. Were the premiums paid by the deceased pensioner? ......

12. If not paid by the deceased pensioner, state the amount of premiums paid by each person who made payment on that account ......

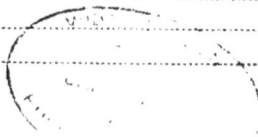

6—1572

2

13. Is there an executor or administrator, or will application be made for appointment of any person as administrator? ....
No

14. Did the deceased pensioner leave any money, real estate, or personal property? ...None

15. If so, state the character and value of all such property ....

16. What was the assessed value (last assessment) of the real estate? ....

17. How was the pensioner's property disposed of? ....
Pensioner had no property

18. Did pensioner leave an unindorsed pension check? (Answer yes or no.) .... Yes

19. What was your relation to the deceased pensioner? .... Son

20. Are you married? (Answer yes or no.) .... Yes

21. What was the cause of pensioner's death? .... Old age

22. When did the pensioner's last sickness begin? ......Died in apparently fair health

23. From what date did the pensioner become so ill as to require the regular and daily attendance of another person constantly until death? ......Was not bedfast before death

24. Give the name and post-office address of each physician who attended the pensioner during last sickness ....
......No physician attended. She had not been sick. She died
......towards morning, the 2nd of November, 1922 while in bed

25. State the names of the persons by whom the pensioner was nursed during the last sickness ....
Pensioner was living with me. We took care of her as she was
blind but she did not go through and period of sickness before
her death

26. Where did the pensioner live during last sickness? ..Pensioner lived with me.

27. Where did the pensioner die? ...At my ranch, abou 12 miles SW of Ardmore, S.D.

28. When did the pensioner die? ..Nov. 2nd, 1922

29. Where was the pensioner buried? ......Chadron, Nebr.

30. Has there been paid, or will application be made for payment to you or any other person, any part of the expenses of the pensioner's last sickness and burial by any State, County, or municipal corporation? (Answer yes or no.) ..No

31. State below the expenses of the pensioner's last sickness and burial. Write the word *none* where no charge is made in case of any item of expense noted.

(Each charge entered below should be supported by an itemized bill of the person who rendered the service or furnished any supplies for which reimbursement is demanded, and should show, over his signature, by whom paid, or who is held responsible for payment, and contain the name of the pensioner for whom the expense was incurred or service rendered.)

NAMES.	NATURE OF EXPENSES.	STATE WHETHER PAID OR UNPAID	AMOUNT.
None	Physician		
None	Medicine		
None	Nursing and care		
None	Undertaker		
John Kelso	Livery	Unpaid	50.00
Chadron Cemetery Ass'n	Cemetery	Paid	217.50
	Other expenses and their nature: Casket	Unpaid	150.00
	TOTAL		217.00

32. Is the above a complete list of *all* the expenses of the last sickness and burial of the deceased pensioner? (Answer yes or no.) ......No

That my post-office address is No. ...., on ....street,

town or city of ......Ardmore......, County of ......Fall River......

State of ......South Dakota......

(When the claimant for reimbursement is a married woman, she is required to sign the application with her own full name, not using the Christian name or the initials of her husband, and all bills should be receipted to her in her own name.)

Charles S Williams
(Claimant's signature in full.)

6—1872

Husband: Perry C. Williams

Born:	1824	in:	Crawford County, Pennsylvania
Married:	February 3, 1848	in:	Crawford County, Pennsylvania
Died:	November 1880	in:	Hartington, Nebraska
Father:	William Williams		

Wife: Martha Campbell

Born:	1829	in:	Pennsylvania, Crawford County
Died:	1922	in:	Indian Creek Ranch, Sioux County, Ne.

CHILDREN

1	Name:	Lewis C. Williams
M	Born:	1848, PA.
2	Name:	Alexander Williams
M	Born:	July 27, 1850, PA.
3	Name:	Franklin Williams
M	Born:	November 28, 1852 or 11-28-55, PA.
4	Name:	Harrison Williams
M	Born:	November 28, 1852 ? MN.
5	Name:	Mark Williams
M	Born:	March 03, 1856, PA.
6	Name:	Miles Williams (Harry ?)
M	Born:	1858, MN.
7	Name:	Elizabeth Williams (Lizzie)
F	Born:	February 01, 1859, IL.
8	Name:	Chauncey Williams
M	Born:	February 01, 1861, IL.
9	Name:	Russell Williams
M	Born:	April 24, 1864, MN.
10	Name:	J. Effie Williams
F	Born:	1866, MN.
11	Name:	**Charles Sidney Williams, Sr.**
	Born:	**September 22, 1869 near St. Charles, Winona County, MN.**
M	Married:	**1893**
	Died:	**May 06, 1938 in Chadron, Nebraska**
	Spouses:	**Lily Thomas, Pearl Johnson, Hattie Blessing, Agnes Quinn, LaVerne Sturdivant**
12	Name:	O.B. Williams
M	Born:	1872, MN.
	Died:	1953
13	Name:	Nellie Williams
F	Born:	1874, MN.
	Died:	About 1885

Grandmother Martha (Campbell) Williams, your granddad's mother, b.1829-d.1922
Picture about 1890

Grandmother Martha Williams, Ardmore, South Dakota, about 1912

Russell Williams (b.1864, d. 1909); killed in Utah

Captain Billy Williams & Robert Williams

Now let's discuss Perry's parents. William Williams, the only son of Robert Williams, was born about 1780, probably in Williamstown, Massachusetts during the latter stages of the Revolutionary War. His mother's name was Seabra. I think this was a given name and not her surname.

Most of the information regarding William Williams was gathered by Clarence L. Burkey, Spring Hill, Florida who married a Williams, one of William Williams' descendants. The information was sent to Dean Williams and then forwarded to me.

William Williams served for 42 days during the War of 1812 and he was generally known as Captain Billy thereafter.

According to Burkey, who interviewed many members of his descendants, many who still reside on Billy's land or the general area, a good many legends abound about his meritorious service. One story involves the saving and carrying of a treasure chest from Washington, and which was supposedly buried along French Creek. The treasure was lost when the creek flooded.

<u>Burkey</u>: "An amusing find. If you go through the "W" Meadville divorce and civil suit record books, you will find only two books: One for WILLIAMS; the other, W. Miscellaneous".

The 1810 census shows Billy living in Fairfield Twp, PA (Fairfield, PA.) (Fairfield, P.411) with a household of 4 males under 10, himself (26-44), 1 female under 10, and his wife (26-44). The 1820 census shows him living in Fallowfield Twp. (Fallowfield, P.580) with a household of 2 males under 10, 1 male (10-15), 2 males (16-25), 1 female (26-44), 1 female over 45. Fallowfield Twp. was subsequently separated to make Greenwood Twp.

"Captain Billy" has been subject of many family legends which have been passed down three generations. Most of these pertain to his War of 1812 adventures as a military Captain and for which he was rewarded with land bordering on the "Great Geneva Swamp in Greenwood Twp.".

Captain Billy married Sarah Seely probably about 1800. We know very little about her. She was born about 1776 in New Jersey and died March 1851 in Crawford Co., Pennsylvania. They had 13 children, 11 boys and 2 girls. The Family Group Sheet on page 32 was prepared by Dean Williams. I have listed the first generation only and not any of the succeeding generations except for those of Perry C. Williams. It is not the intent of this writer to clutter this book with the hundreds of meaningless names and dates of Capt. Billy's descendants. Any interested persons may contact me about the other descendants not listed herein.

Captain Billy succumbed to diphtheria January 28, 1834 in Greenwood Township, Crawford Co., Pennsylvania.

Captain Billy is buried in the Williams Cemetery, Greenwood Township, Pennsylvania. A War of 1812 Veterans marker is on the grave and a privately erected tombstone bears the title, "Captain".

Captain Billy's Last Will and Testament, dated Dec. 2, 1833 is printed on the next page.

WILLIAM WILLIAMS WILL

Registered April 20, 1834

("compared by Me George Le Feire Register") (note: *italicized words are as copied from document copy*)

In the name of God, I William Williams considering the *uncertainlly* of this mortal life and being of sound mind and memory blessed by Almighty God for the same do make and publish this my last will and testament in manner and form following (that is to say) I will that all my just debts, as shall be by me owing at my death, together with my funeral expenses and all charges touching the providing or, otherwise concerning this my last will, shall in the first place out of my personal estate and effects be fully paid and certified, and from and after payment thereof, and subject thereunto, then my will is, that all the grain now in my possessions with hay sufficient to keep two horses, four cows one yoke of oxen together with the above named horses, cows, and oxen with farming *untensials*, household and kitchen furnishings and all the beds and bedding with six swarms of bees, be at the disposal of my beloved wife *Sarah* Williams. As long as she *remaines* my widow and no longer, and that all remainder of my personal property be sold at public vender and the moneys *arrising* therefrom to be applied to the payments of lands or otherwise.

And my real estate consisting of four hundred acres of land situated in Greenwood Township, Crawford County State of Pennsylvania. Adjoining lands owned by Johnathan Tayler and others and also one hundred acres situated in the above named county and township adjoining lands owned by the widow Hearkins and others and also twenty five acres situated in Fairfield Township and Crawford County adjoining lands belonging to Thomas Burchfield and others, be disposed of in the following manner:

First I will that my eldest son Robert have one hundred acres on the West end of the above named acres for his share and *dowery* by his helping to pay the balance due on said land. And that the remaining three hundred acres of said four hundred acre lot remain undivided until my youngest child becomes of age, and at the expiration of that time to have the said three hundred acres as equally divided in respect to quantity and quality as can be among those who are not otherwise provided for in this will. And that remaining one hundred acres before mentioned or the one half of said hundred acres _____ vis the east part I bequeath to my daughter Sarah Brooks by her husband conforming to this former contract, the remaining fifty acres of said one hundred I bequeath to my son John, in case he refuses his equal *quoto* of what is due on the land (NB). It is my desire that my sons use their joint *endeavors* to pay what is due on the land by their industry. And in case my son John refuses to assist as above *mintioned* his *dowery* shall be one dollar (NB) the twenty-five acres in Fairfield Township to be reserved with the three hundred acres until my youngest child becomes of age. And it is my will that my new saw mill be rented year by year for as much as it will demand and keep in repair and profits of said mill be applied for the schooling and clothing the children that are underage if required (NB). Said mill is not to rented when my sons want the use of it, to pay for the land. And it is my will that as long as my sons that are underage till and cultivate the land reserved to profit and advantage they have the *previlage*. And when they fail to do so that it be rented by the executors for the support of the family.

And I make and ordain Robert Williams, Wm. Williams Jr, James Brooks executors of this my last will and testament. (A.C.) And I hereby nominate and appoint Joseph Thatcher overseer of the same. And I hereby commit the *guardianship* of all my children until they shall respectively attain the age of twenty one years, unto my said wife *durning* her life if she shall so long continue my widow. And from and after her decease or second *marrage* unto my executors. And lastly My expressed will and *mealing* is that I do hereby ordain and appoint, that, if any difference, *disbuted* questions, or *controversry* shall be moved, arise or happen concerning any gift or bequest in this my will, given and bequeathed expressed or contrived that there be no suit or suits, in law or equity or otherwise shall be brought, commenced or prosecuted for and concerning the same. But the same shall be referred wholly to three disinterested men appointed by my executors and what thou shall order direct and determine therein shall be binding and conclusive to all and *ever* person and persons therein concerned and I do now declare this is to be my last will and testament.

I witness whereof I have hereunto set my hand seal the second day of December in the year of our Lord one thousand and eight hundred and thirty three. Signed, Sealed, Published and Declared the above name of William Williams to be his last will and testament: In the presence of us who at his request, and in his presence, have subscribed our names as witnessed thereunto.

Samuel Anderson; John Taylor; John Sutton, Jr.   SEAL Wm. Williams

WILLIAM WILLIAMS & WIFE SARAH

Robert

Sarah

John

Williams

CHILDREN OF WILLIAM WILLIAMS and SARAH SEELY are:

i.   ROBERT WILLIAMS, b. October 10, 1803, Geneva, PA; d. January 15, 1849, Crawford Co, PA.

ii.   WILLIAM WILLIAMS, JR, b. 1805, Crawford Co, PA; d. Unknown

      Notes for WILLIAM WILLIAMS, JR:

      A William Williams of Greenwood Township appears in the 1840 census, having a household of one male (60-70?), male age (20-30: probably himself and should have been 30-40); female (30-40); and one female(10-15).

iii. JAMES F WILLIAMS, b. 1809, Crawford Co, PA; d. June 25, 1894, Crawford Co, PA; m. HANNAH.

      Notes for JAMES F WILLIAMS:

      Buried: Methodist Cemetery, Geneva, PA

      Appears in the 1840 Greenwood Twp census with a household of 1 adult male, 1 adult female, and 2 female children.

      More about HANNAH:

      Fact 1: buried: Methodist Cemetery, Geneva, PA

iv.   SAMUEL WILLIAMS, b. August 19, 1809, Greenwood Twp, PA; d. November 12, 1855, Crawford Co, PA.

v.   JOHN PENN WILLIAMS, b. 1810, Fallowfield Twp, Crawford County, PA;
         d. Unknown.

      Notes for JOHN PENN WILLIAMS:

      A John Williams appears in the 1840 census, having a household of himself and one adult female.

vi.   SARAH WILLIAMS, b. 1812, Crawford Co, PA; d. Unknown; m. JAMES L.
         BROOKS, January 20, 1831.

Notes for SARAH WILLIAMS:

A Sarah Williams appears in the 1840 Greenwood Twp census having a household of 2 adult females, 2 male children, and one female child.

vii.   DARIUS WILLIAMS, b. June 07, 1818; d. December 07, 1895, Greenwood Twp, PA.

viii. GEORGE WASHINGTON WILLIAMS, b. 1825, Crawford Co, PA; d. June 03, 1889.

ix.   **PERRY C. WILLIAMS b. 1824, Crawford Co, PA; d. November, 1880, Wynot, Cedar County, NE; m. Martha Campbell**

x.   ARTHUR WILIAMS, b. Unknown, Crawford Co, PA; d. Unknown

xi.   JOSEPH WILLIAMS, b. Unknown, Crawford Co, PA

Notes for JOSEPH WILLIAMS:

A Joseph Williams appears in the 1840 Greenwood Township census, having a household of 1 adult male, 1 adult female, 1 male child, 2 female children.

xii. LYDIA WILLIAMS, b. Unknown, Crawford Co, PA; d. Unknown; m. DANIEL HARKINS.

xiii. PETER WILLIAMS, b. Unknown.

Robert Williams is believed to have been born in Massachusetts between 1745-1755 and died in 1807 in Fairfield Township, Crawford Co., PA. He married a woman named Sarah or Seabra.

I believe the Robert Williams family and an Abraham (his father?) came to what is now Crawford County, Pennsylvania from Williamstown, Massachusetts between 1791 and 1794. This is partly based on Burkey's assertion that Robert took part in the Whiskey Rebellion of Pennsylvania in 1794. The 1800 census shows him living in Mead Township, now part of Crawford County, Pennsylvania with a household comprising one male age 16-25 (our William), one male over 44 (himself) and one female, age 26-44 (Seabra).

According to Burkey there is a land transaction between the Population Company, a Dutch controlled business organization, and Robert and Abraham Williams. An Abraham Williams appears again in Mead Township in the 1800 and 1810 census.

Burkey: "The publication,'Massachusetts Soldiers & Sailors in the War of the Revolution' lists a Robert Williams, Private, Capt. Israel Harris Co., Col, Benjamin Simend's (Berkshire Co.) Regt. enlisted Oct. 12, 1780; discharged Oct. 15, 1780; service 6 days, including 3 days (60 miles) travel home; company marched to Northern frontier by order of General Fellows on an alarm".

"We don't know if this is our Robert, but he could be as we believe he was living in Berkshire County, Williamstown, Northwestern Mass. during the period in question".

THE WHISKEY REBELLION – One interesting purported incident in the life of Robert Williams occurred in 1794, sometime after he and his family arrived in northwest Pennsylvania. Their arrival was when the frontier line was in western Pennsylvania. The frontiersman in this area supplemented their meager income by distilling whiskey and using it for bartering purposes. Cash was very scarce. Finally, the United States government decided a lot of potential revenue could be raised by taxing this liquor. The national debt at this time was fifty four (54) million dollars.

The excise tax on each gallon of whiskey was considered onerous to the settlers because their small, part time and somewhat inefficient distilleries were hit relatively harder than the big, more efficient full time distilleries of the easterners.

The infuriated westerners decided they wouldn't pay the tax. They raised an army of about 5,000 men to resist the "revenuers". Hadn't they recently successfully resisted the British when they had put ruinous taxes on their tea and other items? There was even some talk of withdrawing from the United States.

Well, President George Washington didn't agree, apparently believing that if the rebels succeeded it might result in fracturing the fragile unity of the United States. So, he marched about 13,000 federal troops to the west to defeat the rebels. Some of Washington's troops were draftees and others were Revolutionary War veterans.

The vastly outnumbered rebels must have been intimidated by the federal force because the war soon stopped before it really got started.

Total casualties, from all causes, amounted to less than 20 men.

However, in 1800 during the administration of President Thomas Jefferson the federal government rescinded the tax. So, perhaps in the end the rebels won.

Burkey, by correspondence to Dean Williams said Robert Williams supported the rebellion and he had seen signed petitions with many signatures, one of which was that of Robert Williams.

I have not verified the story that Robert was indeed a rebel.

Robert's Last Will and Testament is listed on next page.

Sept. 11, 1807

LAST WILL AND TESTAMENT OF ROBERT WILLIAMS

(copied as was provided with 'old language' and questionable transpositions indicated by *italics*)

Be it remembered that I Robert Williams of Fairfield Township, Crawford County, and Commonwealth of Pennsylvania, being sick and weak in body and of sound mind, memory and understanding, but thoughtful of my later end, and knowing it is appointed for all men to die. Do hereby make my last will and testament in manner following that is to say First; I will that all my just debts and funeral expenses shall be duly paid and satisfied as soon as *conveniently* can be after my decease.

Item: It is my mind and will that my beloved wife Seabra Williams shall have the use and income of the third part of my estate, real and personal, and have the dwelling house wherein I now live, with a *convenant* garden near the house and one cow with *suficient* food and pasture for the same and as much bedding and household and kitchen furniture as my executors, herein after to be named, shall think proper for her use, *durning* her natural life.

Item: Second it is my will that my grandson Robert meaning my son William Williams, child, is to have one hundred and fifty acres of land to be taken off the west end of the tract of land I now live on. When he arrives at the age of twenty one years, he is to have one hundred *aacres* off it and the remaining fifty after his fathers decease.

Item: It is my will that my son William Williams is to have all the remainder of my estate during his natural life for his use and *benefit* during the same and at his decease it is to be divided equally *amoungst* his children, share and share alike. Except Robert who is herein provided for meaning that my said son William shall have no right title interest or claim of any of my estate farther that for his use and *suport* during his natural life and no longer. It is my will that if my personal estate should not be sufficient to pay my just debts that and in that case I do allow my executors to sell for the best price at public or private sale one hundred acres to be taken out of the southeast corner of the tract of land, I live on so to be the least *ingerous* to the remaining part of the tract and make the *purcher compleat* title for the same, and also to John Treat for a certain piece of ground which I have agreed to let him have at the west end of the place I live on. It being on the west side of a run adjoining land of Robert Powers. Meaning on the bank of the said run reserving the water with the banks to be within the before mentioned Roberts, land it is *suposeds* to contain about six acres more or less. And the said John Treat is to pay at the rate of three dollars per acre for the same.

Item: It is my will that my beloved wife is to have further than what I have in the fore part of this my will, one horse or mare and saddle, to the value of seventy dollars, provided also that what I have hereto for *bequeasted* and given to my said wife is in *lue* and full for all her dower or thirds in my estate and not otherwise, and also what I have before given to and *bequithed* to my son William and *ale* sum of one dollar, provided that it shall be in *lue* and in full satisfaction for his part or dower in my estate and not *otherways* and it is my will that if before mentioned Robert, my grandson shall depart this life before he

43

arrives at full age or without issue, then in that case his land be vested in his brothers and sisters, share and share alike. Then I do nominate and appoint my said wife Seabra, executrix and my friends John McFaden and Robert Powers executors of this my last will and testament and do hereby to allow them or the *surriver* of them do in all things touching the same as what they shall think most advisable.

In witness whereof I have hereunto set my hand and seal this 11th day of September in the year of our Lord one thousand eight hundred and seven. Signed Sealed, Published and Declared by the testator Robert Williams for and his last will and testament in the presents of us.

John Treat

John McFaden   Robert Williams

James Herrington   SEAL

Robert Williams (B1745-1755) Mass., D1807 m. Seabra

William Williams (B1780 Mass., D1834) m. Sarah Seeley

1. Robert Williams (B1803, PA; D1849, PA)
2. William Williams (B1805, PA; D unknown)
3. James
4. Samuel
5. John
6. Sarah
7. Darius
8. George Washington
9. **Perry C. (B1824; D1880, Cedar Co., NE., married Martha Campbell)**
10. Arthur
11. Joseph
12. Lydia
13. Peter

The Early Williams Families

Ithink we are only one or two generations away from getting across the ocean to Wales. Williams is a very common name and whether future family geneologists can succeed in bridging the gap to the old country is questionable. Dad said his father was Welch and his mother was Scottish. Campbell, her maiden name, represents a large clan in Scotland.

Although we can't yet make the jump across the Atlantic Ocean to Wales and Scotland, we can discuss in a general sense Dad's Welch and Scottish forebears. We will start with the earliest known or suspected ancestors and advance to the later generations of Welch and Scotts.

Paleolithic Ancestors

Obviously, one usually cannot trace ancestors for more than a few generations. However, science in recent years has found a way to delve into an individual's deep ancestry through DNA testing. I decided to try and use this approach to discover more about who we are, where we come from and more details and facts as to how it pertains to our Williams line.

Therefore, I contacted the National Geographic Society, one of the sponsors of the testing program, and asked to participate in the Genome study then underway. I paid a small fee and they furnished a DNA kit and I took the cheek swabs and sent them in for analysis. I had a choice of DNA testing to follow the paternal or maternal lines. I chose to follow the paternal line. The paternal line testing involves the 'Y' chromosome which is passed directly from father to son, unchanged from generation to generation for thousands of years, except for slight mutations along the way. Therefore, all my children will show the same lineage along the Williams paternal line.

The mutations, or markers, allow scientists to identify a particular branch on the human tree, where it occurred and when. Each of these markers will be passed down from father to son unchanged for generations.

The results of the study shows that my DNA carries the following 'Y' chromosome markers: M168> P143> M89> P123> M170> P215> P214> M223 and the sub-clade group 12b1 (M223).

Our group called Haplogroup 12b1 (M223) defines one particular branch on the human tree. Tracking our markers provide an intriguing story of a small tribe of modern humans leaving Africa 60,000 years ago, diversifying and becoming a part of, and populating the world.

The following condensed discussion of the analysis results tell the story of how our male ancestors fit within the story of the human journey.

200,000 Years Ago

Humans developed or first appeared in East Africa, probably in present day Ethiopia, Tanzania or Kenya. All living human males, African and non-African carry a genetic marker indicating an East African origin. Archaelogical and linguistic evidence supports this conclusion. This marker suggests an original African Adam.

60,000 Years Ago

Humans made great strides in cognitive abilities and a small group of hunter gatherers found a way to migrate out of Africa. They may have been aided by lowered sea level caused by glaciation in the northern latitudes locking up water in continental glaciers.

50,000 Years Ago

<u>M168</u> – This marker is in our DNA and represents the only lineage to survive outside of Africa. The present day Bushmen of East Africa, hunter-gatherers also carry this marker. All NON-AFRICAN men, world-wide, living today (a sort of non-African Adam) have this marker.

These descendants of M168 used stone tools, and had artistic skills. They were nomads and followed the great herds of game animals across the grasslands of the Middle East.

45,000 Years Ago

<u>M89</u> – Is a marker found in at least 90% of all non-African men. They roamed the grass-lands of the Middle East, which includes present day Iran, Iraq, Arabia, Turkey, etc. Many of the descendants of M-89 remained in the Middle East, but other groups, followed the game herds east and west throughout Central Asia. A smaller group (our ancestors) moved north into the Balkans.

20,000 Years Ago

<u>M170</u> – A man, our ancestor, carrying this marker, was born about 20,000 years ago in what is now the Balkans, perhaps Bulgaria, Romania or Hungary. The Balkans were a place of ref-uge as the waning stages of continental glaciation stopped any northward migration.

These people may be responsible for an advanced technological phase. They were excellent flint knappers. They also may have been the first to weave clothing from natural fibers.

Some of his descendants helped repopulate northern Europe as the great ice sheets began to retreat about 15,000 years ago. Some Vikings, French and Celtic populations carry this marker.

14,000-18,000 Years Ago

<u>M223</u> – The man (our ancestor) with this marker, was born 14,000 to 18,000 years ago in southern France. These descendants repopulated much of northern Europe as the ice sheets retreated.

The famous cave paintings in southern France may have been done by his descendants. About 25% of all northwest European men, including the British, carry the M223 marker. <u>Sub-clade 12b1 (M223)</u>

This subclade marker is also found scattered in lessor amounts throughout northern Europe, but is most common in Germany where about 4.5 million (11%) of all German men carry it.

The Journey to Wales

When our Williams ancestors migrated to Wales remains unknown. Below I present three possibilities:

(A) Stone age tribes migrated to Britain

We may have been part of stone-age tribes that migrated to Britain, including Wales fol-lowing the retreat of the great ice sheets that began melting about 15,000 years ago. The sea between France and England is quite shallow and at times a land bridge connected the two areas. Sea level during the glacial maximum was about 300' lower than it is today.

(B) 'William The Conqueror's' Army

They may have been part of the French king's army that defeated the English about 1,000 years ago. Some of his followers took the name of Williams, hence the origin on our Williams name. British land was promised to the followers of 'William the Conqueror'.

(C) The Anglo-Saxon Invasion

Since the Haplogroup 12b1 (M223) is quite common among northern German men, it is logical to assume some of our ancestors were in the legions of the Anglo-Saxons that invaded England about 1550 years ago.

The stone age tribes that populated the British islands are believed to be the ancestors of the early Celts, ancestors to the Scotch, Irish, Welch, and English. They were excellent flint knappers & left behind many finely worked stone tools and weapons.

I favor theory (A) above as the most likely of the three theories presented. The Welch of 1000 years ago still could have supported 'William the Conquerer' and taken his name.

This is an amazing story. What is obvious now is that we, on this earth, are really brothers and sisters. Also, there really was an Adam(s), sort of.

PART II
DAD'S ENTREPRENEURIAL PURSUITS

Y̲ou now have a general idea of your granddad's predecessors and an outline of his life. Now lets discuss in some detail his early years.

He was in a household of mostly older siblings, and generally under the control of his mother, Martha. Dad's father, Perry, enfeebled because of the Civil War, was frequently gone on preaching tours. He was called a Circuit Evangelist Preacher.

Dad only attended school through the 3rd grade and that was only for a few months each year. Although his formal education was very limited, he later received a first rate education from his first wife, Lily Thomas, who tutored him one on one at home.(1) Lily was said to have been one of Sioux County's first school teachers. Her sister Minnie was supposed to be Sioux County's first school teacher. Although others have also made that claim.

Dad used to tell the story that he had to alternate going to school with one of his brothers as there was only one pair of trousers between them. He also said that he and several of the other children didn't have shoes, so they heated boards behind the stove, fastened them to their feet, and made hurried trips outside to do chores, etc. It is hard to believe that such poverty could have existed. After his father's death, Nov. 1880, his mother took in washing for the neighbors to help make ends meet.

Dad's first job, when he was 10 or 11, about 1879, was gathering cow pies and wood for a neighbor, who constantly nagged the boys to greater and faster efforts. Dad earned a nickel for a day's work. The remaining two children, O.B. (Bern) and Nellie were born in Minnesota, near Brownsville, 1872 and 1874 respectively.

About 1877 the family moved to the area around Ft. Randall, South Dakota and later a short distance south, across the Missouri River to Cedar County, in northeastern Nebr.

In 1886, as mentioned earlier, Sid and his mother moved to Chadron, Nebr. which was then the terminus of the westward advancing railroad. The railroad reached Harrison (then called Summit) in June of 1886. Most of the other children had by then left home and were on their own. Russell, then about 22 was already in Sioux County and operating a sawmill in the Pine Ridge area.(2)

Dad got a job on the railroad building westward from Chadron, the Fremont Elkhorn and Missouri Valley. Your Aunt Ethel thought he was the water boy for the work crews. Your uncle Sid said he either worked on this railroad toward Harrison or the spur that went north from Crawford to Ardmore. He wasn't sure which.

Dad later got a job with his brother Russell logging big pines out of the Pine Ridge until so many sawmills got started that the business floundered.

At one time he owned and operated a butcher shop in Edgemont, South Dakota about the same time that he and his brother Bern were thinking of settling on pre-emption claims in Sioux County near the South Dakota state line, southwest of Ardmore. This was about 1889, a year or two before the Sioux uprising in 1890-91.

(1)   *Lily's father, B.F. Thomas, was Sioux County's first surveyor and school superintendent.*
(2)   *Russell later became a mule train driver in Utah and in 1909 was killed in a saloon brawl when a bartender hit him over the head with a baseball bat. I have Russell's watch which is blood stained and caked with sawdust from the saloon floor. He is buried in the family plot in Chadron.*

The Sioux County court house was built in 1888-89 from brick burned near Tetse Creek, a tributary of Sowbelly Creek in Sowbelly Canyon.(3) Your granddad had a job of hauling the newly fired brick from Sowbelly Canyon to the building site in Harrison. Thirty seven years later in 1926, he occupied the Sheriff's office in this building.

The new courthouse was built on the site of the old building in 1930.(4) The old jail behind the old building was not razed, but continued to house prisoners beyond your granddad's tenure as sheriff. It is no longer used and any prisoners must be jailed in Chadron or Scottsbluff.

(3)   This is only a short distance from the burned residence of Morris and Alda (deceased) Engebretsen, our friends, and Coffee Park in Sowbelly Canyon.

(4)   Some of the used brick from the old courthouse was purchased by Mark Howard and used in the construction of a new blacksmith shop in 1930. When a small boy I observed Mark fit steel rims onto wagon wheels. I now own this building located at 345 Kate St., Harrison and use it as my garage when in Harrison.

Preemptions, Homesteads, and Ranching
in Nebraska, South Dakota & Wyoming

THE PREEMPTION HOMESTEAD

After finishing the courthouse project your granddad decided to settle on a good piece of land as settlers were beginning to move in and were taking up the choice quarter sections. So, during the summer of 1889, at age 19, he settled on a preemption claim of 147.12 acres on Indian Creek, (NW/4 Sec 22-T35N-R55W), Sioux County. The north line is the Nebraska-South Dakota boundary, seven miles southwest of Ardmore, South Dakota. He was under age for filing on the claim as a homesteader, but probably planned to file on it when attaining age 21.

The pre-emption laws of the 1800's allowed squatters (called nesters by the free-ranging cowboys) to move onto unsettled areas and build on land they didn't own. A settler could build, improve and live on the land and had the right to buy or homestead the land ahead of anyone else. Congress abolished the preemption laws in 1891 because of abuses by big land companies.

Uncle Bern Williams settled on the adjacent NE/4 of Section 22 and Uncle Russell settled on the adjacent SW/4 of Section 22. So, now the three Williams brothers controlled 480 acres of the section. A friend, Peter Wiedenfeldt controlled the remaining quarter section (SE/4 of Sec 22).

We don't know how much of the unsettled nearby lands were utilized for grazing cattle by the three brothers. Big cattle outfits, such as the O- Ranch already grazed thousands of cattle in the area, and in fact were already over-grazing the ranges.

Sid Jr. said that he thought Dad had dug a 'dugout' on the side of a hill to live in while constructing a house. This would have been after moving onto the land, early summer, 1889.

Anyone who has ever lived or ranched in northern Sioux County knows that it is virtually impossible to make a living, especially if one has a family, on a quarter section homestead. Thus settlers in such circumstances would attempt to find periodic outside work as cowhands or other jobs while proving up on their homesteads. Most eventually sold out after proving up on their claims.

Dad also found himself in the situation of having to work temporarily off the land and hoped that this would not disqualify him for his homestead.

Your granddad in his 'Homestead Proof-Testimony of Claimant' stated that "he was absent from the land for about three months in 1894 earning money to live and improve the homestead and that the land was cultivated during his absence". This was evidently during the period that he and his brother Bern were ramrodding the Circle Bar Ranch for Dave Anderson. I think they ran the Circle Bar for a much longer time than three months. They raised a lot of horses on this ranch.

The Government Archives in Washington D.C. is a depository of homestead applications, etc. I have the copies of the complete file on Dad's homestead papers. Three pages are listed following and the remaining twelve (12) pages are in Appendix A.

(4—138.)

Receiver's Duplicate Receipt No. *4108*   Application No. *4108*

HOMESTEAD.

Receiver's Office, CHADRON, NEB

NOV 25 1892 , 189

Received of *Charles S. Williams* the sum

of *Fourteen* dollars *no* cents;

being the amount of fee and compensation of register and receiver for the

entry of *Lots 3 & 4 — S² NW⁴* of Section *22* in

Township *35 N.* of Range *55 N.*, under

Section 2290, Revised Statutes of the United States.

C. H. Powers

Receiver.

$14.00   *147 ¹²⁄₁₀₀ Acres*

NOTE.—It is required of the homestead settler that he shall reside upon and cultivate the land embraced in his homestead entry for a period of five years from the time of filing the affidavit, being also the date of entry. An abandonment of the land for more than six months works a forfeiture of the claim. Further, within two years from the expiration of the said five years he must file proof of his actual settlement and cultivation, failing to do which, his entry will be canceled. If the settler does not wish to remain five years on his tract he can, at any time after fourteen months, pay for it with cash or land-warrants, upon making proof of settlement and cultivation from date of filing affidavit to the time of payment.

6610 b—50 m   O—4

54

HOMESTEAD PROOF—TESTIMONY OF CLAIMANT.

Charles S. Williams, being called as a witness in his own behalf in support of homestead entry, No. _4108_, for _Lots 3 & 4 & S² NW¼ Sec 22—35—55_ testifies as follows:

Ques. 1.—What is your name, age, and post-office address?

Ans. _Charles S. Williams, age 28 years, address Ardmore S. Dak._

Ques. 2.—Are you a _native born_ citizen of the United States, and if so, in what State or Territory were you born?*

Ans. _I am a native born citizen of the United States. I was born in the State of Minnesota_

Ques. 3.—Are you the identical person who made homestead entry, No. _4108_, at the _Chadron_ land office on the _25"_ day of _November_ 189_2_, and what is the true description of the land now claimed by you?

Ans. _I am the same person who made H. E. No 4108 at the Chadron Land Office Nov 25" 1892, upon Lots 3 & 4 & S² NW¼ 22—35—55—_

Ques. 4.—When was your house built on the land and when did you establish actual residence therein? (Describe said house and other improvements which you have placed on the land, giving total value thereof.)

Ans. _My house was built on the land in the summer of 1889. I established actual residence therein in the summer of 1889. Frame house 16 x 24 addition 10 x 14, Log stable 15 x 17, Cattle shed 20 x 190, Cellar well & windmill all under fence. No other improvements valued at $1000.00_

Ques. 5.—Of whom does your family consist; and have you and your family resided continuously on the land since first establishing residence thereon? (If unmarried, state the fact.)

Ans. _Myself and wife and two children. We have been absent from the land for short period._

Ques. 6.—For what period or periods have you been absent from the homestead since making settlement, and for what purpose; and if temporarily absent, did your family reside upon and cultivate the land during such absence?

Ans. _We were absent about three months in 1894 earning money to live and improve my homestead. The land was cultivated during my absence._

Ques. 7.—How much of the land have you cultivated each season and for how many seasons have you raised crops thereon?

Ans. _I have cultivated from one to ten acres each season_ _raised crops thereon each season_

Ques. 8.—Is your present claim within the limits of an incorporated town or selected site of a city or town, or used in any way for trade and business?

Ans. _It is not within the limits of any incorporation or used in any way for trade or business._

Ques. 9.—What is the character of the land? Is it timber, mountainous, prairie, grazing, or ordinary agricultural land? State its kind and quality, and for what purpose it is most valuable.

Ans. _It is prairie grazing and farming land. Most valuable for_ _Grazing purposes_

Ques. 10.—Are there any indications of coal, salines, or minerals of any kind, on the land? (If so, describe what they are, and state whether the land is more valuable for agricultural than for mineral purposes.)

Ans. _There are no indications of minerals of any kind on the land._

Ques. 11.—Have you ever made any other homestead entry? (If so, describe the same.)

Ans. _I have never made any other homestead entry._

Ques. 12.—Have you sold, conveyed, or mortgaged any portion of the land; and if so, to whom and for what purpose?

Ans. _I have not sold conveyed, or mortgaged any portion of the land._

Ques. 13.—Have you any personal property of any kind elsewhere than on this claim? (If so, describe the same, and state where the same is kept.)

Ans. _I have no personal property of any kind elsewhere than on this claim._

Charles S. Williams

I HEREBY CERTIFY that the foregoing testimony was read to the claimant before being subscribed, and was sworn to before me this _18_ day of _July_ 189_6_.

M. J. Blewett
Clerk District Court

[SEE NOTE ON FOURTH PAGE.]

* (In case the party is of foreign birth a certified transcript from the court records of his declaration of intention to become a citizen, or of his naturalization, or a copy thereof, certified by the officer taking this proof, must be filed with the case. Evidence of _naturalization_ is only required in final (_five year_) homestead cases.)

NO. 1. HOMESTEAD.

Land Office at ALLIANCE, NEB.,

....189

I, *Charles S. Williams* of *Sioux County*
Nebraska, who made Homestead Entry No. .... for the
Lots 2 & 4 & S½ NW¼

Section *22*, in Township *35*, of Range *55*

West, do hereby give notice of my intention to make final proof to establish my
claim to the land above described, and that I expect to prove my residence and
cultivation before *M.J. Blewett Clerk District Court*
at *Harrison* Nebraska.
on *July 18*, 189 *6*, by two of the following witnesses:

Herman Kroening of *Ardmore S. Dak* Nebraska,
John Messing of " " , Nebraska,
Peter Wiedenfeldt of " " , Nebraska,
John Ostrander of " " , Nebraska.

Charles S. Williams, Claimant.
Ardmore South Dak

Land Office at ALLIANCE, NEB.,

.............*June 8*............., 189 *6*

Notice of the above application will be published in the ....*Journal*.........
........................, printed at ....*Harrison*........., Nebraska, which I
hereby designate as the newspaper published nearest the land described in said
application.

J. W. Wehn Jr
Register.

56

SID WILLIAMS COUNTRY
TRI-STATE AREA
E. WYOMING,
N.W. NEBRASKA &
S.W. S. DAKOTA

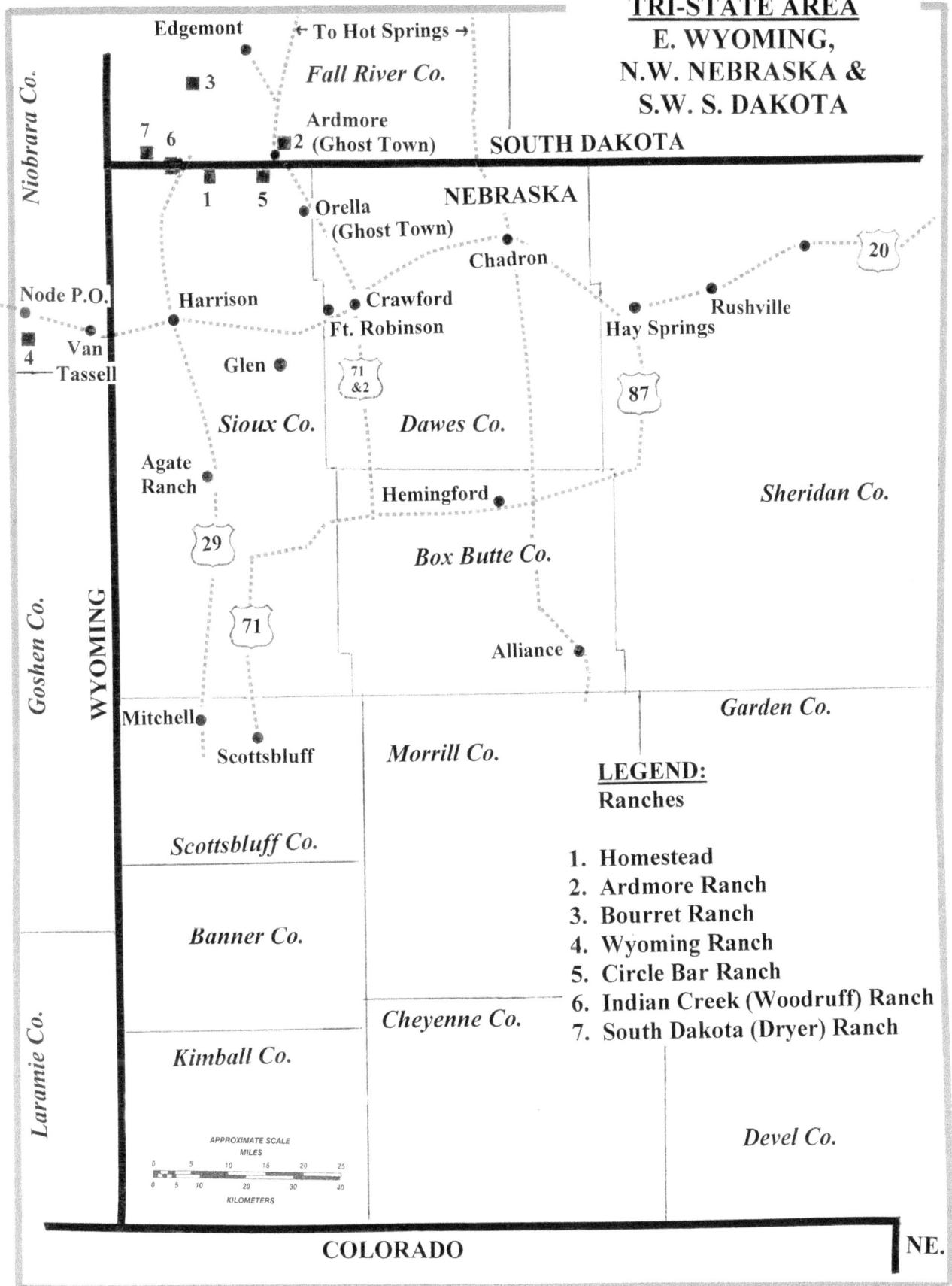

Edgemont

← To Hot Springs →

Fall River Co.

3

Ardmore
2 (Ghost Town)

SOUTH DAKOTA

7 6

NEBRASKA

1 5

Orella
(Ghost Town)

Chadron

20

Node P.O.

Harrison

Crawford

Rushville

Ft. Robinson

Hay Springs

Van
Tassell

4

Glen

71
&2

Sioux Co.

Dawes Co.

87

Agate
Ranch

Sheridan Co.

29

Hemingford

Box Butte Co.

71

Alliance

Garden Co.

Mitchell

Morrill Co.

Scottsbluff

LEGEND:
Ranches

Scottsbluff Co.

1. Homestead
2. Ardmore Ranch
3. Bourret Ranch
4. Wyoming Ranch
5. Circle Bar Ranch
6. Indian Creek (Woodruff) Ranch
7. South Dakota (Dryer) Ranch

Banner Co.

Cheyenne Co.

Kimball Co.

Devel Co.

APPROXIMATE SCALE
MILES
0   5   10   15   20   25
0 5   10   20   30   40
KILOMETERS

COLORADO

NE.

Niobrara Co.

Goshen Co.

WYOMING

Laramie Co.

57

Other Enterprises & The Indian Scare of 1890-91

lso, according to Sid Jr., your granddad owned and operated a butcher shop for a short time in Edgemont, South Dakota. He had the butcher shop during the time of the Indian Scare of 1890-91 because Dad is said to have walked the 22 mile distance from Edgemont to his homestead one night during the peak of the trouble to be with his brothers who had gathered at the homestead.

Although in no direct involvement in the Sioux uprising that winter, he frequently told of one interesting incident at the end of his long walk. Arriving late that night at the cabin, he rapped on the window. The brothers, Russell, Bern and probably Alexander, awakened instantly. Uncle Russell jumped out of bed and grabbing bed slats to ward off the attackers exclaimed: "The rascals-they're here." Hearing Dad laugh immediately put everyone at ease.

After the battle of Wounded Knee the Indian war soon dissipated.

Sid Jr. also said that Dad sometimes took early day tourists on sightseeing trips by horse and buggy to the Hot Springs spa in the southern Black Hills. Quite a trip by horse and buggy. He may have conducted these sporadic or occasional tours during the time he was operating the butcher shop in Edgemont and improving the homestead during the early 1890's. Thus, your enterprising granddad earned money for the homestead.

The homesteads of Dad, Bern and Russell were eventually sold to the Mader family. This is believed to occurred in about 1905 or 06. The Maders eventually sold the land to Ken Loton.

Sid As A Cowhand

t first the large open range ranches, such as the Bar T and the Circle Bar, would not hire the small homesteaders for ranch work and in fact worked against the squatters in various ways. The nesters fenced off the land, water holes and in general impeded the movement of the large cattle herds. The cattlemen cut the fences and the cattle wandered over and destroyed the planted crops. Eventually, the big ranchers realized that discouraging homesteading was a failing endeavor, so they relented and hired some of the "nesters".

Dad also liked to tell the story that one time when the large ranches were having a big roundup and branding project they had one of his homestead calves in the big bunch of calves to be worked and branded. When your granddad contacted the roundup foreman he was reluctantly advised that if they had his calf then it would be up to him to get it out. Dad, on a saddle horse and with a lariat rope, rode into the bunch of bawling calves, found the calf and threw a loop. It looked like a missed toss, but the calf stepped into the loop with a rear foot and Dad was able to haul him out. Dad later got range jobs with some of the big outfits.

Foremen of the Circle Bar Ranch

The famed Circle Bar Ranch was one of the first established in Sioux County after the removal of the Indians to the Dakota Reservations in the 1870's. The ranch headquarters was inside Nebr. and just south of the junction of Hat Creek and Indian Creek.

During the Circle Bar's heyday it ran upward of 20,000 head of cattle. During the time of your grandfather and Bern's tenure as co-managers it was owned by Dave Anderson, then South Dakota State Senator. Anderson's wife, the former Miss Dora Moore had the distinction of having the Village of Ardmore named after her.(5)

We don't know the exact dates of when the Williams brothers operated the Circle Bar but it is believed to have been between 1891 and 1895.(6) The former date marks the end of the Wounded Knee battle and skirmishes when we know Sid was living on a preemption that eventually became his homestead and working as a butcher in Edgemont. Also, we know that Martha V. Williams, my half-sister was born on the Circle Bar Ranch in 1894.

Dad had married Lily Thomas, daughter of B.F. Thomas about 1893. Her father was an early day Sioux County surveyor and School Superintendent. Lily died in 1904 in Springfield, Missouri. She had gone home with the children to be near her parents and where there were good doctors to care for her worsening illness. Dad and Lily were estranged at the time.

After Lily's death Dad went to Springfield, Missouri and got his four children: Martha 10, Sidney 6, Ethel 4, and Floyd 2. Sid's mother, Mrs. Perry (Martha) Williams helped raised the children in Ardmore.

Grandmother Williams had moved from Chadron to Ardmore to be closer to Sid, Russell and Bern who lived in the area. By this time she had a Civil War Pension based on her son Lewis' service in the Minnesota Volunteers. The pension made her day to day existence less problematic.

(5)   Bern Williams was married to the former Miss Evalyn (Eva) Moore, a sister to Mrs. David Anderson. Bern had severely frozen his feet as a youth while herding sheep at Ft. Randall, South Dakota. Dad looked after Bern and assisted him when necessary. However, during his younger years Bern didn't need much assistance. He could operate quite well from a horse.

(6)   When a young fellow I sometimes visited Bern and Evalyn in Edgemont during the late 1940's. At that time he could not walk and got around on his hands and knees. He refused to follow medical advice and have his feet amputated. Ironically, he was the longest lived of the 13 children in his family, living to age 81, dying August 25, 1953 at Yankton, South Dakota. Burial was at Edgemont. Evalyn (Eva) died July 4, 1954, Edgemont, S. Dak., at age 93.

The Lost Six Shooter

Dad lost a 45 Colt 6-shooter while working on the Circle Bar Ranch. The loss occurred after roping a saddle horse from a bunch of horses in the corral preparatory to beginning the work day of rounding up cattle for branding, etc. After mounting, the horse took off on a running buck. A half-mile later after getting the horse settled down he discovered his revolver was missing. An extensive search failed to recover the gun. It was eventually replaced with another colt, a 38 mounted on a 45 frame.

There was considerable justification for packing a sidearm in those days. There was some concern about Indian attacks. The Custer massacre was only 15 years or so in the past; the Wounded Knee battle had happened only 2 or 3 years previously and the 1903 Battle of Lightning Creek was yet to occur. There was concern that renegade bands of Sioux from the Sioux Reservation only 40 miles east could be in the country at any time. In fact bands of Sioux frequently passed through the area on antelope hunting forays. Outlaws passed through the country and considerable livestock rustling took place against the bigger ranchers.

A Bad Injury

Sometime during your grandfather's work on the Circle Bar Ranch he was severely injured. He was driving a team of horses across the Ardmore bridge. Something spooked the horses. He became entangled in the harness or riggings and was dragged across the bridge. He was found unconscious and taken to the Dave Anderson house. Upon regaining consciousness he was found to be paralyzed from the waist down. Eventually, after some convalescence, he regained the use of his legs and regained most of his health. However, back problems, as a result of the accident, bothered him for the rest of his life. Unknown at the time, the accident would be a factor in his death many years later.

The Battle of Lightning Creek-
Last Indian-White Skirmish on the High Plains

(Writer's Notes: this item was taken from the original manuscript authored by this writer which was published in the book: Sioux County History, First 100 years, 1886-1986).

"The Battle Of Lightning Creek"

Last Indian-White Skirmish On The High Plains

Niobrara Co., Wyoming

By Donald R. Williams

Historians agree that the Indian Scare of 1890-91 and the "Battle of Wounded Knee" were the last major Indian-White confrontations in the Great Plains Area.

However, there was one other little known incident called "The Battle of Lightning Creek" that occurred in 1903 in Western Niobrara County, Wyoming.

The Ogallala and Brule Sioux had hunted over the Black Hills Area including western Nebraska since the late 1700's. They had driven out the Apache and Kiowas after they themselves had been displaced earlier from eastern Minnesota by the Cree and Chippewa Indians who had obtained guns from the early fur traders. The Sioux, after obtaining horses, became the scourge of the plains. Then a new more numerous and technologically advanced invader came-the white man. The Sioux and their Cheyenne and Arapahoe allies fought a series of bloody fights with these invaders, largely because of white encroachments on hunting lands set aside for them through various treaties. As a result of the treaty of Sept. 1876, the Black Hills and adjacent areas, including northwest Nebraska, were ceded to the United States and the Sioux relegated to several reservations in South Dakota. The U.S. Gov't in return promised to provide food and supplies to the Indians.

My maternal grandfather, Joseph H. Sturdivant, was involved in one delivery of beef to the Indians.[7] He worked the summer of 1892 for the AU7 ranch near Newcastle, Wyo. He helped drive a bunch of cattle, purchased by the government from eastern Wyoming ranchers, to the Rosebud reservation in South Dakota, just north of Valentine, Nebr.

The Gov't. food allotments were frequently late or sometimes never arrived. The Indians, of a nomadic nature, had a hard time adjusting to reservation life and didn't need much of an excuse to go on hunting forays off the reservations, especially if the Gov't. food allotments were late. These forays continued until the open ranges had been settled up, fenced off and most of the deer and antelope hunted to near extinction by hungry settlers.

My Father, Charles Sidney Williams, Sr., owned and operated a ranch near Ardmore, So. Dak. at the turn of the century. Bands of Sioux frequently hunted on his ranch or passed through on their way to hunting grounds in Wyoming and Nebraska. Failing to procure game, Dad would sometimes give them an old cow to tide them over until they got back to the reservations. This was partly an act of compassion, but also an attempt to keep them from running off his younger livestock. His oldest son, and my half-brother, Charles Sidney Williams, Jr., 88 at the date of this writing (1986) and now living in a retirement center at Hay Springs, Nebr., recalls

---

(7)   *Personal letter, J.H. Sturdivant, AU7 Ranch, dated July 21, 1892 to his wife, who was alone on the Sturdivant homestead, near the headwaters of Sheep Creek, Sioux Co., Nebr.*

that in 1903 or 04, when he was 5 or 6 years old, an old chief gave him a pair of moccasins and a bow with arrows to show his appreciation for an old cow given to his band by Dad.(8)

The Indians supposedly got hunting permits from a Major John R. Brennan, then Indian Agent of the Pine Ridge Indian Reservation.(9) Of course the Indians had no concept of invisible static political boundaries and didn't hesitate to cross over into adjacent states. When hunting in Wyoming or Nebraska they were violating that State's game laws. These Indians were a source of annoyance and concern to the few settlers in the area.

One band of 24 Indians led by Chief Horney Frog, passed through the ranch of Charles M. Hanson, a Fall River County Rancher, in Oct. 1903 on their way to the antelope hunting grounds in eastern Wyo. They told Mr. Hanson, that they would not be stopped, arrested and fined as they had the year before.(10)

The hunting party was soon reported to be hunting illegally to Sheriff Miller of Newcastle, Weston County, Wyoming. He set out after them with a posse of 9 men. Miller intercepted the Indians and attempted to arrest them. Outnumbering the lawmen they refused to be arrested so Miller sent for reinforcements. On October 30 Miller and 12 possemen again caught up to the Indians on Lightning Creek about 12 miles northwest of present day Lance Creek. Miller climbed to the top of an embankment within view of the redskins and demanded their surrender. The answer was a rifle shot and the Sheriff crumpled. The posse took cover and opened fire. After heavy rifle fire from both sides, the Indians began to retreat and during the night slipped away. The posse dispatched a courier to Lusk to telegraph for help and additional posses were organized in adjacent counties. Later it was determined that two whites had died, Sheriff Miller and one of his deputies, Louis Falkenberg. Four Indians were dead, including a Chief Smith, Black Kettle, Gray Bear and a teenage boy. Several Indians were wounded. The dead were buried in shallow graves on the battlefield.

A new posse, headed by Sheriff Lee Mathers of Crook Co., Wyo. and possibly with no legal jurisdiction in So. Dakota, caught up with the renegade Sioux scurrying back to the safety of the reservation. The interception took place east of Edgemont, South Dakota without a fight. The posse took the Sioux to Douglas, Wyo. where 9 bucks were arraigned before a Judge Daniells. However, the persons firing the fatal shots could not be identified and so the case was dismissed. The Indians were escorted back to the reservations.

This skirmish brought to a close a 300-400 year period of conflict with the red man extending over the North American Continent.

(8)   C. Sid Williams, Jr. has told of this incident several times during conversations with this writer the past several years.

(9)   Lusk Herald, Issue of Sept. 1, 1960 describing the "Battle of Lightning Creek".

(10)   This writer and Mr. Tom Broderick, Harrison, Nebr. interviewed Mr. Hanson in Edgemont, So. Dak. in August 1967. I talked to Mr. Hanson again in July, 1968 for additional details. Mr. Hanson was then nearly 92 years of age.

Last Roundups

Your granddad participated in some of the last big cattle roundups for one or more of the large outfits during the last years of the 19th century and the early years of the 20th century. Below is a picture of the roundup of 1905, Duck Creek Camp, southwestern South Dakota.

Open Range Roundup, Ardmore, S. Dakota area; Sid Williams participated, black arrow

Ranches and Other Properties

Ardmore Ranch

About the time of the 1905 roundup your granddad had a chance to buy the land holdings of Ed Jones. This purchase would allow Dad to live in Ardmore and help his mother care for his four children.

Dad, Russell and Bern decided to sell their three homesteads of 480 acres to the Mader family. Dad's share of the proceeds from the sale of his homestead was used to buy the Ardmore Ranch. The new Ardmore Ranch purchase consisted of 760 acres at $5/acre or about $3800. The ranch land was in three sections, stacked in a north-south direction immediately north of Ardmore. A school section, government grazing lands and other leased lands were utilized and other land added later.

The land can easily be seen today as Highway #71 borders most of it along the west side, immediately north of Ardmore.

Webberville Property, Michigan

After Pearl and Dad divorced, 1908, he bought a livery barn-hotel-restaurant in Webberville, Michigan, a town about 50 miles northwest of Detroit (see later section: Marrying a Southern Belle).

It remains a mystery of how he found this property and why he moved so far away from family and friends. Little is known about this property or your granddad's life there. Perhaps he was trying to escape his marital problems. The reasons will probably remain unknown.

Bourret Ranch

About 1910 Dad bought a ranch southwest of Edgemont, South Dakota from one of the Bourret boys, John, Will or James. The Bourrets were expanding out from their Niobrara River properties in Nebraska, but didn't find the South Dakota ranches to their liking, hence sold one of them to Dad. Well, apparently Dad didn't like it either and soon sold it. He still had the Ardmore Ranch. The ranch was traded in 1916 to a fellow from Kansas City, Missouri for a very large house in that city. The house, at 2642 Campbell St., built in 1910, contained 14 rooms and was very modern for the time with indoor plumbing, hot and cold water, electric lights, four mantels and a two car garage.

The house was put up for sale, and the money from the sale was used to buy the Woodruff Ranch.

Woodruff Ranch

Dad bought this ranch from Walter and Carrie Woodruff in 1917. It is located 13 miles southwest of Ardmore, South Dakota and is mostly in Sioux County, Nebraska, but also partly in Fall River County, South Dakota.

The land straddles the South Dakota-Nebraska line and Highway #29 passes through the east portion of the block. The ranch headquarters are west of the highway and can easily be seen before entering South Dakota.

The ranch consisted of 858 deeded acres and cost $10/acre or $8580.00. These lands were sections 23 and 24-T35N-R56W and Sec 15-T12S-R2E in South Dakota. Also, two additional sections of land, one of which was a school section were leased in South Dakota and an additional section of land in Sec 31-T35N-R55W Sioux Co. was purchased at a later date. The Williams heirs own an undivided 50% interest in the minerals under the 858 acres. Twenty five years ago a Leo Sandstone oil play included the above area and a drilling location was selected in Sec. 26 near our interests. The well was not drilled because of too much promotion on the part of some of the partners. I think the prospect is still there.

The Woodruff ranch was sold in 1930 to Jacob Henry. Josie Henry lived on the ranch. It is now known as the Gayle Henry place. Gayle is the son of the late Josie Henry and grandson of Jacob.

The Dryer Ranch

This ranch, in South Dakota, was purchased from Orville Dryer in 1930 after the sale of the Woodruff ranch. It consisted of 800 deeded acres in Sections 12 and 13 of T12S-R1E, and Sections 7 and 18-T12S-R2E in Fall River County. Considerable government grazing rights went with the place. Additional sections were leased, including a school section in South Dakota. This ranch was held until the time of Dad's death in 1938. We called this ranch the Indian Creek Ranch.

I remember this ranch well. The dwelling was a log house with a dirt roof that had a large cactus growing on it.

The Wyoming Ranch

This small ranch was purchased about 1934-35. It was located a few miles south of Node, Niobrara County, Wyoming. It was characterized by good wheat grass and provided a haven for cattle that had run out of grass on the drouth stricken Indian Creek place.

This ranch was sold about the time of Dad's death in 1938. During the 1970's it was part of the ranch operated by Jimmy Serres.

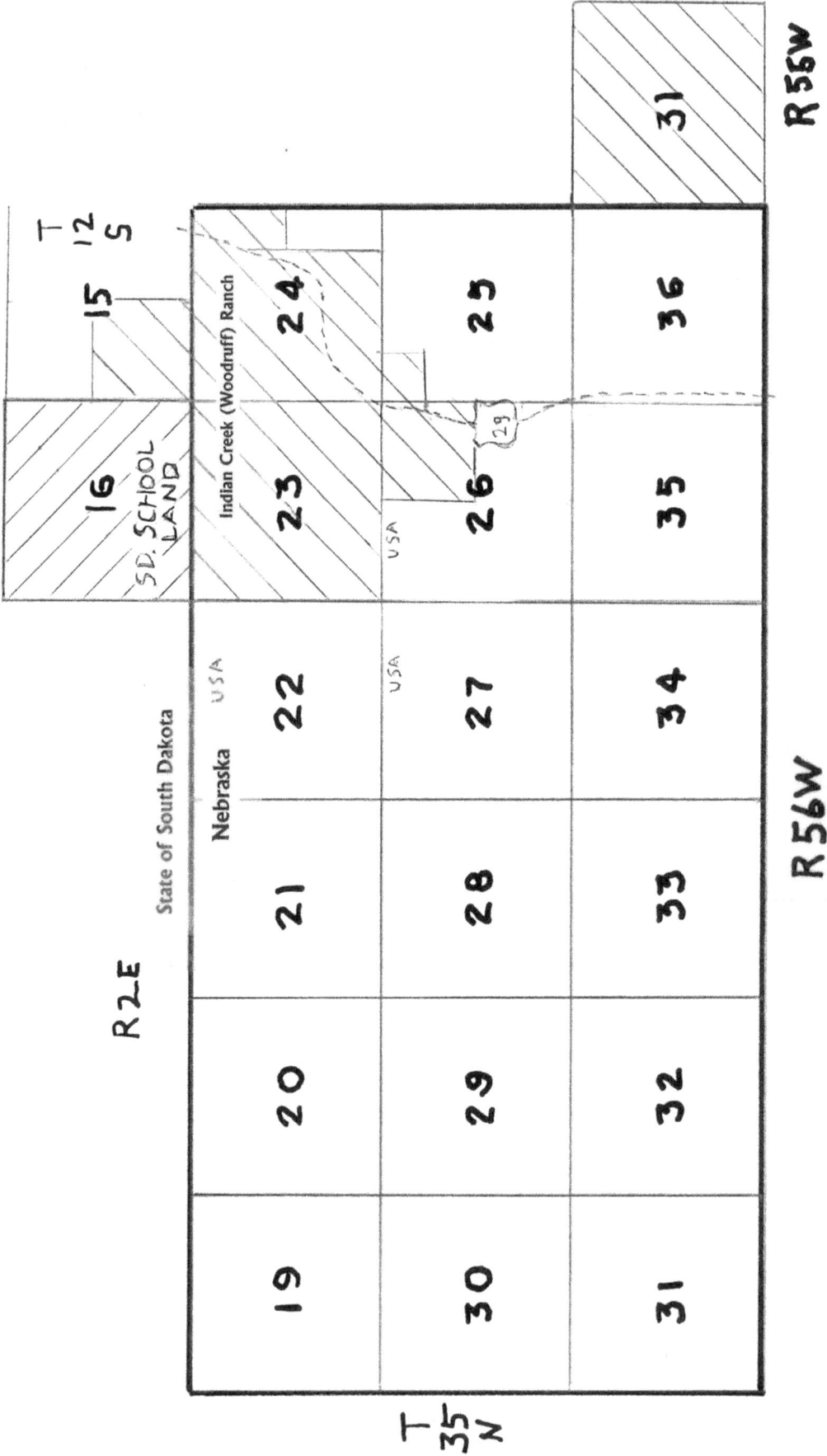

R56W

R2E

State of South Dakota

Nebraska

T 12 S

15

16

S.D. SCHOOL LAND

Indian Creek (Woodruff) Ranch

31

24

25

36

23

26

35

29

USA

USA

22

27

34

USA

21

28

33

20

29

32

19

30

31

R56W

T 35 N

66

Marriages

First Marriage

Dad was first married, 1893, to Lily Thomas, daughter of B.F. and Sarah (Hamlin), Thomas. Lily died in 1904 in Springfield, Missouri. Their children: Martha, Harry (died in infancy), Charles Sidney Jr., Ethel, and Floyd.

Marrying A Southern Belle (Marriage #2)

During 1906-07 Dad shipped a string of race horses to Hot Springs, Arkansas. His horses must have been among the best at this track as Dad is said to have made a lot of money racing his thoroughbreds there. That is another story and more will be said about this in a later section.

While staying at a boarding house during the race meet he met a southern girl, Pearl Johnson and after a short courtship they married March 3, 1907 at Hot Springs, Arkansas. A son, Russell, was born Dec. 30, 1907 at Coffeeville, Kansas. Pearl, pregnant had decided to go to her mother's home to have her baby. The train just got her as far as Coffeeville, Kansas when the birth time arrived. They divorced Dec. 8, 1908, this time in Hot Springs, South Dakota.(1)

A Third Marriage

Sometime after the failed marriage to Pearl, Dad married Hattie Blessing, daughter of Frank Blessing, pioneer Ardmore rancher. However this marriage didn't last long either.

Marriage #4

About the time of Dad's purchase of the Woodruff Ranch he married again for the 4th time to a woman named Agnes Quinn. Legal documents indicate they were man and wife in June of 1917.

The 1920 census of Sioux County lists her name as Agnes, age 27 and their daughter, La Vonne was two. Martha V., Dad's daughter from his first marriage and age 25 was living with them. Agnes was listed as being born in Nebraska while her parents were born in Ireland. I'm not sure when they divorced, but it was sometime before Dad became sheriff in 1926.

(1)   Russell spent several summers at Dad's Woodruff ranch while growing up. He obtained a degree in pharmacy and eventually owned several drug stores in Phoenix, Arizona. He married. He and his wife, Florence had two daughters, Patricia and Linda. Both married and each had children. Patricia married an Arizona Highway Patrolman, last name Rambo.

Marriage #5

The fifth marriage to my mother, LaVerne Sturdivant will be discussed in a later section.

Dad must have had his hands full, taking care of the various ranching enterprises, a stable of race horses; racing in several states; his courtships, marriages, and taking care of his children. Some of his friends described him as a "livewire".

THE
FIVE
WIVES
OF
GRANDDAD
WILLIAMS

Pearl (Johnson) Williams; a native of Hot Springs, Arkansas; estimated date: 1915; second wife of Sid Williams

Lily (Thomas) Williams & daughter Ethel, age two about 1902; Lily was Dad's first wife; they were married about 1893; she died in 1904

Hattie Blessing; wife #3

Agnes Quinn, wife #4;
holding daughter LaVonne

Graves Studio

LaVerne (Sturdivant) Williams; born in 1908 & died in 1981;
they married in Colorado in 1927; she was Dad's fifth & last wife;
she married Fred Davison in 1941, three years after Sid's death

Cattle and Horse Drives

During World War I Dad raised several hundred head of horses on the Woodruff Ranch. He had a lot of dealings with the Army at Fort Robinson. Dad raised top notch saddle horses for the Remount Division of the United States Cavalry. According to Dean Williams, Dad's grandson, the government had a program which allowed thoroughbred breeders in the area to upgrade their stock.

Dad also sold a lot of horses during World War I to the French and British Armies for use in Europe. When the war ended in Nov. 1918 these orders suddenly stopped. We were stuck with a ranch full of horses and little market for them.

Your granddad finally found a rancher about 20 miles south of Atkinson, Nebraska that wanted to acquire the horses. However, because this rancher had little money a trade was arranged. Dad acquired his cow herd and he got the 150 head of horses. Part of the deal was that the horses had to be delivered to the Atkinson rancher's place. This presented a big problem. It was finally decided that the horses would be trailed the 300 mile distance to the ranch. Sid Jr., his brother Floyd, and another cowboy, Penny Vivian, trailed the 150 head of horses from the Indian Creek Ranch. The drive in 1921 or 1922 took 9 days to complete. Much of the route was along present day Highway #20 which in those days was little more than a fenced dirt lane and carried little traffic. Your granddad drove a 1921 Cadillac Roadster which served as a chuck wagon and a bed roll carrier. Dad scouted ahead finding routes around towns and places to water the horses. Some ranchers charged $.05 per head to water them.

Dad wanted the boys to drive his cow herd back to the Indian Creek Ranch, but they didn't think they could do it and I suppose by this time they were tired of the trail. So, Dad found pasturage for the herd and later sent them to market.

Cattle Drive to the 77 Ranch

The Williams boys drove another bunch of cattle for their dad. They drove 700 steers to the 77 ranch located northwest of Lusk, Wyoming. This drive was in about 1934 and was partly across open range country. I asked Sid Jr. about the number of head. He assured me that 700 head was correct. I never understood how we came to have such a big number of steers. The drive covered about 40 miles. Perhaps, he had purchased the cattle on speculation for later sale.

Cattle Drive to the Node Wyoming Ranch

Another drive of about 40-45 miles was the drive to move the cattle herd from the So. Dak. Indian Creek Ranch across northwest Sioux County to the ranch south of Node, Wyoming. This was about 1936. Dean Williams, Floyd's boy, participated in this drive.

71

The Agricultural Depression of the 1920's and '30's

The span of years after World War I through most of the 1930's was about as bad a time as the American cattlemen ever experienced. Many good people lost their places. Some had lived on their farms and ranches for decades, but could not cope with very low commodity prices and extensive drought. This was especially true of those who had borrowed money from lending institutions to expand their operations during the good times. Some could not pay their real estate taxes and foreclosures resulted. This resulted in sheriff's sales. More about sheriff's sales will be discussed under the law enforcement section.

The economic situation got so bad for farmers and ranchers that the government initiated cattle buying programs to help ease their plight. However, the aid was too little and too late for many of them.

The following items taken from the Harrison Sun are informative about these programs. Also, the rainfall given on the following chart shows that the drought was especially severe during 1932 and 1934.

Dad sold some cattle to the government under this program. Some cattle purchased by the government were destroyed and bulldozed under.

Drought stressed cattle were also more subject to tuberculosis and anthrax infections. Dad lost several head due to anthrax and the rest of the herd was expeditiously vaccinated against anthrax.

RELIEF PROGRAM FOR CATTLE INDUSTRY IN DROUTH AREAS

While dry weather conditions continue in this section of the country, government agencies are at work to map out a program to take care of the enormous amount of cattle from the range country that are likely to be placed on an early market, thus demoralizing the market.

Still without rain in this immediate section, although should it come in a few weeks, the grass land will soon recuperate and perhaps carry the stockmen through the season.

Some of the earliest shipments in years from this section, were made last week when four carloads were shipped from this point. The cattle were placed on feed in the eastern part of the state.

While the situation is grave, we have a large number of optimistic cattlemen in the vicinity who assure us that rain will be forthcoming in time to avert disaster, and let's hope they are right.

The following article from the Alliance Times-Herald gives the condition in the Dakotas, and steps to be taken by the government relief administration to care for same:

Heavy purchases of cattle in drouth areas of the north central west and possible transplanting of 3,000 to 4,000 South Dakota families are included in the program for relief of the dry sections of North and South Dakota, Wisconsin and Minnesota.

The Federal Surplus Relief corporation, Harry L. Hopkins, emergency relief administrator, said, will start buying cattle immediately from farmers on relief rolls or those in distress. Within the next three weeks he expects to take the entire surplus in the area. The corporation will do the buying for the agricultural adjustment administration.

In South Dakota where there are hundreds of farms which have not yielded a good living for their owners in years, Hopkins said, from 3,000 to 4,000 families might be moved to state-owned farms on reasonable terms. The state owns approximately 4,000 farms.

The immediate cattle purchasing program will be intensified in four states, Hopkins said, but will not necessarily be confined to them. Other potential drouth areas or sections where there has been no rain in recent months will be included eventually.

Cattle purchases will be many times greater than those already made by the Surplus Relief corporation, Hopkins said.

The cattle will be closely examined for tuberculosis and all tubercular cattle destroyed under the department of agriculture's tuberculoses campaign plan.

Other beef will be canned and distributed to persons on relief rolls.

Harrison Sun, Thurs., May 24, 1934

SPECIALIST INVESTIGATES THE COUNTY DROUGHT SITUATION

W.W. Derrick, animal husbandry specialist in charge of any state organization needed for the government cattle buying program, spent Thursday of last week in Sioux County. The purpose of Mr. Derrick's visit was to investigate the drought and livestock situation in Northwest Nebraska to determine whether or not the area should be declared a primary drought territory and the government emergency cattle buying program started.

Agricultural Agent Swinbank, J. Russell Batie, Dawes County agricultural agent, and Mr. Derrick visited several ranches in the north end of the county where acute feed shortage had been reported. Some cattle were found to be in very poor condition, though most of them were found to be in good shape.

Though no definite action has been taken in starting this program, the Sioux County situation is being brought to the attention of federal authorities in an effort to work out a plan for handling distressed cattle between now and such time as it seems necessary to start the regular cattle buying program.

Should the program be started here, the schedule of cattle prices authorized is as follows:

Condemned animal-2 year old and over $12; 1 year to 2 years $10; under 1 year $4.

Edible animal-2 year old and over $13 to $20; 1 year to 2 years $11 to $15; under 1 year $5 to $8.

Participation, debtor-2 year old and over $6; 1 year to 2 years $5; under 1 year $3.

Participation, creditor-2 year old and over $6 to $14; 1 year to 2 years $5 to $10; under 1 year $1 to $5.

County and precinct committeemen have already been selected, and assurance is given that if an emergency develops the county can be designated to government buying within a few hours notice.

Harrison Sun, Thurs., June 21, 1934

LIVESTOCK PRICES AT SOUTH OMAHA

Beef Cattle Open the Week; Steady to Easier. Top $9.00

GOOD HOGS RULE STEADY

Fat Lambs Hold About Steady With Last Week's Close at $8.50 @ 9.00. Feeder Lambs Stronger at $6.00 @ 6.85

Union Stock Yards, Omaha, June 26, 1934 – Receipts of cattle Monday were 17,000. Including in the arrivals were over 4,500 drouth cattle bought by the packers for processing. Desirable shipping steers were in good demand at steady prices but trade was slow and the trend of the market unequally lower on the bulk of the offerings. Best steers here sold around $9.00. Cows and heifers generally held steady under a broad demand and there was good inquiry and firm market for stock cattle and feeding steers.

Quotations on Cattle: Steers, choice to prime $8.75 @ 9.50; steers, good to choice $8.00 @ 8.75; steers, fair to good $7.00 @ 8.00; steers, common to fair $6.00 @ 7.00; yearlings, choice to prime $7.75 @ 8.40; yearlings, good to choice $6.75 @ 7.75; yearlings, fair to good $6.00 @ 6.75; yearlings common to fair $5.25 @ 6.00; trashy warmed-ups $4.50 @ 5.00; heavy warmed-ups $4.50 @ 5.00; heavy heifers, good to choice $6.25 @ 7.00; light heifers, good to choice $5.75 @ 6.50; heifers, fair to good $5.00 @ 5.75; heifers, common to fair $4.00 @ 5.00; fed cows, good to choice $4.25 @ 5.50; cows, fair to good $3.00 @ 4.25; cutters $2.35 @ 2.75; canners $1.75 @ 2.25; feeders, good to choice $5.40 @ 6.00; feeders, fair to good $4.50 @ 5.35; feeders, common to fair $3.75 @ 4.50; stockers, good to choice $5.00 @ 5.50; stockers, fair to good $4.25 @ 5.00; stockers, common to fair $3.50 @ 4.25; trashy grades $3.00 @ 3.50; stock cows $1.75 @ 2.50; stock heifers $3.00 @ 4.40; stock steer calves $3.50 @ 5.50; stock heifer calves $3.00 @ 4.25.

HOGS OPEN THE WEEK STEADY

Receipts of hogs Monday were 12,500. On good hogs of all weights the market ruled steady with both local packers and order buyers buying freely. Desirable hogs went largely at $4.25 @ 4.50, choice butcher weights up to $4.60. Sows sold at $3.75 @ 4.10 and pigs and light weights were hard to move from $4.00 to $3.50 down.

Harrison Sun, Thurs., June 28, 1934

GOVERNMENT CATTLE BUYING IS CONTINUED IN COUNTY

The strike of workmen in the Chicago stock yards, and congestion in the plants that are processing the government cattle, threatened for a time to suspend government buying of cattle for a time. County Agent J. C. Swinbank was advised by wire the fore part of the week to hold up cattle buying in Sioux County until further notified, but a telegram today rescinded the former order and the buying program is to continue as outlined.

Orders to cut the quota at Harrison last Monday to 200 was later increased to 300. 294 head were delivered here that day and of these 8 were condemned. Buying for the north part of Sioux County was carried on at Ardmore Wednesday, when 300 head were delivered and but three of the number condemned. Deliveries will be made at Andrews tomorrow, the quota being 300 head.

Checks for cattle purchased by the government have begun to arrive, the first payments being received here Monday.

Harrison Sun, Thurs., July 26, 1934

GOV'T. BUYS ALMOST ONE HALF MILLION CATTLE IN NEBRASKA

Final figures given out by officials of the drouth relief cattle buying division of the government show that a total of 477,121 head of cattle were purchased in Nebraska. The total for the United States was 8,156,962, for which an average price of $13.50 was paid to farmers and stockmen.

Harrison Sun, Thurs., Febr. 7, 1935

RAINFALL FOR FIVE MONTHS
NOW CLOSE TO 1934 TOTAL

Additional rainfall during the past week has boosted the total since January 1, 1935, to slightly more than 11 inches, about one and one half inches less than we received here during the entire year of 1934. This puts Sioux County in line with nine other sections of the state which have reported more rain than in normal year to May 31, and there is yet more than a week to go.

A heavy frost visited this section of the state last night, which undoubtedly will result in some damage to plant life, especially to tomato plants that had been set out recently. Fruit trees that were in bloom will also feel the effects of the frost.

Farmers are jubilant over crop prospects, and it is likely considerable farming will be done this season.

The following chart shows the rainfall in inches, beginning with June 1926 to January 1, 1935:

	1926	1927	1928	1929	1930	1931	1932	1933	1934
January		0.7	0.4	0.4	1.3	0.2	0.63	0.15	1.05
February		0.7	1.1	1	0.35	0.8	0.2	0.4	0.85
March		2.35	0.7	3	1.3	2.55	1	1.88	1.25
April		3.85	0.9	4.26	1.68	0.9	3.6	4.5	1.01
May		4.5	3.88	3.15	4.51	1.54	2.64	4.03	0.16
June	2.25	7.05	3.17	2.52	2	2.39	1.1	0.71	3.31
July	2.75	2.1	4.17	2.22	1.18	0.64	0.45	0.8	1.54
August	1.56	3.5	0.33	1.02	3.49	2.48	0.71	3.25	0.68
September	1.23	1.1	0.4	2.34	1.83	0.63	0.47	0.83	0.94
October	1.62	1.73	0.9	2.34	2.88	1.78	1.24		0.9
November	2.05	0.7	0.5	1.45	0.65	0.85	0.33	0.18	0.3
December	0.6	0.85	0.3	0.2	0.3	0.85	0.25	0.03	0.53
Total	12.06	29.13	16.75	23.9	21.47	15.61	12.62	16.76	12.52

Harrison Sun, Thurs., May 23, 1935

LIVESTOCK PRICES AT SOUTH OMAHA

Fat Cattle Open the Week 15-25c Higher-Top $9.90

HOGS GOING STRONG

Sheep and Lambs Fully Steady –

Fat Lambs $8.00 @ 8.50; Feeders

Higher $7.25 @ 8.00. Fat Ewes

25c Higher at $3.50 @ 3.90.

Union Stock Yards, Omaha, Oct. 27, 1936-Receipts of cattle Monday were 18,000 head. A keen demand for desirable yearlings and handy steers featured the opening market this week and prices 15 @ 25c higher than last. A quality was lacking however and best steers here brought $9.90. Plainer cattle and she stock generally sold at firm figures while stock cattle and feeding steers were in active request and 15 @ 25c higher best feeders going around $8.00.

CORNFED STEERS

Choice to prime	.25 @ 10.00
Good to choice	$8.50 @ 9.25
Fair to good	.50 @ 8.50
Common to fair	$6.00 @ 7.25

CORNFED YEARLINGS

Good to choice	$9.25 @ 10.25
Fair to good	$8.25 @ 9.25
Common to fair	$7.00 @ 8.25
Trashy warmed-ups	$6.00 @ 7.00

RANGE HEIFERS

Good to choice	$5.75 @ 6.75
Fair to good	$4.75 @ 5.75
Common to fair	$3.75 @ 4.75

RANGE COWS

Good to choice heavy	$5.00 @ 6.00
Fair to good	$4.00 @ 5.00
Cutters	$3.50 @ 4.00
Canners	$3.00 @ 3.35

CORNFED HEIFERS

Good to choice	$8.75 @ 9.85
Fair to good	$7.50 @ 8.75
Common to fair	$6.00 @ 7.50

CORNFED COWS

Good to choice heavy	$5.25 @ 6.25
Fair to good	$4.00 @ 5.25

RANGE BEEVES

Good to choice	$6.50 @ 7.50
Fair to good	$5.25 @ 6.50
Common to fair	$4.00 @ 5.25

FEEDING STEERS

Choice heavy	$7.25 @ 8.10
Choice heavy	$7.25 @ 8.00
Good to choice	$6.50 @ 7.50
Fair to good	$5.25 @ 6.50
Common to fair	$4.00 @ 5.00

STOCK CATTLE

Good to choice yearlings	$6.25 @ 760
Fair to good yearlings	$4.75 @ 6.25
Common fair yearlings	$3.75 @ 4.75
Trashy yearlings	$3.00 @ 3.50
Wet cows	$3.25 @ 3.50
Feeder heifers	$5.50 @ 6.85
Yearling heifers	$3.50 @ 6.00
Steer calves	$4.50 @ 7.50
Heifer calves	$4.00 @ 6.25

Harrison Sun, Thurs., Oct. 29, 1936

Disposal of the Ranches

At the time of Dad's death in 1938 the Indian Creek and the Wyoming ranches were sold. The cattle, machinery, hay, and all property were sold privately or at auction and the money applied to debt. The assets did not cover all the debts and they were prorated accordingly.

According to law, notices were published in the Harrison Sun for all outstanding bills and debts be submitted for settlement. Some of the claims seemed to be much inflated, but all were paid on a prorated basis as stated above.

PART III
YOUR GRANDDAD'S SPORTING CAREER

Racing Thoroughbred Horses

Sid Williams Sr. was an avid sportsman during his life. He loved owning and racing thoroughbred horses. He also loved the games of baseball and softball.

The first indication I have found in the records of your granddad's racing career was in the notes of the Sioux County Agricultural Society. Mentioned was a horse named 'Chinaman Jim' owned by Sid Williams of near Ardmore, S. Dakota. The date was Sept. 16, 1897 at the one-half mile circular track north of Harrison.

He raced horses, almost continuously every summer from 1897, or earlier, to 1926. These years were quite lucrative and he had some top notch horses during this time.

He was successful enough that Sid Jr. was told by an Ardmore pastor that the financial aid provided by the 'saloon man' and the 'race horse man' assured his continued service in Ardmore. Otherwise he would have to move on.

Dad gave up racing in 1926 when he became sheriff and this continued until 1933 when prohibition was repealed. The national prohibition experiment was in full force when Dad became sheriff and the duties of the sheriff's office demanded his full attention.

The Early Years

During the early racing years, three of his top horses were Rustling Silk, Maud S. and Walter Johnson.

Sid bought Rustling Silk for $800.00 in March 1907 at Hot Springs, Arkansas. This was a lot of money for a horse in those days.

However, according to conversations I had with Sid Jr. before his death, July 22, 1987, Dad had very good success in Arkansas racing Rustling Silk and other good horses. Sid Jr. said Dad won 6 races out of a 7-race program in one day at Hot Springs, Arkansas in 1906 or 1907. The odds on his horse in the 6th race that day were said to be even.

The following newspaper clippings were found pasted to the back of a picture of Rustling Silk, winning in Butte, Montana, 1908.

81

Rustling Silk demonstrated yesterday beyond the shadow of a doubt that she is a race horse of class. Only recently she landed in Butte from Denver, where she won six (6) straight races. Monday she outclassed the field and was made favorite yesterday in the third race of six furlongs, but at that many figured the mare could not come back. She got off fifth and finished first. Lynch was up on Cinnabar, who finished second and Kirshbaum finished third on Sidney F., a horse that had a good play at a long price.

The third race yesterday contained the best class of horses of any one race yet run at the meet, or rather, it contained the biggest bunch of horses that had run well. Snowball, Minna Gibson, S. Nona and Sheen were scratched, leaving Joe Goss, the old reliable, Rustling Silk, the fast and beautiful Berryessa, the 60-to-1 shot, and longest priced horse of the meet thus far; Captain Burnett, Sidney F., Emma Reubold, Antara and Cinnabar. A hard race to guess, don't you think?

If there's anything in the looks of a horse, then Rustling Silk, the bay mare that has caught on with the Butte bettor, is every inch a thoroughbred. The mare is by Mirthful, dam Quiver. Her coat is as fine as silk and she has the keen, clean-cut look-the slender build and symmetrical outline of a model racer. C.S. WILLIAMS, owner, is a splendid trainer and never sends her into a race except in the best of condition.

Sid Williams,
Butte, Montana,
1908, 39 years old

Two Long Shots

There were two long shot winners yesterday that made good money for just a few wise ones and there were likewise four races won by favorite Maud S., the WILLIAMS entry, in the fourth race, was a 25 to 1 shot, but that didn't prevent her from winning as she pleased. And in the last race old Paddy Lynch just romped home all the way in the seventh-eighth of a mile and won for his backers $20 for every dollar invested. The talent couldn't see anything to the race but Alma Boy and Rustling Silk and several hundred went home broke last night, for Alma Boy didn't get in the money at all, while Rustling Silk could do nothing better than show.

-Newspaper, Butte, Montana, about 1908.

82

Rustling Silk first across the finish line; Butte, Montana, 1908
C.S. Williams, owner, standing lower right corner of photograph

Sid Williams in the winner's circle with another winner, Maud S., Butte, Montana, 1908.

Racing During the Depression

Prohibition was repealed in 1933, but the United States and most of the world were still in the depths of the terrible depression. However, with the ending of prohibition, the criminal activity in Sioux County was greatly diminished. Dad felt he could leave the affairs of the sheriff's office in the capable hands of his deputy and son, Sid Jr. while he raced his horses for several weeks each summer.

The later years 1933-38 were not very profitable. Purses were not that great. Also, the competition was greater than ever with a lot of high quality horses. During this period, my memories are quite good of our travels in the racing circuit with two-four horses transported by a Model A Ford truck or towed in a trailer behind a car.

Dad hired 20 year old John Nerud to come to Harrison and train his horses in 1933. John was raised on a ranch near Minatare, Nebr. He eventually became one of the top trainers in the United States and trained many champion horses that raced in the Kentucky Derby, Belmont Stakes, Santa Anita Derby and at other places. John is still training horses in his early nineties in New York, Kentucky and Florida. He credits his racing start and success to your granddad Sid.

We raced a circuit generally starting in June at the Ak-Sar-Ben track in Omaha; followed by racing at Lincoln, Columbus, Mitchell, all in Nebraska. In South Dakota we hit Hot Springs, and Rapid City. In Montana we raced horses at Butte, Billings, Great Falls and Helena.

Later, we usually wound up the racing season at the Sioux County Fair and Rodeo in Harrison.

My job, when I finally got old enough, starting about 1935, was cooling off the horses after a race by walking them around a circular area for about 20-30 minutes.

The Ak-Sar-Ben Fire

In June, 1937 occurred an event that I will never forget. We were having a picnic with friends, John Zimmerman and family, former Sioux County residents, at an Omaha City Park.

Later, in the afternoon, on the way back to the stable, we noticed unusually heavy traffic, and saw several thoroughbred horses running loose around the city. This was all very puzzling, but it soon became apparent as we drew closer to the stables that a terrible fire had engulfed and destroyed the stable where our horses were kept.

The police and fire departments had the area cordoned off, but Dad was able to gain entry to the area when he was able to present proof that he owned horses there.

The stables were just smoking ruins when we got there. One could see a number of horse carcasses in the ruins. Our trainer saved our horses after the fire started, by leading the horses out and turning them loose. Our Model A Ford truck, which was parked next to the stable was moved to safety. We did lose all our racing paraphernalia, such as bridles, saddles, etc.

Our horses were later located running loose in the city, and captured and returned to an alternate stable. Our trainer, Sherman Knight, reported that many of the horses owned by others that were turned loose attempted to return to the barns and some succeeded only to be burned up.

We spent the next several days, driving to stores in Omaha replenishing our racing equipment.

Donald W. Wins

I was quite excited when Donald W. #3, won a race of five furlongs (five-eighths of a mile) at the Ak-Sar-Ben track, June 14, 1937. Everett Brakeman was the jockey who traveled with us under contract.

Everett had a terrible time keeping his weight down. He was frequently over the ideal weight for jockeys.

I was so proud of Donald W. that throughout the rest of my grade school years I signed all my school papers Donald W. or Don W.

Donald W. Sets South Dakota Track Record

My name-sake set a track record for South Dakota at the Rapid City Meet. The exact date is no longer remembered, but I think it was in the summer of 1937. The event was 3 furlongs-and the record setting time was 35 seconds flat. This record stood for many years.

Donald W. after a win at the Ak-Sar-Ben track, June 1937.
Pictured left to right: C. Sid Williams, son Donald (this writer), LaVerne and Ila Mae.

Horse Donald W   Owner L.Williams
Jockey E.Brakeman   Trainer C.S.Williams
Distance 5 Furlongs   1.01
                        June 14, 1937

Charles Sidney Williams Sr., with Donald W.
Ak-Sar-Ben, Omaha, Nebr., May or early June, 1937
Shortly before the big fire that destroyed the stables

Sid's Last Big Win

Dad owned a champion racer for a short time at the Ak-Sar-Ben track in 1937. The horse, with the unusual name of Loafer was purchased at a claiming race in June, 1937. Loafer was entered into one of the big races held that year at the Ak-Sar-Ben track-the Independence Handicap Race of July 3rd, 1937.

Loafer was the last horse out of the gate and Dad said "Well, I guess I better go down and get Loafer". He was surprised to find that Loafer had passed the entire field and won the race. What a thrill! We were awarded an 18" trophy for the win. The trophy was in the possession of my nephew, John Laettner. Recently, John kindly gave the trophy to me.

Dad entered Loafer in a claiming race a few days later. The horse didn't win and was claimed. Dad only owned Loafer for about two weeks.

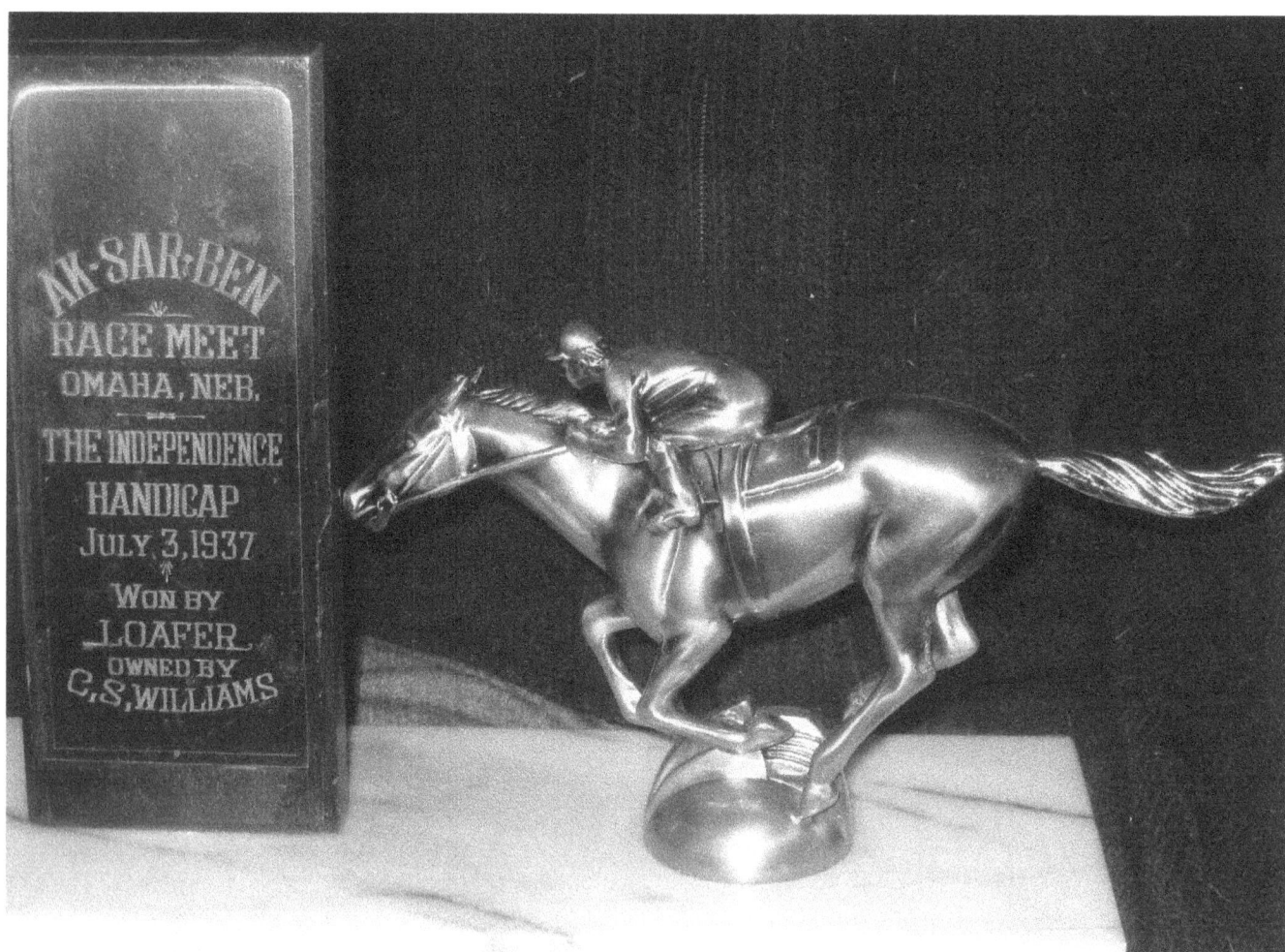

The Last Horses

In early 1938 Sid had several thoroughbred horses in training at the time he became terminally ill. In late May or early June, 1938, a few weeks after Dad's death, my mother, the trainer, Sherman Knight, the jockey, Everett Brakeman and I took two of the horses, Shalina and Hallock to the Ak-Sar-Ben track in Omaha.

That summer, as I remember it, was a mediocre racing year for us. We placed in the money several times and made expenses, but little else.

Racing in Canada

We were still racing during the summer of 1939. Everett Brakeman and Sherman Knight were no longer with us. Mom hired a trainer, Mr. Kerl, from Edgemont, South Dakota. We towed Shalina & Hallock in a trailer behind our 1939 Chevrolet sedan. I remember Mr. Kerl was a heavy tobacco chewer and he would periodically roll down the right front window and spit tobacco juice out the window. I, in the back seat, made sure the right rear window was closed at such times. If I failed I would get tobacco juice in my face. Needless to say, the right side of the green car was stained brown from all that tobacco juice.

We started out racing in Winnipeg, Manitoba. Next was Saskatoon and Regina in Saskatchewan, and then to Calgary and finished in Edmonton, both in Alberta. Again, my job was cooling off the horses after a race and whatever else a 10 year old boy was capable of.

We won several races and placed in the money several times in Canada, but although racing your horses is an exciting sport, Mom decided that there wasn't enough money in the business to justify continued participation in the sport. The horses and equipment were sold and that was the end of our racing experiences.

Media Attention

Your granddad Sid received plenty of media attention during his years as Sioux County Sheriff and as a Nebraska Racetracker. Some of the media mentions came years after his death, the latest in 2002.

I will first list the articles pertaining to our horse racing events, 1930's, that were published in the Harrison Sun, the Sioux County newspaper; the second, articles published in other publications about other family members involved in racing and, finally the many articles concerning your granddad's exploits as Sioux County Sheriff, 1926-1938.

It should be noted that articles have been included in this book exactly as they were published in the various newspapers and magazines.

HORSES WIN AT HOT SPRINGS

Entering two horses in the races at Hot Springs Friday and Saturday of last week, Sid Williams walked off with some of the money. His bay filley, Darling Girl, won second the first day and first the second day in the three-eighths mile race. Another entry in the same event, Sweetheart, placed third each day.

Short Stewart participated in the race meet with two of his gallopers the old favorite, Golden Glow, winning first position in the 4½ furlong event the second day. She also came in ahead the first day but the judges disqualified her on some technicality. Black Air won third in the derby.

Harrison Sun, Thurs., July 20, 1933

WIN AT RAPID CITY MEET

In the four-day race meet held at Rapid City last week, two fillies owned by Sid Williams were consistent winners. Sid reports that there were 150 gallopers at the meet, with a large field of entries for each race. Sweetheart, Sid's sorrel filly, won two firsts and a second in three starts, and Darling Girl, brown filly, won a second and a third in two starts. Sid's gallopers placed in the money in all races in which they were entered.

Harrison Sun, Thurs., June 21, 1934

WINS TWO RACES AT RAPID CITY

Sid Williams has a two-year-old colt that can tear up the turf, according to a report of the Rapid City race meet. Sid purchased this colt from Jack Lacy about four weeks ago, and while the youngster was well broke, he had no track experience and just about three weeks training. But at that the colt stepped out in the three-eighths event for two-year-olds the last day of the meet and tied the track record in his class, stepping the distance in 38 seconds to win the event easily. Darling Girl, Sid's filly, won the five-eighths event the last day, also, making two firsts for the meet. About 150 running horses were entered in the three-day program.

Harrison Sun, Thurs., July 4, 1935

COLT WAS CLOCKED WRONG

In the report of the record made by Sid William's colt at Rapid City last week, we made a slight error in the time. It appeared in the article last week that Donald W., Sid's two-year-old, tied the track record at 38 minutes. This should have been seconds, or a difference of 37 minutes and 22 seconds.

Sid informs us that he will take his four racers, Darling Girl, Sweetheart, Susie Mae and Donald W., to the Hot Springs race meet Friday and Saturday of this week, and as usual there will be plenty of stiff competition at this meet.

Harrison Sun, Thurs., July 11, 1935

"DONALD W." REPEATS

Sid Williams' colt, Donald W., led the field in the two-year-old race at Hot Springs racing meet last week, getting away to a bad start and coming in far in advance of the field. Sid has a most promising running horse in this youngster.

Jack Lacy, superintendent of speed for Sioux County Fair, was a visitor at the Hot Springs races Saturday and he reports there were about 125 running horses in the stables during the three-day meet, and that a number of the owners assured him that they would be on deck at the local fair in August. Jack feels there is every promise of a fine string of race horses for our annual fall show and that every racing event will be well filled.

Harrison Sun, Thurs., July 18, 1935

TAKES RACERS TO ALLIANCE

Sid Williams will represent Sioux County at the race meet in Alliance three days this week, taking his string of gallopers to the Legion show. 125 horses are said to be on hand for the program, and competition will undoubtedly be keen. Pari-mutuel betting will be practiced at this meet, the first in western Nebraska since the law was enacted.

Harrison Sun, Thurs., Aug. 15, 1935

SIOUX COUNTY GALLOPERS TO RUN IN AK-SAR-BEN RACES

Two Sioux County running nags will compete in the Ak-Sar-Ben race meet, which is underway at Omaha and will continue until over July 4th. Walt Warren and Charley Fields left Wednesday of last week with Donald W., Sid Williams' racing colt, and Sweet Memorium, a mare owned by Jack Bourret. Mr. and Mrs. Williams left Sunday of this week for Omaha and will remain there and Sid will look after the entry of his horse in some of the races. Walt Warren is in charge of the Bourret mare and while she has never been entered in a race before, is expected to make a great showing. Donald W., although a youngster, has showed his heels to some pretty fast nags in races during the past year.

Harrison Sun, Thurs., June 18, 1936

WINS HOT SPRINGS DERBY

With a race horse he purchased recently at Omaha, Sid Williams won the derby in the Hot Springs race meet, Saturday of last week. "Strappy," Sid's 6-year-old horse, beat his nearest contender by several lengths in the mile and one-sixteenth event. The day before "Strappy" was declared a second-place winner in the seven-eighths event in a very close race. Aberg's mare, "Scroll," was the winner of the latter event, but finished third in the derby. Sid plans to have his racing nags in shape for the Sioux County Fair in August and later intends to go to Lincoln for the races to be held there.

Harrison Sun, Thurs., June 26, 1936

WILLIAMS RACE HORSES WIN AT THE SCOTTS BLUFF FAIR

Sid Williams' string of racing nags came out very well in the races during the four-day program at the Scotts Bluff County fair in Mitchell last week. Donald W., surprised most of the followers of the turf by winning over some of the best horses from the Ak-Sar-Ben track in Omaha this year, winning a 4 ½ furlong event and also a five-eighths mile race. Cloi Beth came out in the lead in a half-mile race and took second in another half-mile race. Dick Daring won second in a 4 ¼ furlong race and third in a half-mile.

At the Newcastle, Wyo., rodeo and race meet a few weeks ago Sid took six firsts with the three runners, in the two days of racing.

Harrison Sun, Thurs., Sept. 24, 1936

TAKES THREE HORSES TO AK-SAR-BEN RACES AT OMAHA

Sid Williams left Thursday of last week for Omaha, trucking three of his race horses to that point for entry in the races conducted by the Ak-Sar-Ben association. The race meet opened May 27 and continues until July 5. Mrs. Williams and the children went with Sid. The three racers to be entered by Sid are Donald W., Cloi Beth and Dick Darling.

Harrison Sun, Thurs., June 3, 1937

WILLIAMS HORSES SAVED

Although a large number of race horses were lost in the fire which swept Ak-Sar-Ben stables at Omaha last Sunday, those belonging to Sid Williams were not burned as first reported. Mr. and Mrs. Williams were not at the grounds at the time of the fire, but his horses were led to safety and were in the bunch that scattered for miles and not caught up and identified until later. Sid's truck was also moved to safety and all that he lost was some small property left in the stalls.

Harrison Sun, Thurs., June 10, 1937

DONALD W. BREEZES IN

Race reports Monday showed Donald W., one of Sid Williams' string of racers, a winner of first position in one of the races that day at the Ak-Sar-Ben meet. A short time before Donald W. galloped to the line in second place, and begins to look like Sid has one of the front ranked horses in the race meet.

Harrison Sun, Thurs., June 17, 1937

RETURNS FROM RACE MEET

Mr and Mrs. Sid Williams and children returned Wednesday morning from Omaha, where they have been for several weeks taking in the Ak-Sar-Ben summer race meet. Sid brought home two additional race horses, which he bought while at the meet. He expects to leave shortly for Montana, taking two racers, Donald W. and Dick Daring, and will follow a circuit which is in progress in that state.

Harrison Sun, Thurs., July 8, 1937

WILLIAMS HORSES WIN

Sidney Williams received word recently from his father, C.S. Williams, to the effect that Donald W. won first in a five-eighths mile race at Helena, Mont., and in the same race meet Dick Daring won first in the one and one-eighth mile event. Mr. and Mrs. Williams and children left Harrison several weeks ago to take in the Montana racing circuit and were in Great Falls the end of July.

Harrison Sun, Thurs., Aug. 5, 1937

Other Williams Family Members in Racing

The following news item concerns the four generations of Williams family in horse racing, ending with Rob Williams, your granddad's great grandson. He continues the racing tradition of the Williams family that began over 100 years ago.

4 Generations of WILLIAMS FAMILY In Nebraska Horse Racing

Aug. 1974

The Racetracker's News was created with the following types of FAMILY in mind, which consists of four generations of HORSEMEN, this newspaper is 'proud' to run this story and the state of Nebraska Horse Racing was built by RACETRACKERS like the WILLIAMS FAMILY.

First there was SIDNEY WILLIAMS, who in the days of the 'gun-slingers' served as the 'law man of Sioux County' for over 15 years.(1) As sheriff his only hobby was 'racing horses', for those years were the days when the 'equine was master of the highways', he didn't have automobiles or helicopters to chase the outlaws', only his trusted four-legged friend and speed made the difference.

Second came horseman FLOYD WILLIAMS, who raced at every race track in the 'plains states'; he ventured to the 'northwest' where the horsemen of that area quickly learned to respect the quiet little man from Nebraska with his stable of thoroughbreds from the 'cornhusker bushes'. (2) After many years of owning, training, he decided to quit the business, and retire, however, once a RACETRACKER-ALWAYS A RACETRACKER, so he turned to being a 'jockeys agent' which is his present part time job, handling the riding assignments this year for the Peruvian jockey Justo Moreno.

The third generation produced by Floyd and his lovely wife Billie is DEAN WILLIAMS, who like his father before him was raised on and around horses.(3) As a young man he learned every aspect of 'horse racing', galloping, walking, rubbing and training, to even being a 'jockey's agent', who when handling the books for jockey Bob Lee helped his rider fight the scales by wrapping him in a blanket and covering him with 'horse manure', you must remember this was before the days of the 'hot box'. The many years of experiences at racetracks has been the backbone of his present position as trackman for the Daily Racing Form for the Nebraska Racing Circuit.

The fourth generation is the great-grandson, Robert "ROBBIE" WILLIAMS, who just started on his 16th birthday, to gallop and exercise horses in the Nebraska Racing Circuit. This newspaper feels certain that with the 'blood-line' of this youngster, he has just got to be a true RACETRACKER and a credit to the STATE OF NEBRASKA.(4)

(1)   I think the article is in error about the use of the horse in Dad's law enforcement years as sheriff. He always used automobiles, except possibly the occasional use of saddle horses during his first years as sheriff in the 1920's. During the 1920's and 30's the roads were rapidly improving and automobile ownership increased dramatically.

(2)   Floyd Williams, retired to Grand Island, Nebraska and died in 1986 at age 84. His wife, Billie died about 1983.

(3)   Dean Williams, 80, died in 2008 in Omaha, Nebraska.

(4)   The newspaper's prediction was prescient. Robbie has developed into one of the top jockeys in the nation with 4500 wins to date, as of 2009, when he retired from being a jockey at age 51. He now trains race horses for a Mr. Arnold in Texas.

ROB WILLIAMS

Nebraska Veteran Williams Gets Ride in Breeders' Cup

By Mike Patterson
World-Herald Staff Writer
Oct. 25, 2001

After 26 years in the saddle, jockey Rob Williams has ridden in thousands of races.

But none more prestigious than the one he'll ride in Saturday.

The 43-year-old Williams, who grew up in Grand Island, will ride It'Sallinthechase in the $1 million Juvenile as part of the Breeders' Cup card at New York's Belmont Park. It will be the veteran rider's first trip to New York for any reason, and he's hoping to make the most of it.

"It's exciting just to be competing in the Breeders' Cup," he said by phone from his home in Edmond, Okla. "I'm going to need a little luck to win, but you never know what can happen in racing."

Williams, who has won more than 3,000 career races, made his name on the Nebraska racing circuit before leaving for Oklahoma in 1993. He won the jockey title nine times at Grand Island's Fonner Park and twice at Omaha's Ak-Sar-Ben racetrack.(5)

He enjoyed one of his biggest days at Lincoln's State Fair Park, where he once won eight races on the 10-race-card.

But the competition Saturday at the Breeder's Cup – eight races featuring purses of at least $1 million apiece-will be fierce. The Bob Bulfert-trained Officer has won all five previous races and is the heavy favorite in the Juvenile, a race for 2-year-old colts and geldings.

It'Sallinthechase has won one of seven starts and is listed at odds of 50-1.

But Williams isn't ready to wave any surrender flag before the race is run. He's waited too long for this shot, and a victory would bring the rider 10 percent of the purse, or $100,000.

"I could take the rest of the year off if I got there first," the jockey said. "My horse keeps getting better the longer he goes, so who knows?"

Trained by Wilson Brown, the Kentucky-bred colt by Take Me Out has never run as far as Saturday's distance of 1 1/16 miles but has shown the ability to close ground in the late running.

Upsets are also a common occurrence on Breeders' Cup day. At Churchill Downs last year, Spain paid $113.80 to win in the Distaff race and Caressing returned $96 to win in the Juvenile Fillies.

Williams, who is currently riding at Remington Park in Oklahoma, said he is ready to do battle with the top riders in the world. That group in the Juvenile probably will include Pat Day, Kent Desormeaux, Chris McCarron, Jorge Velazquez and Corey Nakatani.

"I don't have any fears about riding at Belmont or riding against those other jockeys", Williams said. "I'm really looking forward to the challenge."

Williams, who will leave his wife and five kids behind in Oklahoma while he goes to work this weekend, said he does have one other concern. He probably won't be able to watch much of Nebraska's nationally televised football game Saturday against Oklahoma.

"We've got to take a lot of guff down here from Sooner fans." He said. "I hope Nebraska gets the job done."

(5)   I recently talked to Sheila Williams, Rob's mother, and she said It'Sallinthechase did not place in the race.

The following article about John Nerud was written by Red Smith, sports writer, and published in the Sunday World Herald, Dec. 24, 1978, Omaha, Nebraska.

NEBRASKA NATIVE JOHN NERUD WILL NOT BOYCOTT RACE AWARDS PARTY THIS TIME

Nerud was the trainer of Dr. Fager, an extraordinary racehorse, who, as a four year old was the first in American racing to win four national championships in a single year-Horse of the Year, Handicap Champion, Sprint Gross Champion. Owner was William L. McKnight, owner of the 3M Company.

The lengthy article goes on, but is omitted here except for what was said about your granddad Sid, which is quoted exactly here:

Nerud grew up on a ranch near Bayard, Nebr. Each boy in the family received a horse as a birthday gift at five. From that age on, horses were John's life. At 18 he became trainer for Sid Williams, who was sheriff of Sioux County in the northwest corner of Nebraska bounded by Wyoming on the west and the Black Hills of South Dakota on the north.

They called him **'BRING 'EM BACK ALIVE SID'**. He was one of the last bold lawmen, wore two pearl-handled revolvers and could use 'em and would use 'em. He was 68 and he had a young wife and little kids. His horses ? they were lousy, but we raced in lousy places-Rapid City, Deadwood, places like that.

After that I left Nebraska on my own with a horse and little money and when the sharpies got through with me I had neither. Couldn't go back home empty, so I took jobs as groom and jockey's agent.

There was much more information before and after these paragraphs that mentioned your granddad.

~~~~~

Another article about John Nerud appeared in the weekly glossy Newsmagazine of Thoroughbred Racing in the issue of January 12, 2002. The Newsmagazine is published in Paris, Kentucky. Excerpts of the article follows:

MAINTAINING A SHARP EDGE –

Approaching his 89th birthday, Racing Hall of Fame trainer John Nerud always speaks his mind.

Thoroughbred Times:

"How has training changed?"

Nerud: "It's all in what happened in the evolution of the horse business. When I was young and starting in the training business, I had a racehorse. I went up to Harrison, Nebraska and the sheriff of Sioux County, Sid Williams, asked me to come up there and train horses. He was 70 and I was 18.(6)

"He was one of those old-time sheriffs like Wyatt Earp. He wore two pearl-handled pistols. And he controlled the town. When any criminal was within a hundred miles, they'd call him. We called him **'BRING HIM BACK ALIVE SID'**. When he went after someone, if they didn't come back, they died. He asked me to come up there and train his horses.

You don't cross him because he'd shoot you. But he was easy to train for. That's when I was 18. I took my horse Dr. Coogle up there. He was a hell of a horse, but I was too dumb to know it.

The lengthy article continued for 20 more paragraphs.

John was born February 18, 1913 in Minatare, Nebraska. He is currently living in old Brookville, New York. According to personal correspondence with him of February 25, 2002 he is still in the thoroughbred training business, training about 20 head.

John, one of the top trainers of all time was elected to the Racing Hall of Fame, 1972; Florida Thoroughbred Breeder's Association, 1981; and also to the Nebraska Hall of Fame.

(6)   *As a small boy I remember John Nerud staying with us and training Sweetheart and Darling Girl. He became one of the top trainers in the United States and credits his training start to working for Sid Williams.*

I think John somewhat embellished his words about your granddad Sid. I remember Dad wearing one, not two revolvers, western style. When not wearing the cartridge belt it was wrapped around the steering wheel column of his car. A high powered rifle was strapped to the left hand door. The revolver was not pearl handled.

*I disagree that Dad would shoot you if you didn't come peaceably. He was always successful in avoiding shoot outs, by using guile, subterfuge and ingenious methods of facilitating an arrest. That's why they called him **"BRING 'EM BACK ALIVE SID"**.*

Sid's Baseball Team

think Dad must have had dreams of owning, and or coaching a good baseball team. He apparently attempted to make this a dream come true as evidenced by a letter that I received February 1968 from Wm. T. Richer, Clerk of Courts, Fall River County, Hot Springs, South Dakota. Mr. Richer said in part:

"I was well and personally acquainted with your father, having got acquainted with him I believe in about 1910, when he brought in a bunch of college baseball players (mostly from Wisconsin), filed them on homesteads, and furnished each and all of them with a team of horses and a wagon, and they in turn were to play baseball for him.(7) I don't recall all of the boys he had, but do remember R.I. (Liz) Farwell, Crumby Herz and his brother, Bill Fitzgerald, and Frank Downey.(8) All of the ball players left this country after they proved up on the homesteads, except that Liz Farwell stayed in business until his death about ten years ago, and Frank Downey died within the past year or two".

"Then I remember that in about 1917 or 1918 your father had a string of race horses, and at one race meet that year in the Hunter Company Derby, your father had entered his horse 'Innovation' with Ross Howard in the saddle. On the pari-mutuel the odds were 71 to 1 on Innovation, and Cal Dalbey and I each took a two dollar ticket, which by the way were the only tickets sold on the horse. The race was run and Innovation was out in the lead, at the finish line, and for a few moments at least Dalbey and I were in the money. It developed that after Ross Howard had weighed in before the race, he was seen slipping his weights to a friend of his, and it was called to the attention of the judges. The judges called the friend up into the judge's stand and closed the trap door. When Ross Howard came to the judges stand to weigh in after the race, he couldn't find his friend and he had to weigh in some several pounds short. (9) The judges called it no race, and Dalbey and I were out for our mutual tickets, and no pay. But neither of us ever forgot the name of 'Innovation'".

"Then after your father was the sheriff of Sioux County, Nebr., he was in my office on many occasions, in connection with cases in Sioux County and in Fall River County".

Very truly yours,

Wm. T. Richer,

Clerk of Courts

(7)   Sid made quite a bit of money racing in these early years and apparently invested it in starting up a top-notch baseball team. Ardmore had one of the top teams in the area.

(8)   Liz Farwell was one of the pall-bearers at your granddad's funeral in May, 1938. Frank Downey married Dad's daughter, Ethel, by his first marriage. Ethel, of course was my half-sister.

(9)   Jockeys were usually under contract and got a percentage of the winnings. Apparently, Howard decided to increase his chances of additional money.

PART IV
SID'S OTHER ACTIVITIES

Sid Williams - Cattle Buyer & Dealer

Your granddad genuinely liked people and he enjoyed dealing and buying cattle with, for, and from them. He had the cowboys and truckers available to him to truck or drive the cattle to shipping points for delivery to the livestock markets in Omaha, Grand Island or other places.

Cowboys that worked for Dad included Ernest Pullen, Penny Vivian, Dad's sons Sidney Jr. and Floyd Williams. Truckers included Ed Clark and others. Partners at various times included Jack Dunlap, John Dieckman of Harrison, a Mr. Siebken of the Van Tassell area and Dad's son-in-law Frank Downey of the Ardmore-Edgemont area, South Dakota. I knew them all except Vivian.

This was a money making enterprise for several years until the bottom dropped out of the cattle market in the late 20's and early 30's. Following are several news items about cattle movement in Sioux County.

The following Sale Barn Commission Co. sales slip supports the contention of very low prices cattlemen received for cattle during the dry summer of 1934.

MALY AND RYAN LIVE STOCK COMMISSION CO.

CATTLE SALESMEN
L. J. (LADDIE) MALY
RES. PHONE HA. 9651
LEO E. RYAN
RES. PHONE WA. 1753

HOG SALESMAN
AXEL H. KNUDSEN
RES. PHONE WA. 0459
SHEEP SALESMAN
ED. GILLEN
RES. PHONE MA. 0651

401 LIVE STOCK EXCHANGE BLDG. PHONE MARKET 3900

REFERENCE
STOCK YARDS NATIONAL BANK

BONDED FOR YOUR PROTECTION

Stock Yards Station   Omaha, Nebr.

No. 3675

STOCK YARDS STATION, OMAHA, NEB. _____ 7/16 _____ 193 4

43e 1 elf

SOLD FOR ACCOUNT OF ___ C S Williams

SHIPPED FROM ___ Harrison, Neb ___ P.O. ___ Same

PURCHASER	CATTLE	HOGS	SHEEP	WEIGHT	DOCK SOWS	STAGS	POUNDS	PRICE	AMOUNT	TOTAL
Heartwell	17 strs			86 00				3 50	301 00	
"	4 "			3 50				3 50	110 25	
"	4 "			20 00				2 50	50 00	
Blanza	1 Hfr			6 00				2 50	15 00	
Cox	2 cows			19 10				1 90	36 29	
Amstead	1 "			6 40				1 75	11 20	
Phillips	1 "			13 50				1 75	23 62	
Amstead	1 "			6 80				1 35	9 18	
Phillips	1 "			8 50				1 25	10 62	
Ardy	1 clf			1 60				4 00	6 40	
Cox x x	11 Hfrs			6 22 0				2 55	158 61	7/17/34
UK+R	1 clf	dead	1 00 #				no value		
	45			76 2 00						732 17

CAR NUMBERS	RAILROAD WEIGHTS	RATE			AMOUNT	
20875	25500	41	TRUCKING			
			FREIGHT	10 5 55	
			YARDAGE	1 5 55	
Bedding		1 00	HAY	9 50	
			CORN NATIONAL LIVE STOCK AND MEAT BOARD FUND TO INCREASE MEAT CONSUMPTION. IF YOU OBJECT THIS WILL BE REFUNDED UPON REQUEST.	2 5	
			INSPECTION & INSURANCE	15	
			HARTFORD STATE } TRANSIT INSURANCE		
			Brand Inspection	4 30	
			COMMISSION	17 00	152 30
			NET PROCEEDS		579 87

Pats Grade 8/17/34

Draft 300.00

279 87

ck

LIVESTOCK SHIPMENTS

Although the cattle shipping season has not as yet reached the peak, indications are that the movement to market will not be as heavy this year as in the past few years. Some of the recent shipments of stock from this point are as follows:

Del Bigelow, one car cattle.

Wilbur Smith, two cars horses.

John Martin, cattle buyer, three cars cattle.

L.A. Witt, four cars cattle.

John Bourret, two cars cattle.

Vernon Dunn, 1 car cattle.

L.D. Hickey, three cars cattle.

Williams & Dunlap, 1 car cattle.

J.W. Davis, three cars cattle.

Saturday of this week the following will ship:

Sam Thomas, two cars cattle.

Shepherd Cattle Company, one car cattle.

Lee Ring, one car cattle.

Harrison Sun, Fri., Aug. 26, 1927

Sid Williams sold 70 head of stock cows to Henry Melgate of Ft. Laramie, Wyo. this week.

Harrison Sun, Fri., Jan. 6, 1928

HOG SHIPMENTS

The following ordered cars for hog shipments this week:

C.S. Williams, one car for Saturday.

Leo DeBock, one car for Tuesday.

J.H. Dunlap, one car for Thursday.

Raymond Riley, one car for Thursday.

Harrison Sun, Fri., Jan. 13, 1928

790 HEAD OF FEEDER CATTLE TO BE SOLD HERE OCTOBER 11

It is well established fact that Sioux County stands at the head of the list in the production of the best quality Hereford cattle, and the public auction of choice feeder cattle to be held at the stockyards in Harrison Tuesday, October 11th, offers cattle feeders an excellent opportunity to supply their demands in this sale.

In the list of 790 head there will be 150 head of cows, 365 head of calves and 275 head of yearlings, mostly steers. They have been consigned from the herds of Grote & Bates, Nick Schaefer, Story Brothers, Sid Williams and Lee Ring. The sale is to be given at one o'clock sharp, and the terms are cash. A.L. Schnurr is clerk of the sale and John Dieckman is auctioneer.

Harrison Sun, Thurs., Oct. 6, 1932

Brand Inspecting

Your granddad was also frequently called upon to inspect brands on cattle being bought and sold. An example following is the sale of 50 steers by John T. Coffee, Harrison, Nebr. to George Rusett, Columbus Grove, Ohio.

NEBRASKA STOCKGROWERS ASSOCIATION
BRAND INSPECTORS' TALLY

Sales Ring or Stock Yards at ....

Sold by _John T. Coffee_ Address _Harrison Neb_

Purchased by _Geo Rusett_ Address _Columbus Grove Ohio_

Date _October 17-1932_ Number Cattle Inspected _50_

Amount Fee $ _5.00_

Copy forwarded with shipment to any public market will be evidence of inspection and fees paid.

Steers	Cows	Bulls	Calves	Brands
50				3

I hereby certify that the above cattle were inspected by me and brands described are correct.

Dated at _Andrews Neb_ this _17_ day of _October_ , 193_2_

C S Williams
Brand Inspector.

PART V
SIDS LAW ENFORCEMENT CAREER

Early Law Enforcement Events

Your granddad Sid became Sheriff in 1926 when the then Sheriff, George W. Hill resigned. It is unclear how Sid got the job. He may have applied for the job, but he may have been approached to see if he was interested in the job. Several incidents in Dad's early life may have been known by the County Commissioners which may have indicated to them that he was the man for the job. Dad was a friend of ranching neighbor, Mert Childs, one of the County Commissioners. The early day incidents are discussed below:

The Doc Middleton Affair

Little is known of the incident concerning Doc Middleton. Who was Middleton? Harold Hutton wrote a book, titled: Doc Middleton, Life and Legends of the Notorious Plains Outlaw, printed 1974. This is probably the most authoritative of several books that have been written about the notorious outlaw. Hutton did a remarkable job of researching the life of Doc Middleton, considering that Middleton went to great lengths to conceal his past. Most of the following on Doc Middleton's life is summarized from Hutton's book, except where noted.

Middleton's real name was James Riley and he was probably born in 1851 in Bastrop County, Texas. He left Texas in 1876 and was on the first cattle drive from Texas, across western Nebraska to Indian Reservations in Dakota Territory, according to Captain James H. Cook, author of Fifty Years on the Old Frontier. According to Cook, Middleton left the drive at the Arkansas River. Cook further states: "During the two months in which I saw Doc Middleton quite frequently when bringing cattle up the trail, I failed to see that he was what I called a first class cow hand, that is, one who first thought was the safety of a cow or herd, and last, the comfort and safety of himself. I met Doc Middleton on numerous occasions after the time when I worked with him on the trail. He preferred gambling and other forms of recreation to trail driving or ranch work."

Middleton had a job of freighting supplies to the Black Hills from Sidney, Nebraska which was then an important stop on the Overland Trail. A wide open town with gamblers, prostitutes, outlaws and soldiers from the nearby military barracks. The Sidney-Black Hills trail crossed the northeast corner of Sioux County, Nebr. Middleton killed a soldier at Sidney in some sort of dispute. He escaped pursuing soldiers and lawmen. This was the first killing of possibly two or three others.

Middleton later headed up a gang of outlaws and made a career out of stealing cattle and horses from Nebraska ranchers and especially horses from the Sioux Indians on the Dakota reservations.

Middleton got into one or more gunfights with vigilantes and lawmen. He was wounded and in turn wounded a law man in one of the encounters. He was captured and spent some time in a Cheyenne, Wyoming jail where he recovered from his wounds. Enroute to the Nebraska penitentiary from Cheyenne by train he was nearly lynched by vigilantes. Quick thinking on the part of the law enforcement officials prevented a neck stretching. Middleton is said to have participated in Buffalo Bill's Wild West Show about 1886.

Middleton was again wounded in some sort of gun battle over a gambling table at Covington, Nebraska in 1891.

During the last major Indian-soldier engagement at Wounded Knee, Dakota Territory, 1890-91 Capt. James Cook accused Middleton of supplying the soldiers with big dressed chickens, each with a bottle of whiskey inside the chicken. He got away with it.

Also, Middleton participated in the 900 mile horse race from Chadron to Chicago in 1893. He was forced to give up part way through the race when his horse gave out.

The Killing of Harry Williams

I had a conversation with Aunt Eva Williams, Uncle Bern's wife, in Edgemont about 1948. She told to me an amazing story. She said Uncle Harry Williams got involved in a brawl in Doc Middleton's Ardmore saloon. She said Middleton hit Harry over the head with a beer bottle when he was backed up against the bar, fatally injuring him. He died a day or two later. This was the source of the trouble between Doc and Dad, according to Aunt Eva. She said the killing of Harry led to an altercation between Doc and Dad and they slugged it out man to man until stopped by bystanders. Hutton in his book, page 200, relates a story of Middleton being in a fight with a younger man and getting the worst of it. The crowd interfered and Doc said: "Keep that man off me or I'll kill him." Possibly this is the described encounter between Dad and Doc as told to me by Aunt Eva. She said Middleton threatened Dad's life. She added that after the encounter Dad always kept the shades down at night while living in Ardmore.

More On Middleton

I might add that I have read where Middleton is said to have lived a short time in a cabin in the hills not far from Glen in Sioux County.

According to Hutton, Middleton purchased lots in Ardmore where he built a home and saloon in 1903. While running the saloon Hutton described six or eight fights that Middleton had with several unnamed persons, some involving gunplay.

Ardmore was a sort of back-wash of the old frontier. It was a stepping off point where some of the last open range roundups were held at the turn of the century.

Ardmore town citizens sometimes called upon Dad to act as special temporary marshal to disarm vociferous cowboys and guntoters during that time. I don't know that any salary was associated with those sporadic duties, but, he as one of the town founders, handled those chores.

I have Dad's holster that he used to carry a concealed six-shooter in an overcoat pocket or hooked inside the trousers. He carried the gun for several years during the early years of the 1900's while both he and Doc lived in Ardmore. See picture of holster following.

The family plot in the northeast corner of the cemetery in Chadron has a tombstone for Harry that reads: Harry, son of C.P. & Martha Williams, born Nov. 28, 1858, died Oct. 16,

1900. This would seem to predate Middleton's 1903 purchase of lots in Ardmore, but I suspect he rented his saloon building before buying or building one.

I have tried to verify Aunt Eva's story, but have been unsuccessful to date. I checked for Harry's death certificate and checked the old newspapers for that time in Harrison, Edgemont and Hot Springs, but could find nothing about the death of Harry Williams. Harry was only 42 years of age, in the prime of life, when he was killed. Was Middleton responsible, someone else, or was his death natural? While researching information for this book I have been able to verify some of the legends or at least found some truth to these family stories.

While trying to verify the story of the Harry Williams killing I asked or arranged to have interviews with two of my half-brothers, Floyd (Stuffy) and Sid Jr. about the incident. Floyd (b.1902, d. 1985), Grand Island, Nebraska was asked about the incident by my nephew Dean Williams. Dean, in replying by letter, Jan. 28, 1981, Floyd stated: "Dad definitely had serious problems with Doc Middleton, but that was before his time and he wasn't sure about the nature of the problem."

Sid Jr. (b. 1898-d.1987) said he thought Dad took Doc's gun away from him after one of Middleton's altercations. He also agreed that serious problems existed between the two men, but he too was vague about the incident.

Sid Jr's. facial expression hardened when I asked him if he knew Middleton. He acknowledged that as a youth growing up in Ardmore he did know him. He described him as a 'snake in the grass'. I detected a reluctance to say more and so I didn't press the issue. However, I sensed that he knew a lot more than he was willing to talk about.

Middleton died in a Douglas, Wyoming jail in 1913 following his arrest for liquor law violations. He died from a severe skin infection and pneumonia.

This story may forever remain an unverified family legend.

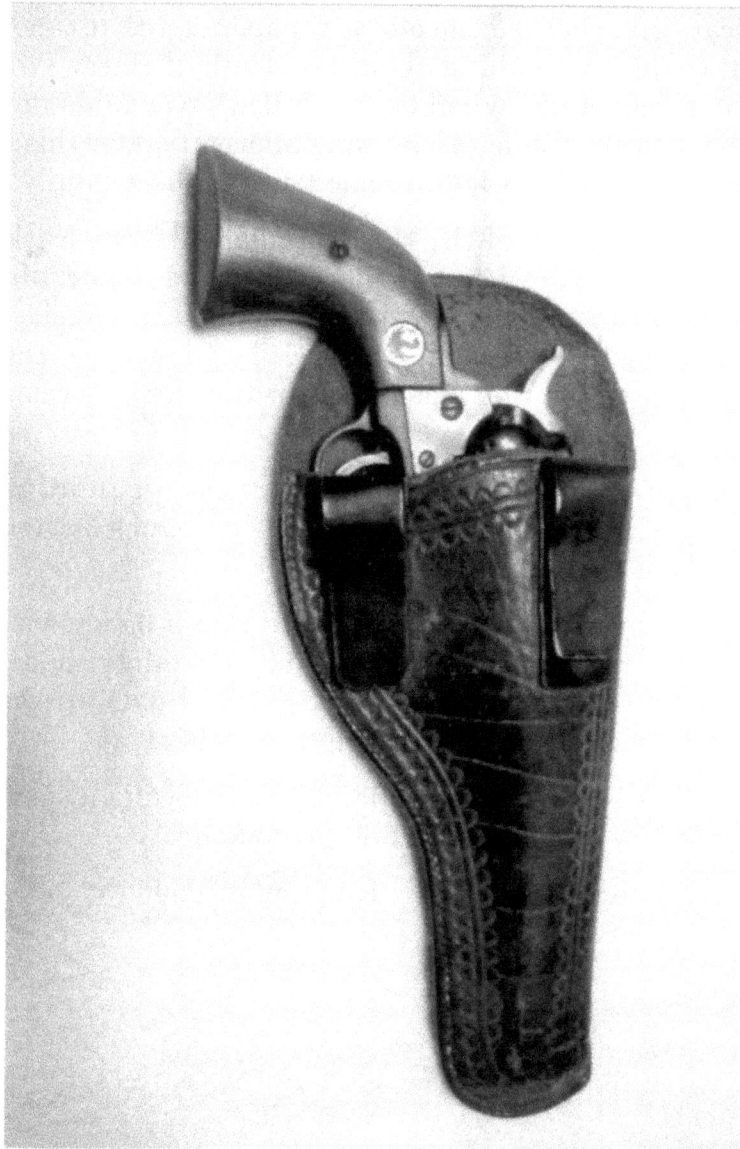

Holster used by Sid Williams Sr., early 1900's when he was feuding with the notorious Texas killer 'Doc' Middleton over the death of Sid's brother, Harry Williams, allegedly killed by Middleton, Oct. 1900. Holster is fitted with clips to fit concealed inside the trousers or an overcoat pocket. The revolver belongs to this writer.

The Bob Wallace Incident

According to my nephew Dean Williams, his father, Floyd told him of a saloon incident that occurred in 1913-14, as follows: "Wallace had the Konraths lined up against the wall and told them he was going to kill them all since they had a long standing feud. No one had the courage to go in and face Wallace, but Sid went in and took the gun away from him.

Sid Jr. added a lot more detail: Here is the story of the incident as told to me in 1986: "About 1913 an Ardmore citizen came running into the hardware store where Charlie Stoop, then also town marshal, was tending the store and hollered: 'Bob Wallace is threatening to shoot the Konraths in the saloon.' Stoop, claiming he couldn't leave the store untended, asked Dad, who happened to be in the store, to investigate. Dad said he would look into it. Upon entering the saloon Dad found that Wallace, wearing western style holsters on a cartridge belt had several of the Konrath boys with arms up against the bar. Dad talked Wallace out of his guns. According, to Sid Jr. he admonished Wallace: "What are you doing wearing pistols into town? Those days are gone forever." I think all the involved people were probably relieved when Wallace handed over his guns.(1)

The Stolen Car

This story was told to me by Ed Meiers, Harrison Chevrolet Dealer and your Uncle, Sidney Jr. It seems that about 1920 Dad owned a big car that Ed described as a Lowsier (sp.) Two men went to the ranch house on the Woodruff place while Dad was gone. They convinced Agnes, Dad's wife at the time, that Dad had sold them the car and that they were supposed to pick up the car from her. She gave them the keys and they drove off. It must be noted that official car titles were not required when transferring ownership until years later.

(1)   According to the Wallace Family History by Merritt Wallace that was published in the book Sioux County-Memoirs of its Pioneers in 1967, his father, Robert Wallace was born in 1859 in Canada.

The family came to Chadron in 1886, then the end of the rail line. They settled in the Indian Creek area, Dakota Territory, just north of the Nebraska line.

Bob Wallace admitted to killing a man in the 1890's; was arrested and placed in jail without bond. Robert Wallace said it was self defence and a jury acquitted Wallace.

When your granddad bought the Dryer Ranch in 1930 they were near neighbors with each other. The Wallaces lived on the south side of Indian Creek and Dad lived on the north side.

I knew Mr. and Mrs. Merritt Wallace and their five children and went to school with them. I chummed around with Jerald and Quentin. Quentin died young before graduating from High School. Carroll, Merritt's daughter, graduated in 1948, Sioux County High School. She married Clarence Schnurr, Sioux County Abstractor. She worked many years for W.E. Mumby, County Prosecutor and Clarence was the son of Al Schnurr, County prosecutor and ranch neighbor to Dad. I remained friends with the Schnurr's throughout the years.

Later, that day, when arriving home he discovered how the con-men had obtained the car. He immediately began an investigation and got leads on the thieves. He found out that they might have gone to Douglas, Wyo. Dad went to Douglas and soon saw his car driving slowly down the main street. The car turned around and came slowly back up the street. Dad quietly stepped into the middle of the street as if he were waiting for the car to drive past so he could safely cross the street. However, when the car was about to drive by he quickly jumped on the running board, pulled out his gun and directed the driver to the police station. At the police station the occupants of the car were able to convince the police that they had recently purchased the car from two men. However, they directed the cops to an apartment complex where the real thieves were believed to be staying. Dad assisted the officers in making the arrests. The car was soon back in his possession.

The Foiled Robbery

During the early 1900's your grandfather was in the horse raising business and annually shipped carloads to eastern cities such as Omaha and Chicago. On one of the trips to Chicago he was accosted by two gunmen who demanded his wallet and a diamond stick pin on a tie. Dad jumped the bandits and during the ensuing fracus succeeded in flooring one, but a gun was discharged by one of the robbers, wounding the small finger of Dad's right hand. The robbery was foiled, but the wound resulted in a permanently stiffened finger. The second bandit succeeded in getting away.

Of course law enforcement officers recommend no resistance to robberies, but the incident serves to demonstrate Dad's fearless approach towards law breakers.

The Noble Experiment That Failed

Following Dad's appointment as Sioux County Sheriff in April 1926, he handily won every election until his death May 6, 1938.

Several deputies served under your granddad during his 12 year tenure as Sioux County Sheriff. These included a Mr. Seaman, Harry Heckert, John Dieckman, Joe Stanek, J.B. Duncan, Sidney Williams Jr. and others.

August 6, 2010 – I met Gloria Stafford, Morrill, Ne., a Harrison visitor, at the Harrison House Hotel. She stated that her father, William L. Newman (b. 1907-d. 1972) served as an occasional special deputy, 1928-1934. This was when an extra man was needed as backup, such as during fair time, for domestic disturbances, etc. Bill grew up on a ranch 14 miles south of Harrison, that later became part of Dan Jordan's holdings.

Dad was also assisted by State Deputy Sheriff Ed Clark, O.E. Forsling, State Prohibition officer and several Federal Prohibition officers.

Some of the local deputies could not or would not perform their duties or found the job so distasteful in arresting friends, neighbors or relatives that were involved in liquor law violations that they resigned or were fired.

My half-brother, Sidney Jr., was efficient in performing his duties as Dad's deputy, but he found it difficult to arrest acquaintances and friends. Some were merely trying to survive the tough dry years of the depression. Despite his desire to continue helping his father enforce the laws he finally resigned after being involved in several moonshine still busts.

Prior to the enactment of the Prohibition Liquor Laws of 1919 our country had been concerned with the question of prohibiting the manufacture, distribution and sale of liquor since the Civil War. The prodding of the Women's Christian Temperance Union, Anti-Saloon League and other groups resulted in several laws against intoxicants. Congress enacted the 18th amendment to the Constitution in 1917 that made the entire United States subject to prohibition. The provisions of the 18th Amendment follows:

Amendment 18

Section 1 – After one year from the ratification of this article the manufacture, sale, or transportation of intoxicating liquors within, the importation thereof into, or the exportation thereof from the United States and all territory subject to the jurisdiction thereof for beverage purposes is hereby prohibited.

Section 2 – The congress and the several states shall have concurrent power to enforce this article by appropriate legislation.

Section 3 – This article shall be inoperative unless it shall have been ratified as an amendment to the Constitution by the legislation of the several states, as provided in the Constitution, within seven years from the date of the submission hereof to the states by the Congress.

The Amendment went into effect on Jan. 16, 1920. The Volstead Act was passed to define alcoholic liquors. The Jones Law was passed in 1929 and provided fines of up to $10,000 for offences against the Prohibition law, or imprisonment up to five years, or both. The Jones Law was amended in 1931.

Sheriff Sid Williams Liquor Law Enforcement Policy

Your granddad Sid was a hater of alcohol and its effect on people and their families. Sid was a strict TEETOTALER, did not smoke and never cursed. One fault which won't be discussed in this section is that he liked the opposite sex too much. I know, because as a kid my sister, Ila Mae could do no wrong, but I had to exhibit exemplary behavior.

Perhaps, the main reason Dad hated liquor so much was that it had a very bad effect on his own family. He had lost one and maybe two brothers in drunken saloon brawls.

Dad, knowing the defects in human character and nature had serious doubts about whether the liquor laws could be successfully enforced.

The time of liquor prohibition, 1920-1933 was probably the most demanding time in the County's history as far as law enforcement was concerned.

Although Sid realized that the prohibition law was a bad one he gave it his best effort, at least for the first few years. This was highly dangerous law enforcement. Moonshiners did not take kindly to seeing their operations confiscated or destroyed. Some had put a great deal of their assets into building, supplying and operating their stills. Dad raided many liquor stills. Some of the raids nearly resulted in shootouts, but he always managed to engineer the raids and arrests in such a manner that such altercations were skillfully avoided.

Other arrests, of a non-prohibition criminal nature were similarly handled even of individuals who swore they would never be taken alive. He early on began to earn the title **"BRING 'EM BACK ALIVE SID"**. These arrests will be discussed in more detail in later sections.

About 1930 Dad realized that no matter how great the effort and diligence of the prohibition officers the illegal manufacture and sale of "moonshine" was not going to be curtailed. The liquor stills in the county were starting up as fast as they were stamped out. The arrest of local citizens consuming, manufacturing, or selling moonshine seemed to be making criminals out of otherwise law abiding citizens. Some people were arrested several times for successive liquor law offences. The same thing was happening state wide and throughout the nation and well organized criminal activity in the large cities developed by gangs led by Al Capone, Bugs Moran and many others. Such big operations did not operate in Sioux and other sparsely populated counties partly because of the diligence of law officers such as your granddad, but more likely because sparsely populated areas did not lend themselves to such large operations.

About 1930 there began to be rumblings in government that Prohibition wasn't working and that the 18th Amendment should perhaps be abolished. Prohibition was also very expensive. It cost a lot of money to investigate, apprehend, prosecute and incarcerate the moonshiners. The prison population very substantially increased because of the incarceration of liquor law violators. The depression exacerbated the problem as low or non-incomes tempted people to become liquor manufacturing entrepreneurs.

About 1930-31 your granddad changed his law enforcement somewhat in regards to Prohibition. He did not go out of his way to find prohibition violators, but once a complaint was filed the law was carried out promptly and efficiently. Even friends of 40 years standing were arrested if a citizen filed a complaint against them. This new policy worked to the general satisfaction of Sioux County residents as a whole.

The moonshiners were ingenious in hiding their activities. Some stills were found in underground caves, chicken coops and other unlikely places. The confiscated liquor was often poured down the gutter in front of the courthouse.

The story was frequently told of Sid Williams refusing to taste confiscated moonshine to identify it as that manufactured by certain home brewers on trial in the county courthouse. However, smelling the liquor usually served to adequately tie in the liquor to the defendants.

I obtained copies of the jail house records for the period that included Dad's tenure as Sioux County Sheriff, April 1926-Febr. 13, 1939, which was 9 months past his death in May of 1938. The late Sioux County Deputy Sheriff Rick Mounts kindly allowed me to see and photograph the records.

Almost 300 people served time in the county jail during the 12 plus years of Dad's service. Most were for liquor law violations during the period of 1926-1933.

I analyzed the arrests records of those arrested for illegal manufacture, possession and selling of moonshine. I knew many of those people and I conclude the violators and the law abiding citizens of the county can be placed in several categories, as follows:

(A) <u>The Prohibition Faction</u>-included those citizens that supported the laws, believed in them and generally aided law enforcement officials. I believe this was a majority of the population.

(B) <u>The Liquor Faction</u>-I believe this was a minority, but sizeable group and these can be divided into several sub-groups, as follows:

    (a) those that liked liquor; were determined to have it and believed the Government had no business telling them they couldn't have it.

    (b) a group that saw an opportunity to help them survive the very tough years of the depression-the drouth and low commodity prices. This is the group I have the most sympathy for.

    (c) this group saw an opportunity to make a great deal of money by operating big liquor stills and bootlegging the stuff. This group included the big gangs of the big cities such as the Al Capone mob. I didn't find any evidence of this kind of operation in Sioux County.

    Only 1 or 2 large stills were found that could conceivably be stretched by imagination to be in this group.

Harrison Sun News Items

A. M. Brown, Editor of the Harrison Sun, during most of your granddad's tenure as Sioux County Sheriff, was an avid supporter of the Prohibition Laws. He was a good friend of Dad and eagerly printed the law enforcement news in the Sun. Criminal activity unrelated to violation of the Prohibition Laws can be found in other sections of this book.

Your granddad was a good politician and realized that favorable news reporting regarding his law enforcement activities would enhance his career in law enforcement.

Dad had a few detractors, but a multitude of friends. Mom described him as a "good mixer" when attending social gatherings. He was of a jovial nature and had an excellent sense of humor and could relate humorous aspects to some arrests despite the seriousness of the crimes. An example would be an incident in which he arrested a high school boy for burglary, and when asked why he burglarized the house, the culprit's reply was "Well, the girls wanted to go to the picture show and I didn't have any money". However, when required he had nerves of steel and a hard nosed attitude toward his duties. Although rare, he was capable of a hot temper when provoked.

The media coverage of the law enforcement activities of the prohibition and depression eras does not cover all the law enforcement events of that time. Some arrests and events occurred that did not make the news.

The following items were taken from the Harrison Sun and pertain to your granddad's exploits while county sheriff. He was involved in all the cases in one way or another. A few items are not related to criminal law violations, but you may find them of interest.(2)

Following are the gathered articles, more or less in chronological order:

GEO. W. HILL WILL RESIGN AS SHERIFF

Geo. W. Hill has filed his resignation as sheriff of Sioux County. The County Board will meet next Monday at which time this matter will come before them. George has been sheriff for a dozen years or more but this year decided not to run again. He had a good position offered him on the police force at Chadron, this job being open at this time although George's term does not expire until the first of the year he feels that he should accept the Chadron job and hence resigned here.

He will move his family to Chadron as soon as possible. This altitude is quite high for Mrs. Hill and no doubt the lower altitude at Chadron will improve her health considerable.

George has made a good sheriff and the many friends are sorry to have this estimable family leave.

Harrison Sun, Fri., April 2, 1926

C.S. WILLIAMS APPOINTED COUNTY SHERIFF

C.S. Williams was appointed Sheriff of Sioux County, by the county board at their regular meeting last Monday, George Hill had filed his resignation and the board accepted it. Sid filed the required bond took the oath of office and he is now our sheriff. He will move to Harrison as soon as possible.

Harrison Sun, April 9, 1926

ANNOUNCEMENT

To the Voters of Sioux County:

I hereby announce myself a candidate for the office of Sheriff of Sioux County, subject to the will of the Republican voters in the Primary election in August.

I have lived in Sioux County for about twenty-five years.

Your support will be greatly appreciated.

C.S. Williams

Harrison Sun, Fri., June 11, 1926

HARRY HECKERT APPOINTED DEPUTY SHERIFF

At the last meeting of the Board of County Commissioners, S.R. Seaman handed in his resignation as Deputy Sheriff, and Harry Heckert was appointed in his place.

We believe that this was a good choice as Harry will make a good officer.

Harrison Sun, Fri., July 16, 1926

(2)   *Some information was gathered from individuals involved in liquor production or by deputies involved in liquor raids. Additional information was found in the records of the County Clerk, Sioux County Courthouse.*

Your granddad, the new sheriff, earned a salary of $100/month. In addition he was paid mileage at the rate of $.15/mile, however he had to furnish his own car. This may be perceived as poor compensation for the highly dangerous job of raiding and arresting the operators of illegal liquor stills. However, this was a time of low commodity prices. For example, a quart of milk and a loaf of bread cost about $.10 each, new cars between $450 and $750 and a top ranch hand earned about $30/month.

C. SID WILLIAMS
Republican Nominee
FOR SHERIFF OF SIOUX COUNTY

Appointed to fill the vacancy occasioned by the
resignation of the former sheriff. Upon the service I have rendered Sioux County in the past I
am basing my campaign, and if that record merits
your support, I respectfully solicit your vote.

Your Support Will Be Greatly Appreciated

Harrison Sun, Fri., Oct. 15, 1926

LIGHT VOTE AT ELECTION

We are giving below a digest of the vote cast at the primary election, this is very incomplete for some of the returns are not in as we go to press, and a few of the precincts did not bring in a sample of the vote cast.

It is certain that A.C. Davis was nominated for County Clerk on the Republican ticket. Henry Hoffman no doubt will be the Democratic nominee for County Treasurer and C.P. Broderick the Democratic nominee for sheriff, and J.C. Lewis landed the Democratic nomination for county commissioner for the third district. The vote between E.F. Pontius and E.B. Lyon for the Republican nomination is so close that the official vote will have to decide that nomination.

The following is the incomplete returns as we have been able to get them:

REPUBLICAN TICKET

County Clerk—

A.C. Davis	263
W.T. Kissack	233

County Treasurer—

E.F. Pontius	220
E.B. Lyon	221

County Sheriff—

L.A. Buckingham	91
Fred D. Mason	70
C. Sid Williams	330

County Attorney—

F.S. Baker	286

County Com. 3rd Dist.—

Harry E. Derby being the

only candidate was

nominated.

Harrison Sun, Fri., Aug. 13, 1926

SHERIFF APPOINTS DEPUTY

John Dieckman has been appointed by Sheriff Sid Williams as the latter's deputy, said appointment having been approved by the board of commissioners at the last session of that body.

Harrison Sun, Dec. 17, 1926

UNOFFICIAL ELECTION RETURNS SIOUX COUNTY

For County Clerk

A.C. Davis r	641
Mary Bonsall d	410

For County Treasurer

H.B. Lyon r	625
Henry J. Hoffman d	416

For County Sheriff

C. Sid Williams r	686
C.P. Broderick d	359

For County Surveyor

F.M. Hall r	817

For County Attorney

F.S. Baker r	462
Albert L. Schnurr d	546

For Co. Commissioner 1st Dist

L.M. Childs r	599
Joseph Konrath d	368

For County Superintendent

Mrs. Elizabeth Emery	552
Nellie Bannan	496

Chasing a Horse Thief and Catching a Bride

Your grandmother, LaVerne L. Sturdivant, a recent May graduate of Torrington High School, Torrington, Wyoming, class of 1927, had just returned home after a horse back ride to the nearby Spoon Buttes in Wyoming. The 10 mile ride was a melancholy one and uneventful except for a bobcat springing out of the rocks in front of her horse, Ginger, startling both rider and horse, and nearly unseating the young woman. She retained control of the mare and continued on her journey. Her mind returned to her thoughts regarding her family's predicament. The Sturdivant's fortunes and future seemed to be very dismal.

Adeline Sturdivant had recently received notice that the foreclosure on her ranch and home of 36 years had been finalized and that the ranch now belonged to the Stock Growers National Bank of Cheyenne, Wyo.

Addy, as she was known, had tried desperately since her husband's death as a result of a heart attack in 1919, to hold onto the ranch. The past eight years had been very difficult. Some of her cattle had been rustled off, beef prices were depressed, and at the time of Joseph Sturdivant's death she was trying to raise and educate her five children, all teenagers or younger. Your grandmother was eleven.

The bank informed Addy that if she could just meet the interest payment for the year that foreclosure on the ranch could be avoided. (See newspaper article regarding foreclosure notice dated May 20, 1927 following). So in order to raise the money she decided to sell the family car, a 1918 Buick sedan. The car was taken to a car dealer in Morrill, Nebr. with the understanding that a buyer would be found and the funds distributed to Addy, less a fee for finding the buyer. Well, she never received a dime for the car. The dealer claimed the "buyer" never paid for the car. So, she lost the car and the interest payment couldn't be made. Therefore, the foreclosure went ahead. This was a time before cars were titled and thus skullduggery was easier.

LaVerne's mother said this was her home and she wasn't going to leave. All this swirled through LaVerne's mind, but she was unable to think of a way to aid her mother and family.

A few weeks later, in early July, a dust cloud was observed moving rapidly on the road leading to the Sturdivant ranch.

A cowboy on a good-looking bay gelding soon showed up at the Sturdivant sod house. He asked Mom if he could water his horse and for directions to Torrington, Wyo. She closely observed the cowboy and horse, mentally noting that something about them didn't seem quite right. He was soon hurriedly on his way after being informed that Torrington was about 18 miles to the southwest.

A day or two later the Sheriff of Sioux County, C. Sid Williams, arrived at the Sturdivant ranch driving a nearly new Model T Ford. He had tracked the cowboy and horse southwestward from the "Chick" Coffee Ranch. Mom was able to give the sheriff an accurate description of the cowboy and horse and that he was probably headed toward Torrington.

Glen A. Hilliard, the name of the cowboy, inadvertently led the sheriff to his soon to be bride. Hilliard was wanted for fraud and for stealing a bay gelding from "Chick" Coffee. The information provided by LaVerne must have impressed the sheriff because he came back a few days later and a whirlwind courtship ensued. They married Aug. 5, 1927 at Greeley, Colorado.

Mom was not yet 19 when she met Dad, age 58. Dad had a way with women and despite the age difference, she fell for him. I suppose this was an easy decision for the Sturdivants as their ranch was foreclosed on and they would soon be evicted. Dad made the case that grandmother Sturdivant would always have a home with them. She did spend considerable time with us during the following years.

I don't believe men, a great deal older than women, should marry because any children that result from such marriages may lose their fathers before they are raised. Such children are at a disadvantage without the guidance and financial support of a father. Here, I seem to be arguing against my own existence. However, despite the fact that Ila Mae and I were quite young when Dad died, I believe we turned out alright.

Soon after Mom and Dad were married Addy received the eviction order and since she refused to leave Dad had the disagreeable job of evicting his new mother-in-law. Her things had to be taken out of the house because she refused to leave. I suppose some of the modest home furnishings were sold and the married children, Joe, Mary and LaVerne took the rest for storage. Addy spent most of her remaining years with us or her other children.

REGULAR MAY TERM OF THE DISTRICT COURT MONDAY

District Judge E.L. Meyer presided over the May term of district court in Harrison Monday, and most of the tasks docketed were disposed of during the day, the balance being passed over to the term scheduled for June 20.

The following cases came to trial and were disposed of as noted:

The Stock Growers National Bank of Cheyenne re Addie Sturdivant, foreclosure sale confirmed, deed ordered.(3)

Harrison Sun, May 20, 1927

(3)   Apparently, the Sturdivants, Addy, Frank, 22, LaVerne, 19, and Charles, 17, were allowed to continue living on the ranch until a buyer could be found. Joe and Mary, now married, had already left home.

The following news article from the Harrison Sun pertains to the Hilliard Case, legal notices and your grandparent's marriage.

WANTED FOR GRAND LARCENY

Glen A. Hilliard, who for some time had been in the employ of Guy Coffee left last month for parts unknown, and Sheriff Williams holds a warrant for his arrest. Last December Hilliard borrowed money from W. L. Hoyt giving as security a mortgage on a number of cattle, and it develops that Hilliard did not have the cattle. The note became due on June 8th, and shortly after Hilliard showed up among the missing; leaving a wife and two small children.

Harrison Sun, Fri., July 8, 1927

SHERIFF HAS NEW DEPUTY

Sheriff Williams has a deputy, although instead of helping the sheriff look after the official affairs of the office, she will look after the sheriff.

On Monday of this week, C. Sid Williams and Miss LaVerne Sturdivant were married at Greely, Colorado, Judge English of that city performed the ceremony.

The groom is well known to the people of this county and the bride is the daughter of Mrs. Addy Sturdivant of Torrington.

Although the bride is not as well known to the people of this community, all join in wishing the newlyweds a very happy future.

Harrison Sun, Fri., Sept. 9, 1927

WARRANT.   Son. Harrison, Nebraska

The State of Nebraska,   SIOUX   County; To the Sheriff or any

Constable of said County, Greeting:

Whereas, before me J.H.Wilhermsdorfer,County Judge.   within and for said County

_____Sioux_____   complaint has been made in writing, signed and sworn to by

W.L.Hoyt,   and filed according to law, that _____

Glen A.Hilliard,_____ of said county, on or about the _____ 6th _____ day

December _____ A.D. 1927, in the County of _____ Sioux _____ in the State of Nebraska

then and there being,did then and there and then and there intending
unlawfully and fraudulently to cheat and defraud one W.L.Hoyt, then and
there did falsely, knowingly,designedly and unlawfully pretend and represent to the said W.L.Hoyt, that he was the owner of Five head of white
face dehorned,4 year old cows,each branded   on left side,One year old
white face heifer branded   on left side, One two year old white face
heifer branded   on left side,located in Sioux County,N ebraska,
that reling upon said false pretenses and representations of said Glen
A.Hilliard, the said W.L.Hoyt, did then and there take and receive from
said Glen A.Hilliard,a promissory note made by said Glen A.Hilliard,
payable to said W.L.Hoyt,said note being secured by a cattle mortgage
upon the above described personal property,and said W.L.Hoyt,did then and
there give to the said Glen A.Hilliard,a sum of One Hundred Dollars in
money,of the value of One Hundred Dollars;that said representations and
pretenses ofsaid Glen A.Hilliard,were wholly false and said Glen A.
Hilliard then and there was not the owner of the personal property in
Sioux County,Nebraska,as he the said Glen A.Hilliard then and there well
knew,and who then and there made said pretenses and representations with
the intent to cheat and defraud the said W.L.Hoyt, contrary to the form
of statutes in such cases made and provided and against the peace and
dignity of the people of the State of Nebraska,

These are, therefore, to command you forthwith to take the said ____ Glen A.Hilliard,

____ if he be found in your county; or if he shall have fled, that you pursue afte

d ____ Glen A.Hilliard, ____ into any other county within the state, and to s

ely keep the said ____ Glen A.Hilliard. ____ so that you bring the body

th before me or some other magistrate having cognizance of the case of said offense so committed, to answer said

int and be further dealt with according to law.

Given under my hand and seal, ____ this ____ 28th ____ day

June ____ A.D. 1927.

County Judge.

County Clerk Records,
Sioux County Courthouse,
June, 1927

County Clerk Records,
Sioux County Court House
Aug. 19, 1927

MAN WANTED HERE APPREHENDED AT TORRINGTON: GIVES $500 BOND

Glen A. Hilliard, for whom a warrant was issued last June, was apprehended last week by the sheriff at Torrington, Wyo., and on Friday Sheriff Williams went after him. Hilliard was charged with obtaining money under false pretenses and in a preliminary hearing before Judge Wilhermsdorfer his trial was continued to a later date, Hilliard giving bond of $500 for his appearance at that time.

Harrison Sun, Fri., Aug. 26, 1927

LIQUOR LAW RAID & ARRESTS

FINED $100 AND COSTS

Billy Preston of North Dakota was arrested Friday night by Sheriff Williams for the illegal possession of liquor. He was brought to County Judge Wilhermsdorfer and given a fine of $100 and costs. He is still lodged in the confines of the county jail, not having paid his fine.(4)

Harrison Sun, Fri., June 24, 1927

DRY LAW VIOLATORS ARRESTED FOLLOWING RAID BY AGENTS

Federal and state prohibition agents have been extremely busy in this part of the state during the past few weeks, and as a result several arrests have been made. Sioux County comes in for a small share of prominence in this respect, a still having been found on the Curt Grimm place and Mr. Grimm was placed under arrest, and upon waiving preliminary hearing was bound over to the district court for trial. Lee Blevens, living near Glen, was also placed under arrest, a quantity of wine and home brew being found on his premises. We are told that several members of the prohibition forces are still at work in this part of the state, although no other arrests have been made here.

Last week at Rushville seventy-five complaints were filed against alleged violators in that vicinity, a number of whom pleaded guilty and fines were assessed aggregating over $3000. Others, we understand have plead not guilty and will stand trial at a later date.

During the past few weeks the sheriff's department of Sioux County has made a number of arrests for illegal possession, and fines were assessed at $100 and costs per head. The work of apprehending violators of the prohibition law has been carried on in a very systematic and sensible manner by officers of this county, and they have the unique record of one hundred percent convictions.

Harrison Sun, Fri., July 22, 1927

JURY FINDS CURT GRIMM GUILTY ON LIQUOR CHARGE

The November term of the district court convened Monday morning, and a number of civil actions were disposed of. Judge Tewell of Sidney substituted for Judge E.L. Meyer, the latter to preside at the district court session at Bridgeport owing to the disqualification of the regular judge to hear certain cases to come up.

The greater part of the three day session was taken up by the case of Curtis Grimm and Florence Grimm, defendants in an action growing out of the alleged violation of the prohibition laws. The case was given to the jury Tuesday night about nine o'clock and a verdict was reached Wednesday morning. The jury found Curtis Grimm guilty as charged and found Florence Grimm not guilty. Grimm was sentenced to serve thirty days in the county jail, pay a fine of $500 and costs of prosecution. L.L. Raymond, counsel for the defense, filed motion for a new trial, which was denied, whereupon he gave notice of appeal to the supreme court. Defense was given until January first to enter the appeal.

County Attorney A.L. Schnurr, assisted by Attorney Moffley, of the attorney general's department prosecuted the case.

Harrison Sun, Fri., Dec. 2, 1927

---

(4)   According to the jail house records Billy Preston served 36 days in the county jail, June 17, 1927 to July 23, 1927.

GRIMM CASE DECIDED

The supreme court of the state passed upon the appeal of Curt Grimm last week, affirming the decision of the lower court. This case was heard before a jury last fall, at which time Grimm was found guilty on a liquor charge and was sentenced to serve thirty days in jail and fined $500 and costs. The account of this decision appeared in a recent issue of the Lincoln papers, although the local authorities have had no official information regarding same.

Harrison Sun, Fri., Oct. 26, 1928

Born to Mr. & Mrs. Floyd Williams of Ardmore, on Friday, August 12, 1927, a son weighing 7 pounds.(5)

C. Sid Williams paid a visit to his new grandson on Tuesday of this week.

Harrison Sun, Fri., Aug. 19, 1927

TWO JAILED DURING FAIR

Although for the most part the fair crowd was orderly, two arrests were made. One was a check artist wanted in Lusk for giving spurious checks, and the other caught red-handed with a gallon of hootch. The moonshine vendor was from Lusk, and plying his trade in Harrison, and he was taken up and fined the usual amount. Upon failure to provide the necessary wherewith he is languishing in jail.

Harrison Sun, Fri., Sept 9, 1927

ARRESTED ON LIQUOR CHARGE

Ed Grimm and Bob Cowell, both of Sioux County, were arrested February 20th by officers in Crawford and charged with illegal possession of liquor. The officers found one gallon and one pint of alleged hootch.

On Monday of this week, County Attorney Fred Crites and Deputy Sheriff McNeff went to Crawford where the trial was held before Judge Hooch. Grimm was fined $100 and costs and Cowell was found not guilty and was released – Chadron Journal.

Harrison Sun, Fri., March 2, 1928

SHERIFF LOCATES STILL ON COTTONWOOD CREEK RANCH

Armed with a search warrant, Sheriff Williams and Deputy Sidney Williams went to the ranch of Ed Hoevet on Cottonwood Creek Saturday night of last week, and uncovered a still. Besides the still, which was not in operation at the time, the sheriff also found two gallons of the completed product and about 75 gallons of mash.

Hoevet was not at home at the time and a trip was made by the officers to Crawford, although their man could not be located. Hoevet was placed under arrest yesterday and brought to Harrison. A hearing is to be held this afternoon, S.L. O'Brien being employed by the defendant to handle his case in county court.

Harrison Sun, Fri., Aug. 17, 1928

SHERIFF GETS FIRST FORD

M.N. Wilhermsdorfer returned Saturday evening from Omaha, where he had gone to get one of the new Ford models. He brought back a sport coupe, which goes to Sheriff Williams, and is the first sale of the new model in Sioux County. The coupe is a keen looking car, has the appearance of being very serviceable, and with its reputed

---

(5)   *This was the birth of Dean Williams. Dean was the source of some of the material used in this book.*

speed bootleggers, etc., will have to take to aeroplanes if they want to escape the stern hand of the law in Sioux County.

Harrison Sun, Fri., April 27, 1928

Sid Williams and son, Sid Jr. drove to Edgemont Saturday and returned Sunday to visit their daughter and sister, Martha. They report her condition very low.

Harrison Sun, Fri., May 11, 1928

MARTHA WILLIAMS PASSES AWAY AFTER LONG ILLNESS

After a long patient suffering of eight months affliction of a cancer, Martha V. Williams passed to her eternal rest Monday morning May 14, 1928, at 11 o'clock in Edgemont, S.D., at the home of her sister, Mrs. Ethel Downey, where she had been.

She was born near Harrison February 14, 1894 and bedfast for several months.(6) She is the daughter of C. Sid Williams, Sr. Sioux County, and has made Sioux County her home, having spent the last four years on her father's ranch near Harrison. Prior to that time she taught school in Ardmore, S.D. and Sidney, Nebr., and on Indian Creek in South Dakota and was a successful teacher. During her illness she was of a sunny disposition, never complaining and until just a few short hours Monday morning before she passed away, did she give up hope of recovering. Martha had an innumerable following of friends; she was always ready and willing to be of service to all with whom she came in contact, and rendering her services in a cheerful manner. The high esteem in which she was held was manifested by the many beautiful floral offerings, also the respect shown by

the business houses of Edgemont closing during the services.

Her father, and one brother, Floyd, were at her bedside at the time of her death. Her sister, Mrs. Downey, was convalescing from an operation at Hot Springs, but was able to attend the funeral and her brother, Sidney, Jr., arrived in Edgemont just after she passed away.

Funeral services were held Thursday morning at ten o'clock at the Catholic Church in Edgemont with Rev. Beaver of Ardmore and Rev. Hoye of Edgemont in charge. Martha had joined the Catholic Church about a month before her passing. Her remains were taken to the Chadron cemetery for burial in the family plot. All arrangements for the funeral services were made by the Royal Neighbor lodge of which the deceased was a member.

Mr. Williams and his family have sympathy of the entire community in the loss of their beloved daughter and sister.

Harrison Sun, Fri., May 18, 1928

BOOZE RAID BRINGS ABOUT ARREST OF SOUTH SIOUX MAN

With the aid of state prohibition law enforcement officers, Sheriff Williams searched several places in the south part of the county Tuesday of this week, and were successful in unearthing a still and quantity of mash. This still was on the place of Orville L. Jeffers, and the man was placed under arrest and County Attorney A.L. Schnurr filed a complaint of unlawful possession and manufacture against Jeffers.

A hearing was given before Judge Wilhermsdorfer Thursday, Jeffers pleading guilty, and the judge passed out a fine of $500 and thirty days in jail. Jeffers is now

(6) She was actually born on the Circle Bar Ranch, Sioux County, near Ardmore. Your granddad and Bernie Williams managed the ranch during the early 1890's.

a guest of Sheriff Williams in the hoosgow, and will remain there for the period of thirty days, and a while longer if the fine is not forthcoming at the end of the first "hitch."

Harrison Sun, Fri., Mar. 16, 1928

TWO CAUGHT IN LIQUOR RAID IN SOUTH PART OF COUNTY

A raid on the farm occupied by Orville Jeffers, in the south part of the county, this week netted the arrest of three men. The officers making the raid were Sheriff Williams and Deputy Sid Williams, and State Deputy Clark. The other two men arrested were Harvey Van Cleef and Frank Behr.

In a hearing before judge Wilhermsdorfer it developed that Jeffers was not implicated in the deal, or at any rate Van Cleef assumed responsibility. The officers found forty-two 50-gallon barrels of mash and forty bags of sugar, which Van Cleef claimed was his and he was bound over to district court on the charge of illegal possession of mash. Fred Cunningham was here to give bond for defendant.

Behr had in his possession a gallon of the finished product and upon pleading guilty he was assessed a fine of $200 and given another jolt of thirty days in jail for good measure. He is at present confined to jail to serve his sentence.

The state's side of the case was very ably handled by W.E. Mumby, associated with A.L. Schnurr in the practice of law, and also serving as deputy county attorney.

Harrison Sun, Fri., July 6, 1928

SHERIFF NABS POOL HALL KEEPER ON BOOZE CHARGE

Armed with a complaint made out by County Attorney Schnurr, Sheriff Williams made a raid on the pool hall Monday morning of this week, and arrested O.D. Housh, proprietor. A search of the ice-box brought to light a quantity of moonshine in a beer bottle, which had been re-capped and placed among the filled bottles in the box, and the officer had some difficulty in locating the forbidden fluid.

Taken before Judge Wilhermsdorfer the same day, Housh plead guilty to the charge of unlawful possession and being in somewhat of a sympathetic mood Monday the judge just granted the offender thirty days in the county bastile, with costs attached, during which period Mr. Housh will have time to reflect upon his misdeed, and at the termination of which issue forth a new man, greatly refreshed. A state officer, who had come up from the south part of the county with some evidence in another raid, aided Sheriff Williams.

Harrison Sun, Fri., Nov. 25, 1927

SHORT RELEASED ON BONDS

Leroy Short, a resident of the south part of the county, who has been incarcerated in the county bastile for the past month, after pleading guilty to possession of a still and manufacture and possession, was released Monday by the county court after serving his thirty-day sentence. There is still a fine of $500 hanging over Short, and in view of the fact that he has a wife and several children who are without support, and have been cared for by the county, the court granted the release after a bond had been given for payment of the fine. Short is to report by letter every week to the court, and to make monthly payments on the fine until the full amount is paid. This would seem a very satisfactory and sensible arrangement for both the family and the county.

Harrison Sun, Fri., June 8, 1928

HOEVET PLEADS NOT GUILTY

In his preliminary hearing in county court Friday afternoon of last week, Ed Hoevet, against whom an information was filed for violation of the liquor laws, plead not guilty and was bound over to the fall term of district court. Bondsmen appeared for the defendant and signed for the stipulated amount of $1000 for his appearance this fall.

Harrison Sun, Friday, Aug. 24, 1928

W.E. MUMBY JOINS A.L. SCHNURR IN LAW PRACTICE

Schnurr & Mumby, Attorneys-at-Law. That is the name of the newly organized professional institution in Harrison.

W.E. Mumby, formerly of Sterling, Nebr., with his bride of but a few days, arrived Tuesday to become associated with A.L. Schnurr in the practice of law. Mr. Mumby graduated from the law school of the University of Nebraska on last Friday, was admitted to the Nebraska bar on Saturday, was married on Sunday morning and left the same day for Harrison, the only mishap of the entire venture being stranded a day because of muddy roads. As a "fast worker" Mr. Mumby reigns supreme and we are glad to welcome both he and his wife to our community. They have taken up residence in the Ralph Schnurr property east of the court house.

The law practice of Mr. Schnurr had grown to such proportions that the partnership makes a splendid arrangement, and Mr. Mumby will receive the appointment of deputy prosecuting attorney to assist Mr. Schnurr in that branch of the work.(7)

Harrison Sun, June 8, 1928

(7)   *W.E. Mumby eventually became County Attorney and worked closely with Dad on criminal cases. I knew him well.*

The Dan Jordan Raid

The Jordan Raid & The Jordan and Williams Family Relationships

The above discussed raid at the Jordan Ranch very nearly resulted in a shootout, but this was avoided and the Jordan father and son team were brought to town by the other father and son team, Sid Sr. and Sid Jr. for a hearing before Judge Wilhermsdorfer.

Before we discuss the raid lets find out who Dan Jordan was, his family and their relationships with the Williams family.

The following information on the Jordans was taken from items written by Mary Jordan and Gertrude Harkin printed in the Sioux County History Book, First 100 Years 1886-1986.

Dad had known Dan Jordan since 1890 when Sarah Jordan & her children, including Dan and Dick arrived in Sioux County. Dan and Sid were friends or at least well acquainted, especially since both were in the ranching business in northwestern Sioux County. The Jordan's had several land holdings in the county, but their main ranch was located a few miles southeast of Dad's ranch at the time of the raid.

Dan (b. 1875, d. 1946) married Barbara Wasserburger in 1898. They were the parents of seven children, raising five to adulthood: Allen, Blanche, Gerty, Della and Dorothy.

Dan, as a young man in the 1890's participated in open range roundups in north central Montana, about the same time your granddad was participating in similar roundups in southwestern South Dakota.

Dan's mother, Sarah, (b. 1850, d. 1932), called 'Grandma Jordan' was a midwife and delivered many babies in the area. She was present to deliver me at our house in Harrison when I was born, May 16th, 1929. Dr. W.H. Priest was late in arriving because he was busy delivering my later good friend, Wendell Leeling at the time, but arrived in time to take charge of my delivery. It was touch and go for me for awhile, but under the expert care of my grandmother Sturdivant I pulled through. The Dr. said later that he thought I was one baby that probably would not survive.

131

Allen Jordan, (b. 1905, d. 1974) Dan's only surviving son, married Mary Doyle and they had three children: Bob (b. 1929, d. 2007), Shirley (b.1930), Rita (b.1932).

I went to school with all three. Bob and Shirley were in my high school graduating class of 1947. We are all good friends. I dated Shirley once or twice. She married Rodney Phipps (b. 1929, d. 1985) one of my good friends, in 1949. Rita married Richard DeHaven. DeHaven, Phipps and I played together on the school football and basketball teams.

I serviced Allen's vehicles many times when he came to the Standard Service Station where I worked, late 1940's, selling him gas, fixing his tires, etc. The Standard Station later became the Senior Citizens Center.

Dorothy (Jordan) married Pete Meiers. Elaine and I managed the Summit Theatre for them while they owned and operated a drive-in theatre in Lusk, Wyo.

Sid Williams Jr. married Sadie Jordan, daughter of Dick Jordan, a brother to Dan Jordan. Unfortunately this union ended in divorce.

Elaine and I look forward to and generally see Shirley and Rita when we make our annual summer journey back to Sioux County. They are among our best remaining friends in Sioux County.

A year or two after Dad died, about 1939 or 1940, Dan Jordan invited me to accompany him to attend the Father-Son Banquet held in the basement of the County Courthouse. I had a marvelous time. I liked Dan. He was always friendly to young folks, such as me.

Now let's discuss the Jordan raid as it was explained to me several times by my mother and Sid Jr. Both stories relate the events with little variance and even though considerable time has passed since I heard the stories I have little doubt about their veracity.

Dad was a teetotaler and realized that alcohol was a destroyer of lives, families and had many injurious effects on society. Some of his brothers had been heavy drinkers and brawlers and so he hated whiskey and what it could do to people and their families. Nevertheless, he considered prohibition a bad law and that people would thwart the law, if possible. However, as a peace officer, he had taken the oath of office and had sworn to uphold the law to the best of his ability.

So, we have two well acquainted middle aged old time cowboys about to confront each other. One believing no 'damn' gov't. had any right to tell him or anyone else what they could or couldn't do on their own place. The other, sworn to uphold the law and determined to do so.

The raiders, consisting of three men, your granddad and his deputy Chas. Sidney Jr., and Federal Prohibition Officer, O.E. Forsling, set out from the courthouse to conduct the raid.

It is now believed that word from Harrison had reached Dan and his son Allen that the law was coming and they proceeded to intercept the law.

Upon arriving at the Jordan place the raiders, for some reason, probably intending to search for the still, split up and agreed to meet at a certain rendezvous point, Sid Jr. had the greater distance to cover.

Sid Sr. scouting ahead was suddenly confronted by Dan holding a pistol and he definitely had the 'drop' on your granddad. The following approximation of the conversation ensued:

Dan: Hold it right there Sid. I've got you covered.

Sid Sr.: Dan, I have a search warrant to search your place for a still. We have complaints that you have one and I'm charged with finding it.

Dan: I think I'll just shoot you right now and call it self defence. No damn government is going to tell me what I can't do on my own place. I think I could get away with shooting you.

Sid Sr.: Well, Dan, go ahead and 'pull' if you think you must, but you better consider this first. I don't think your idea of shooting law officers will fly. That action would result in very serious charges and the penalty would be severe. Also, there are two other officers on this raid and one is a Federal Agent. Do you intend to shoot them too? Remember Judge Wilhermsdorfer has a reputation of giving out light sentences to local first time liquor law violators. The judge is an elected official and he isn't going to make it too rough on local citizens like you. So, before you make this situation any worse you had better hand over that gun and submit yourself to arrest.

Sid advanced toward Dan, extended out his hand and took Dan's gun out of his hand.

Dan: I know you are right Sid (hands gun to Sid), but the government shouldn't be telling people what to do.

Sid Sr.: Well, we both know the Prohibition law is a bad law, but we have to obey the law until it's changed.

Sid handcuffs Dan.

Meanwhile Sid Jr., because of the greater distance to cover, or because he could hear the conversation between Dan and Sid Sr., was running at top speed. With his 6-shooter out in front of him, rounding a corner he collided with Allen. The force of the gun hand hitting Allen in the chest knocked him down. Both were "shook up" over the incident, but Allen's arrest was without further incident.

Liquor and a still were confiscated and the prisoners escorted off to jail. Both received light sentences by Judge Wilhermsdorfer. Dan was allowed to go home at night by Dad, but had to report back to the jail early in the morning. Sid Jr. took Dan with him sometimes when going out of town on cattle theft investigations.

DISTRICT COURT CONVENES MONDAY AND IS STILL ON

With a number of jury cases to be tried in district court, there is indication that the present session, which opened Monday, will continue for several days. There are a number of liquor cases to be heard, and other criminal actions, which require time. Several civil actions have been disposed of, and a divorce was granted to Michael J. O'Connell from Emma O'Connell.

The case of Dan Jordan and Allen Jordan was heard Monday. This case was carried from the county court, where the former plead guilty to a charge of possession of a still and illegal manufacture. It was erroneously stated in the Sun several weeks ago that the defendant had been fined $500 and given thirty days in jail, which was not a fact. The county judge bound the two over to district court, where the fine and sentence as above stated were imposed. The case against Allen Jordan was dismissed in district court.

A jury was drawn Tuesday to hear the case of the state against Fred Cunningham, which proceeded throughout Wednesday, the case going to the jury late in the afternoon. Cunningham was found guilty of illegal possession of intoxicating liquor, and will be sentenced later. In county court some months ago, where Cunningham was given a preliminary, Judge Wilhermsdorfer found him guilty and assessed a fine of $500 and ninety days in jail. An appeal was taken to the district court with the foregoing result.

During the progress of the Cunningham trial, one witness by the name of Baker, a brother-in-law, of the defendant, claimed ownership of the liquor and an order for his arrest was promptly entered. However, the statute of limitation has run out and it was not possible to hold him on the charge.

The case of the state versus Harry Van Cleef is in progress at the time of going to press.

Harrison Sun, Fri., Oct. 26, 1928

MANY JURY CASES HEARD IN TEN-DAY SESSION DIST. COURT

After a ten-day session of district court, Judge Earl L. Meyer left yesterday afternoon for his home at Alliance, leaving the term open, as a number of important cases are still on the docket. This is the longest session of court held for Sioux County for a number of years, and one jury case occupied six of the ten days.

There were six liquor cases on the docket, which were prosecuted by County Attorney A.L. Schnurr and Deputy W. E. Mumby, two being tried by jury and found guilty and the remaining defendants pleading guilty. The first case was that of Dan Jordan, who plead guilty; the jury trial of the state versus Fred Cunningham, who was found guilty and sentenced to sixty days in jail. Defendant placing bond of $500 and arranging for appeal to the supreme court; the state versus Harvey Van Cleef, who was found guilty by the jury and sentenced to thirty days in jail and fined $500 and costs, defendant being committed to jail; the state versus Ed Hoevet, who plead guilty and was fined $100 and costs, which he paid; the state versus Fermin Guilar, who also plead guilty and paid a fine of $100 and costs; the state versus Clarence Farrington, Ray Johnston and George Meyer, who plead guilty and were assessed fines of $100 and costs each, and stand committed to jail until same are paid.

This has been a quite successful term for the county attorney's office, there having been convictions in all liquor cases brought into court, and also the favorable decision of the jury in the damage suit.

Harrison Sun, Fri., Nov. 2, 1928

DAN JORDAN – STILL – JAN. 2, 1929

IN THE DISTRICT COURT OF SIOUX COUNTY, NEBRASKA

The State of Nebraska,   :
      Plaintiff,   :
      vs.   :   J O U R N A L E N T R Y.
Daniel Jordan and   :
Allen Jordan,   :
      Defendants.   :

Now on this 22nd day of October, 1928, the same being one of the regular days of the October, 1928 term of District Court for Sioux County, Nebraska, before the information A.L. Schnurr, County Attorney, in and for Sioux County, Nebraska, said information charging the defendants, Daniel Jordan and Allen Jordan, with possession of still, cash and liquor in violation of the laws of the State of Nebraska.

A.L. Schnurr, County Attorney moved the Court that said information be dismissed as to Allen Jordan, which motion was then and there granted.

The defendant, Daniel Jordan, being present before the court, in the custody of the sheriff of Sioux County, Nebraska, was informed of the charge made against him. Defendant, Daniel Jordan then stated that he was ready to plead to the information, and said information was read to the said Daniel Jordan, and the said Daniel Jordan, then and there entered his plea of guilty.

Defendant was then asked by the Court whether he had anything to say why sentence should not be pronounced, thereupon said defendant produced a petition, which after being considered by the Court, his sentence was suspended to Jan. 22, 1929. At the special request of the defendant it was also ordered by the court that the still and equipment be destroyed by the Sheriff.

It was then ordered and adjudged by the Court that the defendant, Daniel Jordan be fined in the sum of $500.00 and the cost of prosecution, and be imprisoned in the County Jail of Sioux County, Nebraska, until said fine and costs are paid, said sentence to start Jan 2, 1929.(8)

By the Court – E.L. Meyer, Judge.

Endorsed: In the District Court of Sioux County, Nebraska.
State of Nebraska, Plaintiff, vs. Daniel Jordan and Allen Jordan; Defendants
Doc. 7   Page   50, 1468   Journal Entry.
State of Nebraska, County of Sioux – ss. Filed in the office of the Court of District Court of said County this 23 day of November A.D., 1928
                A.C. Davis, Clerk District Court
                By Mary E. Broderick, Deputy.
P.D. Mumby, Deputy County Attorney.
Journal 4 pages 160.

(8)   *A fine of this amount would be equivalent today of about $9,000-10,000.*

SHERIFF WINS SECOND HEAT IN RACE WITH DISTILLERS

Sheriff Williams, apparently, is carrying a little too much flesh for sprinting purposes, or such was indicated in a spirited race over the prairie country northeast of Mitchell, about two weeks ago.

On the night of Sept. 27th, the sheriff and some state men made a raid on a still, but the men who were operating the outfit heard their approach and took to the tall un-cut, and easily outdistanced their pursuers. The still was going nicely at the time, and it appears the moonshiners had buried several barrels of mash at various points in the pasture, near windmills, and when the stuff was ready to run off moved the still to the ground and finished the product. The still was one of the more elaborate kind, and had a capacity of 75 gallons. Seven gallons of moonshine and some mash were procured as evidence.

The men operating the still were known to the officers, but went over into Wyoming, and but recently returned to Scottsbluff. They were apprehended upon their return to Nebraska, and Sheriff Williams went to Gering for them Monday. They are now in the county jail awaiting preliminary hearing, which is set for Monday of next week. They gave the names of Clarence Farington, Roy Johnston and George Meyer.

Harrison Sun, Oct. 12, 1928

MEXICAN CAUGHT WITH STILL

Sheriff Williams was called to the south part of the county last Sunday to get a Mexican who was found with a still in his possession. Upon search of the Mexican's home a still, several gallons of mash and a small quantity of liquor was found under a bed in the house. The Mexican stated that someone else had placed the outfit there without his knowledge. He was arraigned before Judge Wilhermsdorfer Monday, but claiming ignorance of the U.S. language, he was granted continuance to employ an interpreter.

Harrison Sun, Sept. 28, 1928

TWO MEXICANS ARRESTED FOR POSSESSION OF LIQUOR

Two Mexicans, who had been apprehended by J.B. Duncan in the south part of the county last Friday, were brought to Harrison by Sheriff Williams and given a hearing before Judge Wilhermsdorfer Monday, and upon their pleas of guilty the judge promptly assessed a fine of $100 and costs. The Mexicans were caught with a gallon of liquor. They are without available funds and will repose in the county bastile to pay off the indebtedness to the county.

Harrison Sun, Fri., Oct. 26, 1928

HOTEL DE WILLIAMS LOSES MOST OF ITS BOARDERS

Clarence Farrington, Ray Johnston and George Meyer, who have been involuntary guests at the "Hotel de Williams" since the October term of District Court, were released Monday of this week and the sheriff of Scottsbluff County was on hand to take them into custody. Farrington will serve a sentence there on a booze charge, his appeal to the Supreme Court having met with hard luck. Meyer was out on bond in a case at Scottsbluff, where he was caught with about 120 gallons of moonshine, when arrested in the south part of Sioux County on another infraction of the prohibition act. Not being present on the date set for his hearing, Meyer's bondsmen were forced to deliver up the cash. Just what is wanted with Johnson, the third member of the trio, was not stated, although it is presumed he too is mixed up in the liquor traffic the others are charged with.

Two Mexicans, also incarcerated about

137

the same time as the "Three Musketeers," were liberated Monday. They were laying out a fine of $100 each. One was found guilty in district court and the other got his in Judge Wilhermsdorfer's court.

Harvey VanCleff is the sole survivor of the lot, and his stay is of more or less indefinite duration. He got a jolt of thirty days in jail and a fine of $500 and costs.

Harrison Sun, Dec. 14, 1928

OFFICERS FIND SIX BARRELS OF MASH AT LONELY SHACK

Sheriff Williams and Deputy Sidney Williams drove to Scottsbluff Friday afternoon of last week, and were joined there by two Scottsbluff County deputies, the four driving to a point in the sandhills in Sioux County, about thirty miles from Scottsbluff, and searched a small shack in one of the large pastures in that section. The building was a one-room cabin, being unoccupied at the time, but the pronounced odor of "hootch" gave evidence that someone had been there at a recent date. A trap-door covered by a small rug was found under a bed, the hole in the floor leading to a cemented basement, the trap being the only means of getting in or out.

Six barrels of mash were in course of preparation to be "run off," and the officers are of the opinion that they were just a day or so too soon to find a still in operation. Waiting until about three o'clock in the morning, the officers decided no one would show up that day, so the barrels were demolished and the mash poured out on the floor.

The location of the shack is on what is known as the Dineen ranch, and is isolated from other buildings, and provided an excellent place for moonshiners to carry on their work unmolested. Being near to Scottsbluff, the officers of that county have been investigating reports of operation at this point for some time, and gave this information to Sioux County officials, which resulted in the raid.

Harrison Sun, Fri., Febr. 6, 1929

PLEADS GUILTY TO ILLEGAL POSSESSION OF LIQUOR

At his preliminary hearing Monday, in county court, Daily Gayman, of the south part of the county, plead guilty to a charge of illegal possession of liquor and was assessed a fine of $100 and costs, amounting to a trifle more that $126. Gayman paid the amount and was released. L.L. Raymond, Scottsbluff attorney, was present to represent Gayman in court.

Harrison Sun, March 28, 1929

SHERIFF WILLIAMS CAPTURES 300-GALLON CAPACITY STILL

The southern part of Sioux County again comes into the lime-light as the leading center for the manufacture of booze, as evidenced Monday of this week when Sheriff Sid Williams and Deputy Sidney Williams seized one of the largest, if not the largest, still yet taken into captivity by the Sioux County officials.

Following a tip received some time ago, the officers went to the Matthews farm, about twelve miles north of Morrill, and after a search uncovered an elaborate outfit, which had been buried in a field near the house. In the barn there was found a tank containing fifteen barrels of mash, and there was indication that the still had been in use in the barn in running off a batch of "pizen." The still was of 300-gallon capacity and was equipped with a double distilling apparatus. Sid Williams says this is his prize find during his term in office, but is disappointed in not being able to get the owner of the outfit. The place had been rented by John Abrogast, who

138

had gone to town an hour before the officers arrived, and apparently was tipped off that the place had been raided, for the officers remained there two days awaiting his return. Abrogast has a wife and fourteen-day old babe, whom he had left at the farm. It was learned at Torrington that Abrogast had departed for Texas, where he had formerly resided. The still was too big to be brought to Harrison in the car, and a truck will be sent for it when the roads are opened.

Wednesday of this week Sheriff Williams went to the Sheep Creek country and found fifteen barrels of mash buried in a pasture, although no trace of the owner was found. The mash was destroyed.

Harrison Sun, Fri., April 12, 1929

APPOINTED MARSHALL

At the meeting of the town council Wednesday night of this week, Joe Stanek was appointed marshall, and is also to help with the work about the town, on Streets and with the light and water plants. Joe was recently appointed deputy sheriff, and the two jobs will go together nicely, and the salary provided for each job is sufficient recompense to make it worth while for one officer.

Harrison Sun, Fri., May 10, 1929

STILLS AND OTHER MOONSHINE PARAPHERNALIA IS DESTROYED

Sheriff Williams, with the aid of Deputy Stanek, had an extensive party Saturday afternoon of last week, with a large number of people witnessing the ceremonies. A large assortment of moonshine stills, copper pipes, stoves, and other material used in the

manufacture of "moon" was piled outside the jail and such parts that might be used for the distilling process were put out of commission.

In all there were twenty-three booze-making devices, representing the ingenuity of the various manufacturers that have been apprehended during the past year or so. Some were quite elaborate in material and design, while others were ordinary tin cream cans and wash boilers. One worthy of mention was constructed from a dynamite can, suggestive of the brand that might have been distilled therefrom.

Many gallons of hootch were poured out on the ground. This was also on the order of the stills-good, bad, and indifferent. (Editor's note: We arrived at this conclusion from the odor.)

Those who are doubtful of the diligence with which the sheriff and other officers have pursued the moonshiner in Sioux County, would have been convinced of the activity of the law had they seen the pile of booze and machinery Saturday.

Harrison Sun, Fri., July 5, 1929

Mr. and Mrs. Lawrence Leeling announce the birth of a baby boy Thursday evening, May 16th, weighing 7 ¾ pounds.

Mr. and Mrs. C. Sid Williams announce the birth of a son, born Thursday evening, May 16th, weighing 5 ¾ pounds.(9)

Harrison Sun, May 17, 1929

---

(9)   *This was the birth announcement of this writer.*

139

L-R: A.M. Brown, Editor, Harrison Sun; Sid Williams, Sr., Sheriff; Joe Stanek, Deputy
Sheriff; W.E. Mumby, County Attorney, extreme right;
the other two not identified
Photos courtesy of Sioux County Historical Society.

The disposal of 'bootleg' LIQUOR and the
destruction of twenty three 'moonshine' STILLS near
Jail and Old Courthouse, Harrison, Sioux County, Nebraska
Left County Jail, and old County Courthouse built in 1888 and razed in 1930
June 29, 1929.

JURY RETURNS GUILTY VERDICT IN THE HARRY HANEY CASE

In the case of the State of Nebraska vs. Harry Haney on a charge of illegal possession of mash and manufacturing liquor, the jury returned to receive the verdict, although sentence will not be pronounced until the court convenes January 13th.

Harrison Sun, Fri., Nov. 29, 1929

CAUGHT WITH BOOZE OUTFIT

A Mexican was brought here from the south end of the county yesterday by state enforcement officials, and a charge of possession of a still, mash and manufacture of liquor was lodged against him. The offender has not been arraigned as yet, but it is stated that he intends to plead guilty.

Harrison Sun, Fri., June 6, 1930

SHERIFF DIGS OUT STILL AND COPPER COILS IN FLAX FIELD

Searching a field about eighteen miles south of Harrison today, Sheriff Williams found a still and outfit that had been buried in a field of flax. Car tracks leading to the point in the field made it easy to find the location of the "burial ground,' and other tracks led to a ravine where the still had evidently been in operation.

On the strength of the find, and other information, Sheriff Williams had a warrant issued against Frank Parsons, who was arraigned before Judge Wilhermsdorfer today on a charge of illegal possession of a still., and the case was set for hearing on October 10th. The Sheriff also searched the premises occupied by Parsons and found four dozen pint flasks, a quantity of corks, a gallon glass jug that had an odor of liquor,

and what is presumed to be an "aging marhine," whatever that might be.

Harrison Sun, Sept. 26, 1930

DISTRICT COURT CONVENES NEXT MONDAY, NOVEMBER 28

The November term of the district court will convene next Monday morning.

A total of forty-seven cases appear on the docket, forty-five of which are civil actions and three of the latter being divorce cases. Most of the civil filings involve land foreclosures.

Two criminal cases are billed for hearing. One is the state of Nebraska versus Lee Blevens for unlawful possession of mash, and the other is that of the state versus Curtis Grimm and Florence Grimm for unlawful possession of still, mash and intoxicating liquor.

Harrison Sun, Fri., Nov. 4, 1927

FINED FOR POSSESSION

Sheriff Williams arrested a trio of Fair visitors that were quartered in a room at a local hotel Saturday night of last week, when he found a gallon of liquor. The three men were strangers and had been following the concession outfits about the country. At a hearing in county court one of the men, who gave Stanley Jackson as his name and claimed to be from Norton, Kans., confessed ownership of the jug, and was fined $100 and costs, and is laying it out in jail. The other two men were released.

Harrison Sun, Sept. 7, 1928

THIS SHERIFF'S JOB IS BECOMING TOO SOFT A SNAP

A made to order arrest of a man, truck

and a still occurred here Tuesday morning, when Sheriff Williams walked down the street, saw indications of a still protruding from a torn canvas on a truck, and took the whole caboodle to jail.

Lyman Case, driver of the truck, according to his story had slept out on the prairie southeast of Harrison the night previous, and drove into Harrison for breakfast. The truck was parked on Main Street in front of the restaurant, while Case and a twelve-year-old boy went in to eat. Someone saw the still on the truck, notified Sheriff Williams, who parked himself on a bench in front of the restaurant to await the apparent owner of the truck. When Case came out to pursue his journey, the sheriff asked him if that was his outfit, which Case admitted, and the arrest followed. At a hearing Wednesday before Judge Wilhermsdorfer, Case plead guilty to possession of a still and was fined $500 and costs and given thirty days in jail.

Case told the officers that the truck belonged to E.B. Minnick, an Alliance policeman, and that the latter was to have met him at Newcastle, Wyo., near where Case was to go on a homestead. In the truck were 200 pounds of sugar, some bacon, ham and other provisions, and also a phonograph and a few household goods, and a crate of chickens.

Case, who is a brother-in-law of Minnick, also stated that the still outfit also belonged to the Alliance policeman. Word from Alliance is to the effect that Minnick has been temporarily suspended from the police force, pending investigation. When here Wednesday evening, Minnick denied ownership of the still, further stating he had no knowledge of it being on the truck, but applied to County Attorney Schnurr for release of the truck. Mr. Schnurr is not much inclined to respond to the request at the present time.

It developed, after communication with Alliance officers, that Case had had a collision with another truck near Hemingford and was held there most of Monday. In the collision two occupants of the other truck, said to be negroes, were injured and their truck damaged. Case was released with the understanding that the owner of the truck he was driving would pay the damages. Why the still was overlooked at the time of the collision is not understood, as Case claims the outfit was in the ditch at the side of the road after the collision. The boy was held here a day pending the arrival of his father, who took him back to Alliance. The truck is still "in custody" and what disposition is to be made of it has not been stated by the county attorney's office at the present time.

Harrison Sun, July 26, 1929

SOUTHEND DELIVERS UP ANOTHER ON BOOZE CHARGE

Sheriff Williams was called to the south part of the county Saturday to take into custody a Mexican who was caught with a quantity of liquor. Felencio Almanza, together with two sons-in-law, were brought to Harrison and lodged in jail until Monday, when they were given a hearing before Judge Wilhermsdorfer. Almanza plead guilty to possession of liquor and was fined $500 and costs and in addition was given a jail sentence of thirty days. The younger Mexicans disclaimed any part of the liquor, stating they had just arrived from Boulder, Colo., about an hour previous to the raid, to visit over Sunday. Their story was quite plausible and they were dismissed.

Harrison Sun, Aug. 9, 1929

ANOTHER MAN GETS CAUGHT

Sheriff Sid Williams has another Mexican

booze violator stopping at his popular stone palace on courthouse square. The culprit was apprehended in the south part of the county, and also a quantity of Mexican-made "hootch" was confiscated. At a trial in Justice Clark's court, the offender was found guilty of illegal possession of liquor and fined $100 and costs and sentenced to thirty days in jail.

Harrison Sun, Fri., Aug. 23, 1929

SHERIFF PICKS UP LOCAL MAN FOR ILLEGAL POSSESSION

Bob Allen, who has lived here for the past few months, and is employed by Forest Porter on the dray line, was picked up by Sheriff Williams and Deputy Joe Stanek last night and lodged in jail. This morning a complaint was filed against Allen for illegal possession of liquor, to which he plead not guilty when arraigned in county court. Hearing of the case has been set for Tuesday of next week.

Sheriff Williams and Deputy Stanek had been tipped off that a jug of liquor had been cached in the gravel pit on the Walt Woodruff place north of town, and the officers have been spending the nights waiting for some one to call and claim it. (10) Allen went to the place about nine o'clock last night and as he approached the place where the jug was buried, the officers arrested him. He had a glass jar with him at the time, and the officers are of the opinion that Allen had come for a part of the quantity in the jug.

Harrison Sun, Fri., Aug. 9, 1929

Sheriff Sid Williams & Deputy Sheriff, Joe Stanek, about 1929-30.

(10)   *The old Walt Woodruff place is one-half mile north of town and just off of Highway #29.*

143

BOB ALLEN PAYS FINE AND IS RELEASED FROM JAIL

The hearing of Bob Allen, held on a liquor violation charge, was had in county court last week and he was found guilty. The judge imposed a fine of $100 and costs or thirty days in jail. Allen served part of the sentence, and upon payment of the balance of the fine was given his release today.

Harrison Sun, Fri., Aug. 23, 1929

OFFICERS SEARCH RESULTS IN FIND OF 2500 GALLONS MASH

Joe Stanek, Deputy Sheriff, returned to Harrison Sunday morning, after two days and nights vigil, bringing with him Harry Haney and Russel Furbeck, the two being charged with ownership of some 2500 gallons of mash which was found by Officer Stanek and a state prohibition officer on a farm leased by Furbeck.

The search disclosed three galvanized tanks and several barrels of mash in the barn on the place, the mash being poured out by the officers. Stanek arrested Furbeck Saturday and rounded up Haney early Sunday morning, the latter suspected of being interested in the mash in some manner.

When arraigned before Judge Wilhermsdorfer Monday morning, Haney was able to supply bonds and was released. Furbeck is being held in jail, pending a preliminary hearing next Wednesday.

This mash was found in a neighborhood in the south part of the county that has gained considerable notoriety during the past several years for moonshining, although numerous arrests and convictions do not seem to stamp out the persistent violation.

Harrison Sun, Fri., Oct. 11, 1929

HARRY HANEY BOUND OVER TO DIST. COURT ON MASH CHARGE

The preliminary hearing of Harry Haney was heard in county court Wednesday of this week, and upon evidence produced by the prosecution, Haney was bound over to district court.

In a raid by officers last week in the south part of the county, a large quantity of mash, some 2500 gallons, was found, and Haney is alleged to be implicated in the deal. Haney produced bonds in the amount of $1000 and was released.

Russell Furbeck who was also arrested at the time, is still in the county jail, and will be given a preliminary hearing soon.

In giving an account of the raid last week, we neglected to mention the fact that Sheriff Williams was also on the job, he having been summoned from Sioux City, where he had gone with a shipment of cattle.

Harrison Sun, Fri., Oct. 18, 1929

ARRESTED ON LIQUOR CHARGE

Federal Officer Forsling, Deputy State Sheriff Clark, Sheriff Williams and Deputy Joe Stanek drove to the Harry Wasserburger place, three miles southwest of Montrose, Wednesday of this week, and upon search of the place found some beer, parts of what is purported to be a still, and a small quantity of alleged whiskey.(11) Mr. Wasserburger was summoned to appear in county court for arraignment yesterday morning, and

(11) I knew Harry Wasserburger quite well and his daughter, Millie was a member of my 1947 Sioux County High School Class. Another daughter Mary Lou, married John Federle. I worked for them at the Harrison Sun during the early 1950's. Harry was an ok guy.

his hearing was set for November 5th. The specific charges filed, were illegal possession of liquor and possession of a still.

Harrison Sun, Fri., Oct. 18, 1929

MORE MOONSHINE

Sheriff Williams brought back another alleged offender this week; and also five gallons of alleged whiskey. Following a path near the place where Milton Fears resides, the officers dug the liquor from the ground. Fears was brought to Harrison, and plead not guilty, when arraigned before the county judge. The preliminary hearing was set for a later date, and in the meantime Fears is at liberty under bond.

Harrison Sun, Fri., Oct. 25, 1929

TWO BOOZE CASES AIRED OUT IN COUNTY COURT SATURDAY

Harvey Van Cleef, resident of the south part of the county, appeared in county court Saturday of last week to answer to the charge of possession of intoxicating liquor, the complaint growing out of the finding of three gallons of alleged moonshine on the place farmed by Van Cleef. The defendant waived preliminary hearing and was bound over to the district court, and was released on bonds.

Another hearing was that of H.B. Cunningham for possession of wine, which was found on a place where Cunningham has formerly resided. The defendant plead guilty and was fined $100 and costs, which was paid.

Harrison Sun, Fri., Nov. 1, 1929

ALLIANCE EX-POLICEMEN ARE CONVICTED ON BOOZE CHARGE

Harold Jeffryes, a former Alliance policeman, and another ex-policeman of that city, Ellicott Minnick, were found guilty in county court of Box Butte County of sale of intoxicating liquor. A fine of $100 and ninety days in jail was imposed on each. Minnick was the owner of a truck taken up here last summer, which Lyman Case was driving to Wyoming, and on which was loaded a still. Case was fined $500 and sentenced to thirty days in jail. The fine was paid after Case had served the sentence. Minnick was dismissed from the Alliance police force.

Harrison Sun, Fri., Nov. 1, 1929

MEXICAN IS ARRESTED WHEN EXHIBITS DISTILLING PLANT

When officers called at the home of Manuel Guell, a beet worker in the south part of the county, they found Guell to be a most gracious moonshiner. Deputy Sheriff C.A. Nash and J.B. Duncan called at the Guell home and asked the Mexican if he had a still. He replied that he did and showed the officers two boilers on the stove which was in process of "cooking off" a batch of liquor. The Mexican showed them how it worked, and upon request produced several gallons of the finished product which was on the place. He also took them to the place where fifty gallons of mash was in preparation.

When Guell had showed the officers all that was going on, the former was placed under arrest and brought to Harrison Friday of last week. Guell was arraigned before Judge Wilhermsdorfer, but the Mexican claimed he could not understand and the hearing was postponed until an interpreter could be secured. However, two Mexican friends came up today and after a talk with Guell the latter plead guilty and was fined $200 and costs and given an extra dose of thirty days in jail.

It developed at the hearing today that Guell had been talked into making the whiskey by some other parties, the latter claiming to have a "stand-in" with the officers and assured the Mexican he would not be molested. This explains the actions of Guell in being so generous in showing the officers about the place and giving them all the information desired.

Harrison Sun, Fri., Nov. 15, 1929

FALL TERM DISTRICT COURT OPENS MONDAY OF NEXT WEEK

The fall term of district court promises to be a lengthy one, and undoubtedly will be if all cases docketed go to trial.

In the docket printed by the Sun printery last week there appear 56 cases, the greater number equity hearings and most of these will be disposed of in short order. There are 40 such cases on the docket.

Four divorce hearings are scheduled for hearing.

The criminal cases involve complaints of cattle stealing, assault to commit rape, grand larceny, and an unusual number of liquor cases.

The basement of the Odd Fellows building has been fitted up for a court room, the room at the courthouse having been declared unsafe in which to conduct court.

Court opens Monday of next week.

Harrison Sun, Fri., Nov. 15, 1929

LIQUOR LAW VIOLATOR CAUGHT IN SOUTH PART OF COUNTY

Sheriff Williams and Deputy Joe Stanek drove to the south part of the county Sunday,

and in company with Deputy J.B. Duncan, went to the place occupied by Daily Gayman and instituted a search of the premises. The officers found three gallons of alleged liquor in the house and two cans of mash in a haystack near by. They also found parts of a still.

Gayman was brought to Harrison and lodged in jail until Monday morning, when he was arraigned before Judge Wilhermsdorfer, and date for a preliminary hearing was set for March 24ᵗʰ. Gayman supplied bonds in the amount of $1000, and was released from custody for appearance on the above date.

Harrison Sun, Fri., Mar. 14, 1930

PLEADS GUILTY TO ILLEGAL POSSESSION OF LIQUOR

At his preliminary hearing Monday, in county court, Daily Gayman, of the south part of the county plead guilty to a charge of illegal possession of liquor and was assessed a fine of $100 and costs, amounting to a trifle more than $126.(12) Gayman paid the amount and was released. L.L. Raymond, Scottsbluff attorney, was present to represent Gayman in court.

Harrison Sun, Mar. 28, 1930

SHERIFF NABS TRIO WITH CAR AND LARGE QUANTITY OF BOOZE

Sheriff Williams apprehended two men and a woman, driving a Hupp coupe,

---

(12)   Many liquor law violators were fined $100.00 and costs. Adjusted for inflation a similar fine today would be about $2500.00.

According to Sid Jr., the trip to the south part of the county was quite an ordeal during their tenures as sheriff & deputy sheriff respectively, during the 1920's. The trip to the south end of Sioux County from Harrison was on 50-60 miles of unimproved roads (later paved) which entailed opening and closing about 25 barbed wire pasture gates. The trip itself took several hours.

Tuesday night of this week, while the trio were getting gas and service at the White Eagle Service Station. The officers had been tipped off that a car bearing a Douglas county license was traveling through this part of the state, evidently with a cargo of booze, and when it showed up in Harrison Sheriff Williams was on the lookout.

Two men and a woman were with the car, and when they were approached to be placed under arrest one of the men fled down the alley and made his escape. The other man and the woman were placed in jail, and Wednesday the other man was caught in Crawford and returned to this place.

At a hearing today, one of the men gave the name of Raymond Brozoska and admitted ownership of the car and cargo of hootch and plead guilty. He was given a fine of $100 and costs, which he claims he can raise. He was committed to jail until the fine is paid.

Upon being arraigned, Charles Havlik, the other man, admitted he knew the car was carrying liquor and also that he made attempts to sell a part of the stuff, although that since he owned neither the liquor or the car, did not believe he was guilty of bootlegging as charged.

County Attorney Mumby continued the case for twenty days to give Havlik time to think it over. Thirty gallons and three pints of liquor were in the car. The car will be advertised and sold under state statute.

Harrison Sun, Mar. 19, 1931

FOUR ADDITIONAL FILINGS MADE FOR COUNTY OFFICES

More candidates have come into the limelight during the past two weeks, to compete in the August primary election.

A.C. Davis, present county clerk and clerk of the district court, will be a candidate on the republican ticket for the same office. Arch has lived in this county sufficiently long, as has rendered efficient service to the many who call at the office of the clerk, that further comment in these columns would be superfluous.

Sid Williams is also a candidate to succeed himself as sheriff, and his name will appear on the republican primary ballot. Sid has a good record as sheriff, and will have plenty of supporters when election day rolls around.

One of the brand new candidates is W.E. Mumby, candidate in the republican primaries for county attorney. Mr. Mumby has been associated with A.L. Schnurr in the practice of law here during the past two years, and has assisted Mr. Schnurr in the prosecution of cases for Sioux County.

Matt Hall, one of our most highly respected pioneer settlers, will be primary candidate for county treasurer on the republican ticket. Mr. Hall is at present serving as county surveyor.

Harrison Sun, Fri., May 16, 1930

MCQUEEN PLEADS GUILTY

Albert McQueen appeared in county court Wednesday of this week, and withdrew his appeal on a liquor charge, filed some time ago. McQueen was arrested in the south part of the county and brought to Harrison for preliminary hearing, and was found guilty. A fine of $100 and costs was assessed by the county judge, and with the costs of appeal included amounted to $140.60, which amount was paid.

Harrison Sun, Fri., May 9, 1930

C.S. WILLIAMS
Republican Candidate for Sheriff of Sioux County Primary Election August 12, 1930.

Harrison Sun, Fri., July 18, 1930

A daughter was born to Mr. and Mrs. Sid Williams Friday, July 4th. Mother and babe are doing nicely.(13)

Harrison Sun, July 11, 1930

FILES FOR SHERIFF

C.A. Nash was up from the south part of the county Tuesday, and filed as a candidate in the republican primaries for sheriff. Mr. Nash is a Spanish-American war veteran, and for the past twenty years has been a resident of the community in which he now lives. He has been active in the affairs of the water users association under the irrigation project, serving as a director of the board for ten years, and two of which was president of the board.

Harrison Sun, Fri., May 9, 1930

SEVERAL RAIDS MADE DURING WEEK AND BIG STILL FOUND

One of the largest stills to be found in Sioux County was unearthed by Sheriff Williams, Deputy Joe Stanek and O. E. Forsling, state prohibition officer, Friday of last week in the north part of the county. The land occupied by Wm. DeBano and adjoining land was searched, and a large cave about forty feet square was found in a field.

Nothing was found in the cave and the officers were about to give up when Joe Stanek prodded into the dirt floor of the cave and found what proved to be a hole dug deeper into the ground where the still had been concealed. The top was covered with boards and several inches of dirt thrown over to conceal the subterranean cave.

The still is of 100-barrel capacity, and evidently had not been in use for some time. The still was brought to town, and DeBano arrested and arraigned in the county court. DeBano waiving preliminary hearing and was bound over to district court, giving $800 bond for his appearance at the next session of court.

Another search was made north of town, but only parts of what was presumed to be a still were found, although a quantity of liquor was found on adjoining land.

Another arrest made by county officers recently was that of L.E. Pace, a resident of the south part of the county, who was arraigned before County Judge Wilhermsdorfer for illegal possession of liquor, Pace entering a plea of guilty and was fined $100 and costs, which were paid by the defendant.

Harrison Sun, July 4, 1930

WE GOT IT WRONG

In reporting the moonshine outlay unearthed on the DeBano place in the north part of the county two weeks ago, the Sun had about half the facts, and got them wrong. Sheriff Williams informs us it was one of the most complete outfits yet found, and the largest still he has run across during his term of office.

The officers searched over the land in question and only by mere accident found the cave, which had been smoothed over on the surface, giving slight indication of its existence. Evidently when the cave was dug, the dirt was removed some distance, there being a small opening on top for entrance, and that was carefully concealed. The cave is

(13) This was the birth announcement of my sister, Ila Mae. She and I were 1947 Sioux County High School graduates.

She married Ed Laettner, SCHS music teacher in 1949. They had three children: Donald, John and Denise. She later married Grady Mullenix and had one daughter, Stephanie. Ila died January 16, 2005.

18 x 40 feet and was fitted up with necessary articles and presumably when the still was in operation provisions were stored there in order that the operators might stay under ground indefinitely. Ventilation pipes were carefully concealed, and it was complete in every respect for ideal retreat for the moonshiners. Several mash barrels were placed over a hole in the floor of the cave, and in this hole the large still was found. Sheriff Williams believes the still had not been in operation for some time.

Harrison Sun, July 11, 1930

FINED $100 AND COSTS

The Mexican who was caught in the south end of the county last week with a quantity of liquor, was arraigned in county court and upon a plea of guilty was assessed a fine of $100 and costs. The Mexican is a beet laborer in the employ of Mr. Gompert, and has a family of wife and five children.

Harrison Sun, June 13, 1930

HARD-HEARTED SHERIFFS

There'll be no Christmas joy for one Willis Bowman this year, and all because that his tender pleas failed to reach the remote recesses of the hearts of our sheriff and one deputy sheriff. J.B. Duncan, who looks after the dignity of the law in the south part of the county, brought Bowman before the county judge Tuesday, on a charge of possession of liquor. It seems the said Bowman had driven over from Wyoming to carry on a little spree, and supposedly in a drunken stupor stopped his car on the road which divides Scottsbluff and Sioux Counties. Unfortunately for Sioux County, Bowman got sleepy on this stretch of road and pulled the machine to a stop on the north half, which made him a Sioux County violator. Whether the stuff has a little heavier effect on the Sioux

County side of the road, we know not, but it don't speak well for us we'll admit. Deputy Sheriff Duncan was notified of Bowman's condition and as a result the latter was given a hearing before Judge Wilhermsdorfer, who promptly assessed him the jolt of $100 and costs, which amount defendant seemed to be entirely destitute. Turning to Sid Williams, Bowman said: "Now, sheriff, you pay this fine and costs and keep the car and I'll go to Torrington and raise the money." To which Sid said nay. Then he appealed to Deputy Duncan, asking the latter to go his bond, but that didn't work, so Mr. Bowman will partake of Sioux County jail food of his own preparation on Christmas day, and maybe for several days to come.

Several other hearings on liquor charges were heard in local court during the past week, with fine and costs of the $100 variety.

Harrison Sun, Fri., Dec. 26, 1930

ARRAIGNED ON LIQUOR CHARGE

A preliminary hearing was given M.F. Davis of the south part of the county, in county court Wednesday, Davis having been arrested on a charge of possession of a quantity of mash. Further hearing of the case was set for February 16th. Defendant was represented by F.J. Reed of Mitchell.

Harrison Sun, Fri., Jan. 23, 1931

TWO LIQUOR CASES ARE HEARD IN DISTRICT COURT THIS WEEK

With the January term of district court opening Monday of this week, cases on the docket were set for trial, and two liquor violation complaints were first up.

One was that of the state of Nebraska vs. Charles Telander for unlawful possession of intoxicating liquor. After introduction of testimony this case was given to the jury Tuesday morning, and Wednesday evening the jury was called in, reporting a hopeless deadlock, 8 to 4, and was dismissed.

The other liquor case was that of Harvey Van Cleef, the jury going out Tuesday afternoon, and at the time of going to press Wednesday is still out.

The complaint brought against William DeBano for unlawful possession of still has been withdrawn.

Harrison Sun, Fri., Jan. 30, 1931

DISTRICT COURT ADJOURNED

After a five-day session the January term of district court was brought to a close Friday afternoon, with many civil actions that had been on the docket for some time being cleaned up, and all jury cases were disposed of.

The jury in the case of Jas. Bourret vs. D.H. Lawmaster returned a verdict in favor of the plaintiff, which upholds the decision of the county court. The jury in the case of the state vs. Harvey Van Cleef, after some time for deliberation came in with a verdict finding defendant guilty of illegal possession of intoxicating liquor and a fine of $1000 and costs was imposed.

Surplus room in the courthouse came into good use during this term of court, there being two juries out and a third sworn in to hear a jury trial.

Harrison Sun, Thurs., Feb. 5, 1931

OFFICERS FIND 80-GALLON STILL AND OTHER EQUIPMENT

A raid by Sheriff Williams and E.H. Forsling, state enforcement officer, conducted in the northeast corner of the county last week, brought to light a very well equipped moonshine plant. The officers found this outfit in a draw on the land operated by Ray, Albert and Marion Wagner, about a half mile from the house occupied by the Wagners, and complaints were filed against the three in county court, and at a hearing last Friday the defendants plead not guilty and were bound over to district court for trial. Bond was furnished for their appearance.

The still was of 80-gallon capacity, and there was also found plenty of equipment for manufacture on a large scale. Gas and oil stoves, 35 mash barrels, 3 whiskey barrels, and every article necessary for work were in the cave. Two gasoline engines were used for pumping purposes. The plant was located in a cave, around a portion of which brick walls had been built. It is presumed the outfit had seen much service, although was not in operation at the time of discovery.

Harrison Sun, Thurs., Feb. 5, 1931

SELLS CONFISCATED CAR

The car seized by Sheriff Williams a short time ago, when two men were arrested and found guilty of conveying moonshine, was sold at auction Monday and brought $85, Max Federle being the highest bidder. The car was a Hupp "Six" coupe.

Harrison Sun, April 19, 1931

FENCING IN THE JAIL

This week workmen in the employ of Jas. Fullen, contractor, have been building a high woven wire fence around the county jail. The fence is of heavy material and is about nine feet high, has several strings of barbed wire sloped in at the top and will make it a little inconvenient for those who are inclined to hang about the outside and pass articles to prisoners confined inside. A concrete abutment was built around the west and north sides and heavy steel posts set in with lead, which makes a very substantial and serviceable fence.

Harrison Sun, Thurs., April 23, 1931

A Most Persistant Moonshiner

Most manufacturers of illegal brew in Sioux County learned their lesson after an arrest, conviction, fine and/or incarceration and usually decided after their first law-breaking experience that this type of crime didn't pay. They usually refrained from a repeat of this type of illegal activity.

However, Fred Cunningham of southern Sioux County did not fit this mold of the typical Sioux County moonshiner.

Your granddad arrested Fred Cunningham at least six (6) times for illegal liquor possession or for the operation of a still engaged in the manufacture of moonshine during the period 1926-1932.

One of the following news items, that of April 2, 1931 describes the operation of a still in a chicken house that had a capacity of 250 gallons of liquor.

The following sheriff's report is your granddad's account of the conversation with Cunningham on the way back to Harrison after the still was discovered. The report was found in the sheriff's office by then Sheriff Tom Broderick and given to this writer in 1967. Also see news item in following pages dated April 2, 1931:

~~~~~

After officers found 45 gals in one 50 gal. bbl., Fred was asked if that was all, and he nodded his head yes.

On the way to Harrison Fred asked Sid: "It looks tough, if you were in my place what would you do in a case like this"?

Sid: "It is a pretty serious charge, and I don't like to advise you what to do".

Fred: "But I would like to know just what you would do".

Sid: "If I were in your place where it looked like a cinch against me. I would go to the Co. Atty. and tell the truth, and ask him to recommend that my sentence be as light as possible".

Fred: "My God, Sid, do you realize where that would send me"?

Sid: "Yes I do, but if you are stuck and you fight, it seems to me that the easiest way out is the best".

Fred: "Yes, but a man hates to own up to something that will send him to jail. I feel like telling them to go to hell and fight to the last ditch. There might be some little technicality that I might get the case knocked out on. What would happen if some fellow would come up and claim the whiskey"?

Sid: "Fred, I don't believe that you can make that go. You had the still and 250 gallons of whiskey and you couldn't make anyone believe that the holes were bored through the chicken house floor without you knowing it".

Fred: "Yes it looks that way, but if someone would come in and claim the whiskey, why couldn't that work? I can't see why the court should care who is stuck. You shouldn't care, you have done your duty and found the liquor, you shouldn't care who is stuck".

~~~~~

I searched the jailhouse records and these indicate that Fred Cunningham served at least three (3) times in county jail as follows:

    May 26, 1930 – July 31, 1930, 67 days

    March 25, 1931 – March 28, 1931, 4 days

    June 6, 1932 – August 6, 1932, 60 days

My mother told me that Fred Cunningham also served a term in the Nebraska Penitentiary at Lincoln. However, I did not find any evidence of this in the county archives, but this could have been overlooked.

Following are some more articles dealing with some of the other arrests of Fred Cunningham on liquor charges.

DISTRICT COURT DOCKET DISPOSED OF IN SHORT SESSION

District court convened Monday morning, and was dismissed Tuesday evening, with a considerable number of the cases on the docket being disposed of. However, a number of the cases were dismissed, while others were passed to the May term.

In the criminal division, Fred Cunningham was found not guilty by the jury on a complaint filed against him, for illegal possession of liquor for sale and also second offense; while the other complaint in which he was made defendant was dismissed.

Harrison Sun, Fri., Dec. 3, 1926

CUNNINGHAM HOME SEARCHED 20 GALLONS MOONSHINE FOUND

An officer of the state prohibition forces made a raid on the home of Fred Cunningham in the south part of the county Saturday of last week, and twenty gallons of moonshine were found on the premises.

Cunningham appeared before the county judge Monday morning, when a complaint of unlawful possession and second offense was filed against him by County Attorney Schnurr. The second offense filing is based on a conviction of Cunningham in Scottsbluff sometime ago.

A little over a year ago Cunningham was pulled up on a charge of illegal possession, for sale and second offense.

Harrison Sun, Fri., Nov. 25, 1927

CUNNINGHAM APPEALS LIQUOR CASE TO THE DISTRICT COURT

Fred Cunningham, who was picked up on a violation of the prohibition laws last week, was given a hearing before Judge Wilhermsdorfer in the county court Wednesday night of this week, and after the examination of several witnesses for the prosecution, the judge found Cunningham guilty of the charge of possession of intoxicating liquor, also second offense, and pronounced a sentence of ninety days in the county jail and costs of prosecution. Cunningham filed an appeal bond and the case will be taken to the district court.

The raid on the Cunningham home was made Saturday of last week, and in searching the house the officers found a trap door in the floor of a room back of the kitchen. This was the only entrance to a cellar in which was unearthed a quantity of liquor. According to the testimony given by the officers, there was about twenty gallons of moonshine on hand at the time, and most of this was brought in as evidence. It was stated that Cunningham had placed several large barrels in the cellar, through a hole in the foundation of the house, and enclosed the aperture by building a cement wall. A gas pipe was inserted in the cement, through which the liquor was said to be pumped in to replenish the supply be means of a filter pump.

No defense was offered whatever by Mr. Cunningham, and the appeal to the higher court was filed immediately after the verdict was rendered.

Cunningham was found guilty of possession of liquor in Scottsbluff County some time back, and it is on this case that the charge of second offense is based. He has had considerable notoriety in alleged violations of the liquor laws, having been freed on a similar charge in district court last November, and is at present fighting a case in Federal Court, wherein the U.S. district attorney seeks an injunction against Cunningham to restrain the latter from violating the liquor laws of the United States. The injunction, if granted, would place the offender in the position of having been in contempt of court if he made or sold liquor. This case was tried before Federal Judge Woodrough at Chadron in September, and the judge refused to grant the injunction, giving his opinion that such an order would deprive Cunningham of his constitutional right-the right of every man to stand trial before a jury, contempt of court being a case where a jury could not be used.

Harrison Sun, Fri., Dec. 2, 1927

CIVIL ACTIONS GET ATTENTION IN DISTRICT COURT SESSION

The March term of the district court for Sioux County convened on Monday morning and the docket was completed in the afternoon and the court adjourned until the June equity term.

There were but few cases requiring the services of the jury, and as none of these came up for action the jurymen were dismissed until the next jury term in November.

There were two criminal cases docketed, that of the state versus Fred Cunningham, who appealed from the county court when found guilty of illegal possession of intoxicating liquor. The legal representative for Cunningham reported that Cunningham was in a sanitarium and unable to be present for trial and the court granted a postponement of the trial until a later date.

Another criminal filing was that of the state versus Lee Blevens on a complaint for unlawful possession of mash. On request of the prosecution this case was dismissed on account of lack of evidence to convict.

The major part of the docket involved foreclosures and other civil actions.

Harrison Sun, Fri., Mar. 30, 1928

FRED CUNNINGHAM AGAIN IN TROUBLE ON BOOZE CHARGE

Federal, state and county officers have been active in the south part of the county during the past week, in an effort to round up moonshiners and booze peddlers. Armed with numerous search warrants the officers visited various farm places, but were successful in locating but one cache of booze. They found a keg on one place where the whiskey had been poured out just shortly before the arrival of the officers, but not enough for evidence.

A farm which is said to have been leased by Fred Cunningham, and which adjoins the latter's ranch, was searched and thirty-two gallons of peach brandy and other brands of liquor, were found stored in the attic. A man by the name of Albert McQueen and his family are living on the place, and he together with Cunningham were lodged in the jail at Mitchell Tuesday morning, and Wednesday brought to Harrison to be arraigned before Deputy County Judge Jess Newell. L.L. Raymond, Scottsbluff attorney, was present to represent the interests of Cunningham and McQueen and July 17th was set for the preliminary of Cunningham, and at which time the case against McQueen will be tried. The complaint filed against them by W.E. Mumby, deputy county attorney, was for illegal possession of intoxicating liquor. Bond for Cunningham was fixed at $1000 and for McQueen $500, which was supplied and they returned to their home Wednesday.

Cunningham has been arrested several times, and in the district court of Sioux County last fall was found guilty of illegal possession of intoxicating liquor. A sentence of sixty days in jail was imposed by the court, Cunningham appealing to the Supreme Court. Just recently the higher court has passed upon the case sustaining the lower

155

tribunal, and as soon as the mandate can be spread upon the docket, Cunningham will be called on to serve his sentence.

Harrison Sun, July 5, 1929

CUNNINGHAM AGAIN

With scarcely a week intervening since being taken up on a liquor charge, Fred Cunningham was again hauled into court Tuesday to face another charge of violation of the eighteenth amendment.

In a search of the Smith place, which adjoins Cunningham, and which is supposed to be leased by Cunningham, a gallon of liquor and five barrels of mash were unearthed. The raid was made by Sheriff Williams and Deputy Stanek. Walter McQueen, who lives on the place, was also taken by the sheriff. They were brought to Harrison and liberated under bonds. Mrs. Cunningham and A. D. Wilson are the bondsmen on the former charge and Mrs. Cunningham and M.L. Davis on the latter.

Harrison Sun, July 12, 1929

CUNNINGHAM AND McQUEEN BOUND OVER TO DIST. COURT

The trial of Albert McQueen, arrested a short time ago on a liquor charge, was held in county court here Wednesday. McQueen was charged with illegal possession of liquor, a quantity having been found by officers in the house he occupies in the south part of the county. On this charge he was found guilty by Judge Wilhermsdorfer. McQueen took an appeal to the district court.

A few days after the first raid, officers again searched the place and found some mash and some more liquor. The judge found there was probable cause for detaining McQueen on this count and bound him over to district court for trial.

Fred Cunningham was also arrested at the same time as McQueen and similar charges filed against him. The land upon which the liquor was found is leased by Cunningham. A third offense is also included in the complaint against the latter. Both McQueen and Cunningham are represented by Attorney L.L. Raymond of Scottsbluff.

Harrison Sun, Fri., Aug. 9, 1929

CASES DISPOSED OF AT THE SESSION OF DISTRICT COURT

Mandate spread in case of state vs. Fred Cunningham for illegal possession of liquor. Defendant appealed to Supreme Court, but lower court upheld. Sentenced to 60 days in jail and $500 fine and defendant to begin sentence January 13th.

Harrison Sun, Fri., Nov. 29, 1929

LARGE STILL & 250 GALLONS OF LIQUOR SEIZED LAST WEEK

Wednesday of last week a raid was made on the Fred Cunningham farm in the south part of the county, which netted a large quantity of moonshine and the confiscation of material presumably used in the manufacture of liquor.

The raid was made by Sheriff Williams, Deputy Sheriff J.B. Duncan, O.E. Forsling, state prohibition officer, and deputies of Scottsbluff County.

The search of the farm was conducted for several hours before the hiding place of the liquor was found, and the location of the liquor was more by chance, as the officers were about to give up the search when the hiding place was revealed.

When the officers drove into the farmyard, Sheriff Williams noticed the hired man make a dash for the chicken house, and this movement on the part of the man excited the sheriff's curiosity, and while the other officers went to the potato cellar, where the parts of the supposed still were found, Sheriff Williams investigated the chicken house. Neatly coiled on the inside of a hen's nest he found a small hose, evidently used as a siphon, and which was still wet, indicating its recent usage. However, no other signs of liquor were apparent in the building. The other officers returned from the potato cellar and for several hours searched the farm for liquor.

Sheriff Williams was convinced the liquor was in or near the chicken house, and it was here that the search finally settled, resulting in the unearthing of the moonshine. The floor of the building was of concrete, and the roof supported through the center by a row of four-by-fours. There was no sign of an opening through the floor nor along the edge or foundation, and it was by mere chance that one of the officers noticed one of the four-by-fours was loose at the bottom, and hitting it with a crow-bar, the end swung out. The timbers rested on short one-by-four strips and removing one of these, two holes in the cement were revealed. These openings, just large enough for an ordinary garden hose, were plugged with corks, and it was through the holes that liquor was poured into barrels, which were found under the cement floor. There were five holes through the floor leading into as many 50-gallon barrels. An opening was made into the pit, the liquor removed from the barrels, about fifteen or twenty gallons being taken for evidence and the balance poured out on the ground.

A truck was employed to bring the outfit to Harrison that evening, and Sheriff Williams now has the vault at the courthouse fairly full of this sort of material. This latest raid netted a 200-gallon still, 3 pressure tanks, several cases of gallon jugs, two pumps, one for mash and the other to transfer the finished product, gasoline burners, and numerous other articles.

The liquor found last Wednesday was believed by officers to have been run but a short time before the raid, as the refuse mash found in holes in the potato cellar was still warm.

Fred Cunningham was brought to Harrison that night and lodged in the county jail, two counts being filed against him, one for possession of still, and the other a third offense on liquor violation. He was arraigned in county court Saturday, waiving preliminary hearing and bound over to district court for trial. Bonds were fixed at $500 on one count and $1000 on the other. Mr. Cunningham secured bond Saturday and returned to his home.

Harrison Sun, April 2, 1931

FIRE DESTROYS HOUSE AND BARN ON CUNNINGHAM RANCH

Fire believed to be of incendiary origin completely destroyed the house and barn on the Fred Cunningham ranch in the south part of the county Saturday night of last week. Sheriff Williams was called for investigation, and took Mr. Cunningham, who is serving a term in the county jail on a liquor violation charge.

The fire was first observed by neighbors about two o'clock Sunday morning, but too late to save the house and contents or the barn. The chicken house was also in flames, but was extinguished, and those who were on hand at the time report a decided odor of kerosene, which would indicate the fire had been set by humans. Mrs. Cunningham and daughters were in Scottsbluff, where they were spending the night, and it is stated that hired men employed on the farm were in Torrington at the time of the fire. The state sheriff and officials of the state fire marshal's office are investigating the cause of the fire. Some insurance was carried on the buildings and the household goods.

Harrison Sun, Thurs., July 21, 1932

INVESTIGATE CUNNINGHAM FIRE

Horace M. Davis and Henry Mockenhaupt, officers of the state fire marshal's department, have been investigating the fire at the Fred Cunningham place in the south part of the county, which resulted in the complete loss of the Cunningham residence and household effects. This fire occurred several weeks ago and there were indications which pointed to incendiarism. A Mexican was brought to Harrison last week for investigation, but nothing of importance was gained from questioning the man.(14)

Harrison Sun, Thurs., Sept.1, 1932

ARRESTED ON LIQUOR CHARGE

Sheriff Williams and Deputy Stanek arrested Gus Knori last Saturday night, when they found a gallon of liquor in the latter's car. Gus was permitted to go out to the ranch that night and appeared Monday in county court, where he was arraigned and entered a plea of not guilty. A hearing in the case will be had the early part of January.

Harrison Sun, Fri., Dec. 27, 1929

DRY LAW OFFENDER

Sheriff Sid Williams and Deputy State Sheriff Clark made a search of the premises of Louis Havel in the south part of the county Sunday and found a gallon jug containing alleged liquor. Havel was brought to Harrison and Monday arraigned in county court. Hearing on the case was continued to a future date and the defendant is out on bonds in the meanwhile.

Harrison Sun, Thurs., May 21, 1931

BOOZE IS DUMPED

A large quantity of moonshine, of all degrees of quality, was dumped at the county jail yesterday, the officers in charge of the obsequies. Quite a few people gathered to get a last, longing whiff of the departed spirits. Some of it smelled darn good, and some was not so good.(15)

This liquor was a part of the accumulations of past raids and had laid in the store room of the jail for some time.

Harrison Sun, Thurs., Mar. 19, 1931

PROHIBITION PLANK SEEMS TO BE MAIN CONVENTION ISSUE

Following the nomination of Hoover and Curtis as standard bearers for the republican party in the national campaign this fall, and the adoption of a moist-dry-plank in the platform, the democrats will go into the huddle in Chicago next Monday to pick out men for the White House jobs and also thresh out the big issue-prohibition. Undoubtedly this year more will be said and written on this moot question than since the days of 1918 when the dry law was enacted. With the mounting expense of enforcement of the eighteenth amendment, and the questionable headway that is being made, some of the best business minds of the country, heretofore favorable to the law, have taken a decided change and are strongly advocating repeal, or some relief

(14)   I didn't find any evidence that the arsonist was ever apprehended despite the efforts of the state fire marshal's office. Perhaps the fire was started by someone that strongly disapproved of Cunningham's persistent liquor production efforts.

(15)   This was the 2nd destruction of moonshine and still paraphernalia. The first disposal occurred on June 29, 1929 on the courthouse grounds.

from what they term an unworkable law.

Perhaps the statement of John D. Rockefeller, Jr., given out recently, is taken more seriously than any of recent months. Mr. Rockefeller has always supported the amendment and enforcement, contributed liberally to the temperance cause, and his reversal of opinion will have a great influence in the nation when the question is submitted to the people for a change.

Harrison Sun, Thurs., June 23, 1932

LIQUOR CASE IS FIRST UP AT SESSION OF DISTRICT COURT

With the convening of the September term of district court here Tuesday, the docket was set for the term, and the first case called for trial was that of the state against Ray, Albert and Marion Wagner for unlawful possession of a still. The Wagner boys were bound over to district court following a hearing in county court last February. Officers had unearthed a still in a cave near the home of the Wagners, and it was alleged the land on which the still was located was under control of the boys.

The case was heard Wednesday and has been in the hands of the jury since, with no verdict being reached at time of going to press. To determine some point at issue the jury was taken to the land whereon the still was located, which is northwest of Orella.

The state against Dick Witt on complaint of receiving stolen cattle is the next called for trial.(16)

Harrison Sun, Thurs., Sept. 10, 1931

JURY DISAGREES IN WAGNER STILL CASE IN DIST. COURT

After being out over a day and taking a trip to the land on which a still was found last January, the jury in the case of the state versus Ray, Albert and Marion Wagner failed to reach an agreement, standing eleven for acquittal and one for conviction, and was dismissed by Judge E.L. Meyer. The defense brought out the point that the land on which the still was located was owned by a non-resident and the Wagner boys did not have the land rented. The still was not in operation at the time the raid was made by officers and no one was on the land at the time.

Allen G. Fisher and son, Chadron attorneys, defended the Wagner boys.

Harrison Sun, Thurs., Sept. 17, 1931

TWO ARE TAKEN IN RAID WHEN QUANTITY OF MASH IS FOUND

Sheriff Jones of Box Butte County, in company with Sheriff Ridenour and a deputy from Oshkosh and Special Agent Davis of the Stockgrowers Association, made a raid on a place in the extreme southeastern corner of Sioux County Wednesday of last week and found 50 gallons of mash. The place was occupied by George Wright and Glen Stover, the two men being arrested and taken to Alliance. Sheriff Williams was notified and went after them Saturday and upon being arraigned before Judge Wilhermsdorfer Saturday night, Stover claimed the mash belonged to him. The charge against Wright was dropped and Stover entering a plea of guilty was given a jail sentence of thirty days and a fine of $500 and costs were also imposed, which is the minimum under the liquor laws of the state.

Harrison Sun, Thurs., Jan. 14, 1931

(16) *Dick Witt was my wife Elaine's, uncle.*

159

OFFICER NABS FOUR OFFENDERS IN SOUTH PART OF COUNTY

Four violators of the liquor laws were rounded up by Deputy Sheriff J.B. Duncan in the south part of Sioux County Friday of last week, and brought to Harrison Saturday and arraigned in county court. Conrad Kaufman plead guilty to the charge of possession of intoxicating liquor and was assessed a fine of $100 and costs of $59.95, which he paid and was released.

Salvadore Gonsalez plead guilty to possession, he having been caught with about five gallons of the forbidden liquid, and will spend thirty days in jail. It was Gonsalez' place of residence that the party was being held. Another Mexican, Modesto Godenes, seemed to be the life of the party, he being charged with intoxication, and was given fifteen days and costs.

Harrison Sun, Thurs., Jan. 21, 1932

COUNTY ATTORNEY REPORT SHOWS 89 COMPLAINTS IN 1931

During the year January, 1931, to January 1, 1932, the report of County Attorney W.E. Mumby shows there have been 89 complaints filed in his office. The outcome of the complaints were as follows: 41 convictions; 2 acquittals; 6 complainants refused to testify; 8 dismissed account of insufficient evidence; 12 pending in court; 13 of the search warrants issued and nothing found.

A total of $1,099.00 in fines was assessed and $699.00 collected; fines replevied not yet collected, $100.00. Jail days sentenced and served, 305; suspended sentences, 45 days.

The complaints issued were as follows:

Illegal possession of mash—one; dismissed, insufficient evidence.

Operating motor vehicle while intoxicated—one; 30 days in jail, drivers license revoked.

Intoxication—eight; seven paid fines ranging from $2.00 to $15.00 and costs. One served 30 days in jail.

Possession of still and equipment—two; pending in district court.

Possession of intoxicating liquor—eleven; four paid $100 fine and costs, each; one $100 and costs, replevy bond; one thirty days in jail; three in district court; one served 30 days in jail; two served 35 days in jail.

Petty larceny—three; one served 15 days in jail; one 30 days; one case pending.

Bootlegging—one; served 65 days in jail.

Confiscation of automobile—one; proceeds of sale, $85.

Disorderly conduct—fines ranging from $5 to $15 and costs.

Assault and battery—five; one $5 and costs, paid; one, $1 and costs, paid; one acquittal; two, dismissed at request of complainant, costs paid.

Complaint to keep peace—one; found guilty and placed under peace bond.

Defrauding innkeeper—one; complainant refused to testify, defendant paid costs.

Using obscene language—one; complainant refused to testify but paid costs.

Disturbing nursery ponds—one; 30 days and pay costs; suspended.

Unlawful taking of game fish—one.

Forgery—two; one to two years in reformatory and $12 fine; other case dismissed, insufficient evidence.

Horse stealing—one; pending.

Rape—one; prosecutrix refused to testify but paid costs.

Cattle stealing—two; one pending in district court; one dismissed, insufficient evidence.

Receiving stolen cattle—one; acquittal.

Breaking and entering—four; one sentenced one to two years, and three sentenced two to five years each in penitentiary.

Bastardy complaint—one; plea of guilty and costs paid, settlement made.

Maliciously killing cow of over $35 value—two; both dismissed, insufficient evidence.

Interfering with closed irrigation works—one; two defendants, pending in district court.

Insufficient fund checks—six; one, 13 days in jail; two pending; one, plea of guilty, sentence suspended; one, complainant refused to testify but paid costs; one dismissed, insufficient evidence.

Juvenile court cases—two; pending.

Liquor complaint for search warrants—sixteen; one, no return.

Complaint for search warrants, stolen property—three; one, stolen calves; one, stolen chickens, nothing found; one, stolen harness, transferred to federal court.

Harrison Sun, Thurs., Jan. 28, 1932

SERVING OUT FINE

Jack Dunlap appeared in county court this week and changed his plea to guilty of possession of intoxicating liquor. In his preliminary hearing several weeks ago he was found guilty of the charge and a fine of $100 and costs was imposed in county court. He had intended appealing the case to district court, but chose to change his decision and was confined in the county jail in lieu of payment of fine.

Harrison Sun, Thurs., Feb.4, 1932

MEXICAN BREAKS JAIL

Joe Martinez, a Mexican being held on a charge of possession of mash, still and liquor, sawed his way out of jail Monday night of this week and is perhaps dusting his heels for the Rio Grande. Other prisoners in the jail tried to attract the attention of passersby, but the Mexican had been gone for some time before his escape was made known to outsiders. Lou Sherrill heard the shouts of the other prisoners and went to the jail to find out the cause of the noise, and notified the officers. No trace of the saws used in cutting the bars was found and the officers are without a clue as to who helped from the outside, but it is reported a car drove up to the jail just before the prisoner made his get-away and it suspected some of his cronies helped in the delivery.

Harrison Sun, Thurs., May 26, 1932

CUNNINGHAM & CATTLE STEALING CASE IS BEING HEARD IN DIST. COURT

The June term of district court for Sioux County opened Monday of this week, the forenoon being taken up in arranging the docket for the term. Several civil actions were disposed of Monday, as was the criminal case of the state versus Fred Cunningham on liquor law violation complaints. The defendant plead guilty and was given a five-year sentence. This sentence was suspended by Judge Meyer, the defendant being required to report to the sheriff every three months and at every jury term of district court here, he also being paroled to the sheriff.

Mr. Cunningham was arrested Wednesday of last week, following a search of his place in the south part of the county, an alleged still and some liquor being found and also a quantity of liquor on a place adjoining the Cunningham farm. On this complaint defendant entered a plea of guilty and was sentenced to serve sixty days in the county jail.

State of Nebraska vs. Manie Knori

Tuesday morning the court started on

161

the case of the state versus Manie Knori on a complaint for stealing cattle. Most of the day's session was required in the selection of the jury, one witness being examined before adjournment was taken till Wednesday. Several witnesses had been called yesterday, and as we go to press Wednesday evening, the case had not been given to the jury.

Following the Knori hearing the civil action in the matter of the estate of Daniel Slattery, deceased, will be heard, this being a jury trial, an appeal from county court.

Harrison Sun, Thurs., June 9, 1932

SHERIFFS WILLIAMS & MOODY MAKE RAID AND LOCATE STILL

Tuesday afternoon Sheriff Sid Williams of this county and Sheriff Wm. Moody of Dawes, accompanied by two deputies of the latter county, went to a ranch place northeast of Orella and located a moonshine outfit in full operation in a cave.

The sheriffs had search warrants issued in both counties, and the cave was just across the line in Dawes County. Driving up within a short distance of the cave, the officers approached the place and walked in on the operators of the still. Two men were in the cave, Ray Wagner and a Mr. Coleman, the latter being renter of the land. The still was sizzling away at full blast, three full barrels of whiskey having been run off recently, and other quantities of liquor were found in the cave. In an adjoining room in the cave was found ten barrels of mash. The cave was located in a draw, a windmill near the place supplying water for the outfit.

The men were taken to Chadron and were to have a preliminary hearing today.

Ray Wagner was tried on a charge of operating a still in Sioux County about two years ago, the jury in the case in district court having failed to reach a verdict, standing eleven to one for acquittal.

Harrison Sun, Thurs., March 30, 1933

BEER SALES BRING IMMENSE REVENUES TO U.S. TREASURY

That the American people want their beer was fairly well established by the sales as reported the first few days through the daily papers in states where beer can be legally sold. The first two days brought revenues to the United States treasury in excess of $10,000,000 which would mean a tremendous quantity of beer dispensed during that period. This bears out the contention of those who have long advocated taking the beer business from the Capone gang and their ilk and placing it with licensed brewers. Another pleasing phase of the lifting of the beer ban is the large number the United States over who have been given employment to supply necessary materials and equipment for the manufacture and sale of beer.

Many states, still in the dry column, so far as manufacture and sale of 3.2 beer is concerned, are turning their attention to legislation designed to legalize the sale of beer, and several bills are in the Nebraska legislature at the present time and it is understood action will be taken today. Solons from the numerous districts throughout the state have been flooded with petitions requesting favorable action before the session is over. A long list of signers was secured in Harrison and vicinity and mailed in last week.

Nebraska towns along the Colorado border report a steady traffic of Nebraska people to the neighboring state to get a supply of the new brew Saturday, and a consequent falling off in business. May 18th is the date set for the legal sale of beer in Wyoming, and it is quite probable we'll see the same condition here, provided the legislature does not take steps to remedy the situation.

Harrison Sun, Thurs., April 13, 1933

HOUSE PASSES BEER BILL; SENATE TO ACT THIS WEEK

Falling nine votes short in the lower branch of the state legislature to retain the emergency clause, the beer bill was passed by that body Tuesday by a fairly sized crowd of buyers, and provided the measure is not vetoed by Governor Bryan and the senate, it is said July 1st is the earliest date beer can be legally dispensed in Nebraska. The senate is expected to report the bill out and vote on it either the latter part of this week or the first of next week. Indications are that the vote in the upper branch will be close with exponents of the bill having a margin in their favor.

Harrison Sun, Thurs., April 20, 1933

FEDERAL OFFICER HERE

O.E. Forsling, federal prohibition officer for Nebraska, spent several days of this week in Harrison in the interests of his work, assisting Sheriff Williams in investigation work in the county.

Harrison Sun, Thurs., April 20, 1933

OFFICERS LOCATE STILL

Finding of a still on a place in the south part of the county Wednesday of last week led to the arrest of Henry Koch and Conrad Snell, supposed owners of the outfit. Each of the men gave bonds of $500 for appearance in county court for hearing June 9th

Complaint was made by Wm. Walker against Harry L. Davis, the complainant alleging that defendant moved a house from land owned by Mr. Walker. Mr. Davis

was released on recognizance to appear in county court June 26th, at which time the case will be heard.

Harrison Sun, Thurs., May 25, 1933

ORDINANCE ENACTED FOR SALE OF LIQUOR AND BEER IN CITY

At a meeting of the village board Tuesday evening of this week, an ordinance was passed for the regulation of the sale of liquor and beer in this city, the ordinance appearing on another page of this issue of the Sun. Two applications for the sale of beer are also advertised this week, that of W.M. Cox and Joe Kubista, present operators of beer places. The Viele Drug Store was granted a license for the sale of liquor in original packages by the state commission, and a stock of goods was received this week and is now on sale. Sale by the drink requires a special election at the present time, and it will be necessary for twenty percent of the voters at the last village election to petition for the special election, and then a majority of the votes cast will be necessary to make it effective.

Harrison Sun, Thurs., July 4, 1935

SALE OF LIQUOR BY THE DRINK IS ISSUE OF SPECIAL ELECTION

With the filing of a petition calling for a special election to determine the sale of liquor by the drink, this question will be put to the voters of Harrison in the near future. The liquor law passed by the recent legislature empowered incorporated towns and cities to determine the sale of liquor by the drink, although package sale is regulated by the state liquor commission.

The provision of the law as to elections requires the signatures of twenty percent of the number of votes cast at the preceding town election, and upon proper filing of the petition it is mandatory upon the council that a special election be called. Less than fifty votes were cast at the town election in Harrison last spring and considerably more than the percentage of signatures required were secured.

While in the final analysis the state liquor commission has to issue licenses to individuals, the commission has adopted the policy of leaving this matter for town councils to decide.

Harrison Sun, Thurs., Sept. 5, 1935

PART VI
OTHER LAW INFORCEMENT ACTIVITIES

CAR STOLEN SUNDAY NIGHT. THIEF APPREHENDED TUESDAY

Sheriff Williams got quick action on a car thief this week, and County Attorney Schnurr will not be far behind in carrying out his part of the case.

Monday morning O.N. Worley awoke to find that his car, which he had parked just north of the depot, had lifted anchor and drifted out from shore, and immediately got in touch with the sheriff's office. Another car, a Ford roadster, bearing a Wyoming license, was left in place of the Worley car, but the latter being a Tudor sedan, Mr. Worley did not consider the trade a very well balanced one, so sought the return of his own. The roadster had been stolen Sunday evening at Torrington and driven here. Sheriff Williams telephoned to nearby county officers Monday and Tuesday afternoon got word from Rapid City that the Worley car had been found and the driver caught.

Sheriff Williams left Wednesday morning for Rapid City, returning that night with both man and car.

The thief gave the name of W.H. Hanson, age 24, and admitted having stolen the car. From letters found on his person it would appear that his home is Clearwater, Nebr. He also admitted having served time in the South Dakota penitentiary, and a telegram from the warden at Sioux Falls disclosed Hanson had served two years there for transporting a stolen car, and had been released January 26, 1927.

Hanson went into the sheriff's office at Rapid City to inquire for a man he knew at the South Dakota penitentiary, and who was released last March. The sheriff became suspicious and the next morning (Tuesday) a deputy saw Hanson driving through the street and recognized the Sioux County license number. He ordered Hanson to stop, but the latter refused, whereupon the deputy fired a shot over the car, which had the proper effect.

Hanson was arraigned before Judge Wilhermsdorfer yesterday morning when he plead guilty, and the judge bound him over to the district court. Attorney Schnurr got in communication with District Judge Meyer, and arranged to take Hanson to Chadron, where he will plead guilty and be given his sentence.(1)

Harrison Sun, Fri., May 6, 1927

AUTO THIEF GETS MINIMUM SENTENCE IN DISTRICT COURT

W.H. Hanson, the man who was apprehended at Hot Springs last week, for the theft of the Worley car, was taken to Chadron Saturday of last week and arraigned before District Judge Meyer. Upon pleading guilty, the judge sentenced Hanson to from one to ten years in the state penitentiary, the minimum under the state law. Hanson, a second offender, was released last January from the South Dakota penitentiary after serving a two-year sentence on a similar charge.

Harrison Sun, May 13, 1927

CHECK ARTIST DRAWS THREE YEARS IN PEN

James Rogers, who had been convicted of issuing fraudulent checks on several business houses in Town, and was serving a sentence in the county jail, plead guilty to a second offense and was sentenced to from three to five years at Rawlins by Judge C.O. Brown in district court here Wednesday.

(1)   Dad's jail house records indicate that he took Hanson to Lincoln 5-3-27 to serve 1-10 years in the State Penitentiary.

Rodgers wrote at least three checks in town during the Fair and Rodeo, all on the Harrison Bank, and to each of these he signed different names. Judge Brown, in sentencing the prisoner, said that modern business made the accepting of checks a necessity, and he conceived it to be the duty of the courts to protect the businessmen against any who tried to issue checks upon banks where they had no funds or insufficient funds. Lusk Herald-Standard.

Harrison Sun, Oct. 7, 1927

YOUTHFUL FORGER CAUGHT

Issuing checks without funds to back them up is poor business, and a boy from Wyoming, who had just passed his fourteenth year of age, is now thoroughly convinced it doesn't pay to follow such unlawful pursuits. The boy had left home without the knowledge or consent of his parents, about ten days ago, and came to Harrison. After working a few days for a rancher near here, he returned to town and cashed two spurious checks at local business houses, and left for parts unknown. Sheriff Williams apprehended the boy at Crawford Wednesday, and brought him back. The parents, who reside south of Lusk, Wyo., were notified and they arrived here that evening. The checks were made good and the boy released.

Harrison Sun, Fri., Dec. 30, 1927

YOUTH STEALS CAR AT GLEN AND IS CAUGHT AT LUSK

Harry Burns, a young man who has been in the employ of Mrs. Anna Weber on the Shady Nook Ranch near Glen, attempted Sunday to get away with Mrs. Weber's car. He left the ranch about four o'clock in the afternoon, and Sheriff Williams, who had been notified of the theft, apprehended the youth at Lusk and had him safely in the county jail at eleven o'clock the same night.

Burns claims Chicago as his home and said that he took the car to get to Cheyenne, where he intended to beat his way by rail to his home.

He gave several stories about his age, but it is presumed he is about seventeen. He plead guilty to the charge of stealing the car, and will be taken before District Judge Meyer at Alliance to be sentenced.

This is about the first case Sheriff Williams has been called on to handle since he got his new Ford, and as we stated last week, those who persist in violating the law will have to go some to escape the sheriff.

Harrison Sun, Fri., May 4, 1928

YOUNG MAN HELD IN COUNTY JAIL ON STATUTORY CHARGE

Complaint was filed with County Attorney A.L. Schnurr this week, by the relatives of a girl of minor age, against one Everett Hahn, 25, charging the young man with statutory rape. Relatives of the young girl, who is just past sixteen years of age, reside in the southern part of the county.

As reported here, Hahn has worked on ranches for different members of the family for several years, and it is said his mother lives in Canada.

Hahn had gone to Lamar, Nebr. where he had been conducting a restaurant, and was apprehended there and lodged in jail at Imperial, pending the arrival of Sheriff Williams, who drove after Hahn, returning yesterday morning. Hahn will be arraigned before Judge Wilhermsdorfer Aug. 11 for preliminary hearing.

Harrison Sun, Fri., Aug. 5, 1927

"BRING 'EM BACK ALIVE SID"-

EARNING THE TITLE

MEXICAN WANTED IN SHOOTING SCRAPE IS TAKEN BY SHERIFF

Sheriff WILLIAMS went to Orella Saturday of last week, and in company with two officers from Morrill County, arrested a Mexican wanted for the shooting of another Mexican, which occurred about midnight at Bayard.

Following the shooting the Mexican who committed the crime drove to the place of an uncle who is employed by the Burlington at Orella. The Morrill County officers got word of the whereabouts of the man and phoned to Sheriff WILLIAMS to assist them in making the arrest. Driving up to the way car where the Mexican was supposed to be, the other two officers stood outside guard while Sheriff WILLIAMS plunged through the door and made the arrest. The Mexican was asleep on a cot in one end of the car, and when commanded to "come alive" and throw up his hands, he leaped from the cot with both hands as high as he could extend them.(2)

Upon search a revolver, one of the best and most powerful weapons, was found concealed beneath the pillow. The Mexican has the reputation of being a bad man, and perhaps had he not been caught unawares would have given battle to the officers.

At last report the Mexican who was shot was still alive, although little hope was held out for his recovery.

Harrison Sun, Fri., Mar. 16, 1928

RANCH HAND GETS $90 ON THREE FORGED CHECKS

Several Harrison merchants were victimized by a forger last week, who made a haul of about $90 before departing for parts unknown. Wm. Schultz, who has been employed on the Wiley Richardson Ranch for several months past, went first to The Toggery and Dan Davis accepted a check for $30 with the name of Wiley Richardson signed thereto, Dan having knowledge that Schultz was employed by Mr. Richardson, but little suspecting that the name was forged. Schultz then went to Tanner & Davis store where he told Mrs. Davis that Dan did not have the cash to spare and had sent him there to get the check cashed. This one was also for the amount of $30. The next victim was Alex Lowry, who donated $30 to the cause of Schultz.

Schultz's home is at Florence, Nebr., and he has worked on ranches in this locality at various times, and was considered to be honest and industrious. Several of the merchants had extended him credit, Schultz always meeting his obligations before leaving town and for this reason those who cashed the checks did not in the least suspect they were forged.

Schultz bought a ticket for Omaha, leaving the same night on the Northwestern, and officers in the eastern part of the state were notified to be on the lookout for him.

Harrison Sun, Friday, Aug. 24, 1928

ARRESTED ON ASSAULT CHARGE

Upon complaint sworn to by Dan

(2)   I have heard of this arrest several times during the past 60 years from different individuals, but I didn't know the details until I found this news item in the Harrison Sun. I think this event, the Charlie Russell, and the Jordan arrests were the beginning of your granddad earning the title of "BRING 'EM BACK ALIVE SID."

Slattery, Ralph Beeson was placed under arrest Wednesday on the charge of assault to do great bodily injury. This complaint developed from an altercation the night before at the Slattery Ranch, where we understand Beeson had gone with his sister and brother-in-law to assist in the removal of personal effects preparatory to leaving the employment of the Slatterys. It is alleged by the plaintiff that Beeson struck the former with an instrument, inflicting serious wounds. Beeson also bore the mark of having been in a melee, having a gash across the forehead.

The hearing will be held in the county court on September 11th, and if the evidence is sufficient to warrant the charge, Beeson will be bound over to district court for final hearing. The charge is a severe one, carrying a penalty of from one to five years imprisonment in the penitentiary.

Harrison Sun, Fri., Aug. 24, 1928

VAN TASSELL STORES ROBBED

Wednesday night of this week robbers broke into the pool hall at Van Tassell and took about $25 in small change from the safe. The proprietor of the place had put the change in the safe before going home, but did not throw the combination and the money was easy to get.

The same night the Fjordbak store was entered, presumably by the same bunch of crooks, and the safe was blown and the till robbed. We did not learn the extent of the loss at this place.

Harrison Sun, Aug. 24, 1928

ART NEWMAN HELD ON CHARGE OF RAISING P.O. MONEY ORDER

An inspector of the U.S. postal department was in Harrison Wednesday to file charges against, and place under arrest, Art Newman of this place, for the alleged raising of a money order in Wyoming. At a private hearing before the inspector, Sheriff Williams, County Atty. A.L. Schnurr and Deputy Atty. W.E. Mumby, at the county jail, Newman made full confession to the charge.

From all information given out, Art Newman drove to Manville, Wyo., September 14th, where he purchased a money order for the amount of four dollars, using fictitious names in the transaction. From there he drove to Douglas, where he cashed the order at the LaBonte hotel, having in the meantime raised the order to forty dollars.

The manager of the hotel thought the order looked irregular, the word forty being spelled "fourty," Newman having added the "ty" and placed a cipher after the figure 4. A deputy apprehended him about four miles from Douglas and he was taken back to face the hotel manager, but Newman was able to convince them at that time that he was not the man who cashed the order. Later investigation by the postal officials resulted in the arrest and confession Wednesday. Newman is being held in the county jail, pending arrival of a warrant from the department at Omaha, and he will probably be taken before the federal court at Chadron in a short time for sentence. Conviction on this charge carries a sentence of five years in federal prison.

Art Newman has been conducting the mechanical department of the Chrysler Sales Service garage in this city for the past six months, and his guilt of a crime of this nature comes as a surprise to the people of the community.

Harrison Sun, Oct. 12, 1928

A federal officer was here Tuesday to get Art Newman, arrested for raising a money order. An arraignment was had before the federal commissioner at Chadron, and as the crime was committed in another district. Newman's case will be heard at Cheyenne, upon permit of transfer by the commissioner at Chadron.

Harrison Sun, Oct. 19, 1928

CHARGE IS FILED AGAINST GLEN MAN FOR ASSAULT

Mrs. Anna Weber, aged 68, of near Glen, was in Harrison Wednesday to bring action against J.W. Wood, 26, for assault. The specific charge as filed is assault with intent to do great bodily injury. Mrs. Weber alleges that Wood, who was employed on the Weber ranch, struck her in the eye, knocking her down, and again struck her on the mouth, leaving a cut. Mrs. Weber bore marks of a brutal attack upon her appearance at the county attorney's office Wednesday. The attack as stated by Mrs. Weber occurred early in the week. There are conflicting stories current regarding the cause of the altercation, however, when Sheriff Williams went to Glen to arrest Wood he could not be located, and up to the present time has not been served with the warrant.

Whatever, the cause of the argument, we can imagine no good reason whatever for a young man brutally assaulting a woman sixty-eight years of age.

Harrison Sun, Oct. 19, 1928

PLEADS GUILTY TO CHARGE

J.W. Wood, against whom an information was filed the 17th of October, charging him with assault to do great bodily harm, and who was not apprehended at the time, personally appeared before the county judge a short time ago and his plea of guilty of assault was accepted and a fine of $20 and costs, a total of approximately $50, was assessed which was paid by defendant. Mrs. Anna Weber of near Glen was the complainant.

Harrison Sun, Fri., Jan. 4, 1929

SHEEPHERDERS ARE HELD FOR SLAUGHTER OF A COW

Sunday of this week warrants were issued for the arrest of two sheepherders, in the employ of G.E. Sandoz, about 25 miles southeast of Harrison, following a complaint filed by the county attorney's office wherein Dennis Wilkinson and Wilton Wyant were charged with "willfully killing a cow."

The information was brought to the county attorney by Mr. Sandoz, who stated that Wilkinson had told him of having beef and wanted Mr. Sandoz to take some of it. The story as related in a confession by Wilkinson is to the effect that Wyant shot a black cow, presumably the property of Captain Cook, and forced Wilkinson to help him butcher the critter. This occurred sometime between Christmas and New Year's Day. Later Wyant left for O'Neill, taking some of the beef to friends, as he stated it, and was to go on to the home of his parents in Council Bluffs, Iowa, and while there would receive medical treatment for an infected thumb. It was also told that two quarters of beef were hidden in a hay stack, and later thrown in Runningwater *(DRW: Niobrara River)*, as were also the head, feet and hide. Several depositions were taken and signed by men living in that locality, bearing out the story of the killing and butchering of the cow.

Wilkinson shifts all the blame onto Wyant and in a signed statement further accuses Wyant of having made whiskey at the camp. This is supposed to have taken place on the ranch known as the upper Harris place, where Mr. Sandoz had the two men caring for sheep. Wilkinson was placed under arrest and is at present in the county jail. Sheriff C.S. Williams left Tuesday night for Council Bluffs, where Wyant was apprehended, and it is understood Wyant is willing to waive extradition and return for trial.

Harrison Sun, Fri., Jan. 11, 1929

CHARLES ZIMMERMAN AMBUSHED AND SHOT BY A NEIGHBOR

Irvin Zimmerman was notified Tuesday evening of this week that his son, Charles, was in the Lusk hospital following an attack by a neighbor, in which the latter shot Charles with a shotgun.

The following account of the shooting is taken from the Lusk Herald, received this morning:

Charles Zimmerman, a resident of the Hat Creek district, was shot and seriously wounded about 3:00 o'clock Tuesday afternoon, by Charles Frederick, who used a single-barreled shotgun, firing point blank at Mr. Zimmerman from a distance of about 25 or 30 yards.

Mr. Zimmerman is now in the Lusk Hospital in a very serious condition, with seventy-eight No. 6 shot lodged in his neck and shoulder. Dr. Murphy, who is attending the wounded man, says his condition is very serious, and it would be several days before he could determine the exact extent of his injuries. Shortly after arriving at the hospital he coughed up some blood, indicating that some of the shot had penetrated into his throat and plural cavity.

Frederick was arrested Wednesday morning by Sheriff Hassed, and was lodged in the county jail, held without bond, under a charge of assault with the intent to kill, pending the outcome of Mr. Zimmerman's injuries. He gave no reason for the shooting other than to say that some of his neighbors "had been stealing from him."

Considerable mystery surrounds the motive for the shooting. The condition of Mr. Zimmerman at this time would not permit him to make an extended statement. From the evidence it appears that Mr. Zimmerman had been gathering wood and had driven on the corner of the Frederick land to turn his team around. Frederick, it was stated, had concealed himself in the bushes and fired upon Mr. Zimmerman without warning at a distance of not over thirty yards. The entire charge took effect in Mr. Zimmerman's shoulder, one leg, some of the shot penetrating the plural cavity and neck. Mr. Zimmerman upon regaining consciousness, the horses were in a fence corner, one of the animals having its front feet over the wire.

After regaining consciousness, Mr. Zimmerman drove to the Al Bryant home, a short distance away, and Mr. Bryant and Morris Himes immediately brought the wounded man to Lusk with all possible haste, arriving here about 5:00 o'clock. He was taken to the Lusk hospital at once, where his condition was found to be more serious than at first supposed.

Altogether 78 shot took effect; 41 being in the shoulder, and the balance in the neck and leg. The shot in the leg are believed to be accounted for by the fact that Mr. Zimmerman was seated on a low seat, or had one of his legs doubled up in some manner. From indications it would appear that only one shot was fired, as the shooting was done with a single-barreled gun.

Mr. Zimmerman could give no motive for the shooting. He said he scarcely knew Fredericks, and that he had no quarrel of any kind with him, and there had been no business or social relations between the men which might tend to cause bad feeling.

County Attorney Hartwell and Sheriff

Hassed interviewed several residents near the scene of the shooting in an effort to unearth a motive for the deed.

It was at first reported that Fredericks was suffering from shell-shock received in the world war and was not responsible for his act. However, it is stated on reliable authority that, while he was in the overseas service during the war, he did not participate in any engagements, and was not a shell-shock victim.

Mr. Zimmerman is a highly respected resident of the Hat Creek community, and has never been known to have trouble. He has a wife and two small children. His father came up from Harrison Wednesday to be with his son.

Harrison Sun, Fri., Jan. 11, 1929

CHARLES ZIMMERMAN VICTIM OF SHOOTING GOES HOME

Charles Zimmerman, who was shot and seriously wounded Tuesday, January 8, near Hat Creek, by Charles Frederick, was able to leave the Lusk hospital and go to his home Wednesday. Although he was able to be taken home, Mr. Zimmerman has not fully recovered, and it will be some weeks before he will be able to do much work.

The shot had penetrated Mr. Zimmerman's body so deeply that it was possible to remove only three or four out of a total of 78, and he will have to carry around a considerable load of lead the balance of his life unless an attempt is later made to remove them should they cause him trouble.

His assailant, Charles Fredericks, is still held in the county jail. He was given a preliminary hearing before Justice of the Peace W. Boyd Minter last Thursday, when he entered a plea of not guilty to a charge of assault with intent to do great bodily harm.

His bond was fixed at $2,500.00 and it is not believed that he will be able to give the bond. When asked at the preliminary hearing if he wanted an attorney, he declined the proffer, saying that he believed he could "explain the case to the court about as well as any attorney."

The case has not yet been set for trial, but will probably take place when the next jury panel is drawn, some time in February or March.-The Lusk Herald.

Harrison Sun, Fri., Jan. 18, 1929

MAN WHO SHOT CHAS. ZIMMERMAN SENTENCED TO PEN

Charles Frederick, who shot and seriously wounded Charles Zimmerman with a shotgun, at their ranch near Hat Creek, on the 8th day of January of this year, was found guilty by a jury in District Court, and was sentenced by Judge Brown to serve from three to six years in the penitentiary.

Fredericks acted as his own attorney, and the case attracted considerable attention. The court room was filled with interested spectators and there was scarcely standing room, many waiting until after midnight for the jury to bring in its verdict.

After hearing Fredericks testify in his own behalf, the jury apparently were convinced that the defendant was not in his right mind. The jury hesitated to commit a man to the penitentiary whom they deemed mentally unbalanced, yet they did not desire to free him for fear that others might suffer great bodily harm from hallucinations which seemed to be apparent.

At 10:50 o'clock, the jury sent a note to Judge Brown, and asked for instructions in the matter of insanity, saying that they hesitated to bring in a verdict of guilty on a man whom they honestly believed to be either temporarily or permanently insane.

The court instructed the bailiff to bring in the jury, and in addressing them said that the issue of insanity had not been made as a defense, and he could not instruct them on that point, according to court procedure. However, Judge Brown said, if the defendant wanted to enter a plea of insanity on his own volition, he would permit it to be done. In reply to a question of the judge, Fredericks flatly refused to entertain such a proposition, saying "My head ain't just right, but I am not insane."-Lusk Herald.

Harrison Sun, Fri., Jan. 18, 1929

ARRESTED FOR WIFE BEATING

Francisco Cortez, a Mexican section laborer at Orella was brought before Judge Wilhermsdorfer today to answer to a charge of beating his wife. Cortez' wife and son were also brought to Harrison by Sheriff Williams, the woman bearing the marks of a brutal beating, and they are at the home of the sheriff. Cortez is confined in the jail, and will have a hearing next Tuesday, at least a hearing is set for that day, when an interpreter will be supplied to assist the officers in the preliminary.

Harrison Sun, Fri., Febr. 1, 1929

RUNS INTO PARKED CAR ON HIGHWAY EAST OF HARRISON

Sidney Williams' Essex sedan and a Buick car driven by Mr. Norman, Buick dealer at Crawford, were damaged somewhat in a smashup on the highway near the John Lacy ranch Sunday night. Sidney was driving east, and Mr. Norman had stopped to repair a tire and not having just the needed repairs had stopped Wm. Bannan. Blinded by the headlights of one car Sidney was not able to see the tail-light of the other car, and observe that the highway was blocked, and drove into the Buick. The Essex was without bumpers and got the worst of the mix-up, although the other cars were but slightly damaged. That no one was seriously injured in the collision is a miracle. Sidney received a dislocated collarbone, and Miss Gertrude Jordan, who was with him, was cut on the forehead. Mr. Bannan received an injured thumb and Mr. Norman but a slight bruise.

Harrison Sun, Fri., June 18, 1929

WINS BATTLE WITH WIFE BUT LOSES ONE IN COURT

Francisco Cortez may be the victorious gladiator in his own home, but he struck a snag when he came up before Judge Wilhermsdorfer in county court Tuesday afternoon. Cortez is the Mexican who administered a severe beating to his wife, at Orella last week.

Cortez claims to have a perfect misunderstanding of the English language, so to get his side of the story an interpreter was employed. Not having employed counsel for his defense, Cortez was aided by a compatriot, who acted as chief adviser to the defendant, this distinguished interpreter of Blackstone being no other than the Mexican (and perhaps his name is Brutus) who served six months for injecting several inches of the blade of a sharp stiletto into the side of a friend some time back.

During the course of the proceedings it became quite evident that the interpreter, the adviser and the gladiator had had plenty of conversation with each other before the hearing. In other words there was a foul conspiracy afoot, to the dismay of our deputy county prosecutor, W.E. Mumby, who sweat blood, swore inaudibly, and wished he could understand the Mexican dialect, or jargon. The interpreter informed the court that Cortez said his wife received the bruises in a fall from a short flight of steps. However, the evidence brought out by the prosecution must have convinced the judge that it would take at least a fall the entire length from the pearly gates to produce such bumps and bruises, and now Cortez will be off his chili diet for thirty days, while eating some of his own cooking in Sid Williams' all-season home, which nestles snugly under the west wing of the county administration building.

Harrison Sun, Fri., Febr. 6, 1929

FORGER WHO OPERATED HERE LAST AUGUST IS APPREHENDED

After evading officers since the latter part of last August, Wm. Schultz, alleged forger, was returned to Sioux County the first of the week, he having been taken up by officers at Blair, Nebr., and Sheriff Williams went after him last Saturday.

Schultz had been employed by Wiley Richardson at the latter's ranch during the summer months, and on August 15th decided he needed a little more money, so forged the name of Mr. Richardson on three checks, each for $30, and converted them into cash at the stores of Tanner & Davis, The Toggery and Alex Lowry. Schultz boarded a train that night for Omaha, and while he was reported to be with different relatives near there, he succeeded in evading officers until last week.

At a preliminary hearing in county court Monday, Schultz entered a plea of guilty and was bound over to district court by Judge Wilhermsdorfer.

Harrison Sun, Fri., Febr. 6, 1929

SHERIFF GOES TO LINCOLN WITH PRISONER WEDNESDAY

Sheriff Williams left by auto Wednesday for Lincoln. He had in his custody William Schultz, who was sentenced to the reformatory at Lincoln for one to two years for forgery.

Harrison Sun, Fri., May 17, 1929

GIVES BAD CHECK FOR CAR BUT FAILS TO GET AWAY

A stranger breezed into town Monday and putting up a good front, tendered a check to Ed Meier in payment for a car. While Ed was making inquiry by wire at a Thermopolis, Wyoming bank, the stranger slipped out of town with the car. Sheriff Williams and Deputy Stanek communicated with the police officers of Crawford, and the man was apprehended at the railroad crossing. Evidently he was in no hurry for he had taken plenty of time to drive to Crawford.

When arraigned before Judge Wilhermsdorfer Tuesday the man gave the name of E.C. Grunke and is supposed to have formerly resided in Holt county. Prior to coming here it seems he served time in jail at Casper, and from information it has been the practice of Grunke to buy cars on the same terms as he attempted here. At a hearing Thursday Grunke plead not guilty, and will stand trial later on the charge of passing a worthless check. And in the meantime he will probably board at Sid's.

Harrison Sun, Fri., June 14, 1929

PARTIAL LIST OF COMMISSIONER PROCEEDINGS(3)

C.S. Williams, Assigned E.B. Lyon, County Treasurer, Expense	191.50
C.S. Williams, Assigned E.B. Lyon, County Treasurer, Expense	149.25
Mrs. O.H. Wertz, Examination services	12.75
Van W. Westler, Assessing Andrews Precinct	90.00
Mrs. E.E. Whiteaker, Assigned E.B. Lyon, County Treasurer, Examination services	31.75
C.S. Williams, Assigned E.B. Lyon, County Treasurer, Expense	22.50
C.S. Williams, Assigned E.B. Lyon, County Treasurer, Expense	100.00
C.S. Williams, Assigned E.B. Lyon, County Treasurer, Expense	168.00
Mrs. W.B. Woodruff, Assigned E.B. Lyon, County Treasurer, Examination services	23.75
C.S. Williams, Assigned E.B. Lyon, County Treasurer, Expense	186.00
C.S. Williams, Assigned E.B. Lyon, County Treasurer, Expense	243.00
C.S. Williams, Assigned E.B. Lyon, County Treasurer, Expense	83.00
C.S. Williams, Assigned E.B. Lyon, County Treasurer, Expense	157.14
C.S. Williams, Assigned E.B. Lyon, County Treasurer, Expense	38.90
C.S. Williams, Assigned E.B. Lyon, County Treasurer, Expense	147.00
Mrs. E.E. Whiteaker, Assigned E.B. Lyon, County Treasurer, Examination services	19.50

Harrison Sun, June 21, 1929

(3) I've inserted this partial list of Commissioner Proceedings to show the high cost of enforcing the Prohibition laws; the car expenses at 15c/mile; and the cost of incarcerating liquor law violators in the county jail. There was some grumbling in the county concerning these costs because prior to the passing of the Prohibition laws the county had been relatively crime free.

THREE TAKEN UP ON CHARGE OF GRAND LARCENY LAST WEEK

Howard and Richard Mikaelsen and Sammie Knori were placed under arrest Friday afternoon of last week and placed in the county jail on a charge of grand larceny. At a hearing before Judge Wilhermsdorfer Saturday Richard Mikaelsen plead guilty to the charge and the other two not guilty. They were bound over to the district court, which convenes Monday, at which session Richard will receive sentence on his plea of guilty and the other two cases will be heard. All are out under bond.

The arrest of the trio is the result of the loss of personal property from the house of B.C. Gilbert in the Monroe Canyon district. Mr. Gilbert keeps his house furnished, although he has not resided here permanently for several years, and for the past year has been in Omaha.

Harrison Sun, Fri., Oct. 19, 1928

JUDGE WILL ADJOURN COURT UNTIL THE 13TH OF JANUARY

When the case of the State of Nebraska vs. Harry Haney, now being tried on a liquor charge, has been disposed of Judge Meyer will adjourn the district court until January 13th.

During the week three criminal cases have been disposed of, besides a number of equity cases.

At a session Wednesday night, Sammie Knori, Howard and Richard Mikaelsen appeared and plead guilty to petty larceny, and a sentence of thirty days in jail and a fine of $100 each was imposed on Knori and Richard Mikaelsen. This complaint was made against the defendants for breaking into the house of B.C. Gilbert and taking property there-from.(4)

The Haney case, now being heard, together with a number of equity cases, will comprise Saturday's session.

Harrison Sun, Fri., Nov. 22, 1929

MEXICAN TOURIST IS HELD PENDING INVESTIGATION

A Mexican drove into town last week, in a Ford coupe, and being without funds asked to park his car in Lacy's garage over night and sleep therein. The officers were called and upon search found an old shotgun and a "billy" in the Mexican's possession. He was taken to jail and held for two days until word could be received from Pierre, S.D., as to ownership of the car. The car was registered in the name of Mike Ybarra, which seemed to correspond fairly well with the name the illiterate Mex tried to spell and pronounce for the officers, and he was released and allowed to continue on his journey. A gasoline can and a short piece of rubber hose formed a part of the traveler's equipment, which presumably will explain how he is able to make the old car go with no funds to buy gas.

Harrison Sun, Fri., Dec. 6, 1929

TWO ARE HELD IN SOUTH DAKOTA ON CHARGE OF SEED THEFT

Sunday of this week Bob Porter, sheriff of Fall River County, South Dakota, got in touch with Sheriff Williams of this county and the two conducted an investigation of the theft of a number of sacks of alfalfa seed from a warehouse in Ardmore.

Walt Nolan of near Oelrich had purchased a car load of seed, and had some stored in the warehouse awaiting shipment. When ready to load out the car he found

---

(4)   *I was well acquainted with Sam Knori and his family, especially his son Raleigh Knori.*

twenty-one sacks missing and immediately reported the case to the sheriff, and after considerable investigation the clues led them to Sioux County. A search warrant was issued and the officers went to the Lake ranch in the eastern part of the county and found twenty-one sacks of seed in the granary on the ranch. John Konrath, who has the place rented, was placed under arrest and waiving extradition went to Hot Springs, where he was released under $2500 bonds.

Further investigation brought out the fact that a boy by the name of DeJarvis had hauled the seed, and when taken before the court for questioning gave the information that Jacob (Jack) Konrath, a brother of John, had employed him to haul the seed in the DeJarvis truck to the Lake ranch Wednesday night of last week. The seed was loaded out at about two o'clock in the morning. The officers then got out a warrant for Jack Konrath, and he is also out on $2500 bonds, pending hearing.

Harrison Sun, Dec. 20, 1929

STRANGER ADJUDGED INSANE

Thursday of last week Sheriff Williams and Deputy Joe Stanek were called to the farm home of Jacob Forester, in the extreme northern part of the county, to get a man who had appeared there in scant attire. The man was brought to Harrison and placed in jail, and Tuesday a hearing was given the man to judge his sanity.

The man was able to give but scant information concerning himself, although claimed the name of Bela W. Smith, and gave his age as 41. After considering his case, the board adjudged the man insane, and the authorities at Norfolk were notified, but owing to lack of room at the hospital, it will not be possible to take the man there

for some time.

Harrison Sun, July 25, 1930

HE DIDN'T GET IT

Sheriff Sid Williams was in the Sun office this week to collect a balance of something like two thousand dollars, which he claims must be due him, if one is to believe all that appears in this great family journal. But we didn't have the money, and Sid will have to seek elsewhere. In the publication of the commissioners proceedings last week, there appeared in the list of claims allowed, one for C.S. Williams amounting to $2204.17, which was off the $2000 Sid lays claim to. The amount should have been $204.17.

Harrison Sun, Aug. 1, 1930

TAKES MAN TO NORFOLK

Sheriff Sid Williams left Saturday night of last week for Norfolk, where he took Bela Smith to be placed in the state insane institution. Smith was picked up in the north part of the county last July and brought to the county jail here, and a few days later was examined as to his sanity. He was adjudged insane and the officials in charge of the state institution were notified. In the meantime Smith has been confined in the county jail, until last week when officials at the state institution ordered him brought there.

Harrison Sun, Fri., Oct. 10, 1930

CAR OF STOLEN CATTLE RECOVERED AT BELMONT

Ranchers southwest of Chadron were Monday reminded of early days in this country, with an attempted theft of a carload of cattle being checked by officers in

178

the stockyards at Belmont.

According to information of officers here, Rolland Quintard, of Crawford, is charged with stealing a carload of cattle from the Diehl & Sons ranch at Belmont. The cattle were in the stockyards at Belmont, with a railway stock car ordered for shipping the cattle when officers took possession of the cattle and took out after Quintard to secure arrest.

Quintard escaped into the rough lands near Belmont, but was arrested later in the evening by officers.(5)

CHADRON CHRONICLE-

Harrison Sun, Fri, Oct. 10, 1930

FRANK & JOHN PARSONS ARRESTED FOR CATTLE STEALING

On a joint complaint filed by Charley Henry and George Wickersham, John and Frank Parsons were placed under arrest Thursday on a charge of cattle stealing.

Sheriff Williams went to the place of Frank Parsons Wednesday night and found four calves penned in the barn and Ed Clark's truck was sent for to bring them to town. Frank was arrested that night and placed in jail. John was served with a warrant yesterday morning. The defendants were arraigned in county court yesterday afternoon and furnished bond in the amount of $3000 each for their appearance at a preliminary hearing to be held October 29th.

Two of the calves were claimed by Charley

Henry and two by Geo. Wickersham.

Harrison Sun, Fri., Oct. 19, 1928

BOUND OVER TO DISTRICT COURT ON CATTLE STEALING CHARGE

The preliminary hearing for John and Frank Parsons, who were arrested some time ago on a complaint of stealing cattle, was held before Judge Wilhermsdorfer Friday afternoon of last week. The defendants plead not guilty, and after evidence offered by the state the judge bound them over to the next term of district court. E.H. Boyd, Alliance attorney, was present as counsel for the defense.

Harrison Sun, Fri., Nov. 30, 1928

FRANK PARSONS FOUND NOT GUILTY OF CATTLE STEALING

District court opened Monday morning of this week, the first case to come up for hearing being that of the State of Nebraska vs. Frank Parsons for cattle stealing.

All of Monday and a part of Tuesday was taken in the selection of a jury, the original empanel being exhausted before twelve men could be selected and extra summons for service were issued.

A large number of witnesses were examined and the case was given to the jury late Thursday afternoon, the attorneys in the case omitting the customary pleas to the jury. A verdict was reached during the night and Friday was opened, it being the

(5)   I didn't find any jail records of Quintard in the Sioux County Jail. I assume the rustling charges were filed in Dawes County. I knew Quintard when we both lived in Harrison. He and Sid Jr. were friends in later years. He seemed like an alright guy to me.

opinion of the twelve men that defendant was not guilty as charged.(6)

Attorney Prince of Grand Island and E.H. Boyd of Alliance were council for defense. The case was prosecuted by County Attorney A.L. Schnurr, Deputy W.E. Mumby and J.E. Porter of Crawford.

Both Frank and John Parsons, brothers, were under indictment on this charge, the alleged crime having been that of stealing calves from Geo. Wickersham. The latter case was not tried at this time, and there is still pending a similar charge against the defendants for alleged stealing of calves from Charley Henry.

The case attracted wide interest and the room was packed at all times during the trial.

Harrison Sun, Fri., Nov. 22, 1929

HELD FOR CANVAS THEFT

Sheriff George Jones was over from Box Butte County Saturday of last week to arrest Frank Parsons, who is alleged to have stolen binder canvas from the farm of Roy Lockard near Hemingford. Sheriff Jones, in company with Sheriff Williams, went to the farm of Howard Riley southwest of town, where Frank was engaged in combining grain, and served the warrant. He was taken to Alliance and held until Monday, and was released on bond of $700, pending a preliminary hearing set for August 14.

Monday Sheriff Jones returned to Harrison and served a warrant on Lawrence Schutt, who is said to have been with Parsons at the time of the alleged theft. Three sets of canvas were stolen from the Lockard farm, and one set in the possession of Parsons was alleged to have been identified as the property of Lockard. The other two sets were not found here.

Harrison Sun, Fri., Aug. 1, 1930

(6)   *When a lot of smoke surrounds the activities of certain individuals, one may logically assume there is some fire. But when the Parsons noted defense attorneys performed, the smoke cloud soon dissipated.*

However, my Dad said when the 'stolen' calves were trucked to the pasture where the mother cows were kept and released in the presence of the cows, the half starved calves rushed to their receptive mothers and began nursing. My parents said jurors were often quite reluctant to convict local, well known citizens and send them to jail. I knew both Charley Henry and George Wickersham. Both were first class citizens and would not file unjustified theft charges.

The jail house records indicate the Parsons only served a few days in the county jail until their bail bonds could be arranged.

I knew both Frank and Jack, especially Jack. Jack was a likeable, affable man. A few times when I was walking home from work in Harrison, Jack, when driving by, would stop and offer me a ride home. I graciously accepted. I wondered why he did this. Perhaps he thought I might know about his trouble with the law. I did know, having heard it from my folks and others, and he wanted to come across as not such a bad guy. Or maybe he was just trying to do a good deed in his old age.

I never heard of Frank and Jack having any more difficulties with the law after their acquittal of stealing cattle, the canvas thefts and liquor still charges. If indeed they were truly guilty it must have finally dawned on them, after narrowly escaping the penitentiary, of what could happen to them if they continued on their errant ways.

The Parsons eventually became prosperous ranchers south of town and Jack and his wife raised a family of five attractive girls.

180

COMPLAINT AGAINST TWO SOUTH COUNTY BOYS

Deputy County Attorney W.E. Mumby and Sidney Williams Deputy Sheriff, drove to the south end of the county Friday of last week to investigate a complaint of residents there against two boys of minor age. The boys were alleged to have committed criminal assault upon a six-year-old girl, and the evidence was such to warrant the arrest of the boys, who were brought to Harrison and placed in jail. A hearing to arrange bonds was held Monday in the county court, and the boys, whose names are Willie and Floyd Beaver, aged 17 and 14 were released under bonds to appear for a preliminary hearing to be held February 27th.

Harrison Sun, Fri., Febr. 15, 1929

THE MEXICAN MURDER CASE

MAN KILLED BY MEXICAN ON TRAIN NEAR FT. ROBINSON

An unidentified man was shot and killed on a freight train west of Ft. Robinson Wednesday night, and one of three Mexicans who were on the train admits having fired two shots which resulted in the killing.

According to the stories of the fracas as told by the Mexicans, the man killed came from the rear of the freight train just as it was pulling out of Ft. Robinson, walked on by the Mexicans, who were on a tank car, and then came back on the same side and flashed a light on the Mexicans and said "Hands up!" One of the Mexicans states that the man fired a shot, and that he (the Mexican) who was on the other side of the platform, became frightened and ran over the string of cars to the engine and told the engine crew that a man had been killed.

One of the other Mexicans tells that two shots were fired and that he heard the man groan. This Mexican also went ahead to the engine. The third Mexican, Francisco Unzueta, states that the man had fired at him, the shot passing under his arm and he then grappled with the man and wrested the gun from him. The train crew stopped at Andrews and phoned the sheriff's officers to be at the train on arrival in Harrison.

Deputy Sheriff Joe Stanek and John Marking were at the train and Unzueta surrendered voluntarily, handing over a .32 caliber Colt's army special revolver as he approached the officers. That night Unzueta told the officers that the man killed had two guns, and that he had shot the man to resist being robbed. He stated the body of the man rolled off the tank car a short distance west of Ft. Robinson.

The section men at Ft. Robinson were called out at two o'clock Thursday morning to hunt for the body, which was found beside the track about a mile west of the station at four o'clock. County Attorney A.L. Schnurr was notified of this and with Dr. Priest, W.E. Mumby and Joe Stanek, went to conduct an inquest.

From the position of the body it appeared that it had been rolled from the car after the shooting, there being no marks in the dirt to indicate a struggle although it is presumed the man was not dead at the time he was rolled from the car, as the grass and weeds on the right side were beaten down, supposedly by the movement of the right arm.

The ground around the body was searched carefully, and directly over the point where the body lay, and about twenty feet away, were found an improvised holster, a flashlight and a small tobacco sack containing four .32 caliber shells and two keys. About one hundred yards east of the body along the track a cap was found.

181

After summoning a jury of six men, Mr. Schnurr ordered the body moved to the depot at Ft. Robinson where an examination of the body was made and the inquest was held.

When the clothing was removed two bullet holes were disclosed on the left side, one penetrating at a point below the seventh rib and the other below the twelfth rib. One bullet passed through the body and the other lodged in the right side. The shots followed a downward course through the body.

Major Hassed, of the U.S. medical corps, stationed at the Fort, was called, and the body opened for careful examination, and to remove the bullet. The bullet was a .38 caliber, which verified the story of the two guns, as told by the Mexican. The victim of the shooting was judged to be a man about 35 years old, medium build, five feet six inches, had light roached hair, blue eyes; a double cross tattooed on the left shoulder, which Major Hassed said might be the Lorain Cross, an insignia of a certain detachment of American forces in Alsace-Lorraine during the World War. A long deep scar on the inside of the right leg, just above the knee, was another mark of identification.

The clothing was examined carefully, but no papers that might definitely establish the man's name or home address were found. He wore a pair of overalls and a jumper over his other clothing, and on the inside lining of the trousers the name "Robertson" was stamped, evidently the mark made by some cleaning establishment that had cleaned the trousers. On a strip of paper was written "Happy Jack" and under this the name "Mrs. C.L. Wells, Nebraska City, Nebr." A safety razor, two towels, a five dollar bill, a small mirror and a few other articles were taken from the pockets of the clothing. Later the initials "M.C.R."

were found on the underwear, this perhaps being the laundry mark.

With this information the jury proceeded with the inquest, examining several witnesses, and returned a verdict that the unidentified man's death was caused by two gunshot wounds, inflicted by unknown person or persons, but presumably by one of three Mexicans being held at Harrison, Nebr.

Thursday officers from the fort and representatives for the railroad company, together with Mr. Schnurr, cross examined the Mexicans, and were able to get a signed statement from them, Unzueta confessing the killing, but stoutly maintaining he acted to prevent being robbed. One of the Mexicans, Eriberit Contreras, said he met the other two at Rapid City Wednesday morning, and had rode the same train until they were taken off at Harrison. He appears to be telling a straightforward story. The other two, Unzueta and Manuel Cardenas, had been working in the beet fields near Nisland, S.D., they stated.

In Unzueta's effects was found another small tobacco sack, identical to the one found at the scene of the murder and which contained the two keys, and in the former there was an express receipt made to Unzueta for shipment of two suit cases to Denver. It would appear that if these keys happen to fit any lock on the suitcases, this would also establish the ownership of the .32 caliber gun.

Unzueta also told the officials Thursday that he buried the second gun while the train stopped at Andrews. This morning Deputy Attorney Mumby and Deputy Stanek went to Andrews and found the gun buried near the track, as told by the Mexican. Later a call from L.C. Holt at Crawford established the fact that the .38 caliber revolver had been stolen from a car at the depot at Crawford the night before and was the property of one of the operators employed there. The chamber of the gun gave evidence that two shots had been fired from this gun, while the .32 did not appear to have been fired recently. The .38 was empty while there were four cartridges in the .32.

Attorney Schnurr communicated with the U.S. district attorney at Omaha today and was advised that the federal department would take over the case, since the crime was committed on the reservation, and officials will arrive in the morning to take the Mexicans to Chadron, where the trial will probably be held at an early date. A charge of murder will be filed against Unzueta, and the other two will be held in custody as witnesses.

The body of the unidentified man was taken by Mr. Huston to Crawford and prepared for burial. Photographs and fingerprints were taken and an effort is being made to locate relatives and establish identity.

Harrison Sun, Fri., July 26, 1929

FIRST DEGREE MURDER CHARGE IS FILED AGAINST MEXICAN

Arraigned before the federal commissioner at Chadron Monday, Francisco Unzueta was bound over to the grand jury for trial at the next session of the federal court, and is held without bail, he having been charged with first degree murder for the killing of an unidentified man Wednesday night of last week. County Attorney Schnurr and Deputy Sheriff Joe Stanek were called in to assist with the investigation, the case having been taken over by federal authorities since the crime was committed on the government reservation.

Erlberit Contreras and Manuel Cardenas, two other Mexicans who were on the freight train at the time of the killing, are held under $5000 bonds each as material witnesses.

No further information has been gathered, aside from that given last week,

either as to the motive for the shooting or as to the identity of the man killed. Several stories are current regarding the victim of the shooting, one being to the effect that he was C.L. Wells, a garage mechanic of Nebraska City, and another states that he was known at Valentine, Nebr., and another story is to the effect that he had stopped frequently at a rooming house in Crawford, and was there the evening of the murder. However, these seem to be without foundation.

A wallet containing some checks was found along the railroad track east of Glen, but whether this has any connection with the crime is not stated.

Harrison Sun, Aug. 2, 1929

U.S. DIST. COURT ADJOURNED

The jurymen called for service at the term of U.S. district court at Chadron returned home yesterday, having been excused when the court was adjourned until the latter part of November. The case of the Mexican held for murder was postponed until that time. J.H. Lacy and Vern Hanson were also rung in for jury service, besides those heretofore mentioned from this community.

Harrison Sun, Fri., Sept. 27, 1929

MEXICANS MAY BE TRIED IN DISTRICT COURT HERE

County Attorney A.L. Schnurr has recently received a copy of an opinion given by Judge Woodrough, of the United States district court, with reference to the three Mexicans held for the murder of an unknown man, on the Northwestern right-of-way near Ft. Robinson. It is the decision of Judge Woodrough that the federal government is without jurisdiction in the trial of the Mexicans, and has given the federal officials thirty days in which to appeal to a higher tribunal. As a matter of precaution Mr. Schnurr has filed charges against the Mexicans in Sioux County, and in event of their release by the federal authorities, the Mexicans can be brought to Harrison to stand trial.

The opinion given by Judge Woodrough is a lengthy document, a part of which cites the fact that the state of Nebraska turned the land embraced in the reservation over to the United Sates for military purposes, the government later ceding a right-of-way to the Northwestern Railway company, and the crime having been committed on the railroad right-of-way is outside the jurisdiction of the federal government.

Harrison Sun, Fri., Nov. 8, 1929

MEXICAN ACCUSED OF MURDER BROUGHT TO SIOUX COUNTY

Under a decision by Judge Woodrough, of the federal court, Francisco Unzueta, a Mexican held on a murder charge, was released by the federal authorities Tuesday of this week and Sheriff Williams was at Chadron armed with a warrant from this county for his arrest, a charge of murder having been filed against Unzueta and also two companions, who are being held in Omaha. Sheriff Williams left last night for Omaha for the latter two.

Unzueta has been in custody since the finding of a dead unidentified man on the Northwestern right-of-way just west of Ft. Robinson last July. Believing the crime was committed within the area of the government reservation, attorneys for the government took over the case, but a short time ago a ruling was made that the government was without jurisdiction, since the crime was actually committed on the right-of-way of the railroad. An appeal was perfected and permission granted to carry same to the supreme court of the United States for decision. In the meantime, Unzueta was to have been released

on his own recognizance, as were also the two companions in Omaha, and as a precautionary measure County Attorney Schnurr is holding them on the murder charge for trial in the district court of Sioux County.

This case presents a unique situation, since it is possible for the defendants to demand trial within a limited time, and then should the high tribunal rule it is a government case a mess of legal technicalities could develop.

Unzueta was arraigned yesterday and bound over to district court.

Harrison Sun, Dec. 6, 1929

MEXICANS' HEARINGS SET FOR 20ᵀᴴ OF JANUARY

The fore part of the week the three Mexicans held for murder of the unidentified man near Ft. Robinson were brought before Judge Wilhermsdorfer, but the preliminary hearing was extended to January 20ᵗʰ. Attorney A.G. Fisher, representing Francisco Unzueta, appeared in behalf of his client and filed objections to the jurisdiction of the county court and also to the district court of Sioux County, and further alleges that the crime was committed in Dawes County. The question of jurisdiction in the case has been carried to the supreme court of the United States for decision, and it is probable no further action will be taken until an answer is returned.

Harrison Sun, Fri., Dec. 20, 1929

MEXICAN HELD FOR MURDER IS TRANSFERRED TO CHADRON

This week marks another move for Francisco Unzueta, Mexican held for the murder of a man presumed to be Omer Robertson, and which occurred July 25ᵗʰ last. The body was found on the railroad right-of-way just west of Ft. Robinson station, and being on the military reservation it was first determined the federal court held jurisdiction. A contrary decision was rendered and an appeal taken to the supreme court of the United States.

In the meantime A.L. Schnurr, representing Sioux County, had a survey made of the ground near where the body of Robertson was found, and F.M. Hall, county surveyor of Sioux County, and Hal Mead, for Dawes County, returned the report that the location in question is 590 feet east of the Sioux County line. It now appears that if the Nebraska courts have jurisdiction, it will be up to Dawes County to proceed with the prosecution. Unzueta, who had been held by federal authorities in Omaha, was recently transferred to the jail at Harrison, and Manuel Cardenas and Elberto Cantreras, two Mexican companions on the night of the crime, were brought here from Dawes County jail. County Attorney F.A. Crites has filed a complaint against Unzueta, and the Dawes County sheriff came Wednesday to take the Mexicans to Chadron, where they will be held for trial. Mr. Crites expects to proceed with the case at the March term of district court, in Chadron. A.G. and C.A. Fisher of Chadron are the attorneys for Unzueta.

Harrison Sun, Jan. 10, 1930

TRIAL OF MEXICAN FOR MURDER IN PROGRESS AT CHADRON

Quite a number of men from this community were called to Chadron Monday to be present at the hearing of the Mexican, Francisco Unzueta, who is being tried for the killing of an unidentified man near Ft. Robinson last July. Several were called for jury service, and three were sworn in as jurors, namely: W.A. York, John Bell and I.S. Zimmerman. Dr. Priest, A.L. Schnurr, John Marking, Joe Stanek and W.E. Mumby were called as witnesses. Joe Stanek, deputy sheriff, was on the stand for several hours during the first day of the trial, being one of the government, the case being heard in federal court. A.G. Fisher, Chadron attorney, is counsel for defense. Most of those called for witnesses have returned and report the case is likely to last the balance of the week. This is the only case to be heard at this session of court, and fifty witnesses were subpoenaed.

Harrison Sun, Fri., May 30, 1930

MEXICAN IS ACQUITTED BY JURY OF MURDER CHARGE

Francisco Unzueta, the Mexican who was indited for the murder of Omar Robertson, last June, was acquitted by a jury in Federal court at Chadron.

This case had been in progress before Judge J.W. Woodrough of Omaha for more than a week, during which time a large number of witnesses were called to testify, several of whom were from Harrison.

Unzueta with two Mexican companions were riding a freight train out of Ft. Robinson, when they claimed Robertson approached them with a gun and attempted to rob them. Unzueta claimed Robertson fired at him and his companions but missed, and the gun was taken away from Robertson by Unzueta who admits shooting Robertson, but in self defense. Robertson was armed with two guns, and the Mexicans all claim Unzueta acted in self defense.

One of the Mexicans, who was without a passport, was ordered deported.

Harrison Sun, Fri., June 6, 1930

MEXICAN FILES CLAIMS AGAINST SIOUX COUNTY FOR $4007.75

Claims amounting to $4007.75 against

Sioux County were rejected at the meeting of the board of county commissioners on December 16th. These claims were filed by Eriberto Contreas, one of the trio of Mexicans apprehended here in July, 1929, and held for the murder of a man on a freight train on the Ft. Robinson military reservation.

This case was tried in federal court at Chadron this year and the Mexicans were acquitted. One claim amounting to $3683.25, filed by Contreas, is for sickness contracted while in confinement, improper medical care, and numerous other reasons stated in the petition. Another claim is for $324.50 from the Verges sanitarium in Omaha, where Contreas was confined and treated. There were also claims for witness fees. Claims for witness fees and other claims were also filed by Contreas against Dawes County, and the witness fees were allowed we understand, but the other claim rejected by the commissioners of that county.

Contreas is represented by Attorney Allen G. Fisher of Chadron, and it is probable appeal from the rejected claims will be made to the district court.

Harrison Sun, Dec. 26, 1930

OTHER DAMAGE CLAIMS FILED AGAINST COUNTY BY MEXICANS

This week additional claims have been filed against Sioux County and the state of Nebraska, as an outgrowth of the arrest and trial of the Mexicans held for the murder and as witnesses, in the death of Omar Robinson in July, 1929.

The recent filing of claims covers those of Francisco Unzueta, who was tried for the murder in the federal court at Chadron several months ago, the jury hearing the case having acquitted the defendant. Unzueta, through his attorneys, is seeking to recover $5100 from Sioux County, for mental anguish and several other reasons stated in the petition; and a claim of over $10,000 is filed with the legislature against the state of Nebraska.

Harrison Sun, Fri. Jan. 9, 1931

CITY OFFICIALS WILL MAKE AUTO LICENSE COLLECTIONS

Sheriff Sid Williams expects to go to the south part of the county this week, to enforce the motor vehicle statute relative to payment of auto licenses in the county of residence.

The apportionment of the state gasoline tax, one-fourth of which is paid back to counties of state, is based on the car and truck registry of the various counties. It is noticeable that Sioux County has been getting but a small portion of this fund, and investigation developed the fact that upwards of one hundred car owners of the south part of the county have been procuring their licenses from adjoining counties. By this practice Sioux County is not getting the amount of refund to which it is entitled, and also a greater part of the license money is paid into the county fund.

Section 8365, Compiled Statutes of Nebraska, reads:

Every owner of a motor vehicle shall, for each motor vehicle owned, except as herein otherwise expressly provided, make application for registration on a blank to be furnished for that purpose by the county treasurer of the county in which the owner resides, in addition to such other particulars as may be required by the Department of Public Works......

Section 8396—The violation of any of the provisions of this article . . . . .shall be deemed a misdemeanor punishable by a fine of not less that ten dollars and costs, nor more than fifty dollars and costs, or imprisonment not exceeding sixty days in the county jail for each subsequent offense, or both fine and imprisonment; provided, however, if any person operating a motor vehicle in violation of the provisions of this article, shall by so doing seriously maim or disfigure any person or persons, he shall upon conviction thereof be fined not less than two hundred dollars and costs, nor more than five hundred dollars and costs, or be imprisoned in the penitentiary for not less than one year or more than ten years.

The penalties attached to violation of these statutes is pretty severe, and it behooves all car owners to give strict observance of same before procuring their licenses.

Harrison Sun, Fri., July 19, 1929

COLLECTING AUTO LICENSES

Sheriff Sid Williams spent Wednesday and Thursday in the south part of the county, collecting auto license fees from a number there who had procured their licenses from neighboring counties. Settlement is being made on the basis of a half year's fee. The law stipulates that car owners must get licenses in the county in which they reside.

Harrison Sun, Fri., July 26, 1929

TEN DAYS MORE IN WHICH TO GET DRIVERS' LICENSE

The law requires that every driver of an automobile in the state of Nebraska must have a driver's license on the first day of October, 1929, or suffer the indignity of being hauled into court to tell the why and wherefores. Regardless of what you think of the newly enacted legislation, it will be much safer and expedient to get the license and wear it about your clothes, same as you do your hunting and fishing license, and there's no better time to get it than RIGHT NOW.

There is considerable controversy over the financial side of the law. So many seem to be of the opinion that the county treasurers, who get a small portion of the fee, will become suddenly wealthy. In the more populous counties the fees may aggregate quite a sum, but in the more sparsely settled counties no one will get overly rich. Any way, it imposes additional work on the treasurers, and if there is to be a fee charged, such as the law provides, who in the world is entitled to it but the ones who do the work? A driver's license is good "from now on," unless revoked for good and sufficient cause. The first cost is the last, provided you don't mix too much hootch with the gasoline, or do some other fool things. Whether the law is a good one will depend upon rigid enforcement.

Harrison Sun, Fri., Sept. 20, 1929

WARNING TO CAR DRIVERS

We will soon begin to call for your driver's license, and those who have not complied with the new law should do so at once and avoid possibility of trouble.
C.S. WILLIAMS, Sheriff.

Harrison Sun, Fri., Oct. 18, 1929

SHERIFF WILL MAKE EFFORT TO COLLECT PERSONAL TAX

More than two hundred distress warrants for collection of delinquent personal taxes have been issued by the county treasurer's office, and turned over to Sheriff Williams for collection. Under the law the sheriff can seize such property and sell same for satisfaction of taxes, and this procedure will be carried out. Notices will be sent to those having delinquent personal taxes, and if immediate response is not forthcoming, seizure and sale will follow.

It is to the advantage of the delinquents to make settlement and avoid further costs.

There are several thousands of dollars due the county from this source.

Harrison Sun, Fri., Dec. 6, 1929

HARRISON STATE BANK CLOSED TO PROTECT ITS DEPOSITORS

We unhesitatingly say that due to malicious talk and propaganda circulated in Wyoming, the Harrison State Bank of this city closed its doors Wednesday noon, and was placed in the hands of the State Department of Trade and Commerce. The action taken by Geo. L. Gerlach, president of the institution, and Jesse L. Gerlach, cashier, was a precautionary measure, and not because of a low reserve.

The propaganda had had some effect and a number of the bank's depositors had begun to make withdrawals, some of which were fair sized amounts, and to protect the bulk of the loyal depositors the officers determined temporary closing, at least, was necessary.

It is not boastful to say that Harrison has two of the strongest banks in the state, and both are absolutely solvent in every way, shape and form. However, steady withdrawal could have a devastating effect upon most any bank.

As a matter of fact, the Harrison State Bank had a cash reserve of more than twenty percent when the doors were closed, all its paper is in the vaults, and has not one dime of borrowed money, and it has been a surprise to those familiar with the banking business, especially correspondent banks and state officials, that the bank was closed.

Mr. Lau, one the of the state examiners arrived Thursday, and Mr. Wood will be here Saturday, at which time a meeting of the depositors will be held, and some action taken. Those who have done business with the bank for years, and have known the Gerlachs most all their lives, are back of the officers one-hundred percent. There is a great feeling of confidence in the institution and many feel that the bank should be re-opened.

The stock of the bank is all owned by people in this community, Dave Hamaker, the vice-president, and Wiley Richardson, both substantial ranch owners, being among the stockholders.

It is likely a committee will be chosen from the depositors of the bank, and together with the state examiners will make a thorough investigation of the bank's condition, and report same to the depositors at a later date. Definite action will depend upon this report.

Harrison Sun, Fri., Dec. 20, 1929

SHERIFF HAVING SUCCESS COLLECTING DISTRESS WARRANTS

Sheriff Williams informs us that he is meeting with splendid cooperation in the collection of delinquent personal taxes, a large number having been issued by the county treasurer and turned over to the sheriff for collection. Notices were sent to all and at the present time about $4000 has been collected. It is the opinion of Sheriff Williams that it will be necessary to force collection of small percentage of the amount.

Harrison Sun, Fri., Dec. 20, 1929

The old original courthouse, 1888-1930, made from Sioux County brick and timber. Sid and his brother, Russell felled some of the pine trees and Sid hauled some of the brick, fired at a kiln on Tetse Creek, Sowbelly Canyon to the building site in Harrison.

The new courthouse, built 1930, on the site of the razed old courthouse. Your granddad was the first sheriff in the new building.

JURY FINDS FOR DEFENDANT IN SIOUX COUNTY-MEYER CASE

District court for Sioux County opened Monday morning of this week with Judge E.F. Carter, of the 17th judicial district, supplying for Judge Meyer, who is holding court in Dawes County.

The civil action wherein Sioux County sought to recover from F.W. Meyer, former county treasurer, and the surety company in which Mr. Meyer was bonded, monies alleged to be due the county, was the first case to be heard.

Some time ago audit of the books and records kept by Mr. Meyer during his terms of office was made by the public accounting firm of Campbell & Company of Lincoln, and the report of the company originally showed a shortage of some $7800. However, some corrections were later made in this report and the amount sued for by the county was $4334.75. The case was heard by a jury, Mothersead & York of Scottsbluff were attorneys for the defendant and County Attorney A.L. Schnurr and E.D. Crites of Chadron represented Sioux County.

During the course of the trial numerous witnesses were presented by the plaintiff, most of whom were officers of school districts throughout the county. After several days of examination and cross-examination of the witnesses of the plaintiff, the defense rested and the pleas of the attorneys were heard at a night session Wednesday. Judge Carter read his instructions to the jury Thursday morning, following which the jury proceeded to the jury room for deliberation, and at 11:30 last night the sealed verdict was returned to A.C. Davis, district clerk, who had been designated by Judge Carter to receive same. This morning the verdict was read and found to be generally for the defendant. In an action of this nature, if after six hours of deliberation the jury is unable to come to a unanimous agreement, five-sixths of the jury can return a signed verdict. In this case there were eleven signatures, one member of the jury dissenting.

Thursday morning the case of the state of Nebraska vs. Frank Parsons was called for trial, counsel for defendant asking for continuance owing to inability of some of the witnesses to be present, and same was taken under advisement. Following this, court was adjourned until Monday of next week, because of the extremely cold weather and threatening snow storm.

Harrison Sun, Jan. 17, 1930

THREE YOUNG MEN HELD FOR THEFT OF CHICKENS

Warrants were sworn out yesterday for the arrest of Merle Cheney, Charles Eversaul and Charles Havlik on complaint of D.C. Hanks, Jr., resident of the east part of the county, alleging the theft of chickens from the premises of the latter.

Cheney was located in the county jail at Chadron, where he is serving a sixty-day sentence and a fine of $100 and costs for bootlegging. Havlik was arrested by Chief of Police Hill at Crawford upon advice of County Attorney Schnurr, and is being held for the Sioux County officers. According to word from the Crawford officers today, both Cheney and Havlik have admitted guilt and had sold the chickens to Ernest Mahlman. Sheriff Williams will go to Crawford tomorrow for Havlik and Eversaul and bring them to Harrison for hearing.

Harrison Sun, Fri., April 4, 1930

SIXTY DAYS AT HARD LABOR

Appearing before Judge Wilhermsdorfer in county court Monday, Charles Eversaul and Charles Havlik plead guilty to the charge of stealing chickens from D.C. Hanks and were sentenced to sixty days in jail at hard labor. Merle Cheney, a third member of the gang, is serving a term in the Dawes County jail for liquor law violation and did not appear for hearing.

Harrison Sun, Fri., April 11, 1930

THIRTY DAYS AT HARD LABOR

Nathan Dather, a young man who has been employed on various farms in this community, was apprehended near the Wyoming state line the fore part of the week by Sheriff Williams and brought back to town to answer a charge of removing property from the home of Gordon Bartell. Dather had been employed at the Bartell farm for a short time, but tiring of the farm grind he picked up a watch, a leather coat and some other articles, and hiked out. The theft was reported in time to pick Dather up before he left the state, and at a hearing in county court was found guilty and sentenced to jail for thirty days, with the additional penalty of hard labor.

Harrison Sun, Fri., May 16, 1930

PETER SWANSON IS DRAGGED TO DEATH BY SADDLE HORSE

Sheriff Williams was called to Glen Friday of last week to investigate the cause of death of Peter Swanson, old time Sioux County settler. It was rumored that Mr. Swanson may have been murdered, but a thorough examination revealed the facts as set forth in the article following, which was written by the Sun's correspondent at Glen:

The community was shocked Friday with the news of the tragic death of Peter Swanson, which occurred on Thursday in a terrible manner. Thursday morning Mr. Swanson went to the Petersen place to look after his cattle and noticing something after his young calves, went back to the ranch for a rifle. He failed to come back that evening, but as he had mentioned going up to the Sam Chrismen place on business, Clay McIntosh and wife, who were working for him, thought he must have gone on up there and was delayed in getting home. As he did not appear in the morning an alarm was raised and George James and his riders, Sam Chrismen and sons, and Eldon Lambert started out on horseback to search for him.

George James found him late that evening in a rough spot near the line fence. Evidently he had been killed Thursday morning, as he was found tied to his horse and in a battered condition. The supposition is that he tied the horse to his wrist so that he could hold it if it got frightened while he shot at a coyote or some marauding animal, and the horse becoming frightened jerked him down and ran with him. He was dragged into a canyon where he struck some sharp rocks, as the bruises on his head and scalp and flesh on the rocks indicated. His arm was dislocated and head badly crushed and wrist deeply cut where the rope was tied. The horse was badly frightened and was walking around in circles when they found it. Mr. Swanson's hat, gun and field glasses were found at the spot where he must have fired the gun, but the body was dragged some distance away.

Funeral services were held Monday afternoon at Crawford with interment made by the side of his brother, George, who died a little over two years ago.

Mr. Swanson was an early settler of Sioux County, being associated with this brother, George, on the Soldier Creek ranch, but left here some years ago and moved to Arkansas. At the time of his brother George's death, he was willed the old Fred Pullen ranch and had been making his home there ever since.

Harrison Sun, Fri., April 25, 1930

EARLY HISTORY OF SIOUX COUNTY

Compiled by John H. Newlin

July 17, 1930

In territorial days before 1867, Western Nebraska was divided into two subdivisions with no distinctive border between the two. The West section was known as Beauvais Terra, or Bad Lands, and the East portion as The Great Sand Hills. The county was then much larger than at present. About the only evidence of civilization was the proposed wagon road from Fort Pierre to Fort Laramie, in the northwest corner and roughly paralleling the present Hat Creek.

March 1, 1867, when Nebraska became a state, Sioux County came into existence. Its eastern boundary was the west line of Holt County, and the south line the forty second degree of latitude, its present boundary. It was attached to Cheyenne County for taxation, administrative and judicial purposes for nearly a score of years. By 1883 the eastern part had been divided into four counties: Rock, Brown, Keya Paha and Cherry counties, so that Sioux County comprised the territory now known as Sioux, Dawes, Box Butte, and Sheridan Counties. The legislature of 1885 divided it into Sioux, Dawes, Box Butte and Cherry Counties leaving Sioux County with its present territory.

The first white people to visit Sioux County were the Mallet brothers, then the trappers came. Sage, as early as 1845 made a visit here in connection with the American Fur Company. The next, the establishment of Fort Robinson and the Red Cloud Agency. Edgar Beecher Bronson, tarried on Soldier Creek for a few weeks. Emmons & Brewster established the first ranch in Sioux County, the Warbonnet Ranch, on Warbonnet Creek, north of Harrison. Charles F. Coffee started the 010 Bar Ranch on Hat Creek in 1879. Dr. Graham established the Agate Springs Ranch on Niobrara, or Runningwater about that time.

The first real settlers arrived about 1880, L.E. Beldon being the first man to take a homestead, filing on what is now the Lake Ranch, near the Fort Robinson reservation. Dan Klein came in 1881, and as also did Theodore Trimoue, Henry Kreman, John Foxwell, John Tucker, and Dan Colville, all settling along the banks of White River. Joe Morris, W.H. Zimmerman, Peter and Jake Henry and the Serres brothers all settled in the Hat Creek valley from 1884 to 1887-8. Miss Sadie Morris was the first white child born in the county. Mrs. Katherine Graham was the first white woman to make her home permanently in the county. The first death, and burial in the Harrison Cemetery, was an elderly stranger who died alone in a tent here. The next was Mrs. W.E. Fiddler who was taken sick and died while passing through Harrison. The first wedding was Carl Lux and Rena Fellers. The first religious services held in the county was held at the home of Mrs. Graham at the Agate Springs Ranch.

In June 1886, the Fremont Elkhorn & Missouri Valley railroad reached the present site of Harrison building from Chadron to Casper. The townsite had been named Summit on account of its altitude. But later it was changed to Bowen and in the fall of 1887 was changed to Harrison. The courthouse was built in 1888 by Whitney and Murphy, the brick being burned in Sowbelly canyon. The cost was about $10,000 and was paid by Bowen and Hat Creek precincts. The first paper printed in Sioux County was the Bodarc Record by Charles F. Slingerland.

The first school was taught by Miss Mary Delahunty, in the neighborhood of Fort Robinson. There were forty two pupils enrolled, five white children and the rest half-breeds and quarter bloods.

Ed Satterlee was the first postmaster at Harrison. The first post office established in the county was Warbonnet, at the Warbonnet Ranch with B.E. Brewster postmaster. The Bodarc Record was the newspaper in the county, Charles Slingerland, editor. The first doctor was George J. Shafer. The first ordained minister to hold services in the county was Rev. J.A. Schamahorn. B.F. Thomas was the first county superintendent, and also the first surveyor.(7) J.G. Morris, J.F. Pfost and D.H. Griswold, were the first commissioners, they were appointed by the governor. The first elected officers were: county judge, C.E. Verity; clerk, Charles C. Jamison; treasurer, Edmund C. Lockwood; attorney Edward D. Satterlee; superintendent, Benjamin F. Thomas; sheriff, J.F. Pfost; surveyor, W.M. Pennington; coroner, Charles H. Andrews; commissioners, A.J. McGinley, J.G. Morris and Daniel Klein. The county seat was located at Harrison.

Chief Yellow Hand was killed by Buffalo Bill (W.F. Cody) in the fall of 1876 on Warbonnet Creek. This portion of what was known as Warbonnet Creek is now known as Hat Creek.

The last battle between the Indians and soldiers occurred early in 1879, near what is now the Story post office.(8)

One hundred thousand dollar bonds were voted for the new court house on February 18th, 1930.

The county officers when this was placed here July 21, 1930, were: Sheriff, Charles Sidney Williams; Deputy Sheriff, Joseph Stanek; clerk, Arch C. Davis; deputy clerk, Mary E. Broderick; superintendent, Mrs. Elizabeth Emery; Judge J. H. Wilhermsdorfer; treasurer, E.B. Lyon; deputy treasurer, Anna Lyon; attorney, Albert L. Schnurr; deputy attorney, W.E. Mumby; commissioners, I.D. Hickey, chairman, L.M. Childs and J.C. Lewis; E.L. Goldsmith & Company, Architects, of Scottsbluff, Nebr., and James Fullen, General Contractor, of Gering, Nebraska.

Address to the public and laying of cornerstone by Honorable E.L. Meyer, Judge of the Sixteenth Judicial District of which Sioux County is a part.

Harrison Sun, July 25, 1930

(7)   *B.F. Thomas, first Sioux County superintendent of schools, was your granddad's father-in-law by virtue of his first marriage to Lily Thomas.*

(8)   *This was the last stand of a group of Cheyenne Indians that had broken out of confinement at Ft. Robinson, Jan. 9, 1879. After a two week running fight in the butte country west of the Fort, a remnant band of 31 Cheyennes made a desperate last stand north of Harrison. Most of them were killed.*

Many years ago, as I recollect, Charley Henry, a northern Sioux County rancher, brought into town a human skull he had uncovered when constructing a dam for stock watering purposes. Not much was made of the find at the time. However, years later, Charles Umphenour, a county official, was examining some old surveys and found that the surveyor had meticulously recorded the location of the last stand site of the Cheyennes. Henry's find at the dam site seemed to correlate well with the site described by the surveyor.

Perhaps the Sioux County Historical Society or some other organization should look into the feasibility of placing a marker or monument on the last stand site before time again obscures the memory of the battle location.

POLITICAL ANNOUNCEMENT

C.S. WILLIAMS

I have filed for the nomination of Sheriff of Sioux County on the Republican ticket, and respectfully solicit your support at the primary election in August. Having served for several years in this capacity, I refer you to my record during that time.

Harrison Sun, Fri., July 18, 1930

C.S. WILLIAMS

Republican Candidate for Sheriff of Sioux County

Primary Election August 12, 1930.

In soliciting the support of the voters of Sioux County for the office of Sheriff, I present the following:

> If nominated and elected I will continue the policy of law enforcement as indicated by my record of the past four years—a sensible enforcement with a square deal to all concerned.

> Last year, according to the report of the state sheriff's department, Sioux County ranked near the top in enforcement, based on population.

YOUR VOTE AND SUPPORT APPRECIATED

Harrison Sun, Fri., July 18, 1930

THIEF MAKES GET-AWAY

Upon advice from Torrington the fore part of the week, a man was sought here for the theft of two saddles. It developed that the thief had disposed of one of the saddles to Alex Osback, who upon learning of the fact, hunted the man and found him camped on the roadside west of the Wiley Richardson Ranch. Approaching the stranger, Axel told him what was wanted and while in the act of helping roll up the bed clothes the fellow slipped away in the darkness, leaving his car and has not been heard from since. The car is in possession of the sheriff, and an attempt will be made to bring him back here to answer the charge.

Harrison Sun, Sept. 19, 1930

CAR THIEF IS APPREHENDED AT HEMINGFORD THIS WEEK

The young fellow who made his escape here last week, after selling some stolen saddles in this vicinity, returned last Friday and that night stole Martin Koch's car. The theft was discovered a short time later, and it was possible to track the car about ten miles south of town. Word was sent out to surrounding towns by Sheriff Williams and Monday the marshal at Hemingford phoned that he had the man in custody. Sheriff Williams went after him that day, and found several officers of the law on the job, also wanting the culprit for other thefts.

The young fellow says his name is Edwin Wilkins, and confessed the theft of the Koch car, and also of stripping a model T Ford belonging to John Tangen. Wilkins said he drove out west of the Wiley Richardson ranch to get the car he drove here a few days before, but this car had been brought to town by the sheriff. While out that way he and a partner he had picked up, stripped Tangen's car of the tires, battery and generator, and drove east toward Alliance. They stopped at daylight about fourteen miles northwest of Alliance and cut the back off Koch's car and also dismantled the top, as a matter of precaution, and proceeded on to Hyannis. Leaving Koch's car near that town, they stole a model A Ford and drove back to Hemingford, where Wilkins was caught. Appearing before County Attorney Schnurr, Wilkins signed a confession and he will be taken before Judge Meyer for sentence.

Wilkins not only proved too agile for those who had him cornered southwest of town last week, but also resorted to his fleetness to skip away from the Hemingford marshal, and it was two hours later before he was again in custody.

Wilkins has been following a carnival outfit, and is suspected of having induced two young girls to steal from a residence in Alliance several weeks ago, that they might be provided with gasoline money to travel to the surrounding fairs.

Harrison Sun, Sept. 26, 1930

DRW: Sioux County High School where my sister Ila Mae and I graduated, 1947.

DRW: This is the old grade school where Ila Mae and I attended the First Grade, 1935-36. The building was razed and a new school was built in 1936.

BANK ROBBING BECOMING AN EVERY DAY AFFAIR IN STATE

With four big bank robberies in less than a week, the hold-ups being perpetrated in broad daylight, Nebraska seems to be the mecca for this class of criminals at the present time. Banks at Merriman, Lincoln, Hay Springs, and North Platte have been victimized, and people throughout the state are wondering which will be the next town to be visited.

The robbery at Hay springs yesterday noon had the people of this corner of the state and southwestern South Dakota in a fever of excitement. Last night Harrison and vicinity were aroused when the report came in that the car carrying the bandits was on the road here from Ardmore, and posse(s) were hastily organized and went out to block the roads leading into town from the north and northeast. However, nothing developed throughout the night vigil, and it is fairly well established that the gang got away to the northwest into Wyoming, or else doubled back east through the Black Hills region.

Towns are becoming aroused over the situation, and there is talk of organizing to defend the banks against these gangs of marauders. Most banks are carrying burglary insurance, but none of them like the idea of having a bunch of stick-ups coming in and running off with the money. It seems possible to organize in some manner to protect the banks from hold-ups, and steps to effect prevention of robberies should be taken at once.

Harrison Sun, Sept. 19, 1930

DISTRESS WARRANTS GIVEN SHERIFF FOR COLLECTION

Delinquent personal taxes are collectible by law under a statute providing for the issuance of distress warrants by the county treasurer, and this week a large amount has been turned over to the sheriff for collection in this manner.

There is a total of more than $28,000 of delinquent personal taxes in Sioux County; for the year 1929 and prior years. Last year the amount was about half of the present amount, and there was about $9000 collected.

Harrison Sun, Sept. 26, 1930

THIEVES BREAK INTO OFFICE OF WHITE EAGLE SERVICE STATION

Monday night of this week the office of the White Eagle Service Station was broken into, the perpetrators entering through a window which had been pried open. Breaking the lock on one of the gasoline pumps, the tank was found empty, so the thieves broke the lock on another pump and evidently filled their car. Five bottles of oil were taken from the office, as well as a rim wrench, a flashlight, some tire patch repairs, and about 150 pennies that were in the cash register. Tracks of the car were discernable in the frost when Mr. Lushbough opened the station Tuesday morning, but the identity of the car or persons who did the job has not been established.

Harrison Sun, Thurs., Feb. 26, 1931

FIRST GROUP OF OFFICIALS TO OCCUPY NEW COURTHOUSE

Back row, left to right—J.C.Lewis, County Commissioner; A.L. Schnurr, County Attorney; Mrs. Elizabeth Emery, County Superintendent; I.D. Hickey, Chairman Board of County Commissioners; L.M. Childs, County Commissioner; Anna A. Lyon, Deputy County Treasurer; W.E. Mumby, Deputy County Attorney.

Front row, left to right—Joe Stanek, Deputy Sheriff, C. Sid Williams, Sheriff; Mary E. Broderick, Deputy County Clerk; A.C. Davis, County Clerk and Clerk of the District Court; J.H. Wilhermsdorfer, County Judge.

Harrison Sun, Thurs., March 12, 1931

MEXICAN A SUICIDE

County Attorney W.E. Mumby was notified by phone yesterday morning of the suicide of a young Mexican beet laborer in the south part of the county. According to the report given by Deputy Sheriff J.B. Duncan, the Mexican, who had been employed on the Perkins farm, walked from the house he had been occupying and deliberately shot himself through the head. No motive was given for the Mexican's rash act. He was unmarried.

Harrison Sun, Thurs., March 5, 1931

SHERIFF WILLIAMS GETS MAN FROM ILLINOIS FOR OFFENSE

Sheriff Sid Williams returned from Alton, Ill., yesterday morning, bringing with him Louis H. Hickey, a former soldier at the Fort, who was wanted here for breaking into a farm house northeast of town a short time ago. A warrant was issued for Hickey, who was accused of breaking into the house of Henry Fricke and taking property therefrom, including a check that had been given to Mr. Fricke in payment for some hay. The check had been endorsed and presented for payment by someone other than Mr. Fricke. Hickey admitted to Sheriff Williams that he had taken some property from the Fricke house, but denied having cashed the check.

Hickey is a young man about 24 years of age, and was discharged from the army last November. He had been living in the neighborhood northeast of Harrison. He is being held in jail here and will be given a hearing later.

Harrison Sun, Thurs., March 12, 1931

DISTRICT COURT DOCKET DISPOSED OF IN SHORT SESSION

In the case of the state versus, Jesus Monjarez, the complaining witness failed to appear and defendant was given his freedom. He had been in confinement for several months.

Following is a list of the divorce and civil actions, which were heard and acted upon.

Ila Mae Steele vs. Andrew Thomas Steele, divorce. Dismissed.

Enos Sloan vs. Elizabeth Sloan, divorce. Dismissed.

Theresa Altig vs. William Henry Altig, divorce. Dismissed.

Sylva M. Parmely vs. Arthur G. Parmely, divorce. Continued.

Mona Mae McKim vs. Clyde M. McKim, divorce. Divorce granted the plaintiff.

Wm. S. Nicholson vs. John W. Getchell, foreclosure. Objections overruled, sale confirmed. Defendant given 40 days to file bill of exception.

In the matter of the Estate of Joseph Studivant, deceased, by E.F. Pontius, Admr. Confirmed.(9)

Caroline M. Harris vs. John W. Getchell, foreclosure. Sale confirmed.

The Royal Highlanders vs. Edward Leathers, foreclosure. Sale confirmed.

Carl Ehrdardt vs. John Watts and John A. Anderson, money judgement. Found for plaintiff.

Harrison Sun, Fri., Dec. 3, 1926

CAR STOLEN SUNDAY NIGHT IS LOCATED AT EDGEMONT

The W.J. Lacy & Son Garage was broken into early Monday morning, the intruder gaining entrance by smashing a glass at the rear of the building. John Marking, who runs the power plant on the night shift, heard a disturbance at the garage and went over to investigate. Before he reached the building a car was driven through the alley and John found the front doors ajar and phoned Mr. Lacy, who came down but at that time determined nothing was missing. The next morning, however, it was found that an Essex coupe belonging to Carl Dallam was gone, and Sheriff Williams phoned nearby places to be on the lookout for the car. Yesterday afternoon the sheriff was advised the car had been found beside the road near Edgemont, and he and Clint Townsend left last evening to bring it to Harrison.

Harrison Sun, Thurs., May 28, 1931

FIFTEEN DAYS FOR BUM CHECK

Guy Millburn, claiming Lusk as his home, was arrested last Wednesday on a charge of passing a bad check at the Oxford Hotel. At a hearing in county court he plead guilty and was given fifteen days in the county jail, plus costs.

Harrison Sun, Thurs., June 18, 1931

---

(9)   *The above article was split into two sections. The section pertaining to Fred Cunningham is under that part dealing with the Cunningham problem. Grandmother Sturdivant, as already discussed, lost the ranch due to foreclosure in 1927.*

ALBERT T. GLADE ARRESTED ON CHARGE OF STATUTORY OFFENSE

Rosa Sage, a woman about sixty years of age, filed a complaint against Albert T. Glade, 55, charging the latter with statutory assault, the offense allegedly having been committed Monday night of this week. Glade has been employed at the Warneke ranch for about a year, and the complainant, whose home is in Mitchell, came to the ranch Sunday to serve as housekeeper. Sheriff Williams brought Glade to town Tuesday and the latter was arraigned in county court and entered a plea of not guilty. His bond was fixed at $1500 pending preliminary hearing July 6th. Glade is being held in custody upon failure to procure the bond.

Harrison Sun, Thurs., June 25, 1931

Russell - "I'll Never Be Taken Alive"

The two cases we are mostly concerned with here are that of Dick Witt and Charley Russell. Dick Witt, my wife's uncle, was arrested three (3) times, and will be discussed in a later section.

Charley Russell, was also arrested three (3) times and is the man who said he would never be taken alive and is also believed to have originated the story of the dynamite blast set off to scare away the sheriff.

Who was Charley Russell? The following information was taken from an article written by Wilbur M. Westler and printed in the Sioux County History Book, First 100 years, 1886-1986. (10)

Charley M. Russell was born during the civil war in 1863, Marshall County, Iowa.

He came west with his parents and siblings, Frank, Belle, Mae and Harvey Jr. They filed on a 640 acre homestead on White River, 15 miles southeast of Harrison. They added another two sections later.

He always carried two 44 colt revolvers, just as he had in the wild west days. These served as a backup when having numerous quarrels with his neighbors and others. He apparently had little regard for the law because he never got law enforcement officers involved in his squabbles.

One day, Harvey Jr. failed to show up for supper and Charley rode out, fearing the worst. He found him shot in the back. He placed the lifeless body over the horse and took Harvey home. Westler does not state if the killer was ever identified.

(10)   In 2009 at Harrison, Keith Mumby, Grand Junction, Colo., and son of the late W.E. Mumby, former Sioux County attorney, related to me an incident concerning his father and Charley Russell. I don't know the exact date of the incident, but it was probably sometime after Mr. Mumby became county attorney in 1928.

Keith said Mr. Mumby was working at his desk in the court house when Charley Russell came into the office, introduced himself, and banged down a cartridge, (likely that of a 44 caliber taken from a revolver) on Mumby's desk and announced: "This is my calling card." I don't know what the county attorney's response was, but we can surmise that if this bizarre form of introducing himself was meant as a form of intimidation it was a dismal failure as all arrest warrants against Charley Russell were successful and he was prosecuted according to the law.

A few months later a neighbor was found shot to death and Charley having been overheard making threats against the victim was arrested and a jury convicted Russell. He was sentenced to the State Penitentiary at Lincoln for a life term. Five years later another man admitted to the murder and Charley was released. Linda Staudenmaier in the same history book identifies the murdered man as Alois Staudenmaier shot to death by a horse thief on March 29, 1900.(11)

Charles was also a gunsmith, a great reader, philosopher, ran a sawmill and free with lots of advice.

Frontier Model 44-40 caliber six shooter used by my grandfather,

Joseph H. Sturdivant, 1880's-1900. Joe carried this revolver

while trailing large herds of cattle on the Chisholm Trail, Texas

to Nebraska during the 1880's. This revolver is very similar to

the 44-40 caliber six shooters carried by Charlie Russell when

he was arrested(3) times by your grandfather.

(11)   I knew Alois' son Charlie Staudenmaier and went to high school with Alois' grandson, Charles Staudenmaier. The grandson had lost his feet in a mowing accident; was fitted with artificial feet; although he had a bad limp-got around ok.

My wife, Elaine (Witt), who was raised about 10 miles south of the Russell place, states that to the best of her knowledge Russell didn't have a car or truck. Charles made occasional trips to town on a saddle horse or with horses and wagon for ranch supplies and to replenish ammunition for his weapons.

During the blizzard of 1949 they ran out of firewood and nearly froze to death. He died in the hospital Feb. 1949, aged 85 years, 7 months.

I remember seeing Charley Russell once. The year was about 1947-48. He was in the office of the Morrison Lumber Co. and was using crutches. He was pointed out to me by one of my friends, Ralph Hildebrand. He wasn't wearing his guns then, probably knowing better.

Released after serving five (5) years in the Nebraska State Penitentiary he vowed never to go to jail again or be taken alive.

The first arrest of Russell by your granddad was on a charge of assault by a Henry Sweezy on Jan. 27, 1931. He got out of it with only two days of jail time.

The second arrest was made only seven months later on Jan. 25, 1932 on a charge of forced entry. The charge was by the Cutlers. It appears that one of Russell's cows was killed and butchered by someone and he thought the Cutlers had done it. He forced his way into their house, wearing his guns, scared them half to death, busted up some of their stuff and threatened retribution. Apparently, it never occurred to Russell to get the law involved in the cow killing incident.

As soon as the Cutlers could extricate themselves from the situation they went to Harrison and swore out a warrant for Russell's arrest. Again your granddad somehow made the arrest unaided and brought Russell in. He served three days for this incident in county jail and bound over to district court.

Russell, on being released from jail, told your granddad that that was the last time he would ever allow himself to be arrested. Dad asked him if that was a threat. Russell's answer was silence.

The next arrest of Russell was made six (6) years later on a charge of threatening to shoot J.B. Bravard. It is intimidating enough to get in an argument with someone wearing guns, especially so if that person draws his gun, cocks it, points it at you, and then threatens to blow you away. Bravard wasted no time in getting to town and swearing out a complaint.

Dad, already suffering from the ailment that would take his life seven (7) months later was now faced with how to arrest Russell without getting into a shoot-out. Several of your granddad's friends advised him not to go after Russell because of the danger of a shoot-out.

However, Dad devised a plan. He knew that Russell had blooded horses. Everyone knew that Dad was interested in race-horses and that he had even bought an excellent colt from Jack Lacy. The horse 'Donald W' turned out to be a record setter. This was generally known by the public because news items had appeared in the Harrison Sun about the horse purchase and his racing ability. So, it wouldn't appear unreasonable to others that Sid was looking for other horses to buy from local residents.

How the meeting with Russell was arranged is unclear. The arrest warrant shows a mileage charge of 60 miles or $4.80 @ $.15/mile. This would indicate two trips to Russell's place – 15 miles out and 15 miles back – two times. The first trip may have been an exploratory trip to see what kind of horses Russell had and to give Russell a few days to round them up and get them in the corral for inspection.

The arrest warrant was dated Oct. 25, 1937 and the arrest was seven days later on Nov. 1. The warrant shows French in attendance. He was a newly hired town marshal and not well known in Harrison or the county. I suspect Dad may have presented French as his horse trainer.

The other possibility for the first trip is that Dad found no one home, necessitating a second trip.

The arrest – The horses were in the corral. Russell and Dad had their arms on the rail and were busily engaged in discussing the merits and characteristics of the horses. Russell had his cartridge belt and guns on as usual. Dad was unarmed having left his gun in the car to lay to rest any suspicions that he was at the Russell place to make an arrest.

During the conversation Dad edged closer to Russell, who was absorbed in boasting of his horses' merits. This move did not raise any suspicions by Russell. Suddenly Dad grabbed one of Russell's guns and at the same time gave him a shove, momentarily throwing him off balance. By the time Russell recovered Dad had Russell's gun cocked and pointed at him with the warning not to move. I suppose at this point French moved in and removed Russell's other gun.

According to the jail house records Russell served 65 days to Jan. 4, 1938. The following documents indicate considerable legal activity regarding Russell.

Your grandmother, LaVerne Davison, and Sid Jr. told me this story several times with little variance. Of course, Dad being the source of this version, one would not expect much difference.

Never was any mention made to me about the dynamite story or by any of the other county officials. I suspect Russell, being very upset about being arrested, had concocted a plan of what he would do if the sheriff ever came around again. This plan was told often enough that people began to believe that it actually happened.

I searched through all the courthouse files for the period of your granddad's tenure as sheriff, April 1926-May 6, 1938. I found that all the arrest warrants sworn out for Russell's arrest, as well as all other warrants for that matter, were carried out efficiently and effectively. There is absolutely nothing to the dynamite story.

Thus, the title: **BRING 'EM BACK ALIVE SID** continued to grow.

One further note concerning the Russell story: We had been to Harrison on vacation and were preparing to leave for our ranch in Okfuskee County, Oklahoma. The date was the morning of Monday, July 29, 1996 and I was in Herren's Ranch supply store to buy a styrofoam cooler to transport some perishables and was introduced by Dick Herren to George Wasserburger whom I already knew (he didn't seem to know me). However, when I explained that I used to wait on him when I worked at Leslie DeKay's Standard Service Station part time while attending high school in the late 1940's and that I was the youngest son of Sid Williams, Sr. George W: "Well, I guess then that I knew Sid a lot better than I knew you." He proceeded to tell me a story of Dad and Charley Russell, a gunslinger who always carried two guns, western style. The conversation went about as follows:

George W: "Charley Russell ranched on White River. I was just a boy living in the White River Valley at the time and Russell scared me the way he would come galloping toward you carrying those guns. The Cutlers, neighbors, killed and butchered one of Russell's cows which the Cutlers claimed they mistook for a deer. Seems Russell took the law into his own hands – invaded the Cutler house; smashed their rifle over a stove and generally raised hell and terrorized the Cutlers. The Cutlers filed charges. Russell said he would never be taken out alive and he could only be taken out DEAD. Sid went down, and by G___ he brought him in."

Don: "Well, Dad arrested Russell several times. I don't know which arrest it was but on one occasion he went to Russell's place on the pretext of buying horses. While they were at the corral examining Russell's horses, Dad managed to sidle close to Russell without raising suspicion and at the opportune moment suddenly grabbed Russell's revolver and pointed it at him and succeeded in making the arrest."(12)

Dick H: "Someone should write all this down. Don, maybe that someone should be you."

Don W.: "Well, maybe – I haven't thought much about it."

I went immediately to our house and wrote down the conversation, as related here. There was no mention of any dynamite story.

George Wasserburger died June 11, 1998, aged 81 years.

(12)   *After doing all this research, I now believe the episode related here occurred during the 3rd arrest.*

Following are news items and court records regarding the Charley Russell problem:

SEVERAL CASES ARE HEARD IN COUNTY COURT DURING WEEK

Henry Sweezy of near Glen swore out a complaint against Charley Russell accusing the latter of assault. It developed that Mr. Sweezy and Mr. Russell had a few words and the former attempted to hit the latter with a cane, and Mr. Russell said he took the cane from Sweezy and poked him in the ribs a couple of times. Mr. Russell was placed under bonds to keep the peace. Another neighborhood misunderstanding near Glen resulted in a warrant being sworn out for Mrs. Guy Yohe, she being accused by Mrs. Anna Weber of assault. This hearing will be heard later in the week.

Dan and Bill Slattery are summoned into court Tuesday on a complaint filed by the water commissioner, the Slatterys being charged with disturbing a lock placed on a headgate from the stream that is used for stock and irrigation purposes by residents below the Slattery ranch. This case will go to the district court for final hearing. There has been some disagreement between the Slatterys and Clarence Dout, the latter having a ranch just below the Slatterys, the latter claiming full right to the water that is said to originate from the springs on their land holdings. This case was argued in several courts and an appeal to the supreme court of Nebraska developed that Mr. Dout had riparian rights to the water from the creek.

Harry Baldwin was brought before the judge on complaint brought by the Lowry Hotel, on a charge of attempting to beat a board bill. Baldwin had been given several weeks to make proper adjustment of the account but on failure to do so was again brought into court and assessed costs, including the account which amounted to $34.

Harrison Sun, Thurs., July 30, 1931

GIVEN 60 DAYS IN JAIL FOR MAKING MENACING THREAT

On a complaint made by J.B. Bravard, Charley Russell was taken into custody Tuesday and at a hearing in county court Wednesday was given a sentence of sixty days in the county jail and assessed the costs of prosecution amounting to $15.(13)

The complaint grew out of a neighborhood quarrel, and Bravard stated that Russell made threat of shooting the former. Both are residents of the Glen community.

Harrison Sun, Thurs., Nov. 4, 1937

JAIL HOUSE HISTORY-CHARLES RUSSELL

Arrest #1 – Charley Russell arrested June 27, 1931 on a charge of assault. He was in county jail 2 days to June 28th.

Arrest #2 – Charley Russell arrested Jan. 25, 1932 and was in the county jail to Jan. 27, 1932 on a charge of forced entry.

Arrest #3 – Charley Russell arrested Nov. 1, 1937 on a charge of threats & served 65 days to Jan. 4, 1938.

(13) *The late Rick Mounts, Deputy Sheriff, allowed me to examine the jail records for the period 1926-1938 that includes Dad's tenure as sheriff. See text that follows about Charles Russell and a later text about the Dick Witt arrests.*

210 – COMPLAINT   Printed and for sale by the Omaha Printing Company, Omaha

IN THE County   COURT OF   Sioux   COUNTY, NEBRASKA.

THE STATE OF NEBRASKA,
vs.
                                        } Complaint for   Assault and Battery
Charles M. Russell

STATE OF NEBRASKA,
County of Sioux   } ss.

Count 1

The complaint and information of   Henry Swezey
of the county aforesaid, made in the name of the State of Nebraska, before me, the County Judge, within and for
said county, this   27th   day of   July   A. D. 19 31, who being duly sworn,
on his oath, says that   Charles M. Russell   on the   24th   day of
July   A. D. 19 31, in the county aforesaid then and there being, did then and there

unlawfully and wilfully threaten the said Henry Swezey in a threatening manner

Count 2

And the said Henry Swezey, being further sworn on oath, doth say that the said
Charles M. Russell, then and there being, then and there on or about the 24th
day of July, 1931, did then and there unlawfully and wilfully strike the said
Henry Swezey

contrary to the form of Statutes in such cases made and provided, and against the peace and dignity of the people
of the State of Nebraska.

X Henry Swezey

(SEAL)   Subscribed in my presence, and sworn to before me, this   27th
           day of   July   , 19 31 .

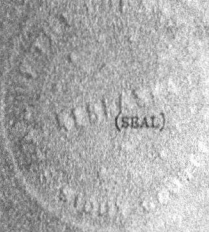

                                        County Judge.

No. 43.

WARRANT

THE STATE OF NEBRASKA
vs.

Charles M. Russell

Returned and filed this

28th day of July 19___

J.H. _____
County Judge

275 — Printed and for sale by Omaha Printing Co., Omaha

STATE OF NEBRASKA,
Sioux } ss.
COUNTY

Received this warrant July 27 1931
and pursuant to the command thereof I have

arrested the within named

Charles M. Russell

and now have his body before the Court.

Dated this 28 day of July 31.

C. S. Williams

Sheriff of Sioux County

FEES

Arrest	$	1.00
Mileage 30 Miles	$	4 50
Attendance	$	
Total	$	5 50

WARRANT

IE STATE OF NEBRASKA

vs.

Charles M. Russell.

and filed this

4 day of *January* 19 32.

[signature]

County Judge

STATE OF NEBRASKA,
COUNTY *[ink blot]* Sioux } ss.

Received this warrant 22 nd Jan. 19 32

and pursuant to the command thereof I have

arrested the within named

Charles M Russell

and now have his body before the Court.

Dated this 25 day of Jan 19 32.

C. S. Williams

Sheriff of Sioux County

FEES

Arrest	$1.00
Mileage 70 Miles $	10 50
Attendance $	1 00
Total $	12 50

IN THE County COURT OF Sioux COUNTY, NEBRASKA Ex-1

THE STATE OF NEBRASKA,
vs.

Charles M. Russell

Complaint for Feloniously entering
Building- Section 28-539

STATE OF NEBRASKA,
County of Sioux
} ss.

The complaint and information of C.S.Williams, County Sheriff of the county aforesaid, made in the name of the State of Nebraska, before me, the County Judge, within and for said county, this 20th day of January A. D. 1932, who being duly sworn, on his oath, says that Charles M. Russell on the 20th day of January A. D. 1932, in the county aforesaid then and there being, did then and there

wilfully, unlawfully and feloniously enter the dwelling house of Jennie Cutler armed with a dangerous weapon, to wit: a revolver, with the intent to rob and steal, and did then and there threaten to disfigure, maim and kill Hugh Hiatt and Glenn Cutler, and then and there ordered the said Hugh Hiatt to relinquish and hand over to the said Charles M. Russell certain personal property, to wit: a 25-35 caliber Winchester rifle, then and there being situate in said dwelling house, and the property of the said Glenn Cutler

contrary to the form of Statutes in such cases made and provided, and against the peace and dignity of the people of the State of Nebraska.

C. S. Williams
County Sheriff.

Subscribed in my presence, and sworn to before me, this 20th day of January , 1932 .

(SEAL)

J H Williamson
County Judge.

943—COMPLAINT—(Long Form) **Any Court**

STATE OF NEBRASKA, } ss.
Sioux County, IN County COURT, OF
Sioux COUNTY,

THE STATE OF NEBRASKA, vs.
Charles M. Russell

FOR

COMPLAINT

Menacing Threats

The complaint and information of J. B. Bravard of Sioux County aforesaid, made in the name of the State of Nebraska, before me, the undersigned Magistrate, within and for said County of Sioux, State of Nebraska, this 25th day of October A. D. 1937, who being duly sworn, on oath says, that Charles M. Russell

on or about the 23 day of October A. D. 19 37, in the County of Sioux and State of Nebraska, then and there being did then and there unlawfully and knowingly assualt and threaten in a menacing manner the said J. B. Bravard and did then and there in a menacing manner threaten to shoot and kill the said J. B. Bravard.

contrary to the form of the Statutes in such cases made and provided, and against the peace and dignity of the State of Nebraska.

J B Bravard

Subscribed in my presence and sworn to before me this 25 day of October 19 37.

County Judge

No. 209 Doc. 1 Page 216

State Complaint
Sioux COURT

THE STATE OF NEBRASKA

Charles M. Russell

Filed this 25th day of October A. D. 1937

WITNESSES FOR THE STATE
N. B.—Get full name, address and telephone number of Witnesses.

No. 209-Doc. 1, Page 216

WARRANT

THE STATE OF NEBRASKA vs.

Charles M. Russell

Returned and filed this 2nd day of November 1937

County Judge

STATE OF NEBRASKA, } ss.
Sioux County

Received this warrant October 25 19 37 and pursuant to the command thereof I have arrested the within named Charles M. Russell

and now have his body before the Court.

Dated this 2nd day of November 1937

C. S. William
Sheriff of Sioux County.

FEES

Arrest		$1.00
Mileage 60 Miles	$	4.80
Attendance French	$	3.00
Total	$	8.80

IN THE COUNTY COURT OF SIOUX COUNTY, NEBRASKA

State of Nebraska

       Plaintiff

    Vs   PEACE BOND

Charles M. Russell

       Defendant

State of Nebraska, County of Sioux, SS: Be it remembered that
on the 3rd day of January, 1938, Charles M. Russell as principal
and _____Van W. Westler_____ and _____Frank S. Russell_____
of Sioux County and State of Nebraska, aforesaid appeared personally
before the undersigned J. H. Wilhermsdorfer, County Judge in and
for the County of Sioux and State of Nebraska and jointly and
severally acknowledged themselves to be indebted to the State
of Nebraska in the sum of One Thousand Dollars ($1000.00) to be
made and levied on their respective goods, chattels, lands and
tenements, to be void however, if the said Charles M. Russell
shall personally be and appear before the District Court of Sioux
County, Nebraska, on the first day of the next term thereof or
forthwith if it be term time of said District Court and in the
meantime be of good behavior generally and especially toward J. B.
Bravard and shall further deliver to the Sheriff of Sioux County
all the fire arms owned by him or in his possession or under his
control to be kept in the vault of the Sheriff of Sioux County
pending the final outcome of the final disposition of this action,
and to do and receive what shall be enjoined by said court upon
him and shall not depart from said court without leave.

    Witness our hands this 3rd day of January, 1938.

                              Charles M. Russell.
                              Principal

Witness:

_____*W. Elm...*_____   *Van W. Westler*
                           Surety

                           Frank S. Russell
                           Surety

1-3-38

213

PLEADS GUILTY TO DISTURBING FISH IN NURSERY POND

Lee Blevins of near Andrews plead guilty in county court this week to disturbing fish in a nursery pond and was sentenced to thirty days in jail and assessed the costs of prosecution. A charge of seining trout from White River, in the preserve area above Andrews was also placed against Blevins, although this charge was dropped because of insufficient evidence.

Officials of the game and fish department and local sportsmen have experienced considerable difficulty during the past few years in stocking streams in this vicinity with trout. There has been illegal trapping and seining of fish and those who have put in considerable time and effort to increase the supply of fish in the streams are about to give up hope.

Harrison Sun, Thurs., July 23, 1931

SUICIDE CASE IN SOUTH PART OF COUNTY LAST SATURDAY

County Attorney W.E. Mumby and Sheriff Williams were called to the south part of the county last Saturday to investigate a suicide case. William Vaughan, who had been employed on the Clark Jones place north of Henry, died as a result of self-inflicted gunshot wounds, the investigation proved. Mr. Vaughan, who was about 34 years of age, had come from Illinois about five months ago to work on the Jones place, and according to testimony given by Mrs. Vaughan, he had made the statement that morning that he was not doing himself nor Mr. Jones any good and wanted to leave. Mrs. Vaughan discouraged him of this notion, telling him he just felt despondent.

Vaughan secured a gun and walked out of doors and shot himself in the head, dying a few hours later.

Harrison Sun, Thurs., Aug. 20, 1931

FILLING STATION ROBBED

Thieves entered the Barnes filling station Tuesday night of this week, but did not take anything of much value. Some oil was taken, a gallon measure can, and also some tire and tube patching material.

There was evidence that someone attempted to break into the White Eagle station the same night. Marks on the north window showed an effort was made to pry open the sash. At the Barnes station the lock was removed from the door.

Harrison Sun, Thurs., Aug. 20, 1931

BOUND OVER TO DISTRICT COURT

In the preliminary hearing of Manie Knori on a charge of cattle stealing, held in county court last week, the defendant was bound over to district court.

Harrison Sun, Thurs., Oct. 30, 1931

ARRAIGNED ON CATTLE THEFT

Following the killing and butchering of a heifer on the L.C. Sine place northwest of Harrison October 12th, Manie Knori was arraigned in county court yesterday, the complaint against the defendant being cattle stealing. The date for the preliminary hearing was set for October 30th. The defendant was released under bond following his arrest early in the week. Pete Maguire, who was also taken up in connection with the alleged stealing, is being held in the county jail.(14)

Harrison Sun, Thurs., Oct. 22, 1931

PROPERTY TAKEN FROM RANCH IN SOUTHEAST PART OF COUNTY

George Schnell, rancher in the southeast corner of the county, last week asked the sheriff's office to investigate the looting of his ranch two weeks ago, when property valued at several hundred dollars was taken. No one was at the place at the time the robbery was committed and Mr. Schnell reports the loss of two truckloads of rye, two truckloads of hogs, a cream separator, two sets of harness, a rifle, $35 worth of groceries and some well tools. Sheriff Williams was busy in district court at the time the report came in and Deputy Sheriff J.B. Duncan went to the ranch to investigate the robbery. No trace of the property has been found at the present time.

Harrison Sun, Thurs., Sept. 17, 1931

PROPERTY TAKEN FROM RANCH IN SE PART OF COUNTY

A young fellow giving the name of S.W. Warren, a transient who had been doing odd jobs at the Oxford Hotel, was arrested last Saturday night by Sheriff Williams on advise from Chadron that a few items of clothing had been stolen from the way-car of the stock train while on the siding here Saturday afternoon. Search of the garage, where Warren had been sleeping, resulted in the finding of a pair of shoes and a rain coat.

Warren admitted the pair of shoes he was wearing had also been stolen by him from the car. In county court Monday morning Warren plead guilty to petty larceny and was sentenced to two weeks in the county jail at hard labor.

With others incarcerated in the jail, the village has been making good use of the prisoners, who have been raking up the rock on the streets south of the county property and the back street.

Harrison Sun, Thurs., Sept. 17, 1931

FOUR MEN ATTEMPT ROBBERY OF KOCH STORE SUNDAY NIGHT

Quick justice was meted out to the four men who attempted the robbery of the Koch Mercantile store early Monday morning. All four of the men were caught Monday, arraigned before County Judge Wilhermsdorfer that afternoon, when they entered pleas of guilty to the grand larceny indictment of breaking and entering, and taken to Alliance to appear before District Judge E.L. Meyer Tuesday and receive their sentences.

The men gave the names of James McCoy, Golden, Colo., Arthur Blake and Ralph Johnson of Lawton, Okla., and Richard Arnold of Mannington, W.Va. McCoy, who was the first caught and seemed to be new to this sort of game, was sentenced to the penitentiary for a term of from one to two years. The other three received sentences of from two to five years each for their part in the crime.

MARSHALL ON THE JOB

The apprehension of the four robbers the frustration of their plans to rob the Koch store of approximately $1000 worth

(14)   *The jail house records do not indicate that Manie Knori served any county jail time. Pete McGuire on the other hand served time from Oct. 16, 1931 to March 17, 1932 when a bond was arranged.*

215

of merchandise is due to the fact that John Marking, who is employed by the village to operate the power plant on the night shift and also serve as marshal, was "on the job."

Coming down the alley about two o'clock Monday morning, John noticed a car parked at the rear door of the Koch store and stepped around the corner of the building to watch developments. One of the men came out to the car and John drew his gun and ordered the fellow to "stick 'em up," which request met immediate response. Another of the men came to the door at that time, and had an armload of shirts which he intended to put in the car. Not knowing whether or not the men were armed, John shot in the air, thinking he might be able to arouse somebody nearby, but this sent the other three robbers out the front door and they made their get-away. The captured man was taken to the jail and word was sent to Sheriff Williams, who came down immediately, and with the assistance of other men of the town who had been summoned a search was made for the three men who had made their escape.

A second member of the gang was found in the fire-escape at the grade school. Meanwhile the remaining two men had taken to the railroad track east of town, and most of the search was directed in the vicinity of Andrews and Glen. Monday afternoon the men were found east of Glen and the officers had no difficulty in making the arrest, although the men denied they had been in Harrison at the time of the robbery and knew nothing about it. However, when brought before the two who had been previously captured, the latter admitted they were the ones wanted, and later they told Sheriff Williams they were guilty.

Finger prints of the men were taken, and in an interview with County Attorney Mumby, all four men signified a willingness to plead guilty to the charges placed against them, thus saving the county considerable expense of trial.

The older man of the gang, McCoy, was in Harrison a short time ago and had been befriended by John Marking, who permitted him to remain in the office at the power plant one cold night, and John is quite certain another of the gang has been in Harrison before. The men had evidently formed their plan of robbery while in Casper a few days before, and coming to Harrison broke in Ed Meier's garage and stolen the car to use in making away with the merchandise.

In telling the officers of the attempted robbery, one of the men said they had been in the store for an hour and a half, and had spent the time in picking out the more valuable class of merchandise. Shirts and shoes were taken from the boxes, and the empty boxes placed back on the shelves. A quantity of the goods had been placed in the car when John arrived at the scene, but a larger amount was in piles on the floor ready to be taken to the car.

Harrison Sun, Thurs., Dec. 31, 1931

THIS MAN'S BUSINESS OPERATIONS REQUIRES MANY ALIASES

Barton Ackley, the man of many aliases, was apprehended in Mitchell Saturday of last week by Sheriff Sid Williams and returned to Harrison to answer for the passing of a couple of bum checks. Presenting a check to the Koch Mercantile company in October, he received $12 in cash, using a small part of the amount to pay for some small purchases. The check was given on C.R. Wasserburger, payable to Jack Mitchell.

The check was turned down at the bank, there being no such account carried at the bank. Later in the week he passed another check, using the same names, at

Marstellers and the following day this check was also denied payment at the bank. Vern Marsteller made inquiry and learned the said "Mitchell" had departed early that morning for the town of Mitchell, and notified Attorney Mumby, who got out a warrant and Sheriff Williams went after the check artist.

It developed Ackley had opened an account at the bank in Mitchell under the name of "Gordon Carter," he drawing out his balance before returning with the sheriff. He has been in this community for several weeks, and was known as Smokey Acton and at other places as Smokey Vernon. He had registered at a local hotel under the name of George Knori.

Ackley was arraigned in county court Monday morning on two counts, one of forging checks and the other indictment was for forging an endorsement to checks. He plead guilty and was taken to Alliance to be arraigned before District Judge E.L. Meyer for sentence. Ackley was sentenced to serve not more than one nor less than two years in the state reformatory on each count, the sentences to run concurrently.(15) A fine of $12 on each count was also imposed, and Ackley made restitution of the amounts of the checks. He claims his home is in the Cherokee country of Oklahoma.

Harrison Sun, Thurs., Nov. 12, 1931

BEGIN PENITENTIARY SENTENCES

Sheriff C.S. Williams and W.E. Mumby left Monday evening of this week for Lincoln, in charge of the four men who plead guilty to burglarizing the Koch Mercantile, where the latter were delivered to the warden of the state penitentiary to begin their terms in the state penal institution. The four men were James McCoy, sentenced to one to two years; Arthur Blake, Ralph Johnson and Richard Arnold, the three latter to serve from two to five years.

Harrison Sun, Thurs., Dec. 14, 1932

SHERIFF WILLIAMS HURT IN CAR WRECK NEAR CROOKSTON

Failing to make a turn in the highway just at the edge of the town of Crookston, Sheriff Williams was seriously injured in a car wreck Monday morning of this week. Sheriff Williams was en route to Norfolk and had as his passenger Charles Root, whom he was taking to the state sanitarium.

Mrs. Williams and Mrs. Ferd Federle left that afternoon for Valentine, where both Mr. Williams and Mr. Root were taken and placed in a hospital for medical attention. W.E. Mumby and Judge Wilhermsdorfer also left for Valentine Monday evening, returning Tuesday evening and brought back word that Sid is pretty badly hurt, but it is thought he will be able to return home in a few days. Sid was unable to give any cause for the accident, but from information gained by those who saw the accident it is thought that Sid was going too fast to make the complete turn and the car went into the embankment, throwing the men through the windshield, although the car did not turn over. When help arrived both Sid and Root were unconscious, with blood streaming from wounds about the head, and were rushed to the Valentine hospital. Root soon regained consciousness, but Sid was irrational until about seven o'clock that evening.

(15)   *I believe the original article in the Harrison Sun was miswritten and that the sentences of Barton Ackley should read: Ackley was sentenced to serve not more than two years nor less than one year in the state reformatory on each count, the sentences to run concurrently.*

217

Sid's chest was crushed when thrown on the steering wheel, and he received several bad cuts on the head, and bruises about the body. Root was also cut about the head, although not as seriously injured as Sid.

The car was badly damaged.

J.B. Duncan from the south part of the county and former deputy sheriff, is in charge of the sheriff's office during the absence of Sid Williams.

Harrison Sun, Thurs., June 23, 1932

Sid Williams returned home Friday morning of last week from Valentine, where he had been in a hospital for several days following an auto accident. Sid is pretty much bruised up and has several bad cuts, but says he feels fortunate that the accident did not prove more serious.(16)

Harrison Sun, Thurs., June 30, 1932

PICKS 'EM UP IN A HURRY

Sheriff Williams had two calls last week from sheriffs in adjoining counties, and in each case the parties to be apprehended fell right into the waiting arms of the law. Thursday of last week the sheriff at Torrington phoned to be on the lookout for Earl Green, wanted there for appropriating a Hudson car. Sheriff Williams went to the Oxford hotel to inquire of him, Green having been employed there some time ago, and while he was at the hotel Green drove up in the car. The Torrington sheriff came that day to take Green back to answer the charge of car theft.

Tuesday Sheriff Williams just stepped from the courthouse following a call from the sheriff at Lusk to be on the lookout for a young girl who was leaving home to see the world, and observed a car driving into town with the girl a passenger. She had been picked up by tourists, telling them she was coming to Harrison to see her grandmother. However, her grandmother does not live here. She was returned to her home.

Harrison Sun, Thurs., Aug. 18, 1932

SEPT. TERM DIST. COURT COMPLETED IN DAYS SESSION

Judge E.L. Meyer came over from Alliance Tuesday and held a term of district court, this being an equity term with no jury summoned. Most of the cases heard before Judge Meyer were civil actions, although Fred Brothwell, who has been held for complicity in the stealing and butchering of a heifer in the south part of the county, was brought before the court. The original charge of actual participation in the crime was altered to accessory after the fact to which Brothwell plead guilty. He was sentenced to sixty days in jail at hard labor, fined $100 and ordered to pay costs.

But one case occupied any great length of time, that being the State of Nebraska vs. E.J. Emmons, an action brought in behalf of the Department of Public Welfare to enjoin Mr. Emmons from practicing medicine or surgery in the state of Nebraska. The defendant in the case contended he was practicing physical healing which does not

---

(16) Your granddad was injured quite badly, as indicated by the newspaper article, on Monday, June 20, 1932. He came home early, against the doctor's advice, four (4) days later on Fri., June 24.

The doctor was fearful and warned that Sid needed a few more days of recuperation or the injuries could lead to more serious problems. The warning was prophetic. The accident had dire consequences and was a factor in his death six years later.

conflict with the statutes pertaining to any of the healing arts as set forth therein. Several witnesses were examined and at the conclusion of the hearing the court granted a temporary injunction, and the matter of a permanent injunction was taken under advisement by the court. This order will enjoin the defendant from practicing medicine or surgery or any of the healing arts, or representing himself to be a doctor in any of the healing arts.

Harrison Sun, Thurs., Sept. 8, 1932

RECOVERS STOLEN CAR

Some prowling individual entered the editor's back yard, early Monday morning, and shoved the latter's car into the alley. To be safe from interference, the thief wheeled the car by man-power for some distance, later taking off and leaving for parts unknown. Buck Jordan saw the car cross the main street intersection, heading west, but attached no significance to it at the time. Monday morning Sheriff Williams wired information to surrounding towns, and Tuesday morning Sheriff Hassed phoned from Lusk that the car had been found there Monday evening. After herding the wreck that far the thief evidently concluded he could pick up a better one and abandoned it in the rear of the lumber yard at Lusk. Aside from taking the jack from the tool-box nothing more was missing and the car was none the worse for the trip.

Harrison Sun, Thurs., Sept. 8, 1932

BREAK INTO OIL STATION

The Standard Oil Company's station was broken into Monday night and it was found that the thieves had taken ten gallons of kerosene from the service truck, evidently of the opinion they were helping themselves to gasoline. A quantity of lubricating oil was also missing. The empty cans and the funnel were found on the Agate highway south of Bigelows.

Harrison Sun, Thurs., Sept. 29, 1932

CAR PURSUIT

Upon request from the sheriff at Lusk, Wyo., Sheriff Williams stopped a car in which four people were leaving Lost Springs, Wyo., for Mississippi. They were being pursued due to having left the Wyoming town without making settlement for a garage bill, which Sheriff Williams collected.

Harrison Sun, Thurs., Dec. 1, 1932

WOMAN & CHILDREN WANTED IN WYO. FOUND HERE SAT.

Mrs. Ruby Bostrom and three daughters were located here by Sheriff Williams Saturday of last week, and turned over to Sheriff Hassed from Lusk, who took them back to the Wyoming city. Mrs. Bostrom was under court order to turn her three daughters over to the officer, the court having decided the mother was not capable of properly caring for them. The children range from one to four years of age. Under order of the district court of the Wyoming County the children are to be placed in custody of the state board of charities and reform for a period of six months, and will be returned to the mother if she is adjudged physically and mentally capable of caring for them.

Evidently anticipating the action of the court, Mrs. Bostrom brought her children to Harrison, Monday of last week, first leaving them at the home of Frank Bailey, and returned later in the week and rented rooms at the L.C. Larsen home where she was located by Sheriff Williams, who notified the Wyoming officials.

Harrison Sun, Thurs., Jan. 19, 1933

JUDGE MEYER DISPOSES OF MANY CASES IN DAY SESSION COURT

Judge E.L. Meyer opened the January term of district court for Sioux County Monday, and by eliminating the jury was enabled to go over the docket and complete the session in one day.

Russel Locker, who pleaded guilty to branding a heifer belonging to a neighbor in the Glen community, was given a suspended sentence and paroled to the sheriff, defendant to pay costs of the action.

All other cases taken up were civil actions.

Harrison Sun, Thurs., Jan. 26, 1933

MANI KNORI ACQUITTED COMPLAINT FOR STEALING CATTLE

The jury on the case wherein Manie Knori was tried in district court for stealing cattle returned a verdict of not guilty, after being out several hours. Charles Fisher was attorney for defendant, and W.E. Mumby and R.R. Wellington prosecuted the case.

Hearing of the case contested will of Daniel Slattery, was opened Thursday morning of last week and continued until Saturday afternoon. This was a jury trial, but after all testimony had been presented a directed verdict was handed the jury by Judge Meyer, finding for the proponent, Mrs. Marie Slattery. Application for a new trial was denied. Schnurr and Mumby and E.E. Crites were attorneys for Mrs. Slattery and A.G. Fisher and F.A. Barrett represented the contestants.

Harrison Sun, Thurs., June 16, 1932

CAR OWNERS TAKE NOTE

Having been very considerate with car owners with regard to securing license plates for this length of time, I hereby give notice that effective at once, car owners must secure license plates for the year 1932, or be subject to arrest.

C. SID WILLIAMS,

Sheriff of Sioux County

Harrison Sun, Thurs., April 21, 1932

FOUR ARE BOUND OVER TO DISTRICT COURT FOR CATTLE THEFT

Sheriff Williams was called to the south part of the county the fore part of the week to investigate the theft and butchering of a heifer belonging to Wm. Fanning. Information was given officers that evidence pointed to the Fred Brothwell place nearby, and a search of the place disclosed sufficient information to warrant the arrest of Fanning, his son, Harry, Harvey Massengale and Cecil Wilson. Upon being arraigned in county court the four plead guilty, the first three to stealing and butchering the heifer and Wilson was held as an accessory to the fact.

According to the story told the sheriff, Massengale shot the heifer and he and Harry Brothwell did the butchering, while all four took the carcass to the Brothwell place. The four were bound over to district court, their bonds being set at $1000 each, excepting the one for Wilson, which is $500. They are being held in the county jail in lieu of bonds.

Harrison Sun, Thurs., Aug. 19, 1932

THREE TO SIX YEARS IN PEN GIVEN PAIR FOR THEFT OF COW

Harry Brothwell and Harvey Messengale, two of the four arrested several weeks ago for the theft and butchering of a heifer belonging to Wm. Fanning, were sentenced to indeterminate terms of three to six years each in the state penitentiary of District Judge E.L. Meyer Wednesday of last week. Cecil Wilson, a relative of the Brothwells, who had but recently returned from California, was paroled, he pleading guilty as an accessory after the fact. Fred Brothwell, father of Harry Brothwell, refused to enter a plea of guilt in the stealing and butchering of the heifer, but admitted helping to hang the meat up after young Brothwell and Massengale had killed and butchered the heifer.

The elder Brothwell is being held in the county jail pending action of the county attorney in the matter. The pair who were sentenced last Wednesday will be taken to Lincoln as soon as word comes from the warden that all necessary arrangements have been made.

Sheriff Williams and County Attorney Mumby drove to Alliance, taking the four men for a hearing before Judge Meyer.

Harrison Sun, Thurs., Sept. 1, 1932

TO STATE PRISON

Sheriff Williams, accompanied by his son, Sidney, drove to Lincoln Friday of last week, taking Harvey Massengale and Harry Brothwell, the latter two to serve from two to five years in the state penal institution for theft of cattle.

Harrison Sun, Thurs., Sept. 29, 1932

CAR & TRUCK DRIVERS MUST HAVE 1933 PLATES BY APRIL 5

Sheriff Williams received word this week from the state sheriff's department, advising him that all car drivers in Sioux County must have the new 1933 license plates by April 5th, or arrest will be made.

This order applies to cars, trucks, and particular attention is called to equipping trailers with plates. It makes no difference the nature of the trailer, if used on public roads, it must carry plates. There is an additional charge for the use of trailers, with special plates for same.

Under the new law the cost of license plates has been reduced to an amount where it seems inexcusable for a motor vehicle driver to operate his car without them.

Those who bought license plates before the new law became effective will be compelled to "hold the sack" for their rebates, it now seems. Collections made by county treasurers were disbursed to the various funds under former requirements, as per order of the state department, and it also seems the money has been spent, as it will be necessary to wait until money accumulates from sales since enactment of the new law is available to make the refunds. At the present time no definite plan for making application for rebates has been provided.

Harrison Sun, Thurs., March 23, 1933

FIRE & DEATH THREAT USED TO EXTORT MONEY FROM RANCHER

One of the most fiendish methods of extortion was used by three robbers who invaded the ranch home of Erik Scherven Monday night of this week, in an effort to get their victim to reveal the hiding place of money.

In relating his harrowing experience to the Sun editor, Mr. Scherven said he had been in bed for some time when about ten o'clock someone knocked at his door. Erik got out of bed and the stranger said he needed gasoline for his car, but when the door was unlocked a flashlight was thrown in

Erik's face and he was commanded to about face and do as commanded. The intruder took a dishcloth and wrapped it over Erik's eyes and another cloth was used to bind his hands. He was then commanded to sit in a chair, and not make any effort to move, upon threat of being shot. There were three men in the gang, and the spokesman demanded of Erik the hiding place of his money, and upon being informed he had none about the place, the leader said he knew a way to "make him talk a plenty," and started a fire at his feet. Upon Erik's insistence that they would find no money there, the three men proceeded to make a search of the house, tearing out drawers, emptying sacks of flour and other goods in the pantry and made a thorough search of trunks and all through the house. They then went to the garage and other outbuildings and while they were gone a heavy quilt that had been tossed on the fire on the floor of the kitchen begun to smoulder and Erik said he called to the men outside to return and put out the fire, as the smoke was suffocating him and feared they would permit the floor of the room to catch afire.

As near as he could determine, Erik stated the men remained at his place about two hours, using all sorts of threats to make him produce money. The leader is the only one who did any talking, the other two men conversing in a whisper all the time they were at the place. Upon leaving the men gathered a quantity of food stuff, some clothing, a set of new harness and collars, and tools. They cut the telephone wire before entering the place, and before leaving took the distributor head from his car. As they left the place they warned Erik if he reported the case to the officers within five days they would return and "get him." They neglected, however, to turn his saddle horse loose and he rode over to the Oscar Story Ranch and got in communication with Sheriff Williams, who was located at Edgemont. Sheriff Williams went to the place immediately and began to work on the case. Officers over the state were notified by telephone to be on the lookout, although no trace of the men has been found to date.

The Scherven Ranch is about twenty-five miles northwest of Harrison.

Harrison Sun, Thurs., May 4, 1933

QUICK JUSTICE METED OUT TO TRIO WHO ROBBED SHERVEN

Prompt and well-planned action on the part of Sheriff Sid Williams has resulted in bringing to justice the three men who, Monday night of last week, drove to the home of Erik Scherven, twenty-five miles north of Harrison, and by threats of burning and cutting his throat attempted to force Erik to reveal the supposed hiding place of money.

Sheriff Williams had tracked the car used by the robbers and was quite positive of the identity of the trio who had pulled the job. Tuesday afternoon of last week he went to the Dunlap place north of Harrison and arrested Chester Dunlap, placing him in jail here. Upon questioning Dunlap said he knew nothing about the affair. Reports from Crawford and Alliance that the men wanted had been in the two towns proved wrong, and Sheriff Williams went into Wyoming to search for the other two he had suspected of the crime. He found Edwin Wilkins at the Wamper place north of Lusk and Oliver Dunlap at the Ernest Paulson place in the near vicinity. Both men were brought to Lusk Friday of last week and held in the county jail at that place.

Keeping the men separated and questioning them finally brought results and Monday Oliver Dunlap confessed his part in the crime, and implicated the other two. They were brought before County

Judge Wilhermsdorfer Monday and all upon being arraigned plead guilty to the charge of feloniously entering a dwelling, threats of violence and death upon the person of Erik Scherven. Sheriff Williams and Deputy State Sheriff E.E. Clark took the men to Alliance, where they entered a plea of guilty before Judge Meyer, who sentenced Wilkins and Chester Dunlap to 15 years in the penitentiary and Oliver Dunlap was given ten years in the state reformatory for men. The first two are each 24 years of age and the latter 22 years old.

Wilkins has served time in the reformatory in Wyoming and also a term of 17 months in the Nebraska penal institution for theft of Martin Koch's car about two years ago.

It developed in the grilling of the men Monday, that they had perpetrated a like robbery in Box Butte County on April 17, according to a confession of Wilkins. The victim was Jim Butler, a rancher living about 20 miles west of Alliance, from whom they secured $237.50 in cash and a quantity of provisions. They took the money and went to Denver, where they bought the car used here, according to the story of Wilkins. This robbery was never reported to the Box Butte county officers and only became known as a development of the Scherven robbery and the subsequent apprehension and confession of the trio.

The hiding place of the property taken from the Scherven ranch was revealed by one of the men, who was taken to the place about thirty-five miles northeast of Lusk by the officers to assist in locating it.

By unrelenting vigilance and putting in days and nights on the job Sheriff Williams has brought to an abrupt end a case that may have caused the county considerable expense in prosecution.(17)

Harrison Sun, Thurs., May 11, 1933

TRACING WYOMING ROBBERIES

Sheriffs Harold Dewitt of Torrington and Wm. Hassed of Lusk were in Harrison Tuesday to interview Edwin Wilkins and Chester and Oliver Dunlap in connection with some recent robberies near Torrington. Some of the loot in possession of the trio was thought to be a part of property stolen from homes near Torrington. The Wyoming officers went to Alliance that evening to question the three young men.

Harrison Sun, Thurs., May 11, 1933

HOT CHECK ARTIST LOCATED TUESDAY AT WORLAND, WYO.

Sheriff Sid Williams left this morning for Worland, Wyo., to get J.S. Robinson, wanted here for issuing short checks. Complaint was made against Robinson by Buck Jordan and E.M. Pedersen June 20th of last year and sheriffs in nearby states were notified by the local office. On a tip that the man wanted was in Wyoming, Sheriff Williams sent out additional notices a few days ago and yesterday received word from the sheriff at Worland that he had Robinson in custody.

Apparently Robinson has worked the same game in many other towns, as Sheriff Williams has been advised by authorities at Scottsbluff and Grand Island and Lamar, Colo., that they would very much like to

---

(17) The Eric Scherven Ranch was only a few miles from Dad's Indian Creek Ranch. Dad being well acquainted with everyone in that area quickly solved the case. After their release, Chester and Oliver Dunlap were in the Harrison area and I got to know who they were. I also knew the victim, Erik Schervan.

have him to answer to similar charges. Robinson was in the horse buying business, giving checks on the Platte Valley State Bank of Scottsbluff to several here, the bank protesting payment on account of lack of funds.

Harrison Sun, Thurs., Feb. 9, 1933

FIRST COMPLAINT IN COUNTY FOR BOOTLEG GASOLINE FILED

Officers working under the Department of Agriculture, to which the Motor Fuel Tax division has been transferred under a new law, have been working in this part of the state and Wednesday filed a complaint against Howard E. Frye, who was apprehended the day before just north of Henry, in Sioux County, with about 350 gallons of gasoline, which the officers state in their complaint was transported into the state "without notice of the importation of said motor vehicle fuel oil having been given to the Department of Inspection, and with intent to evade paying tax on the sale or use of gasoline." Sheriff Williams went to the south part of the county today to serve a warrant for the arrest of Frye.

Under the new law a conviction calls for a fine of from $100 to $2,000 and imprisonment of one to five years.

Harrison Sun, May 4, 1933

AFTER SADDLE THIEVES

State Deputy Sheriff E.E. Clark and G. Ridenour, Sheriff of Garden County, stopped overnight in Harrison Monday. They were enroute to some point in Wyoming to search for some saddles stolen in Garden County. During the past year there has been a run on saddles by thieves, several having been stolen in this locality, and it is believed by the officers that a regular organization has been formed to handle the stolen property.

Harrison Sun, May 25, 1933

SUFFERS HEART ATTACK

Sid Williams is able to be around again after suffering from a serious heart attack Saturday, Mrs. Williams and children, who were visiting relatives at Wheatland, Wyo., were called home due to his illness, as was also his daughter, Mrs. Frank Downey of Edgemont, S.D.

Harrison Sun, Thurs., June 8, 1933

HELD FOR SHEEP THEFT

Sheriff Hassed of Lusk came to Harrison last Friday, and with Sheriff Williams went to the country to serve a warrant on Henry Plumb, who was suspected of the theft of ten head of ewes from Albert DeGehring. Upon questioning by the officers Plumb admitted he took the ewes from DeGehring's flock while herding sheep for Leo Dunlap, on the latter's place north of Lusk, and brought them to a place north of town. Plumb is held for hearing in district court at Lusk.

Harrison Sun., Thurs., June 8, 1933

ADMITS HORSE THEFT

Being suspicious of a young man trailing three head of horses near Indian Creek Thursday of last week, Sheriff Williams went out Friday morning and dickered with the stranger for the purchase of two of the horses, which were delivered to town. The young fellow gave the name of Paul Anderson, but after a grilling by the sheriff the young man admitted he had stolen the horses. Sheriff Petty of Fall River County, S.D., was called by phone and further questioning developed the fact that two of the horses had been stolen from Tom Richardson, who lives north of Edgemont, and the other from Art Montgomery. It was also learned that the man's rightful name was George Robinson. He also had a saddle horse which he claimed as his own. Sheriff Petty took Robinson back to South Dakota, where he will answer to the charge of horse stealing.

Harrison Sun, Thurs., June 22, 1933

SHERIFF WILLIAMS CALLED TO SCENE OF SHOOTING TODAY

Newton Brandon made a hurried trip to town this afternoon to advise Sheriff Williams of trouble in the community southeast of Agate. Reports are somewhat confusing, but from more or less authentic information obtainable this evening, it seems two men were engaged in an altercation, one slapping the other, who picked up a piece of iron and crushed his assailant's head. Later, it seems, a shooting scrape developed, one man reported to have been shot and the man with the gun still on the rampage. Sheriff Williams and Dr. McNeil left for the scene of the trouble about five o'clock, and as there are no telephone lines to the neighborhood, it is impossible for the Sun to have an accurate account of the trouble this week.

Harrison Sun, Thurs., June 29, 1933

NOBODY SHOT; NOBODY KILLED

Following the filing of a complaint against Wm. LeLaCheur for assault on the person of one Harold Wallace, it develops that the fracas in the Canton community Thursday afternoon of last week was an unfriendly gesture of fists between the above mentioned parties. Sheriff Williams brought LeLaCheur to Harrison on complaint filed by Newton Braden, near whose place the fight occurred. From information given the sheriff, the difficulty between the men arose over the difference of money one owed the other, and Wallace climbed on LeLaCheur's wagon to carry on the argument. One hit the other and the fight ensued. The team ran about three-quarters of a mile, with the men in combat on the wagon. When Braden, only witness of the fight, caught up with the team, he found 'Wallace had evidently come out second best, although both men bore bruises of battle'.

Sheriff Williams found Wallace at the Braden home with his eyes swollen entirely shut and otherwise bruised. LeLaCheur was brought to Harrison and arraigned in county court. He gave bond for his appearance July 10th, for preliminary hearing.

Harrison Sun, Thurs., July 6, 1933

ASSAULT CASE DISMISSED DEFENDANT ASSESSED COSTS

After listening to a portion of evidence in the complaint against Wm. LeLaCheur, charged with assault on the person of Harold Wallace, and following consultation of attorneys and persons interested in the case, the complaint was dismissed and defendant assessed costs of the action. From evidence submitted it was apparent both parties in the altercation were somewhat at fault, and rather than to pursue expensive legal procedure, and the possibility of appeal to the district court, with conviction doubtful, this action on the part of the court would seem the proper course to pursue.

Harrison Sun, Thurs., July 13, 1933

APPREHENDED PAIR WANTED IN MISSOURI FOR BURGLARY

Sheriff Sid Williams and Deputy State Sheriff Clark yesterday rounded up a pair of young fellows wanted in Missouri for burglary. Sheriff Williams was advised a short time ago that the men might be found near here, one having relatives in Wyoming, and the other, Harold Kephart, had been working for Harry Wasserburger. They are being held in the county jail here, waiting arrival of an officer from Rockport, Mo., who will take them back to stand trial on several burglary jobs they are suspected of being guilty of.

Harrison Sun, Thurs., July 13, 1933

RETURNS PRISONERS TO MISSOURI

Officers arrived Tuesday from Rockport, Mo., to get two men apprehended here last week by Sheriff Sid Williams, and who are wanted in the Missouri town for burglary. The officers had the necessary extradition papers and left Tuesday night with their men.

Harrison Sun, Thurs., July 20, 1933

FINDS STILL AND MOONSHINE

Sheriff Williams made a search of the place occupied by Joe LaMay, east of Harrison, Wednesday of last week and in a cave near the house found a five-gallon keg containing three gallons of alleged moonshine, and also a still ready for operation. LaMay was released on bonds to appear for hearing at a later date.

Harrison Sun, Thurs., Aug. 3, 1933

JOE LAMAY TAKEN UP ON COMPLAINT FILED BY HIS WIFE

Out on bond pending hearing on complaint for possession of liquor and operating a still, Joe LaMay was again taken into custody this week, following a complaint filed by Mrs. LaMay, who charges that her husband became violent following his release on the former charge and made violent threats. The complaint brought against LaMay this time is that he is a dipsomaniac and a hearing before the insanity board is scheduled for Friday of this week.

Harrison Sun, Thurs., Aug. 10, 1933

TWO TAKEN TO NORFOLK SANITARIUM DURING THE PAST WEEK

Sid Williams left for Norfolk Saturday of last week, taking Joe LaMay who Friday was adjudged a dipsomaniac by the county board of examiners. LaMay will be confined there for treatment.(18)

Monday of this week Albert Scott, 17 years old, was brought before the board and upon examination it was found the young man was suffering from dementia and was ordered confined in the Norfolk institution for treatment. The parents of the boy who reside in the south part of the county, gave the information that their son had suffered a fall a short time ago, striking on his head, and complained of a peculiar sensation similar to electrical currents passing through his head, as the boy explained it. Fred Mason left on the Monday passenger, taking the boy to Norfolk.

Harrison Sun, Thurs., Aug. 17, 1933

(18)   *A dipsomaniac is one who has an uncontrollable liking of alcoholic drink.*

REX COFFEE HOME LOOTED SUNDAY; TRUCK IS APPROPRIATED

A ranch hand recently employed on the Rex Coffee ranch, broke into the Coffee home Sunday, while the family was spending the day on a trip to the Black Hills, and after taking what articles of clothing and other property he wanted, loaded same into the Coffee truck and left for parts unknown. Upon his return late Sunday evening Rex found the house in disorder, and came into town immediately, and tracks indicated the truck was driven west from here. Accompanied by John Marking, they drove to Casper, where a search was made, but upon returning to Harrison learned the truck was located in the Burlington railroad yards at Alliance. A trip was made there that afternoon, but no information as to the driver of the truck could be given by officers there.

The thief took about all of Rex's clothes, three razors, some blankets, several hundred pennies, but aside from the foregoing Rex could not account for any other loss of property.

Upon applying for work at the Coffee ranch about three weeks ago, the man gave his name as Buck Chandler and had worked around Chadron before coming here. A card found in the bunkhouse bore the name of Ralph Hancock, and was issued by an election district at Klamath Falls, Oregon.

Harrison Sun, Thurs., Aug. 17, 1933

RETURNED FROM KANSAS TO ANSWER BUM CHECK CHARGE

Jack Ewing, who more than a year ago gave a bad check to the Lowry Hotel, was apprehended at Lansing, Kansas, last week and Sheriff Williams went after him to answer to the charge. Ewing posed as a salesman for the American Steel & Wire Co., and while here gave the hotel a check on the First National Bank of Kansas City. When the check was returned unpaid, investigation revealed the fact that Ewing was not known by the company he purported to represent, and also that no such bank as the one the check was drawn on existed. It later developed that Ewing was engaged in buying and selling second-hand butcher equipment. He was arraigned in county court Friday of last week, pleading guilty to the charge of issuing bad checks.

Harrison Sun, Thurs., Oct. 9, 1933

EWING GETS YEAR IN PEN

Jack Ewing was taken to Alliance last Friday to appear before Judge E.L. Meyer, Ewing entering a plea of guilty to a charge of giving a bad check to the Lowry Hotel about a year ago in payment of a board bill. He was sentenced to serve a year in the penitentiary.

Harrison Sun, Oct. 16, 1933

SENTENCED FOR WATCH THEFT

Sheriff Williams returned last week from Burke, S.D., where he went to get two men who were accused of the theft of a watch from the home of W.F. Rowland, in the Curly community. They admitted the theft and were taken before Judge Meyer at Alliance for sentence. Glen Briggs was given one year in the state penitentiary and Joe King a year in the reformatory.

Harrison Sun, Thurs., Oct 12, 1933

AGATE POST OFFICE ROBBED

Harold Cook was in Harrison today and reported that the post office at Agate had been entered last night and some money and stamps had been taken. The extent of the loss was not reported.

Harrison Sun, Thurs., Sept. 14, 1933

TRIO ADMITS ROBBERY OF THE AGATE STORE LAST SEPTEMBER

Information picked up by Sheriff Williams some time ago resulted in the apprehension of three young men who robbed the Agate store and post office last September. Clyde Cotton, 20, was picked up at Gering a few days ago and told the officers the whole story of the affair. Later Floyd Marquis, 24, was arrested at Scottsbluff and the third member of the trio, Kenny Waln, 24, was arrested at Cheyenne.

Waln, although young, has somewhat of a police record, and when first questioned held firmly to a story of innocence, but finally admitted his guilt. Arraigned in county court here the three young men were bound over to district court on complaints of breaking and entering. They were taken to Alliance yesterday and plead guilty before Judge E.L. Meyer, who sentenced Waln and Marquis to the state reformatory for terms of one to three years. Cotton was paroled to Chief of Police Guy Carlson of Scottsbluff.

U.S. Post Office Inspector Hornsby of Hastings was here to investigate for the government but the federal charge was dropped. In the robbery of the Agate store about $7.50 in money, some cigarettes and an inner tube were stolen, and also about 200 pennies of the post office money.

Harrison Sun, Thurs., April 26, 1934

MEXICAN HELD FOR SLASHING YOUNG MAN WITH BEET KNIFE

Sheriff Williams was called to the south part of the county the fore part of the week to get a Mexican beet worker, who had slashed a young man, employed at the place, with a beet knife. Sheriff Williams investigated the case yesterday and learned that another Mexican was also implicated in the altercation and will go after him this week.

The young fellow who was cut up in the fracas, was taken to the hospital at Scottsbluff, where the doctors report his condition as serious. A knife wound across the back of one hand and a deep cut across the forearm was inflicted by the Mexicans. The deeper cut on the arm severed all the larger veins and cords and the doctors are of the opinion he will lose the use of the hand entirely.

The young fellow, who is 22 years of age, says his home is in Alabama, and that he was employed on a farm in the south part of the county, and was running a beet puller when the trouble started. One of the Mexicans took him to task for damaging beets when he crossed an open irrigating lateral in the field, according to the story told to Sheriff Williams, and when suggested that the Mexican run the puller the latter became angry and took a large jack-knife from his pocket and slashed the young man across the back of one hand. He took a wrench from the puller and struck the Mexican across the head and at that time another Mexican came up from behind and slashed his arm with a beet knife. The young fellow ran to an adjoining field for help, and to escape further punishment from the Mexicans.

Harrison Sun, Thurs., Oct. 19, 1933

MEXICANS IN STABBING FRACAS BOUND OVER TO DISTRICT COURT

Two Mexican beet laborers, Ed Mendoza and Joe Yxta, who became involved in a cutting fracas in the south part of the county several weeks ago, were arraigned in county court Friday of last week on a complaint of assault with intent to do great bodily injury.

Herman Freeman, the complainant, and C.R. Howell were witnesses for the state. Freeman received two bad cuts on the arm and hand, and one hand has been rendered permanently useless and two fingers of the other hand are permanently injured since his encounter with the Mexicans, when a large beet knife was used in the fight.

Harrison Sun, Nov. 9, 1933

FOUR CAUGHT IN ACT OF STEALING POTATOES AT GRAGG FARM

Four young men, Henry Wathen, James Smith, Jack Barnett and William Labbo, were caught last Friday night when they were taking potatoes from a storage cellar, which they had broken into on the Forrest Gragg farm in the south part of the county. When arraigned in county court this week they entered pleas of guilty to the charge and were bound over to district court for sentence.

Harrison Sun, Thurs., Febr. 4, 1934

MANY CASES DISPOSED OF IN THREE-DAY SESSION OF COURT

The February term of district court convened Monday of this week, and in the three days of its session most of the cases on the trial docket came in for some form of action.

While this was a jury term, but one case called for the service of a jury, that of Bushnell vs. Thompson, et al, and this case was declared a mistrial. But one criminal case was on the docket for trial at this term, that of the state vs. Ed Mendosa and Joe Yxta. The defendants were alleged to have been involved in a cutting affray, the outcome of a controversy between workers during the beet harvest in the south part of the county last fall, but the complaining witness who charged the Mexicans with slashing him with knives left a short time ago for Alabama and failed to put in appearance for the trial.

Harrison Sun, Thurs., Feb. 22, 1934

BOYS ARRESTED FOR THEFT

Sheriff Williams went to the south part of the county Thursday of last week to get three boys who were suspected of having stolen a washing machine from a farm home in that vicinity a short time ago. A farmer residing in the south part of the county had purchased a new washing machine at Scottsbluff and taken it to his home. That same evening the machine was stolen. The three boys arrested for the theft were Clarence Majors, Clarence Bearbower and Carl Johnson. The original charge placed against the boys was breaking and entering, constituting grand larceny. This complaint, however, was later changed to petty larceny and at a hearing in county court the boys plead guilty to the latter charge and Majors and Bearbower were given thirty days in the county jail, while Johnson was sentenced to ten days.

Harrison Sun, Thurs., March 8, 1934

FILES FOR SHERIFF

C.S. Williams is the latest to file for county office, and will seek re-election to the post he now has, county sheriff, filing as republican candidate in the primaries. Sid has held the office of sheriff of this county for two terms by election, and was previously appointed to fill an unexpired term.

Harrison Sun, Thurs., March 29, 1934

OFFICERS BELIEVE SATURDAY NIGHT FIRE INCENDIARY ORIGIN

The fire in the Jim Lacy property last Saturday night is believed to be of incendiary origin, and a charge of attempt to commit arson has been filed against Ernest Ritchie, who has been living in the house for a short time. Smoke was observed coming from the house about 10 o'clock Saturday night and the fire fighting apparatus was rushed to the scene in time to extinguish the blaze before much of the building was burned. After the fire was put out, an examination revealed the fact that a pile of wood in one corner of the kitchen had burned the interior of this room but had not reached through the ceiling. Another fire was in the attic, where a pile of pitch wood and some cotton had caused the blaze. Cotton was also found in the pile of burning wood in the kitchen. The manner in which the fires were laid pointed suspiciously to an attempt to burn the building and Sunday morning Ritchie was placed under arrest pending an investigation by the state marshal's office. M.H. Mockenhaupt, deputy state fire marshal, arrived Tuesday and after an investigation of the property had the above charge filed against Ritchie. When arraigned Wednesday in county court Ritchie entered a plea of not guilty and was released under bond for his appearance at a preliminary hearing to be held Friday.

Harrison Sun, Thurs., April 5, 1934

BOUND OVER TO DIST. COURT

The preliminary hearing of Ernest Ritchie, who was held on a charge of attempt to commit arson, was heard in county court Friday evening of last week and the defendant was bound over to district court. The defendant was released under bond for appearance at the next term of court. (19)

Harrison Sun, Thurs., April 12, 1934

WM. DeBANO

Candidate in Democratic

Primaries for Sheriff

Born and raised in Sioux County. Served in U.S. Army during the World War.

Feel confident that I can satisfactorily serve the people of Sioux County, and earnestly solicit the support of all in the primaries.

Harrison Sun, Thurs., March 8, 1934

CANDIDATE FOR SHERIFF

Forrest Gragg, resident of Townsend precinct in the southern part of the county, made filing Tuesday as a democratic candidate in the primaries for the office of County sheriff. With the filing of Mr. Gragg, there are now three candidates on the democratic ticket for this office and one republican candidate. Mr. Gragg is a farmer in the irrigated section of the county, and has been a resident of Sioux county for a number of years.

Harrison Sun, Thurs., May 17, 1934

MORE CANDIDATES FILE

Monday of this week two more filings were made for county office, C.M. Rich, present commissioner for the third district, filed as republican candidate for that office. J.B. Duncan, also a resident of the south part of the county, is a candidate for sheriff on the republican ticket.

County Attorney Mumby today announced his filing, seeking nomination for county attorney on the republican ticket. Mr. Mumby has served one term in this office.

Harrison Sun, Thurs., June 21, 1934

---

(19)   The defendant served about 6 days in the local jail before being released under bond.

ANNOUNCEMENTS

SID WILLIAMS FOR SHERIFF

As a candidate in the republican primary for sheriff I earnestly solicit the support of the voters of Sioux county in the election Tuesday, August 14th. During the past nine years that I have served as sheriff, it has been my endeavor to fulfill the duties of the office in a conscientious manner, and if the service I have given during that time meets the approval of the people of Sioux county, I will appreciate your continued support and vote.

Harrison Sun, Thurs., June 21, 1934

Harrison Sun, Thurs., July 26, 1934

STOLEN CAR RECOVERED

A Chevrolet car, stolen in Denver Saturday of last week, was recovered by Sheriff Williams Monday night, although the parties driving the car were not apprehended. Sheriff Williams spotted the car on the ridge road northeast of Harrison, where it had been left when the gasoline supply was exhausted. It was brought to Harrison and will be held pending arrival of the owner from Denver.

Harrison Sun, Thurs., June 21, 1934

Harrison Sun, Thurs., Aug. 9, 1934

FOR SHERIFF

To the voters of Sioux county: Having filed in the Democratic primaries for Sheriff of Sioux county, I earnestly solicit your support.

FORREST GRAGG

Harrison Sun, Thurs., July 26, 1934

233

PRIMARY *ELECTION RETURNS SIOUX COUNTY*

Both party candidates are listed below, the r represents Republican and the d Democratic candidates.

FOR COUNTY CLERK		TOTALS
A.C. Davis	r	363
Press L. Wilson	d	262
Paul B. Britt	d	195
Jesse L. Gerlach	d	191
Earl G. Hutchinson	d	163
Roy S. Emery	d	123

FOR COUNTY TREASURER		
F. M. Hall	r	415
J.H. Christian	r	92
Elver Shinbur	d	434

FOR COUNTY SHERIFF		
C.S. Williams	r	334
J.B. Duncan	r	156
Neil Jordan	d	374
William DeBano	d	199
Forrest Gragg	d	138
George Dilling	d	106
W.F. Walker	d	35

FOR COUNTY ATTORNEY		
W.E. Mumby	r	391

FOR COUNTY ASSESSOR		
John L. Wilson	d	289
Henry Hoffmann	d	265
Rose Houx	d	222

FOR COMMISSIONER 1ST DISTRICT		
Jacob Wasserburger	d	83
George Meng	d	120

FOR COMMISSIONER 3RD DISTRICT		
C.M. Rich	r	38
John S. McClure	r	15
Harry Morris	r	101
D.A. Hoy	d	42
H.C. Lamb	d	7
C.E. Thomas	d	45
V.C. Luth	d	45
J.C. Lewis	d	90
A.D. Wilson	d	68

Harrison Sun, Thurs., Aug. 16, 1934

PRIMARY DEMOCRATIC TICKET

For County Sheriff

Neil Jordan	374
William DeBano	199
Forrest Gragg	138
George Dilling	106
W.F. Walker	35

Harrison Sun, Thurs., Aug. 16, 1934

PRIMARY REPUBLICAN TICKET

For County Sheriff

C.S. Williams	334
J.B. Duncan	156

Harrison Sun, Thurs., Aug. 16, 1934

UNOFFICIAL *ELECTION RETURNS FOR SIOUX COUNTY*

FOR COUNTY CLERK

Press L. Wilson	d	894
A.C. Davis	r	876

FOR COUNTY TREASURER

Elver Shinbur	d	547
F.M. Hall	r	1210

FOR COUNTY SHERIFF

Neil Jordan	d	792
C.S. Williams	r	966

FOR COUNTY ATTORNEY

W.E. Mumby	r	1288

FOR COUNTY ASSESSOR

Henry Hoffmann	d	992

FOR COMMISSIONER 1ST DIST.

Jacob Wasserburger	d	274

FOR COMMISSIONER 3RD DIST.

J.C. Lewis	d	253
H.E. Morris	r	293

FOR JUDGE SUPREME COURT

Edward F. Carter	883
James L. Tewell	480

FOR STATE SUPERINTENDENT

Charles W. Taylor	972
John A. Jimerson	415

FOR BOARD OF REGENTS

Orval L. Fox	765
Del J. Bigelow	668
Earle A. Ellicott	334
Ernest W. Baldwin	408
FOR REPEAL	843
AGAINST REPEAL	670

Harrison Sun, Thurs., Nov. 8, 1934

FEW CHANGES MADE IN PERSONNEL AT THE COURT HOUSE

Today is the day set for changes of county officials at the court house, and three officers were inducted into office in Sioux County.

H.E. Morris was sworn in as commissioner from the third district, taking the place of C.M. Rich, who has served during the past four years. Miss Thelma Lawler has taken her place as the newly elected county superintendent, succeeding Mrs. Elizabeth Emery, who has held the office for the past twelve years. Henry Hoffman, newly elected assessor, will take the place held by Mrs. Wm. Houk during the past two years.

Other officials elected at the recent election and succeeding themselves are A.C. Davis, county clerk and clerk of the district court, F.M. Hall, county treasurer, W.E. Mumby, county attorney, and C.S. Williams, sheriff.(20) Mary Broderick was reappointed deputy county clerk and Jess Newell deputy county treasurer.

On the board of regents of the Sioux County high school O.L. Fox and Del Bigelow will be the incoming members, serving with V.L. Hanson and Oscar Skavdahl, holdover members.

The county commissioners opened a session of the board Wednesday to wind up the business of the past year, and the new board will organize today.

Harrison Sun, Thurs., Jan. 3, 1935

MORISON LUMBER CO. SAFE IS BLOWN, YEGGS GET ABOUT $30

The safe at the Morison Lumber Company office was blown some time during Saturday night, and about $30 in cash and a number of checks were taken from the money drawer of the safe.

Discovery of the burglary was not made until Sunday morning about eleven o'clock, when Joe Morison, manager of the concern, came downtown. Entrance had been made through the window facing the alley and from indications they had entered the building before the snow began falling that evening, which was about eleven o'clock, as the window pane taken from the frame was lying on bare ground and was covered with the full fall of snow, or about four inches.

The safe was rolled to the middle of the floor, where it was turned over on a sack of feed to deaden the sound, and the burglars evidently went about the business in a methodical manner, as the explosion was heard by people in the neighborhood about twelve-fifteen. No importance was attached to the noise made by the explosion, however, those hearing it believing it to have been made by the firing of a gun.

The biggest loss, Mr. Morison says, was the damage done to the safe. The combination dial was knocked off and the door was wrecked beyond usefulness. No trace of the burglars has been found as yet.

Harrison Sun, Thurs., Dec. 20, 1934

---

(20) *Your granddad won re-election again against a popular democrat, Neil Jordan. The election this time was somewhat closer. Perhaps the county voters, in part, perceived that your granddad was in declining health. Sid was now 65 years of age, had been in a serious car accident, and had suffered a heart attack the previous year.*

There may also have been some grumbling because Sid would appoint his capable son, Sid Jr. as deputy to take care of the sheriff's office while he took off for a few weeks in July to race his horses at the Ak-Sar-Ben, Omaha and other race tracks. However, most of the voters were apparently satisfied with his job performance. Even sheriffs need and are entitled to vacation time.

UNITT HARDWARE AND THE E.G. MEIER FILLING STATION ROBBED

The C.H. Unitt Hardware store was entered early Monday morning, the robbers getting away with 15 to 20 boxes of high powered shells, a shotgun, a .22 rifle, a BB gun, a small amount of change from the cash register and around 15 or 20 gallons of gas. Nothing else in the store seemed to have been molested. Entrance to the building was gained by removing a pane of glass from one of the front doors. This same place of business was robbed last year, abut a year ago, and practically the same amount of goods stolen.

A quantity of gas, about 20 gallons, had been taken from the pump at the E. G. Meier Garage that same morning, and it is thought was perpetrated by the same outfit that pulled the Unitt job.

Officials are working diligently to solve these robberies.

Harrison Sun, Thurs., Oct. 25, 1934

J.T. COFFEE'S CAR STOLEN

About seven o'clock last Friday evening J.T. Coffee's Ford coupe was stolen from in front of his residence. An abandoned car was found on the Agate road with a license plate from Hitchcock County, and getting in communication with authorities at Trenton, it was learned the car, a V-8 sedan, had been stolen from Culbertson Thursday evening. A connecting rod burned out which had forced the abandonment of the car, and it is quite evident the Coffee car was used for the purpose of getting away from this vicinity.

Police at McCook sighted the Coffee car in that city and gave chase, but were unable to recover the car, but several days later it was discovered near Beverly, Nebr., hidden in willows along Frenchman Creek.

The party who got away with Mr. Coffee's car and the Culbertson car, has not been apprehended, but it is thought that an arrest will be made soon. Little damage was done to the Coffee car, but all the tools and a quantity of vaccine had been removed. A saddle was still in the car.

W.E. Mumby and Mr. Coffee left early Wednesday morning to recover the stolen property, returning that same evening. Officials and the owner of the car from Culbertson were in Harrison Wednesday to claim their car.

Harrison Sun, Thurs., Oct. 25, 1934

HOLDING SUSPECT

Sheriff Williams received word from officials of McCook, that they have taken into custody a man by the name of Price, whom they suspect of being implicated in the robbery of the Unitt Hardware, in Harrison, in the early morning, October 22nd. The man in question was caught with guns and ammunition in his possession, which are thought to be part of the haul.

It has not been learned whether the suspect will be brought to Harrison to stand trial or not, as it is understood that Red Willow County also has charges against the man being held.

Harrison Sun, Thurs., Nov. 1, 1934

RETURNS WITH PRISONER

Sheriff Williams left for McCook Saturday, returning Monday with Burto Harris, who was apprehended there and held for robbery of the Unitt hardware store a short time ago. The guns and ammunition were found in Harris' possession. Harris is also suspected of being one of the men who stole J.T. Coffee's car.

Harris was arraigned before county court yesterday, pleading not guilty to the charge lodged against him, and his hearing has been set for Nov. 13.

McCook officers informed Sheriff Williams that Harris has served a hitch in the pen, and that he is thought to be a member of a gang of thieves that have been operating in western Nebraska for some time.

Harrison Sun, Thurs., Nov. 8, 1934

PRISONER TURNED OVER TO WEBSTER COUNTY OFFICER

Burto Harris, who has been held in the county jail here since the fore part of November, was turned over to Sheriff I.W. Crowell of Webster County Thursday of last week. Harris is wanted in Webster County on several charges, the more serious being for holding up a filling station, three witnesses identifying him as the man who pulled the job. Other charges lodged against Harris in Webster are burglary and auto theft. Harris is being held here awaiting trial for breaking into the Unitt hardware, and while he has been turned over to the Webster County authorities on the more serious charge of holdup, the charge against him here is still pending, and in case he is acquitted in Webster County, will be held for this county to answer the charge against him here.

Harrison Sun, Thurs., Dec. 6, 1934

HARRIS GETS SIX YEARS

Burto Harris, who was returned to Webster County from here a short time ago, was sentenced to six years in the penitentiary, following a plea of guilty of holding up a filling station attendant at Red Cloud several months ago. Harris plead guilty to burglary.

Harrison Sun, Thurs., Dec. 13, 1934

LONE BANDIT KILLED FOLLOWING HOLDUP OF BANK

Bullet From Long Range Rifle Halts the Career of Man Who Had Fled With $685 Taken In Raid on Sioux National Bank.

~~~~~

Just one hour after a lone bandit staged a day-light holdup of the Sioux National Bank of this city making away with $685 in currency, checks and money orders, the perpetrator of the crime had paid for his indiscretion with his life, the money returned to the bank, and the case a closed incident as far as police annals are concerned, although a man supposed to be Marion R. Jensen of Denver, is dead, a victim of his own folly.

Returning to the bank shortly before one o'clock Monday, Harold Jeffrey, assistant cashier, had reopened the institution following the noon hour closing and had just opened the vault door when the bandit entered the bank and drew a gun on Mr. Jeffrey, ordering him to "Stick 'em up," and then asked where the money was. Jeffrey replied that it was in the vault, and he was ordered to hand it out, which he did and then the bandit ordered him into the vault, closing the door but did not turn the bolts.

At this time H.H. Thompson, cashier of the bank, Zada Clark, bookkeeper, and Ferd Price of Van Tassell, entered the bank, and menacing them with his gun the bandit backed to the door and fled.

Seizing a gun from the vault Mr. Jeffrey gave chase and fired a shot at the bandit's fleeing car, which had been parked along the south side of Whiteaker's store a short distance from the alley. At this time the alarm was spread and nearby towns telephoned to be on the lookout. The bandit car was seen to go west from town on highway 20, and hastily organized posses went in pursuit. At Van Tassell it was learned no car had passed through that town, so it was evident the bandit had taken a side road and the posses returned to Harrison. A short time later the car was reported to have gone east on the highway. The bandit had hidden out along the highway west of town and waiting until he thought all pursuing cars had gone west he doubled back east.

The posses again took up the chase and meeting a car of police officers from Crawford about five miles east of town it was learned a car similar to that used by the bandit had passed them a short distance east. E.E. Whiteaker took the lead with his car and gave chase. With him in the car were Harold Jeffrey, Albert Moody and the latter's son, Lawrence, the latter two having come up with the Crawford posse and got in Whiteaker's car.

The Crawford officer said the party in the car they had passed was wearing a cap, smoking a pipe and was wearing dark glasses, and was traveling at a leisurely pace. When staging the holdup the bandit wore a hat, did not have on glasses, but the car fitted the description of the one he had used.

BANDIT CAR OVERTAKEN

A hot chase followed and the bandit was overtaken about fifteen miles east of town. The pursuing car pulled up close and the horn was sounded to attract his attention. To this he pulled a little to the side of the road but also speeded up his car. A warning shot was fired in the air, but failed to make the bandit stop and both cars were traveling at a fast pace when approaching a curve in the highway, and his car went over the shoulder of the road and swerved to the top of the cut-bank along the highway. Whiteaker's car went a short distance past, where it was stopped, and at this juncture the bandit was getting out of his car on the opposite side from the pursuers.

OPENS FIRE ON POSSE

Being deliberate in his movements the possemen were of the opinion the bandit intended to surrender, but as he straightened up after emerging from the car, he pulled a Luger .38 pistol and opened fire. The first shot fired struck the rear window of Whiteaker's car and fragments of glass were thrown over the occupants. One large piece of glass struck Albert Moody in the face and caused him to fall forward. Another shot lodged in the heavier part of the frame of the car, this shot being in direct line for Mr. Whiteaker in the driver's seat and another shot pierced the body of the car near the end, the bullet grazing the upholstering of the back of the car and lodged in the other side of the body. This bullet was in line for Mr. Moody, although the latter had fallen forward when hit by the heavy piece of glass.

The possemen got out of the car as quickly as possible and ran to cover. They are of the opinion four or five shots had been fired by the bandit before they could get in a position to return the fire. The bandit was on higher ground and also had the advantage of keeping his car between him and his pursuers, who shot at the car but could see nothing more than the bandit's feet and legs below the body of the car.

BANDIT FELLED BY RIFLE SHOT

As the shots were being fired another car arrived and the bandit was seen to run toward the timber on the other side of the hill, and it was observed that he was re-loading his gun. Albert Moody, who was armed with a long range .30 caliber army rifle, ran to the top of the fill and fired a shot at the fleeing bandit to head him off from reaching the timber. Mr. Moody's intention was to aim low and cripple the bandit if possible, but at his position the lower limbs of the bandit were not visible and the bullet pierced the bandit's body, entering about an inch from the spine and emerging from the lower part of the abdomen. Half turning he fell to the ground, and when the possemen reached the spot he was lying full length, with arms outstretched, and while a faint beating of the heart could be detected, he made no struggle. The shot that brought him down was fired from a distance of about 200 yards.

When searched a .32 caliber pistol was found in the bandit's pocket, one he had taken from the bank, and the Luger pistol used in firing at the possemen had been reloaded with five shells. He evidently intended to get to the pine timber and would have given further battle to his pursuers. His every action was positive proof that he did not intend to be taken alive and would battle the possemen to the last.

The body was placed in the car used by the bandit and brought to town, and search of the man's clothing made to establish identity. In a billfold were found papers bearing the names of Marion R. Jensen, and M.R. Jensen, and some of the papers gave his address at 5135 Osceola St., Denver. A scar about three inches in length on one thigh and a tattoo mark U.S.M.C. on the right shoulder were found on the body. An identification card showed him to be 30 years of age last February.

This information was communicated to the captain of detectives in Denver, and investigation established his identity. It was found that he had a wife and ten-months old baby living at the address given. The Denver officers also informed Sheriff Williams that the man was suspicioned of being implicated in a bank robbery in Iowa last summer, officers from that state asking for an investigation of him at the time. However, so far his conduct in Denver was concerned, they reported they had nothing

on him. Jensen had worked as a traveling salesman. He formerly lived at Northfield, Minn., and about two years ago moved to Denver for his wife's health, who is afflicted with tuberculosis.

In the car were found another gun, shells for a .22 high-powered rifle, Nebraska and South Dakota license plates, several rolls of bandages and adhesive tape. The hat and overalls he wore were found in the car. He had evidently made the change when hiding out west of town. The high-powered rifle, inquiry revealed, had been pawned a short time ago in Scottsbluff.

The car used by the bandit was a 1934 model V-8 sedan, tan colored, and a license plate on the rear of the car carried Nebraska license No. 21-6929. This license was issued to a party working at the experimental farm near Mitchell, but the car for which it was issued had since been junked. A Colorado registration card showed Jensen had purchased the car in Denver last August.

BODY TO BE SHIPPED TO DENVER

Arrangements were completed to have the body of Jensen shipped to Denver for burial. The body will be taken to Crawford tomorrow and shipped over the Burlington to the Colorado city.

Jens Jensen, father of the man, lives at Pipestone, Minn., where he is employed in a butcher shop. The mother lives with a daughter in Kalamazoo, Mich. Young Jensen was a graduate of the high school at Latimer, Iowa.

WIFE PROSTRATED WHEN NEWS OF HUSBAND'S DEATH REPORTED

Mrs. Dorothy Jensen, wife of the dead bandit, was prostrated when the detectives informed her at her Denver home of the death of her husband. She asserted her husband had always provided well and knew of no reason why he should turn bank robber, and while she said the description given Denver officials of the dead man corresponded with that of her husband and was undoubtedly him, she refused to believe he had robbed the bank.

Mrs. Jensen said her husband left Denver about a week before the robbery, saying he was going into Wyoming on a business trip. She received a telephone call from him at Cheyenne and he told her he would probably be home Christmas eve.

STAYED OVER NIGHT WITH GEORGE DAVIS

George Davis, rancher living about five miles south of town, after he had seen the body of the bandit, informed the officers that the man had stayed over night with him last Thursday night. Caught in the snowstorm that afternoon, Jensen was stalled in a drift and Mr. Davis told him he had better stay over night. Mr. Davis stated that the man informed him his name was Hill, that he formerly lived in Denver but had moved to Scottsbluff, and was a traveling salesman. Mr. Davis further said the man was of quiet demeanor, and by the general conversation carried on during his stay in the Davis home, would far from suspect him of being a bank bandit.

The next morning Mr. Davis loaned the man a scoop shovel in case further drifts were encountered on the trip to town, which was left at the Lacy garage. Friday Jensen had a new water pump put in his car at the Lacy garage, and was seen by several about town that day. And a number of others are positive they have seen him here even before last Thursday.

CAR SEEN AT DEPOT MONDAY NOON

It also develops that the car was parked at the depot between eleven and twelve o'clock Monday morning, and while those observing two men in the car paid no particular attention, the description of one tallies fairly well with that of Jensen. It is also reported that the other man purchased a ticket to Chadron, leaving on the 12:25 passenger, and that the two men were noticed holding a quiet conversation on the west side of the depot.

Marcie Howard is positive in his knowledge of having seen Jensen loitering about the mail box in front of the post office not long before the bank reopened Monday afternoon, and said the man had his hat pulled well over his eyes and appeared to be extremely nervous.

While the foregoing has no bearing on the outcome of the robbery, it tends to show the man had been through here before and had probably planned the robbery during those visits and was making mental notes of general conditions, and the best way to get away. It is now believed he was trying to get to the south, but close pursuit prevented him leaving the highway. Figures on a note pad found in his pocket indicated the distances between turns and the directions of the turns on the Harrison-Mitchell road.

CORONER'S INQUEST FOR JENSEN DEATH HELD WEDNESDAY

Although County Attorney W.E. Mumby is convinced that the shooting of Marion R. Jensen, bank bandit, was fully justifiable, a coroner's inquest was conducted by Mr. Mumby Wednesday to establish an official record showing the cause of his death. After examination of several witnesses, the jury consisting of F.J. Lacy, F.D. Viele, Henry T. Dunn, V.E. Marsteller, Norris A. Pedley and

P.H. Unitt, returned the following verdict:

"That Marion Jensen was killed by a gunshot wound inflicted by Albert Moody on the 24th day of December, 1934, while the said Marion Jensen was attempting to escape arrest after committing a felony, to-wit: the robbery of the Sioux National Bank of Harrison, Nebraska; that said Marion Jensen was resisting arrest and apprehension and had shot five or six times at the persons who were pursuing him a few moments before the time he was wounded; that said Jensen was killed by a bullet from a Springfield army rifle in the hands of Albert Moody; that said shooting was justified and was not felonious, and we recommend that no complaint be filed against said Albert Moody."

Harrison Sun., Thurs., Dec. 27, 1934

DEPUTY SHERIFF CLARK COMMENDS WORK OF POSSEMEN

Deputy State Sheriff Clark, who came to Harrison Tuesday to work on the bank holdup case, is high in praise of the local men who participated in the pursuit and capture of the bandit. Sheriff Clark stated the methods used by the pursuers and the manner in which they handled the case when coming onto the bandit would have done credit to seasoned officers, and the community could well be proud of the men who considered it their civic duty to assist in apprehending a criminal who had made a raid on the bank.(21)

This expresses the sentiment of the community, and while none of us favor the killing of a criminal if he can be taken otherwise, we fully appreciate the harrowing experience of the men giving chase, and it is miraculous they survived the raking fire from the bandit's pistol.

TRY TO LINK JENSEN WITH BANK HOLDUP AT KEARNEY

The description of Jensen tallying somewhat with one of the bandits who held up a Kearney bank a short time ago, two employees of that bank and a lady customer who was in the bank at the time came to Harrison today to view the body. It is understood all three were of the opinion Jensen was not one of the men staging the Kearney robbery.

Harrison Sun, Thurs., Dec. 27, 1934

IMPLICATED IN ROBBERIES

Sheriff Williams recently received a letter from O.C. Lee, Sheriff at Worthington, Minn., in which the latter wrote that he and other officers had solved a number of bank robberies in Minnesota in which Marion Jensen, bandit who held up the Sioux National Bank last December, and Jensen's brother-in-law, a man by the name of Wolcoth, were said to be implicated. Jensen paid with his life for his misdeed here, and Wolcoth is serving time in the Minnesota penitentiary after confessing to theft of a car and planning to hold up a bank. Wolcoth, although strongly suspected with participation in Minnesota holdups, could not be proved guilty of the actual crime. Sheriff Lee stated in his letter that Jensen and Wolcoth had stolen a car at Fairmont, Minn., which was found abandoned at Sioux Falls, S.D. The two were said to have robbed a bank at Bricelyn, Minn., and Jensen was positively identified by a bank official as the long bandit who later robbed the bank at

---

(21) Your granddad Sid received some criticism for not being in the sheriff's office when the robbery occurred. However, it must be remembered that much of the sheriff's work takes place in the field away from the office. So, it is not surprising that he wasn't in the office.

Frost, Minn. Jensen and Wolcoth are also accused robbing the bank at Elmore, Minn., in 1932. Of robbing the bank at Elmore, Minn., Lee would tend to dispel the idea that Jensen was inexperienced in banditry.

Harrison Sun, Thurs., June 13, 1935

ANOTHER BANK ROBBERY

Western Nebraska seems to be the field of operation for bank bandits of late, a second robbery having been committed in a little more two weeks in this section of the state.

Four bandits armed with machine guns held a large crowd at bay in the First National Bank of Scottsbluff Tuesday afternoon about two o'clock, and got away with $11,600, taking four of the bank's employees as hostages. Word sent out to nearby towns failed to stop the bandits, who it appears have made their escape, with little if any clues for officers to follow.

Harrison Sun, Thurs., Jan. 10, 1935

QUARANTINED FOR SMALLPOX

Sheriff Sid Williams was called to the south part of the county Tuesday of this week to post smallpox placards. Several families are under quarantine against the malady in that part of the county. One case is reported in the valley north of Harrison, also.

Harrison Sun, Thurs., Jan. 17, 1935

BROUGHT FROM FREMONT TO ANSWER A CHARGE OF FRAUD

Sheriff Williams returned this morning from Fremont, bringing with him J.B. Rochelle, against whom complaint was made about a year ago for fraudulently obtaining money. Rochelle has in past years solicited insurance in Harrison and vicinity, and about September 1, 1933, he is alleged to have sold a policy to Geo. Story, taking the latter's note for the amount of $79.35 in payment of same. Rochelle later sold the note to W.L. Hoyt, and the policy had not been issued to Mr. Story at the time of the sale of the note. Rochelle was recently located at Fremont, where he has been engaged in the insurance business. Unless some settlement is made in the meantime, Rochelle will be arraigned in county court.

Harrison Sun, Thurs., Feb. 28, 1935

VAN TASSELL HAPPENINGS

Sid Williams of Harrison was mingling with friends in town Friday afternoon.

Harrison Sun, Thurs., April 4, 1935

ADJUDGED INSANE

Mrs. Nina Baldwin, who eluded a nurse at Lusk last week and came to Harrison, was taken into custody here by Sheriffs Hassed of Lusk and Sid Williams, and later transported to Newcastle, where a jury adjudged the woman insane. Mrs. Baldwin has been a familiar figure in court at Lusk for a number of years, and insanity charges had been pending for some time. She had demanded a change of venue, which was granted. Mrs. Baldwin had been placed in the care of a nurse last week, but contrived in some manner to escape and cross the state line to Harrison, where she thought she would be safe from the Wyoming officers. She was committed by the court to the Evanston hospital.

Harrison Sun, Thurs., April 4, 1935

OFFICERS CALLED TO MEETING

Strained relations between opposing

factions in one of the school districts in the south part of the county, led some of the patrons to believe the best way to prevent trouble was to have an officer present at the meeting, and Sheriff Williams was called in to attend the meeting, which was held Monday evening. Difference of opinion as to the conduct of the district's business has been at high pressure in this district for some time. Miss Thelma Lawler, county superintendent, was also asked to attend the meeting. Occurrences of this nature are regrettable and it is to be hoped the difficulties have been ironed out. In the final analysis it is usually the pupils who are damaged the most from such controversies.

Harrison Sun, Thurs., June 13, 1935

PASSES THREE BUM CHECKS

A man who has been employed by Glenn Cutler in the hay fields for a short time passed three worthless checks on merchants last Saturday, using the name of Roy Toft, George Forge and Albert Hilder. The checks, each for a small amount, were drawn on the account of Glenn Cutler. The culprit is being sought to answer to a charge of forgery.

Harrison Sun, Thurs., Aug. 29, 1935

WANTED FOR CAR THEFT

Norman Ross, 17-year-old Watford City, N.D. lad, was apprehended here Tuesday by John Marking, following a phone call from Crawford officers, who stated the young man had driven away from a filling station there without the formality of paying for some gas he had purchased. Following his arrest it was ascertained Ross had stolen the car he was driving at Bismark, N.D., Sept. 7th,

and officers from there are expected tonight to get the boy and the car. Ross was on furlough from the state training school at Mandan, N.D., and stole the car and headed westward.

Harrison Sun, Thurs., Sept. 12, 1935

DELINQUENT TAX COLLECTIONS

I have in my hands distress warrants issued from the county treasurer's office of Sioux County, for collection of delinquent personal taxes in the county. Notices of delinquency are being mailed this week, and prompt attention to these notices should be given, to avoid incurring additional expense to those owing personal taxes. A short time will be allowed for remittance, after which I will begin to levy against property for tax collection.

C.S. WILLIAMS, Sheriff.

Harrison Sun, Thurs., Nov. 21, 1935

NEW MARSHAL APPOINTED

At the meeting of the town council last Tuesday night the resignation of John Marking as marshal of the town was accepted and Lynn Barkus was appointed to fill the position. At best, the job of marshal in a small locality has its unpleasant features, but we are constrained to remark, from our own observations during a period of several years, that John Marking has rendered the community some very valuable service, and we are pleased to inform the public that he will continue to watch over the community during the hours from midnight till dawn.

Harrison Sun, Thurs., Jan. 9, 1936

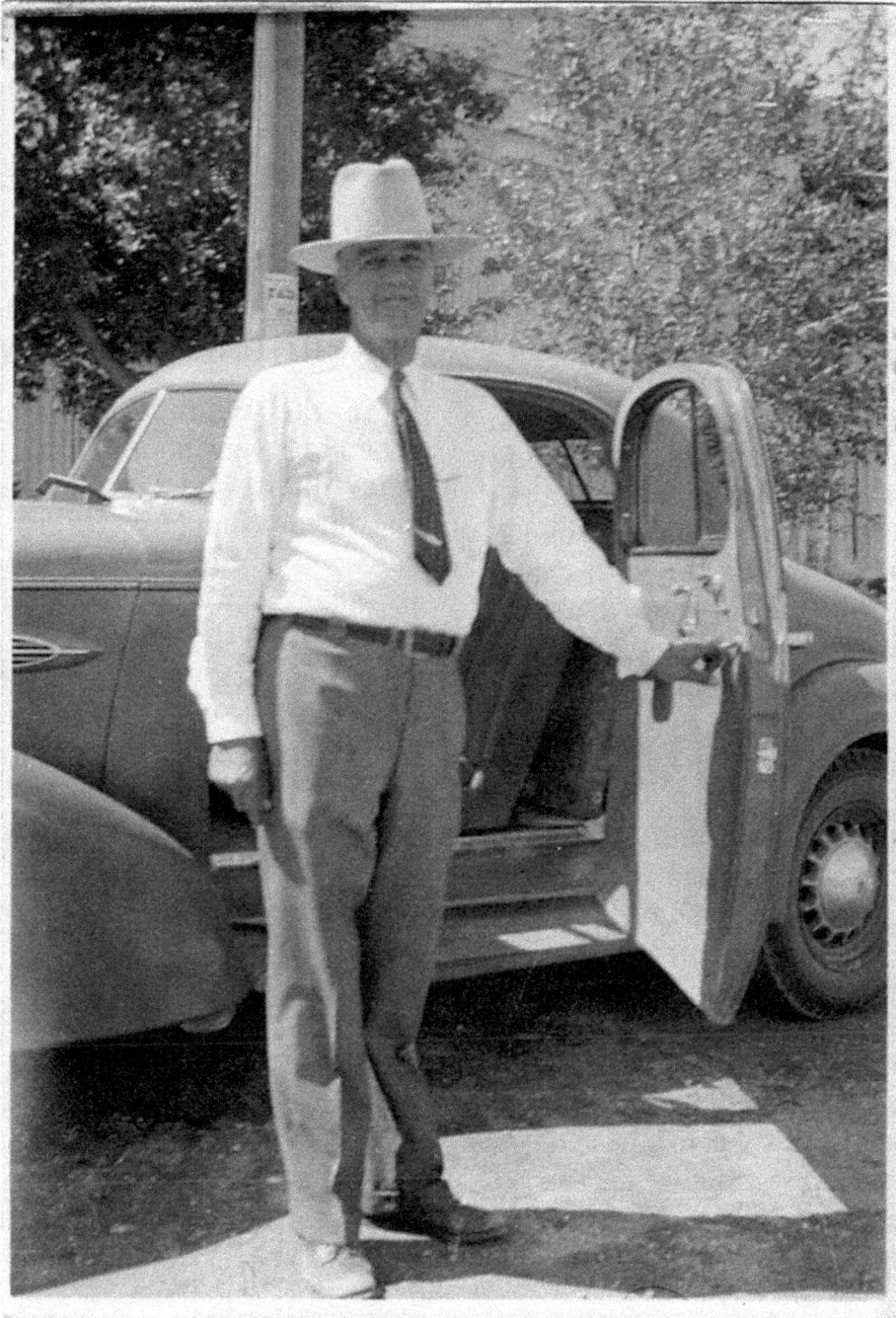

Charles Sidney Williams, Sr., age 67
Summer, 1936
Photo taken by Mary Coffey, Deputy County Clerk or County Clerk
In front of Sioux County Courthouse
Car is a 1935 Oldsmobile Coupe
Note Sheriff's badge on belt-right side

THREE YOUNG MEN GIVEN SEVEN YEARS FOR STATUTORY OFFENSE

County Attorney W.E. Mumby was called to Scotts Bluff County Monday to question three Scottsbluff young men, who were held on a serious complaint, involving the alleged statutory offense against a fifteen-year old girl.

According to signed statements made by the men, the three, John Pauley, 18, Kenneth Cain, 19, and Adam Bretthauer, 21, left Scottsbluff Sunday afternoon driving to Mitchell, and then to Morrill, and from the latter point took the road north into Sioux County, where they persuaded a young girl to get in the car with them. They continued north for a short distance, where the offense was committed and later returned the girl to her home. The boys then drove to Mitchell and were in a beer parlor when officers found them and made the arrest.

Upon questioning by County Attorney Mumby, the boys confessed and were brought to Harrison and arraigned in county court Tuesday when they entered pleas of guilty and were bound over to district court.

Sheriff Williams and Mr. Mumby took the boys to Alliance yesterday for appearance before District Judge E.L. Meyer, who sentenced each to seven years imprisonment in the reformatory for men at Lincoln.

Harrison Sun, Thurs., Oct. 24, 1935

GIVEN ONE TO TWO YEARS

Sheriff Williams and County Attorney Mumby drove to Alliance Wednesday to arraign Jess Chilson before District Judge

E.L. Meyer. Chilson plead guilty to a charge of misrepresentation in the transfer of some horses to the Gillette brothers south of Glen recently, and upon his plea of guilty was sentenced to one to two years in the state institution at Lincoln. Chilson was apprehended in Colorado.(22)

Harrison Sun, Thurs., Jan. 23, 1936

THIEVES BREAK INTO BULK OIL WAREHOUSES MONDAY NIGHT

Both the White Eagle and Standard Oil company warehouses were broken into Monday night, and Lou Sherrill, manager of the latter company, reports 45 gallons of kerosene and 5 gallons of lubricating oil were taken from his warehouse. Nothing was taken from the White Eagle warehouse. Similar robberies were reported in Crawford the same night, when three retail stations were broken into, and also a warehouse of the White Eagle company, the latter firm reporting the loss of 150 gallons of gasoline and a barrel of oil.

Harrison Sun, Thurs., June 18, 1936

JAIL BUSINESS HITS SLUMP

Sheriff Williams informs us that business at the county jail has been poor for quite some time, it having been several months since the bastile has been occupied, except for the confinement of local culprits who have been temporarily indisposed and given safe lodging for the night. Not a warrant for criminal offense has been issued in the county for many months. Why not organize a pool and poker club and get some use of the building?

Harrison Sun, Thurs., Dec. 10, 1936

(22)   *Served 3 days in jail before going to the pen.*

WILLIAM RAUTZ ENTERS PLEA GUILTY OF FELONY CHARGE

Although the total value of several miscellaneous theft items amounted to little in dollars and cents, William Rautz made the mistake of breaking and entering, which constitutes a charge of felony, and upon his plea of guilty faces the possibility of penitentiary term.

According to the admission of guilt to a series of thefts Monday night of this week, as made to Sheriff Williams, Rautz was having a very fine night of it. He first stopped at the Lake Ranch in the east part of the county, where he drained a quantity of gasoline from a car standing in the yard, and before leaving helped himself to a suit of underwear from the clothes line. Later he stopped at Mike Ruffing's place and picked up two coyote traps. From there he proceeded to Glen and attempted to get some more gas from the tank at the Marshall store, but the tank was empty. Rautz then proceeded to a school house south of Glen and broke into a building and loaded the back end of his pick-up with coal.

Rautz was arraigned before Judge Wilhermsdorfer in county court yesterday and entered a plea of guilty to the theft of the coal, and will be taken before Judge Meyer at Alliance Friday for sentence.

Rautz was brought before County Judge Wilhermsdorfer last March on a complaint of non-support of his family and was ordered to make monthly contribution to his wife, which he complied with for a time.

Harrison Sun, Thurs., Jan. 28, 1937

RAUTZ GIVEN PEN TERM

William Rautz, who plead guilty in county court here last week, to a charge of breaking and entering, was taken to Alliance Saturday by Sheriff Sid Williams and County Attorney W.E. Mumby, and was sentenced by Judge E.L. Meyer to serve from one to two years in prison. Rautz was taken directly to Lincoln from Alliance by Sheriff Williams.(23)

Harrison Sun, Thurs., Feb. 4, 1937

ADMIT KILLING OF ANTELOPE

On their appearance in county court Monday of this week, Ted Hammond and George Schraeder plead guilty to a complaint filed by Leon Cunningham, deputy state game warden, charging the young men with unlawfully killing an antelope. According to evidence secured by the game wardens, the antelope was shot January 10 and the carcass taken to a cellar on the Riggins place in the east part of the county, where the animal was butchered. Investigation made recently by Sheriff Williams in company with the wardens disproved the allegation that others were implicated in the deal. The young men were released on their own recognizance to appear Saturday of this week for sentence. The statute provides a penalty of $1000 fine or 30 days imprisonment for the killing of an antelope.

Harrison Sun, Thurs., Jan. 1, 1937

TWO SERVE OUT FINES

Ted Hammond and George Schrader elected to serve out the fines of $100 each, assessed against them in county court last week, when they plead guilty to charges of shooting antelope. They were committed to the county jail Monday. An error appeared

(23)   *Rautz served two days in jail before being taken to Alliance for sentencing.*

in last week's Sun in connection with this case, it having been stated the fine for killing antelope is $1000, which should have been $100.

Harrison Sun, Thurs., Feb. 4, 1937

GIVEN TEN DAYS FOR DISTURBANCE

"Monk" Barkus ran afoul of the law last Friday night and upon appearance in county court Monday morning was given a sentence of ten days in jail and assessed the costs on the charge of disturbing the peace, which had been lodged against him.

Harrison Sun, Thurs., Feb. 4, 1937

DISTRICT COURT CONVENES MONDAY; JURY IS DISMISSED

Lawyers, litigants and many others will flock to Harrison Monday of next week when Judge Earl. L. Meyer will open a regular term of the district court for Sioux County. Although a jury term, those who had been called for service have been notified not to appear, as such cases scheduled for a jury trial will be heard by the judge, upon agreement of the attorneys.

There are 53 cases registered on the docket, most of which are foreclosures. The Sioux County docket is entirely free from criminal actions, and there are but two divorce cases.

Harrison Sun, Thurs., Feb. 11, 1937

FISHING WITHOUT LICENSES

Two young fellows of Lusk were picked up on Sowbelly Creek last Saturday, by Leon Cunningham, game warden, and taken before Judge Wilhermsdorfer for a hearing on the charge of fishing without non-resident licenses. The boys now realize the importance of having one of those little tags, containing a permit to fish in the streams of the state, as they were assessed a fine and costs, amounting to $4.50 each. This should be a warning to numerous others who do not have fishing licenses. The cost to resident fishermen is only a dollar each, and the money is used for a good purpose-to aid in re-stocking the streams, and none should expect to have the privilege of fishing without a license.

Harrison Sun, Thurs., April 15, 1937

HOME ROBBED; SHERIFF NABS TRIO, WHO ADMIT THE CRIME

Upon receipt of information that a robbery of the home of A. C. Cullers, in Cottonwood precinct this county, had been planned, Sheriff Williams drove to Crawford Saturday to learn that the robbery had actually taken place that afternoon, and a box containing $77 in cash, $90 in postal saving certificates and other valuable securities had been taken from the house. Mr. Cullers, 80 years old, who lives alone on his farm, had gone to Crawford that day and the robbery was perpetrated during his absence.

Tire tracks in the yard of this farm place furnished a clue which took Sheriff Williams to Hemingford and to several other points, and it was not until Monday that he rounded up Earl Stoneking, who was suspected of having committed the robbery. Ethel Franks, who had been seen with Stoneking Saturday, was picked up for investigation and upon questioning she admitted having gone to the Cullers place with Stoneking and another man. She was brought to Harrison to face Stoneking, who had steadfastly denied having any part in the robbery, but when he realized the woman had told the facts to the sheriff he admitted his guilt.

The other man in the trio was Ralph Beers, who was arrested in Crawford Monday night and is being held in jail there.

After the robbery Saturday the men and the woman drove to Horn and then west over the Cottonwood road and near the O.L. Fox Ranch; the box was hidden in a gulch. Sunday, however, Stoneking drove to the point and got the box hiding it in a clump of trees along the highway about twelve miles east of Harrison. After admitting the crime Stoneking took Sheriff Williams to the new hiding place of the box and it was recovered.

Harrison Sun, Thurs., March 25, 1937

REVERSES STORY WHEN TAKEN BEFORE THE DISTRICT JUDGE

When arraigned before District Judge E.L. Meyer at Alliance yesterday, Earl Stoneking, who was arrested last week for robbing the home A. C. Cullers in the east part of the county, entered a plea of not guilty and was brought back to the Sioux county jail, where he will be held until the September term of court, or until bond is forthcoming for his release.

Stoneking had previously made a full confession of guilt to Sheriff Williams and County Attorney Mumby, and later Ralph Beers and Ethel Franks were arrested for complicity in the robbery, both of whom confessed having had a part in the robbery. The latter two, however, plead guilty before Judge Meyer but sentence was withheld. Attorney Charles Fisher of Chadron appeared before Judge Meyer at Alliance yesterday in behalf of Stoneking.

Harrison Sun, Thurs., April 1, 1937

STONEKING CHANGES PLEA; SENTENCED 1 TO 4 YEARS

Earl Stoneking, who was apprehended for robbery of the home of Amos Cullers in the east part of the county several weeks ago, and who had previously entered a plea of not guilty when arraigned before Judge E. L. Meyer in Alliance, has taken a change of heart and decided to plead guilty to the charge. He was taken before Judge Meyer, who has been conducting a term of district court in Chadron, and was given a sentence of from one to four years in the state penitentiary.

Ethel Franks and Ralph Beers, who were with Stoneking when the robbery was committed, and who plead guilty, were given suspended sentences of two and three years respectively. Either of the latter two can be brought in for sentence to penal institutions unless they follow the straight and narrow path, under requirements imposed by the court. They are to remain in either Sioux or Dawes Counties unless permitted by the court to leave, and are to make frequent reports to Sheriff Williams or the court. They are also required to pay the costs of prosecution.

Stoneking is in custody of Sheriff Williams and will be taken soon to Lincoln to begin serving his sentence.(24)

Harrison Sun, Thurs., April 15, 1937

ESCAPED CONVICT CAPTURED

Charles Vincent, who escaped last June from the state prison farm at Riverton, Wyoming, was on his way back to the Wyoming pen at Rawlins last Monday, he having been apprehended at Crawford last Saturday. Vincent had beaten his way to Harrison on the

(24) *Stoneking served 30 days in the county jail before going to the pen. Franks and Beers served 25 days before being placed on probation.*

local freight that morning and while the crew was unloading merchandise he stepped into the depot and purloined a suitcase belonging to George Wickersham, while the latter was at the stockyards loading cattle. John Marking phoned to the police officer at Crawford and Vincent was taken off the train, and had the grip in his possession. Officer Eschenbrenner noted Vincent's likeness to that of a card he had received from the Rawlins prison and a check-up proved Vincent to be the man that the Wyoming authorities were offering a reward of $50 for.

Harrison Sun, May 20, 1937

TOWN BOARD CONSIDERS APPLICATIONS FOR MARSHAL JOB

Several applications for the job of marshal of the village were considered at the regular meeting of the village board Tuesday evening, and the board has taken under advisement the matter of employing an outsider for the position. Under a law enacted at the last state legislative session, the salary a village is permitted to pay its marshal was raised from $25 to $50 per month. Added to this would be other odd jobs, and the total salary per month be made worth while for a competent man.

Harrison Sun, Thurs., Sept. 9, 1937

FRENCH CHOSEN MARSHAL

At a special meeting of the town council, held Tuesday, Mr. French was elected to the position of marshal, and he is to begin his duties October 1. Mr. French has been employed as night marshal at Bayard, Nebraska, for some time. In addition to his work as marshal, he will have the job of reading meters, making out light and water statements, and other duties. He comes well recommended for the position.

Harrison Sun, Thurs., Sept. 16, 1937

PLEAD GUILTY PETIT LARCENY

Two young men were taken up this week and lodged in jail on a complaint brought by Frank Hrasek, of the south part of the county, charging the young men had stolen 1960 pounds of oats and taken the grain to a valley town elevator and sold it. The young men are Gerald Blair and Jack Bourbon, who claim Arkansas as their home. In county court they plead guilty to a charge of petit larceny and were sentenced to thirty days in jail.(25) The stolen grain was returned to Mr. Hrasek. The boys claimed this was their first offense and said they expected to use the money to return to their home in Arkansas.

Harrison Sun, Thurs., Dec. 16, 1937

SHERIFF WILLIAMS STARTS PERSONAL TAX COLLECTION

Sheriff Williams says there's no foolin' about the collection of delinquent personal taxes, and he has already started levying on property for the collection of same. This follows in the wake of an order issued recently by the board of county commissioners, that legal procedure be instituted at once to bring the treasurer's ledger up to date. Foreclosure proceedings are to be brought against certain tracts of land for collection of real estate taxes.

In another column of this issue Sheriff Williams calls attention to delinquent property taxpayers of his action, and further states that those delinquent can save themselves costs of levying if they will come in at once and make settlement.

Harrison Sun, Thurs., Jan. 27, 1938

(25)   *The jailhouse records indicate that the two men were indeed incarcerated for 30 days.*

NOTICE TO DELINQUENTS

Have received a written notice from the Board of County Commissioners to proceed at once with the collection of delinquent personal taxes in Sioux County, and have already levied on some of the property for collection of taxes.

Those delinquent can save the costs if paid before the property is levied on.

C.S. WILLIAMS,

Sheriff, Sioux County

Harrison Sun, Thurs., Jan. 27, 1938

SHERIFF WILLIAMS PICKS UP TWO-GUN MAN WEDNESDAY

A man giving the name of Malcolm Douglas was picked up by Sheriff Williams at the Oxford Hotel Wednesday evening, following a telephone call from Mrs. Bell, operator of the hotel. Mrs. Bell stated the man was in the hotel lobby when the hotel was opened Wednesday morning and remained there during the day, and she became suspicious of him when he hid his face behind a paper whenever anyone came in the hotel. He told Mrs. Bell his car had broken down near town and he was waiting for his brother to arrive that evening to help him out.

Following the telephone call Sheriff Williams entered the building through the back entrance and when he came into the office, the man had his hat pulled over his face. The sheriff lifted his hat and told the suspect that he wanted him. A search revealed no weapons, but when the man said he wanted his overcoat, which was hanging near, Sheriff Williams beat him to it, and in a side pocket was a loaded .38 caliber revolver. A search of a package

Douglas carried was made at the jail and another gun was found, besides a box of cartridges, and also a number of cartridges were found in the man's pockets. He had but a few cents on his person.

That same day a new Ford V-8 coupe was taken up on the highway about a half mile west of town, bearing an Alliance dealer's license plate, and it is believed the car was stolen by Douglas and driven here. A leak in the oil plug had drained the motor and the engine was stuck.

The car had been stolen from the storage room of the Alliance dealer and had not been missed until Sheriff Williams notified them that the car was here. It had been driven 106 miles, according to the speedometer.

Upon questioning, the man in custody said his name was Malcolm Douglas and that he had come from Casper the night before and was enroute to Arizona, and steadfastly maintained he had nothing to do with the stolen car. Two money order receipt stubs were found on his person, issued by the Spearfish, S.D., post office. A call there elicited the information that the orders were issued to one Donald Price, and later the man confessed his name was Price.

Price said he was born at Spokane, Wash., and his present home was Missoula, Mont. He is 25 years old, brown hair, slender build, about six feet tall. He had served in the navy and said he was "kicked out" for misbehavior. He evidently had a yen for decorating his skin, for he has tattoo marks pretty well over his body. On his right forearm he has a mark of "Horseshoe, Idaho" and a combination snake, skull and crossbones. Left forearm is tattooed with skull and crossbones and also an eagle and USN 1931. Left leg tattooed Panama 1933. Right leg, "Rose." Back of right hand, skull and crossbones.

Fingerprints were taken of Price, and Sheriff Williams will hold the man in custody until a thorough investigation can be made to determine if he has a criminal record and is wanted at some other point. (26) The sheriff of Box Butte County came over with a garage mechanic for the Ford car, and offset impressions were made of fingerprints on the car, to compare them with the ones taken of Price.

Harrison Sun, Thurs., Feb. 3, 1938

(26)   The arrest of Two-Gun Price and the arrest of Charley Russell three (3) months earlier completed your granddad's earning the title: **"BRING 'EM BACK ALIVE SID".**

GETS $300 FINE FOR GUN TOTING; TO SERVE SENTENCE

Donald Price, the man who was picked up here a short time ago as a suspicious character, was arraigned in court this week and upon a plea of *guilty* to carrying concealed weapons, was fined $300. Price was remanded to the county jail until the fine is paid. Failure to produce the money means one hundred days in jail.

Harrison Sun, Thurs., Feb. 17, 1938

MEIER GARAGE BROKEN INTO LAST NIGHT; CAR IS STOLEN

A thief or thieves broke into the Edw. Meier garage last night, and loaded up a lot of tools, a radio and drove away with Rudie Hartman's Chevrolet coupe, which was stored in the garage. The car was found about seven miles west of town, alongside the highway, where the thieves were forced to abandon it when the engine stuck. There was no water in the radiator and when the engine got hot, the car was stalled. An electric drill, a hoist, and some other valuable tools were taken from the garage, but all these items, including the radio, were still in the car. The only articles lost were a sheep-skin coat and a rifle, which the thieves must have taken with them. The motor was damaged by over-heating. No trace of the pilferers has yet been found.

Harrison Sun, Thurs., March 10, 1938

LACY GARAGE LOOTED SAME NIGHT PRISONER DISAPPEARS

Just what connection a county jail prisoner may have with the looting of the Lacy Garage is not at the present time known, but Donald Price, held in the county bastile on a charge of carrying concealed weapons and sentenced to serve a $300 fine, sawed his way out of the jail and his whereabouts are unknown.

The thievery of the Lacy Garage followed shortly after the pilferage of the Ed Meier's garage, when a car was taken and driven almost to the Wyoming line and later recovered, with most of the articles he had stolen.

It is suspected that Price was aided by an outsider, and the two pulled the Lacy job. When opening the garage Sunday morning Verne Hutchinson discovered someone had been in the place during the night and upon investigation there was found a new Ford car had been stolen, as well as a typewriter, an adding machine, a radio, and two electric drills. The car is insured but the other loss will amount to about $300.

No locks were broken in the Lacy garage and it appears that the party who did the job must have concealed himself in the building before the place of business was closed Saturday night. Footprints in the alley at the rear of the garage indicated that a watcher was on duty until the opportune time to commit the robbery.

Price was apprehended here February 2 by Sheriff Williams. At about the same time a new Ford coupe was found west of town and later identified as a car stolen from the Alliance Ford dealer. Price could not be proven as the perpetrator of the thievery but was taken up as a suspicious character and found to be packing two revolvers. Later information revealed the fact that he has served two terms in Arizona for car theft and robbery, and it is also known that he is wanted in Fresno, Calif., for highway robbery. However, the Fresno authorities would not stand the expense of coming after him.

It is possible that Price's confederate has been here for some time, and in some manner got some hacksaw blades to him.

The case has been turned over to the

federal department of justice, as it is supposed the stolen car was transported from the state and which would constitute a crime under the jurisdiction of the federal government. Officials of the department are now working on the case.

Harrison Sun, Thurs., March 17, 1938

STOLEN CAR, JAIL BREAKER WERE PICKED UP IN ARIZONA

Officials of the Federal Bureau of Investigation notified County Attorney W.E. Mumby that Donald Price, the man who sawed his way out of the county jail two weeks ago, had been picked up in Phoenix, Ariz. The new Ford car, stolen from the Lacy garage at the same time Price disappeared, was found on the streets of the Arizona city. Later information was to the effect that Price had admitted theft of the car, and also the missing articles from the garage. Price told the officers that he sold the radio at Cheyenne, one of the electric drills at Rock Springs, another drill, a typewriter and an adding machine in Salt Lake City.

Transporting a stolen car to another state constitutes a federal crime and it is likely Price will be turned over to the U.S. Department of Justice for indictment and punishment.

Harrison Sun, Thurs., March 24, 1938

COUNTY STOCKMEN TO MAKE FIGHT AGAINST RUSTLING

A petition is being circulated among Sioux County stockmen, asking for cash subscriptions to a fund to be offered for the arrest and conviction of cattle thieves. Quite a number have reported the loss of cattle the past fall and winter, and while no one stockman has lost a large number of cattle, a few from each herd has made the total run to quite an amount. One ranchman reported the loss of eight head of heifers recently, and another a like number of mixed cattle. The annual loss represents a large sum of money, and the stockmen promoting the organized effort to stop this leak are desirous of forming a county stockmen's association, and have arranged to hold a meeting in Harrison Friday, February 18, to perfect a permanent organization. All stockmen should be interested in this movement and should make it a point to be here on the above date.

Harrison Sun, Thurs., Feb.10, 1938

YOUR GRANDDAD'S FINAL ILLNESS & DEATH

SHERIFF WILLIAMS ILL

Sid Williams was taken ill Tuesday and taken to Lusk, Wyo. for medical treatment. His illness is due to a heart ailment and he is also being observed for symptoms of other disturbances to his general health. While in Lusk he is staying at the home of Mrs. Reuben Galloway.(27)

Harrison Sun, Thurs., March 3, 1938

C.S. WILLIAMS CRITICALLY ILL

Sheriff C.S. Williams who had been a patient at Lusk, Wyo., for several weeks, was moved to the hospital at Chadron last Friday evening. After removal to the hospital at Chadron additional x-rays were taken and the doctors found Mr. Williams to be suffering from an injured vertebra. He is also suffering from an enlarged heart.

The members of the family were called to his bedside Saturday, but since that time he has shown improvement.

Harrison Sun, Thurs., March 17, 1938

(27)   Dad had been ailing for several months and after discussing it with my mother said he was going to Hot Springs and consult with a Dr. and take some hot bath treatments while there. Mom offered to go with him, stating that Mrs. Goodsin Lacy would probably take care of the kids, but he went alone.

On the way home he took a little traveled road to Crawford or Chadron (we aren't sure which) and his car, a 1937 DeSoto, broke down and quit running. No one came along and so he started walking, and traveled many miles before he caught a ride to town. He made arrangements for his car to be fixed and finally got home late at night, the last day of Feb. or early in the morning of March 1, 1938.

Apparently, the very long walk aggravated his spinal condition and he was in a great deal of pain. That day, March 1, Mom and Dad went to see Dr. Reckling in Lusk and they spent several days in Lusk with Mom's sister, Mrs. Reuben Galloway. When no improvement was noted he was transferred by ambulance to the Chadron hospital.

At Chadron, a gradual paralysis set in until he was eventually paralyzed from the waist down. X-rays indicated this was due to a honey-combed and collapsed vertebrae. This damaged vertebrae is attributed to the accident that occurred in the 1890's while foreman of the Circle Bar Ranch on Hat Creek, near the South Dakota line. Dad had been dragged by a team of horses across the Ardmore bridge and was for a short time paralyzed. That old injury was traumatized again June 20, 1932 the bad car accident that occurred while taking a man to the sanitarium at Norfolk, Nebraska.

A few weeks before his death he contacted pneumonia and although he had a "robust physique" and an "Iron Constitution" most of his life, at almost age 69, he could not overcome the paralysis, a heart condition and pneumonia, and passed away Friday evening, May 6, 1938.

Following are the news items printed in the Harrison Sun regarding his illness and death.

DEATH COMES TO SHERIFF SID WILLIAMS AT CHADRON MAY 6

Stricken with a heart illness March 1, and taken to the Lusk hospital for medical treatment, later being removed to the Chadron hospital, Sheriff Sid Williams passed away at the latter institution Friday evening of last week, after an illness of more than two months. Sid fought a valiant fight for life, but the ravages of his affliction gradually encroached upon a robust physical constitution, when he was forced to answer the final call.

Coming to this western country as a youth, Sid grew up through the early pioneer period and has been identified in various pursuits. He has worked as a cow-hand, conducted a ranching business for himself, and in later years devoted much time to the development of race horses, more for the love of the game than for profit.

In 1926 he was appointed sheriff of Sioux County to fill the unexpired term caused by the resignation of George Hill, and at the election following was voted into the office, as he has been in subsequent elections, and at the time of his death he was still the county's sheriff. In this capacity Sid was known as a fearless official, and at no time hesitated to do his duty as he saw it.

A familiar figure in Harrison and Sioux County for a number of years, Sid will be missed from our ranks, and the community deeply sympathizes with the bereaved ones in his passing.

Funeral services were conducted from the Methodist church at Chadron Monday afternoon of this week. Rev. E.C. Mitchell delivering the sermon. Burial was made in the Chadron cemetery, the remains being laid to rest beside the mother, a daughter and four brothers of deceased. Pallbearers were Dick Pfeister of Edgemont, Ray Farwell of Ardmore, Chris Wasserburger of near Montrose, and A.L. Schnurr, L.M. Childs and J.H. Wilhermsdorfer of Harrison.

The following obituary has been prepared by relatives:

Charles Sidney Williams was born at St. Charles, Minnesota, September 22, 1870, and passed away May 6, 1938, at the Chadron Municipal hospital, after an illness of two and one-half months.

As a youth he came to Hartington, Nebr., with his parents and later came to Sioux County, Nebraska, where he entered business with his brother, also taking a homestead near Ardmore, S.D., which became known as the Circle-Bar ranch. He continued in the cattle business in Fall River County, S.D., and Sioux County until 1926, when appointed sheriff of Sioux County to fill the unfinished term of George Hill and was still sheriff at the time of his death.

He leaves to mourn his loss his wife, LaVerne; five sons: Sidney, Jr., of Harrison, Floyd of Chadron, Russell of Parker, Arizona, Royal of Palisade, Colo., and Donald of Harrison; three daughters: Mrs. Frank Downey of Chadron, Mrs. Gayle Heming of Palisade, Colo., and Ila Mae Williams of Harrison, and one brother, O.B. Williams of Edgemont, South Dakota. (28)

Harrison Sun, Thurs., May 12, 1938

(28)   There are a few errors in the obituary printed in the Harrison Sun on Thursday, May 12, 1938.

My research, backed up by 1870 census data, indicates that his actual birth date was Sept. 22, 1869. Also, the Circle Bar Ranch was already in existence when he took out a homestead. He and his brother had run the Circle Bar for Dave Anderson.

Following is a RESOLUTION by the Board of County Commissioners concerning your grand-dad that was printed in the Harrison Sun. My family received a copy of the Resolution.

Harrison, Nebraska, May 16, 1938

Board of County Commissioners met pursuant to call of the Clerk. There were present, John Lacy, Jr., Chairman, Harry Morris and Jacob Wasserburger, Commissioners, and A. C. Davis, Clerk.

The following Resolution was offered and adopted, to-wit:

RESOLUTION

Charles Sidney Williams, Pioneer Settler and Rancher of Sioux County, Nebraska, died at Chadron, Nebraska, May 6, 1938. Mr. Williams was born at St. Charles, Minnesota, September 22, 1870. Mr. Williams was appointed Sheriff of Sioux County, Nebraska, on April 5, 1926 and continued in office until his untimely death. In the passing of Mr. Williams, Sioux County loses a sincere and fearless officer.

WHEREAS, it is the desire of this body to render tribute to the memory of our departed friend and colleague,

BE IT RESOLVED BY THE BOARD OF COUNTY COMMISSIONERS OF SIOUX COUNTY, NEBRASKA, That the Public Service which he rendered was marked by faithfulness and honor; that he guarded zealously his oath of office and was noted as an efficient peace officer and we can pay no higher tribute to our departed colleague.

THAT The County Clerk of Sioux County, Nebraska, be directed, forthwith, to send to his bereaved family, a copy of this RESOLUTION after the same shall have been spread upon the records of the proceedings of this body, as an expression of our reverence to his Memory.

Attest: _A C Davis_____
          County Clerk.

          Clerk's Seal
          Sioux County,
          Nebraska.

_John Lacy Jr_____
          Chairman.
_Jacob Wasserburger_____
_Harry Morris_____
          Board of County Commissioners.

Dated this 16th day of May, 1938.

This special session of the Board of County Commissioners of Sioux County, Nebraska, was called for the purpose of appointing a County Sheriff to fill vacancy.

It was moved, seconded and carried that Sidney Williams, Jr. be appointed Sheriff for the unexpired term. Sidney Williams, Jr., being present, accepted the appointment, took the Oath of office, and presented his Bond which was duly approved and ordered filed.

There being no other business, on motion, Board adjourned to meet June 6, 1938.

_John Lacy Jr_____   _A C Davis_____
          Chairman.   Clerk.

######

257

TWO FILE FOR SHERIFF

Two more filings for the office of sheriff of Sioux County have been made recently, bringing the total primary candidates for this job to four. Harold Skavdahl filed as a republican candidate while John Marking will fly the democratic banner in the primary race. Other candidates are Joe Stanek, republican, and John Buffington, democrat.

Harrison Sun, Thurs., April 21, 1938

CAR THIEF TURNED OVER TO CUSTER COUNTY FOR FORGERY

Clinton Fields, alias Dee Clinton, was apprehended at Hyannis Friday of last week, by Grant County officers, and returned to Sioux County. Fields had been working as a sheep-herder for Jerry McCarthy, leasor of the Mortensen ranch in the northwest part of the county, and Thursday night of last week made away with McCarthy's V-8 pickup. Reporting the theft to Deputy Sheriff Sidney Williams the following afternoon, word was sent out and Fields was located at Hyannis. He was brought back to Harrison Saturday and later advise came from Custer County officers that Fields had been wanted in that county for several months on a forgery charge. He was released to Custer County for prosecution under the former charge. The pick-up was returned to Mr. McCarthy, and it is stated that the latter holds money due Fields which is sufficient in amount to pay some bad checks floated here by Fields and also pay mileage expense of the sheriff's office.

Harrison Sun, Thurs., April 28, 1938

TWO FILINGS FOR SHERIFF

The sheriff's job in Sioux County seems to be much in demand, with four filings having been made some time ago and two additional filings during the past week. The roster reads John Buffington, democrat; Joe Stanek, republican; Harold Skavdahl, republican; John Marking, democrat; and the two new entries are Joe LaMay, democrat, and M.R. Wallace, republican.

Very few filings for the other elective county offices have been made to date, although there is yet plenty of time for aspirants to get into the running. Filings must be made forty days before the primary election date, which is August 9th.

Harrison Sun, Thurs., May 5, 1938

FOUR CONVICTED FROM SIOUX CO. APPLY FOR COMMUTATION

In this week's issue of the Sun are published four applications for parole and commutations from sentences to penal institutions.

Adam Breethauer, Kenneth Cain, and John Parley, convicted on October 23, 1935, for rape are asking for commutation and parole, Earl Stoneking, convicted on April 14, 1937, for breaking and entering is seeking a parole.

Harrison Sun, Thurs., March 17, 1938

PART VII
OTHER EVENTS AND INCIDENTS

A Skeleton In Our Closet

I have presented here a number of news items concerning Dick Witt, my wife's uncle because he was arrested several times by your granddad dating back to July, 1931. Most of the items presented occurred after your granddad's death, but since he had started the cattle theft investigations before his final illness and the investigation finished and the arrests made by your uncle Sid Jr., the information is therefore provided.

The Dick Witt Arrests

More than an ordinary amount of discussion is presented here about Richard (Dick) Witt and I wanted to tell about everything in this book even if it exposes all the skeletons on both sides in the family closet.

Dick Witt, the son of a Lutheran Pastor, was a brother of your other granddad, Art Witt.

He was arrested three (3) times, twice by your granddad Williams, Sheriff, and the third time by your uncle, Sid Jr., who assumed the sheriff's duties for a short time after the death of your granddad Sid. The arrest summaries are presented below:

Jail House Records:

Arrest #1: Dick Witt – arrested for cattle stealing July 21, 1931 and served two days in jail to July 22, 1931

Arrest #2: Richard Witt – arrested for stealing government harness – Oct. 5, 1931 and served four days in jail to Oct. 8, 1931

Arrest #3: Dick Witt – arrested for cattle stealing – Dec. 15, 1938 and served two days to Dec. 17, 1938

Arrest No. 3 resulted in a trial of Dick Witt, and other Sioux County residents, Lee Blevens, Raymond Schneringer and Marvin Rising. All were sentenced to the Nebraska State Penitentiary at Lincoln. Dick was sentenced to four years.

The three arrests of Dick Witt were not the only scrapes he had with the law. Art Witt, your other granddad, was able to get Dick out of all his lawless activities except the last one. One incident that I am aware of was that Dick Witt shot a wandering bull, belonging to the Gillett family that had gotten in with Art Witt's cows.

While in the penitentiary Dick left behind a wife and four children that lived in Glen. Your grandmother, Henrietta Witt, kept a huge garden and they kept Dick's family supplied with all the fresh vegetables they needed.

The following news items detail some of the legal problems of Dick Witt and the others involved in cattle and harness thefts:

SEVERAL CASES ARE HEARD IN COUNTY COURT DURING WEEK

The county court has been the scene of much activity in the criminal division during the past week, with four cases to be heard before Judge Wilhermsdorfer.

Monday a hearing was held for Dick Witt of near Glen, who with two boys of minor years were charged with cattle stealing.(1) Witt was bound over to district court, and the two boys will be heard later before the juvenile court.

The complaint was brought by Frank Bannan, who accuses defendants with the theft of two calves.

Harrison Sun, Thurs., July 30, 1931

MORE ON DICK WITT

Another criminal trial in district court last week was that of the state versus Dick Witt, on complaint of having received stolen cattle. Selecting the jury to hear the case was started Thursday and the introduction of evidence and pleas of attorneys lasted until Saturday evening when the case went to the jury. A sealed verdict was delivered during the night and read Sunday morning which was for acquittal. Two youths of minor age alleged to be involved in the stealing of calves from Frank Bannan some time ago, and will be tried in juvenile court some time later. J.E. Porter of Crawford was attorney for Witt in the above trial.

Several civil cases were aired before Judge Meyer during the term and a number continued. Court was adjourned Tuesday morning, the term being left open and the jury subject to call.

Harrison Sun, Thurs., Sept. 17, 1931

ARRESTED ON CHARGE OF TAKING GOVERNMENT PROPERTY

A search warrant was issued the fore part of the week to locate certain items of government property, believed to be on the place occupied by Dick Witt, near Glen. Sheriff Williams and Deputy J.B. Duncan went to the Witt place Tuesday and concealed in a draw about a half mile from the house uncovered several sets of harness, some halters and items of clothing. This property was taken from Fort Robinson. A federal officer and an army officer from the fort were here today to quiz Witt, and it is presumed the officers will take the case into federal court. Witt is being held in the county jail pending further action of the officials.

Harrison Sun, Thurs., Oct. 8, 1931

SHERIFF WILLIAMS ROUNDS UP SEVEN FOR CATTLE THEFT

The old west rides again, but in a modern manner. In place of galloping steeds, trucks are used to convey stolen cattle from fenced pastures to nearby marts, where the stolen plunder is disposed of.

For several years this manner of cattle rustling has been pursued on a profitable basis, but it appears the day of reckoning has come to a certain gang operating in Sioux and Dawes County, with the arrest of seven suspects during the past week.

Last May Sheriff Sidney Williams, Jr. of Sioux County became suspicious of the sale of a steer through a nearby sales ring, and since that time has been working on the case which involved a number of cattle

---

(1)   This article was split and the other part may be found concerning the Charles Russell news items.

thieves, and this week the case cracked with the arrest of the seven men. Lee Blevins, Raymond Schneringer and L.L. Dyer were taken before the county judge at Chadron Wednesday and signified they would plead guilty to the charge of stealing five head of cattle from the Lloyd Thomas ranch in Dawes County. The cattle were recovered. Others are in jail at Chadron at the present time and efforts are being made by officials to clear up the theft of numerous other cattle. County Attorney W.E. Mumby spent two days in Chadron to assist in placing charges that will bring a well organized gang of cattle thieves to justice.

DICK WITT ADMITS GUILT

Dick Witt of Glen was returned to Harrison Wednesday evening and today entered a plea of guilty to the theft of six head of cows and calves from the Henry Kreman place near Glen. This occurred in the late spring of this year. The cows and calves were taken to Scottsbluff, according to Witt's confession, where the calves were disposed of, although the buyers refused to take the cows which were later trucked to South Dakota and traded for horses. Witt was arraigned in county court here and bound over to district court.

Numerous cattlemen have reported the loss of cattle recently, and it is probable the efforts of the officials working on the case will uncover evidence implicating several others than those in custody.

Harrison Sun, Thurs., Dec. 15, 1938

THREE SENTENCED FOR CATTLE THEFT; ANOTHER IN CUSTODY

Following a plea of guilty of theft of cattle from the Lloyd Thomas ranch near Crawford, Loren L. Dyer and Lee Blevins appeared before District Judge Earl L. Meyer at Chadron last Friday and were sentenced to three years in the penitentiary. A third party in the deal, Raymond Schneringer, was sentenced to three years in the reformatory.

Marvin Rising was arrested yesterday and brought to Harrison as a suspect in the theft of cattle from the Kreman place near Glen and his hearing is set for Friday in Sioux County court.

In connection with the cattle rustling that has been going on in Dawes and Sioux Counties of late, Jay N. Woods of west of Hemingford was arraigned in Box Butte County court Tuesday on a charge of receiving stolen cattle. He plead not guilty and his hearing is set for Thursday of this week.

WITT DID NOT PLEAD GUILTY

In the last issue of the Sun there was recorded an article in regard to cattle thievery in Dawes and Sioux Counties, and there appeared in our columns a paragraph in which it was stated that Dick Witt had plead guilty to the theft of cattle from Henry Kreman. The Sun acknowledges the erroneousness of this article, as Witt did not enter a plea of guilty. However, he was taken before the county court on a charge of cattle theft and plead not guilty and was released on a bond of $1,000 for appearance Wednesday, Dec. 21. Since that date the time for hearing has been extended. On Thursday evening of last week, just before going to press, the editor inquired of the status of the case from a party whom he thought knew of the developments, and in the course of the conversation misunderstood the information given.

Harrison Sun, Thurs., Dec. 22, 1938

TWO PLEAD GUILTY, 2 OTHERS STAND TRIAL IN CATTLE CASE

With district court convening Monday, a number of civil actions were disposed of while arrangements were being made to hear four criminal cases on the February docket.

Arraigned before the court Monday, Raymond Schneringer plead guilty to a charge of cattle stealing, while Lee Blevens plead guilty to receiving stolen cattle. Both had plead guilty to similar charges in Dawes County some time ago for cattle taken from the Thomas ranch. The charges filed against Schneringer and Blevens in Sioux County were in connection with the theft and disposal of six head of cows and five calves from the Kreman ranch near Glen.

WITT FOUND GUILTY BY JURY

Two others taken up in connection with the theft and disposal of the Kreman cattle were Dick Witt, who was charged with receiving stolen cattle, and Marvin Rising, charged with cattle stealing. Witt stood trial, with a jury sworn in Tuesday to hear the case and after submission of evidence of various witnesses and the pleas of the attorneys, the case was given to the jury this afternoon. After a few hours deliberation the jury returned a verdict of guilty as charged. County Attorney W.E. Mumby and E.D. Crites of Chadron were attorneys for the prosecution while Porter, Skaggs & Porter represented the defendant.

The case against Rising will start tomorrow, a jury having been sworn in to hear the case.

Harrison Sun, Thurs., Feb. 16, 1939

JURY FINDS RISING GUILTY OF CATTLE THEFT CHARGE

A jury last Saturday returned a verdict of guilty against Marvin Rising indicted for cattle theft. With two admitting guilt in connection of theft or receiving stolen cattle from the Kreman place near Glen, and two found guilty in district court here, unless the motions for new trials in the cases of Dick Witt and Rising are sustained by the court, this about clears the docket of criminal cases.

Loren L. Dyer pleaded guilty to a charge of implication of cattle theft in Dawes County. Lee Blevens also entered a guilty plea in this connection, and on a charge filed against him in Sioux County, he also plead guilty. Raymond Schneringer entered a guilty plea of connection in the theft of the Kreman cattle.

Court adjourned Saturday until Monday morning of next week, at which time Judge Meyer will probably pronounce sentences.

TWO MORE JURY CASES

A jury of six have been called for 10:00 Monday morning to hear the damage case of Sarah E. Barnes et al versus the Department of Roads and Irrigation for settlement of right-or-way for the road from Harrison north.

Another jury trial which may come before the court next week is that of John A. Macumber vs. Jerome C. Gillette et al. This case involves the title to a piece of land in the eastern part of the county.

Harrison Sun, Thurs., Feb. 23, 1939

WITT SENTENCED TO FOUR YEARS; OTHERS GET THREE

Overruling motions for new trials for both Dick Witt and Marvin Rising, Judge Meyer pronounced sentence following verdicts of guilty. Rising was sentenced to three years in the state reformatory for men and Witt was given four years in the penitentiary.(2)

In pronouncing sentence on Rising, Judge Meyer said it was apparent the defendant had many friends who felt Rising should be shown leniency, and also the jury had recommended such in the return of their verdict. However, since the defendant had refused to enter a plea of guilt, as had others implicated in the theft of the Kreman cattle, and had placed the county to the expense of a trial, he felt he had no other course to pursue than to impose the minimum sentence. Judge Meyer also added that when the time came for consideration of parole, if circumstances at the time were favorable, he would not object to such action on the part of the parole board.

Raymond Schneringer, who plead guilty to participation in the theft of the Kreman cattle, was sentenced to three years in the state reformatory for men, this sentence to run concurrently with a sentence interposed in Dawes County, for theft of cattle from the Thomas ranch. Lee Blevens, who had plead guilty for participation in the disposal of the Thomas cattle, and who also plead guilty to a part in the Kreman cattle in Sioux County, was given a three-year sentence to run concurrently with the Dawes County sentence.

Harrison Sun, Thurs., Mar. 2, 1939

(2)   *World War II was on when Dick Witt was released from prison and as a result the country was booming. Witt was able to utilize his considerable talents into a successful ice plant business in Scottsbluff, Nebraska. He later sold out at a big profit and settled in Washington State where he lived the rest of his life.*

The Liver, Ear, Mudhole and Other Incidents

Liver, Its Whats For Dinner –

Nearly 300 people were arrested and went through the county jail during the tenure of your granddad as Sheriff 1926-1938. The burden of caring for the prisoners in the county jail became onerous, especially since more and more time was required of the law officers trying to do field investigations of liquor law violators and other criminal activities.

Therefore, at one point the jail and the prisoners were supposed to do their own cooking. This worked for awhile, but one day the sheriff found the inmates had broken up the stove and all the kitchen paraphernalia. So the next time the sheriff brought in groceries, it was liver. Sid told the prisoners that: "here is dinner and to prepare it to suit yourselves". I never learned what happened next, but I suppose the meal burden fell on my mother to prepare eats for the prisoners. I know that at times she did prepare meals for the prisoners.

The Ear And Mudhole Incidents

Harrison had a few habitual drunks and occasionally the sheriff was called out to arrest the drunks that were making a nuisance of themselves. Sid got one as far as the jail house steps when the drunk decided he didn't want to spend another period in jail sobering up and he sat down on the steps and wouldn't budge. Dad got behind him and grasping the top of each ear with thumb and forefinger began lifting him up. The drunk immediately changed his mind and was led to his cell.

On some occasions Dad drove them home with the admonishment that they were to stay home until they sobered up and not to be seen on the streets any more that evening. Most obeyed.

On one occasion a drunk after being arrested laid down in the street and refused to get up. Near where the drunk rested was a mudhole. Dad grabbed a leg and started to drag him into the mudhole. The drunk immediately changed his mind and offered no more resistance to the sheriff.

The Big Fight

Dad got a call one evening that a fight was in progress in one of the saloons downtown. There, he found Guy (Chick) Coffee and one of the Hill boys engaged in a vicious fist fight. These were big strapping fellows and Dad was an old man. Nevertheless, Dad stopped the fight and said: "If you two insist on fighting then be at the fairgrounds tomorrow morning at 10 o'clock and you two can settle your differences there. I want you two to go home-that's all you will do now otherwise I'll put you in jail. I'll referee the fight tomorrow". Both agreed to go home and settle their argument tomorrow.

The next day at the fairgrounds a large crowd had gathered, as well as the two contestants. Dad set out the rules, but the people I remember talking to about the fight didn't seem to remember what the rules were. They did say the fight appeared to be evenly matched with each fighter giving about as much as he received. However, Mr. Hill (I don't remember his first name) suddenly declared he had enough and quit. Mr. Coffee was therefore declared the winner.

The Big Riot

This was a big fight involving five cowboys at one of the downtown saloons. According to the jail house records this occurred Sept. 2, 1933 and those arrested spent 5 days in jail on a charge of rioting. This date would have been during fair time or shortly afterwards. Anyway, Dad got the call of several cowboys mixing it up. He stopped the fight and put all five in jail.

I worked in the Harrison Sun office during the early 1950's. One day during that time a Mr. Wasserburger (his first name escapes me), of the Edgemont, South Dakota area came into the office to renew his subscription to the paper. Upon learning that Sid Williams was my father he proceeded to tell me about the fight. He said he was in the saloon when the big fight was taking place. He said the cowboys were really mixing it up. Dad arrived and Wasserburger quoted Sid as saying: "You fellows have done all you're going to do. Now you are all under arrest and coming with me". Wasserburger stated he had never seen anything like it. "The cowboys just wilted and meekly submitted themselves to arrest". Wasserburger added: "I suppose these men, individually would probably have been more than a match for Sid because Sid was an old man. It was amazing to me how he controlled a bad situation".

The jail records list those arrested as: Happy Sankey, Max Hedges, Red Pholen, Dave Hunt, and Summartore. Hap Sankey is the only one that I knew.

CONCLUSIONS REGARDING
THE LIFE OF YOUR GRANDDAD, SID

Sid Williams was a hard-nosed, no-nonsense, liquor hating enforcer of the law. He was a historical figure locally as well as in adjoining parts of Wyoming and South Dakota and well known in ranching, horse racing and law enforcement circles.

Distinguished and effective service as Sioux County Sheriff earned him the title of **"BRING 'EM BACK ALIVE SID"**, as he was described by his friends. He arrested and brought in gun-toters who swore they would never be taken alive. At least one, Charley Russell, was a hold-over from the wild west days. Frequently without backup, Sid had to devise creative and innovative ideas to make arrests and avoid shoot-outs.

Again, one reason for this literary exercise was to determine if there is any credence to a persistent story I have heard several times during the last 50 years. The last time I heard the story was at our 50th wedding anniversary party held in August, 2000, Harrison, Nebr. About 100 people attended including a number of old timers. The story is that Charley Russell set off a charge of dynamite at a gate entry-way into the ranch yard, thwarting arrest and scaring away the sheriff.

I carefully researched the records at the Sioux County courthouse. I found that the court ordered arrest warrants three times for the arrest of Charley Russell during the tenure of your granddad as Sioux County Sheriff. These were June 1931, Jan. 1932, and Nov. 1937. Your granddad efficiently and promptly carried out the arrests. No mention was made of any resistance by Russell, although each time he was armed with his Colt 44 caliber revolvers. I think there would have been additional charges against Russell if there had been any resistance by explosives or by any other means.

I believe the dynamite blast story was a figment of Russell's imagination and might have been an idea, planned and expressed to his friends as to what he would do if the sheriff ever came around. The planned surprise was told often enough that it finally became a fact in the minds of his listeners, especially those that resented law enforcement authority. The dynamite blast event never happened.

Sid handled the sheriff's job superbly, considering that a large segment of the population didn't want to obey the prohibition laws. Of course he had his difficulties because some in this group simply didn't like being arrested and who resented law enforcement authority no matter how courteous the officer might be.

Dad's courage and judgement as sheriff were unquestionable. Physically robust and temperamentally suited for the tough law enforcement demands of the Depression and Prohibition eras he still related to others easily, even those he arrested.

The toughest part of the sheriff's job for your granddad were the sheriff's sales, conducted by court order on the front steps of the courthouse. These were homesteaders, ranchers, etc. who could not pay their real estate taxes and were losing their land. Sid, raised in poverty himself, sympathized with them. When these dispossessed settlers complained that they didn't know how they were going to feed their families, your granddad told them he had an account at Koch's grocery store and that they could charge groceries to his account until they could arrange something else.

I remember that Bob Koch, son of Gladys and Luther Koch, grocery store owners, once showed me a roll of paid receipts representing groceries charged to Dad's account. Also, on one occasion Dad's bill at Koch's store exceeded $300 which would equate to about $5,000 in today's value. Yes, Sid helped many with encouragement and aid to get through the harsh years of the depression even though we weren't in great shape ourselves.

Morris Keel, Sioux County rancher, living a few miles north of Harrison, stopped in at the Harrison Sun newspaper office where I worked in the early 1950's to pay his subscription to the paper. When he found out that I was Dad's youngest son, he said: "Your dad was a fine old man and don't let anyone ever tell you differently". I didn't press him for any details, but I often wondered what kind of experience he had with my Dad. I heard other stories of how he helped others get through the Depression years.

I think the stress and strain of the sheriff's job during Prohibition-the search for illegal stills, stakeouts, arrests, combined with the injuries sustained in the automobile accident while transporting a man to the State Sanitarium in Norfolk, Nebraska substantially shortened his life.

Sid was an example of law enforcement at its best.

While his performance as sheriff was exemplary I think his personal life could have been better.

He owned several different ranches during his lifetime. I think, perhaps, he should have stayed with one of the better places-such as what is now the Gayle Henry (Woodruff) place. He would have been better off using his considerable talents in adding to, and building up one place. Of course no one knew then that hard times for the cattlemen would cover almost the entire 21 year period between the World Wars, 1918-1939.

Although he made a lot of money in the early years racing thoroughbreds this was not the case in the Depression Years. Owning and racing thoroughbred horses is an exciting sport, but I think we would have been better off without them. Dad had a tendency to bet too much money on his own horses at the pari-mutuel betting booths. Of course, if he won, he won big, but conversely, if he lost he lost big.

The most critical and worst fault of your granddad was that he liked the opposite sex too much. Marital infidelity was a factor in the dissolution of some of his earlier marriages. The relationship with my mother was the longest and most stable of his five marriages. The one time she suspected he might be starting to stray she calmly, but sternly informed him that she would not tolerate another woman in his life. Otherwise, she and the kids would be gone. That ended the matter. He must have realized that he was much too busy enforcing the liquor laws to pursue such illicit activities. Besides, he needed a stable home life if he was going to be an effective enforcer of the law. Also, being an older man, he was probably a little mellower and grew to appreciate a good home life.

Well kids, that tells you just about everything I know about your granddad. Now, you probably know more about him than the other three grandparents that you did know.

I think if there was one bit of advice he might give his grandkids it would be this: "If you obey the laws, even laws you don't believe in, or dislike, then you are unlikely to get into trouble with the law. If you don't like the law, obey it anyway, but work to get it overturned or changed".

APPENDIX A

C.S. WILLIAMS
ADDITIONAL HOMESTEAD DOCUMENTS

HOMESTEAD AFFIDAVIT.

Office of the Clerk of the District Court of Sioux County,

Harrison, Nebraska, November 22 1892

I, *Charles S. Williams*, of *Ardmore S.D.* ~~Nebraska~~, having filed my application No. *4108*, for an entry under section 2289, Revised Statutes of the United States, do solemnly swear that I am not the proprietor of more than one hundred and sixty acres of land in any State or Territory; that I am over the age of twenty-one years, *a single man, and a Native born* citizen of the United States: that my said application is honestly and in good faith made for the purpose of actual settlement and cultivation, and not for the benefit of any other person, persons, or corporation, and that I will faithfully and honestly endeavor to comply with all the requirements of law as to settlement, residence, and cultivation necessary to acquire title to the land applied for; that I am not acting as agent of any person, corporation, or syndicate in making such entry, nor in collusion with any person, corporation, or syndicate to give them the benefit of the land entered, or any part thereof, or the timber thereon; that I do not apply to enter the same for the purpose of speculation, but in good faith to obtain a home for myself, and that I have not directly or indirectly made, and will not make, any agreement or contract in any way or manner, with any person or persons, corporation or syndicate whatsoever, by which the title which I might acquire from the Government of the United States should inure in whole or in part to the benefit of any person except myself ; and further, that since August 30, 1890, I have not entered under the land laws of the United States, or filed upon, a quantity of land, agricultural in character, and not mineral, which, with the tract now applied for, would make more than three hundred and twenty acres; that owing to distance I do not appear at the District Land Office to make this affidavit; that I never before made a Homestead Entry under the land laws of the United States.

Charles S. Williams

Sworn to and subscribed before me this *22nd* day of *November* 189*2*

Conrad Lindeman

Clerk of the District Court.

273

HOMESTEAD.

—o—

LAND OFFICE AT CHADRON, NEB.,

November 22 1892

I, *Charles S Williams* of *Ardmore, S. D*
~~Nebraska~~, do hereby apply to enter, under Section 2289, Revised Statutes
of the United States, the *Lots 3 and 4 and S² NW¼*

of Section *22*, in Township *35-N*, of
Range *55* west, containing *147.12* ~~160~~ acres.

Charles S Williams

—o—

LAND OFFICE AT CHADRON, NEBRASKA.

NOV 25 1892

_____ 189

I, *W H McCann* Register of the Land Office,
do hereby certify that the above application is for surveyed Lands of the class which
the applicant is legally entitled to enter under Section 2289, Revised Statutes of the
United States, and that there is no prior valid adverse right to the same.

W H McCann

Register.

HOMESTEAD APPLICATION.

Charles S. Williams

CHADRON, NEB

NOV 25 1892 _____ 189

Sec. *77*, Town. *35*, Range *55*

g.g.
63 - 16

(4—137.)

HOMESTEAD.

RECEIVER'S RECEIPT, No. 4108   APPLICATION, No. 4108

Receiver's Office, CHADRON, NEB

NOV 25 1892   , 189 .

Received of *Charles S. Williams* the sum of *Fourteen* — dollars *no* — cents;

being the amount of fee and compensation of Register and Receiver for the

entry of

Lots 3 and 4 and S r N W

of Section *22* in

Township *35 N* of Range *55 W* , under

Section No. 2290, Revised Statutes of the United States.

J.T. Brown
Receiver.

$ 14

147 ¹²/₁₀₀ *Acres*

NOTE.—It is required of the homestead settler that he shall reside upon and cultivate the land embraced in his homestead entry for a period of five years from the time of filing the affidavit, being also the date of entry. An abandonment of the land for more than six months works a forfeiture of the claim. Further, within two years from the expiration of the said five years he must file proof of his actual settlement and cultivation, failing to do which, his entry will be canceled. If the settler does not wish to remain five years on his tract, he can, at any time after fourteen months, pay for it with cash or land warrants, upon making proof of settlement and of residence and cultivation from date of filing affidavit to the time of payment.

(4897—50,000.) o 6—012

See note in red ink, which Registers and Receivers will read and EXPLAIN THOROUGHLY to person making application for lands where the affidavit is made before either of them.

276

Land Office at

July 20 , 18_96_

I, _J. W. Wehn Jr._ , Register, do hereby

certify that a notice, a printed copy of which is hereto attached, was

by me posted in a conspicuous place in my office for a period of

thirty days, I having first posted said notice on the _8_

day of _June_ , 18_96_

J. W. Wehn Jr
Register.

G—3?

277

CERTIFICATE AS TO POSTING OF NOTICE.

PROOF OF PUBLICATION.

Notice hereby given that the following named settler has filed notice of his intention to make final proof in support of his claim, and that said proof will be made before M. J. Blewett, clerk of District Court, at Harrison, Neb., on July 18, 1896, viz:

Charles S. Williams, of Ardmore, S. D., who made H. E. No. 4108 for the lots 3 & 4 and s. ¼ nw. ¼ sec. 22, tp. 35 n., r. 55 w.

He names the following witnesses to prove his continuous residence upon and cultivation of, said land, viz:

Herman Kroening, John Messing, Peter Wiedenfeld, John Ostrander, all of Ardmore, S. D.

[40-45]   J. W. WEHN, JR., Register.

STATE OF NEBRASKA,
COUNTY OF SIOUX. } ss.

L. J. Simmons, being first duly sworn, deposes and says he is the publisher of THE SIOUX COUNTY JOURNAL, a newspaper of general circulation, published and printed once each week at Harrison, Sioux County, Nebraska: that the notice hereto attached and which is a part of this affidavit and a part of the proof of *Charles S. Williams* was published in said paper for 6 consecutive weeks, the first publication having been made on the 11th day of *June* 1896, and the last on the 16th day of *July* 1896: that said notice was published in the regular and entire issue of every number of the paper during the period of publication, and that the notice was published in the newspaper proper and not in a supplement.

L. J. Simmons

Subscribed and sworn to before me this 18th day of July 1896

Dwight H Griswold

Printer's fee $............   *Notary Public.*

HOMESTEAD.

Land Office at

July 20", 1896

FINAL CERTIFICATE, } No. *1882*

{ APPLICATION, No. *4108*

It is hereby certified That, pursuant to the provisions of Section No. 2291, Revised Statutes of the United States, *Charles S. Williams* has made payment in full for *Lots 3 and 4 and S² NW¼*

of Section No. *22*, in Township No. *35 U*, of Range No. *55 W*, of the *Sixth* Principal Meridian *Nebraska*, containing *147 and 12/100* acres.

Now, therefore, be it known, That on presentation of this Certificate to the COMMISSIONER OF THE GENERAL LAND OFFICE, the said *Charles S. Williams* shall be entitled to a Patent for the Tract of Land above described.

J. W. Wehn Jr

Register.

ELECTRO'S.

279

HOMESTEAD PROOF—TESTIMONY OF WITNESS.

John Messing , being called as witness in support of the Homestead entry of _Charles J. Williams_ for Lots 3 & 4, S½NW¼ Sec 24, Tp 35 55, testifies as follows:

Question 1.—What is your name, age, and post-office address?

Answer: _John Messing, Age 34 Years, Address Ardmore South Dak._

Ques. 2.—Are you well acquainted with the claimant in this case and the land embraced in his claim?

Ans. _I am well acquainted with both claimant and land._

Ques. 3.—Is said tract within the limits of an incorporated town or selected site of a city or town, or used in any way for trade or business?

Ans. _It is not within the limits of any incorporated town or selected site of a city or town or used in any way for business_

Ques. 4.—State specifically the character of this land—whether it is timber, prairie, grazing, farming, coal, or mineral land.

Ans. _It is prairie grazing and farming land._

Ques. 5.—When did claimant settle upon the homestead and at what date did he establish actual residence thereon?

Ans. _Claimant settled upon the land under the Preemption laws in 1887. He established actual residence thereon in the summer of 1889._

Ques. 6.—Have claimant and family resided continuously on the homestead since first establishing residence thereon? (If settler is unmarried, state the fact.)

Ans. _Claimant and family have been absent for short period._

Ques. 7.—For what period or periods has the settler been absent from the land since making settlement, and for what purpose; and if temporarily absent, did claimant's family reside upon and cultivate the land during such absence?

Ans. _Settler was absent about three months in summer of 1894. Settler was absent earning money to live and improve his homestead._

Ques. 8.—How much of the homestead has the settler cultivated and for how many seasons did he raise crops thereon?

Ans. _Settler has cultivated about 18 acres, raised some crops each season._

Ques. 9.—What improvements are on the land and what is their value?

Ans. _Frame house 16x24, Addition 10x14, Log Stable 15x17, Cattle shed 20x100, Well and windmill, Cellar, all under fence. Valued at about $1000.00_

Ques. 10.—Are there any indications of coal, salines, or minerals of any kind on the homestead? (If so, describe what they are, and state whether the land is more valuable for agricultural than for mineral purposes).

Ans. _There are no indications of coal or minerals of any kind on the land._

Ques. 11.—Has the claimant mortgaged, sold, or contracted to sell, any portion of said homestead?

Ans. _Not to my knowledge_

Ques. 12.—Are you interested in this claim; and do you think the settler has acted in entire good faith in perfecting this entry? _has acted in entire good faith in perfecting this entry._

Ans. _I am not interested in this claim and I think settler_

John Messing

I HEREBY CERTIFY that the foregoing testimony was read to the witness before being subscribed, and was sworn to before me this _18th_ day of _July_ 1896.

W. J. Blewett
Clerk District Court

[SEE NOTE ON FOURTH PAGE.]

(The testimony of witnesses must be taken at the same time and place, and before the same officer as claimant's final affidavit. The answers must be full and complete to each and every question asked, and officers taking testimony will be expected to make no mistakes in dates, description of land, or otherwise.)

280

HOMESTEAD PROOF—TESTIMONY OF WITNESS.

Peter Wiedenfeld , being called as witness in support of the Homestead

entry of _Charles A. Williams_ for _Lots 3 & 4, S. NW. Sec. 22_, testifies as follows:

Question 1.—What is your, name, age, and post-office address?

Answer _Peter Wiedenfeld Age 37 Years, address Ardmore S. Dak_

Ques. 2.—Are you well acquainted with the claimant in this case and the land embraced in his claim?

Ans. _I am well acquainted with both claimant and land,_

Ques. 3.—Is said tract within the limits of an incorporated town or selected site of a city or town, or used in any way for trade or business?

Ans. _It is not within the limits of any incorporated town or selected site of a city or town, or used in any way for trade or business,_

Ques. 4.—State specifically the character of this land—whether it is timber, prairie, grazing, farming, coal, or mineral land.

Ans. _It is prairie grazing and farming land,_

Ques. 5.—When did claimant settle upon the homestead and at what date did he establish actual residence thereon?

Ans. _Claimant settled upon the land as a pre emption in 1889 Claimant established actual residence thereon in the summer of 1889,_

Ques. 6.—Have claimant and family resided continuously on the homestead since first establishing residence thereon? (If settler is unmarried, state the fact.)

Ans. _Claimant has been absent for short period,_

Ques. 7.—For what period or periods has the settler been absent from the land since making settlement, and for what purpose; and if temporarily absent, did claimant's family reside upon and cultivate the land during such absence?

Ans. _Settler was absent about three months during the summer of 1894 earning money to live and improve his homestead,_

Ques. 8.—How much of the homestead has the settler cultivated and for how many seasons did he raise crops thereon?

Ans. _Settler has cultivated about 10 acres, raised some crops each season,_

Ques. 9.—What improvements are on the land and what is their value?

Ans. _Frame house 16 x 24, Addition 10 x 14, Log stable 15 x 17 Cattle shed 20 x 100, Well & windmill, Cellar, All under fence, valued at $1000.00_

Ques. 10.—Are there any indications of coal, salines, or minerals of any kind on the homestead? (If so, describe what they are, and state whether the land is more valuable for agricultural than for mineral purposes).

Ans. _There are no indications of coal or minerals of any kind on the land_

Ques. 11.—Has the claimant mortgaged, sold, or contracted to sell, any portion of said homestead?

Ans. _Not to my knowledge,_

Ques. 12.—Are you interested in this claim; and do you think the settler has acted in entire good faith in perfecting this entry? _acted in entire good faith in perfecting this entry_

Ans. _I am not interested in this claim and I think settler has,_

Peter Wiedenfeld

I HEREBY CERTIFY that the foregoing testimony was read to the witness before being subscribed, and was sworn to before me this _18th_ day of _July_, 189_6_

M L Bennett

Clerk District Court

[SEE NOTE ON FOURTH PAGE.]

(The testimony of witnesses must be taken at the same time and place, and before the same officer as claimant's final affidavit The answers must be full and complete to each and every question asked, and officers taking testimony will be expected to make no mistakes in dates, description of land, or otherwise.)

HOMESTEAD PROOF.

LAND OFFICE AT

Original Application No. 4108

Final Certificate No. 1882

Approved: J. B. Weber Jr., Register

F. M. Broome, Receiver

Charles S. Williams

FINAL AFFIDAVIT REQUIRED OF HOMESTEAD CLAIMANTS.

SECTION 2291 OF THE REVISED STATUTES OF THE UNITED STATES.

I, Charles S. Williams, having made a Homestead entry of the Lots 5 & 4 & 13 NW¼ Section No. 22 in Township No. 35 of Range No. 55, subject to entry at Alliance Land Office under section No. 2289 of the Revised Statutes of the United States, do now apply to perfect my claim thereto by virtue of section No. 2291 of the Revised Statutes of the United States; and for that purpose do solemnly Swear that I am the head of a family and a native born citizen of the United States; that I have made actual settlement upon and have cultivated and resided upon said land since the 14th day of October 1889, to the present time; that no part of said land has been alienated, except as provided in section 2288 of the Revised Statutes, but that I am the sole bona fide owner as an actual settler; that I will bear true allegiance to the Government of the United States; and, further, that I have not heretofore perfected or abandoned an entry made under the homestead laws of the United States, except

State of Nebraska } ss.
Sioux county

Charles S. Williams

I, M. J. Blewitt Clerk of the District Court at Harrison Neb, do hereby certify that the above affidavit was subscribed and sworn to before me this 15 day of July 1896.

M. J. Blewitt
Clerk District Court

282

no conflict

Final Certificate No. *1882*

Homestead Application No. *4108*

LAND OFFICE

4T

July 20, 18*96*

Sect. *22*, Town. *35*, Range *55*

Approved *Sept 2*, 18*96*

E. G. Fraser & , Clerk,

Div. C, List No. **53**

Patented *Sept 16*, 18*96*;

Recorded, Vol. *4a*, page *3174*

116

Final Receiver's Receipt No. *1882*   Application No. *4108*

HOMESTEAD.

Receiver's Office,

July 20, 189*6*

Received of *Charles S. Williams* the sum

of *Three* dollars + *68* cents,

being the balance of payment required by law for the entry of

Lots 3 and 4 and S² NW4

of Section *22* in Township *35 N* of Range *55*.

containing *147 and 121/100* acres, under Section 2291 of the

Revised Statutes of the United States.

F. M. Broome

Receiver.

$ *1 82* Testimony fee received. Number of written words, *1200*

Rate per 100 words *15* cents.

o-4

APPENDIX B

MARTHA WILLIAMS

ADDITIONAL

AFFIDAVITS

FOR

CIVIL WAR PENSION

GENERAL AFFIDAVIT

JUNE 22, 1886

State of Pennsylvania, County of Crawford, SS.

In the matter of Pension Claim of Martha Williams, mother of Lewis C. Williams in Company H of the 1ˢᵗ Regiment, Minnesota Volunteers on this 22 day of June A.D. 1886 personally appeared before me, a Justice of the Peace in and for the aforesaid County, duly authorized to administer oaths, A. Campbell aged 64 years, a resident of Greenwood in the County of Crawford and State of Pennsylvania well known to me to be respectable and entitled to credit, and who, being duly sworn, declared in relation of aforesaid case as follows; that he was present at the marriage of Perry Williams and Martha Williams, formerly Martha Campbell and that they were married at the residence of Mark Campbell in or about the year 1848 and he further saith that William Porter was a Justice of the Peace and that they were married in Greenwood Township, Crawford County and state of Pennsylvania and his Post Office address is Custard, Crawford County, Pennsylvania and he further declares that he has no interest in said case and is not concerned in its prosecution.

G.W. Lopes

S.H. Seley

(Signature of Affiants)

A. Campbell

(Signature of Affiant)

GENERAL AFFIDAVIT

JUNE 22, 1886

State of Pennsylvania, County of Crawford, SS

In the matter of Pension claim of Martha Williams, mother of Lewis C. Williams in Company H of the 1st Regiment, Minnesota Volunteers, on the 22 day of June A.D. 1886, personally appeared before me, a Justice of the Peace in and for the aforesaid County duly authorized to administer oaths, G.W. Lopes, aged 59 years, a resident of Greenwood in the County of Crawford and State of Pennsylvania well known to me to be reputable and entitled to credit, and who, being duly sworn, declares in relation to aforesaid case as follows: that he was present at the marriage of Perry Williams and Martha Williams, formerly Martha Campbell and that they were married at the residence of Mark Campbell in or about the years 1848 and his Post Office is Custard, Crawford County, Pennsylvania and he further declares that he has no interest in said case and is not concerned in its prosecution.

S.H. Seley

A. Campbell

(Affiants)

G.W. Lopes

(Affiant)

GENERAL AFFIDAVIT

AUGUST 28, 1888

For the testimony of EMPLOYERS or NEAR NEIGHBORS of soldier, (other than relatives) who have known him before his enlistment, or since his discharge and return from the army.

State of Minnesota, County of Winona, SS. In the matter for pension of Martha Williams for pension.

On this 28th day of August A.D. 1888; personally appeared before me, a Notary Public in and for the aforesaid County, duly authorized to administer oaths Ira Cunfield aged 67 years, a resident of Saratoga in the County of Winona and State of Minnesota whose Post Office address is Troy, Winona County, Minnesota and well known to me to be respectable and entitled to credit, and who being sworn, declare in relation to the aforesaid Case as follows: That he has been well and personally acquainted with Perry C. Williams and that from the years 1863 to 1873 and that he has known the said claimant, Martha Williams during all the such time above mentioned. And that he knew his said son, Lewis C. Williams from 1863 until he enlisted in the army in the spring of 1865.

That said soldier, Lewis C. Williams was the son of the claimant and her husband, Perry C. Williams; that he was never married and left no widow or children surviving him. That his father, Perry C. Williams was a very feeble man and totally unable to labor or support the family. That the parent at the time of the soldier's death was about 45 years; that he was a farmer by occupation; that he had no income during the years, 1863, 1864, and 1865 except what was derived from the labor and earnings of said soldier and that neither of the parents of said soldier had any property or income from 1863 to 1873 except the earnings of the said son, Lewis C. Williams. That he knows the facts above stated from being all of said time a near neighbor and being intimate with the parties. That said soldier worked for him from time to time and that he paid his father the said Perry C. Williams therefore.

OCT. 15, 1888

GENERAL AFFIDAVIT

Territory of Dakota, County of Charles Mix, SS.

In the matter of Pension Claim of Martha Williams.

ON THIS 15th day of October A.D. 1888, personally appeared before me, a Notary Public in and for the aforesaid County, duly authorized to administer oaths, Cary H. Jaclyn age 59 years, a resident of Jackson Township in the County of Charles Mix and Territory of Dakota well known to me to be reputable and entitled to credit, and who, being duly sworn, declares in relation to aforesaid case as follows:

That he has known Martha Williams the above named applicant for a pension for more than five years. That during this time he has lived on adjoining farm to her residence. That he and his family have visited and neighbored with her and affiant has been well acquainted with her and familiar with her family affairs for more than five years last past and during all this time she has remained a widow and has always so represented herself and has been so represented by her friends and members of her family who know her:

Affiant further states that said applicant has a daughter about fourteen years of age who is entirely dependent on applicant for support, said daughter being both physically and mentally deficient to such an extent as to or unable to even dress herself and required the constant care of an attendant. This affiant knows by seeing her at home (?) and having her at his own house for six weeks to care for.

His Post Office address is Bertholdi, Charles Mix County, Dakota Territory.

He further declares that he has no interest in said case and is not concerned in its prosecution.

Eva Glarchin (SP)   Cary H. Joslyn
H.M Carroll   (Signature of Affiant)
(If affiant signs by mark,
two persons who can write
sign here)

GENERAL AFFIDAVIT

August 4, 1888

State of Nebraska,   SS

County of Cedar

   I George W. Ramsey being first duly sworn before and say that I was acquainted with the claimant herein, Martha Williams, and have been acquainted with her since April 1880; that on the 3rd day of November 1880 the said Martha Williams became a widow by the death of her husband, Perry C. Williams; that I have been continuously acquainted with the said Martha Williams, during the period lapsing since that time, and in a position to know all her domestic relations and that of my own personal knowledge the said Martha Williams has remained a widow since the 3rd of November, 1880 and the widow of the said Perry Williams.

George W. Ramsey
(signature)

Subscribed in my presence and sworn to before me this 4th day of August 1888.

J.C. Zigler,
Justice of the Peace

GENERAL AFFIDAVIT

AUGUST 28, 1888

State of Minnesota, County of Winona, SS.

In the matter of Claim of Martha Williams

ON THIS 28th day of August A.D. 1888, personally appeared before me, a Notary Public in and for the aforesaid County, duly authorized to administer oaths, E.B. Gerry age 52 years, a resident of Saratoga in the County of Winona and State of Minnesota well known to me to be reputable and entitled to credit, and who, being duly sworn, declares in relation to aforesaid case as follows: that he was intimately acquainted with Perry C. Williams, the husband of the above named claimant, Martha Williams from 1865 to 1873; that he lived within one mile of him during said time and that the said Perry C. Williams was in feeble health during all of that time.

That the said Williams and his family were very poor during all the time above mentioned.

His Post Office address is Troy, County of Winona and State of Minnesota. He further declares that he has no interest in said case and is not concerned in its prosecution.

E.B. Gerry,
(Signature of Affiant)

State of Nebraska

County of Cedar   SS.

  I, Hansen E. McKruzir, being final duly sworn depose and say, that I am a duly registered and practicing physician under the laws of said state and that I have been a practicing physician under the laws of the said state for the period of sixteen years. That on or about the 27 or 28 day of Oct. 1880 I was called as a physician to attend one Perry C. Williams and found upon a proper diagnosis of the case that the said Perry C. Williams was afflicted with inflammation of the lungs. On the third day of November, 1880 while suffering from the said affliction, the said Perry C. Williams died leaving as his widow Martha Williams the claimant herein.

                Signature,
                H.E. McKruzir, M.D.

Subscribed in my presence and (sp) to before me this 4th day of September, 1888.

                (Signature)
                Geo W. Ramsey,
                Justice of the Peace

SEPTEMBER 4, 1888

State of Nebraska

County of Cedar   SS.

    I, Lizzie E. Ramsey being first duly sworn depose and say that I am acquainted with the claimant herein, Martha Williams, and that I have been acquainted with her for the period of at least twenty nine years; that on the 3rd day of November, 1880 the said Martha Williams became a widow, by the death of her husband, Perry C. Williams; that I was present at the death of the said Perry C. Williams; that I have been continuously acquainted with the said Martha Williams since November 3rd, 1880, and am and have been in a position to know of her domestic relations; that to my personal knowledge the said Martha Williams is and has been the widow of the said Perry C. Williams since November 3rd, 1880.

                                               Lizzy E. Ramsey
                                               (Signature)

Subscribed in my presence and sworn to before me this 4th day of September, 1888.

                                               (Signature)
                                             Geo W. Ramsey,
                                             Justice of the Peace

OCT. 15, 1888

GENERAL AFFIDAVIT

Territory of Dakota, County of Charles Mix, SS.

In the matter of Pension Claim of Martha Williams

ON THIS 15th day of October A.D. 1888, personally appeared before me, a Notary Public in and for the aforesaid County, duly authorized to administer oaths, William Dinsmore age 31 years, a resident of Bartholdi P.O. in the County of Charles Mix, Dakota Territory; and Jos L. Scroggins of same place, both well known to me to be reputable and entitled to credit, and who, being duly sworn, declares in relation to aforesaid case as follows: Each for himself says that he has lived near said Martha Williams for more than five years last past. That during all this time she has remained a widow and has so represented herself and her friends and relatives who are supposed to know so represent her. The affiant have each visited at claimant's house and are familiar with her family affairs and affiants each for himself states that claimant has a daughter wholly dependent upon her for support. That said daughter is about fourteen years old and is so mentally and physically afflicted as to be entirely helpless not being able to dress herself and needing the constant care of an attendant and affiant Scroggins says his age is 30 years and each affiant says his Post Office is Bartholdi, Dakota Territory. They each further declares that they have no interest in said case and are not concerned in its prosecution.

Signed:

Bill Glarehen   Wm. M. Dinsmore
H.M. Carroll   Jos L. Scroggins
(If affiant signs by mark,   (Signature of Affiant)
two persons who can write
sign here.)

APPENDIX C

CHARLES M. RUSSELL

ADDITIONAL LEGAL DOCUMENTS

ARREST #1

1931

IN THE COUNTY COURT OF SIOUX COUNTY, NEBRASKA

The STATE OF NEBRASKA,

as. <u>Henry Sweezy</u>

<u>Sioux</u> County

being first duly sworn, on his oath says that he has just cause to fear

and does fear that one <u>Charles M. Russell</u> will commit the

offense of <u>assault with intent to do great bodily injury</u>

_____

_____

_____

_____

_____

_____against the person of this complainant.

Subscribed in my presence, and sworn to before

me this <u>27th</u> day of <u>July</u>

(signed by)

X <u>Henry Sweezy</u>

A.D. 1931.

(signed by)

<u>J.H. Wilhermsdorfer, Cty. Judge</u>

Section 267 Criminal

THE STATE OF NEBRASKA,

ss.   *TO THE SHERIFF OR CONSTABLE OF*

Sioux   *County.*   *SAID COUNTY, GREETING.*

WHEREAS, before me **J.H. Wilhermsdorfer, County Judge,** *within and for said County of* **Sioux** - - - - *complaint has been made in writing, signed and sworn to by* **Henry Sweezy,** - - - - *and filed according to law,that* **Charles M. Russell,** - - - - *of said county, on or about the* **24ᵗʰ,** *day of* **July,** *A.D. 19* **31,** *in the County of* **Sioux** - - *, in the State of Nebraska,* **then and there being, did then and there unlawfully and willfully threaten the said Henry Sweezy in a threatening manner.**

Count 2

And the said Henry Sweezy, being further sworn on oath, doth say that the said Charles M. Russell, then and there being, then and there on or about the 24ᵗʰ day of July, 1931, did then and there unlawfully and willfully strike the said Henry Sweezy, contrary to the form of the statutes in such cases made and provided and against the peace and dignity of the people of the State of Nebraska.

These are, therefore, to command you to forthwith to take the said **Charles M. Russell,** - - - *if he be found in your county; or if she shall have fled, that you pursue after the said* **Charles M. Russell,** *into any other county within the state, and take and safely keep the said* **Charles M. Russell.** *So that you bring his body forthwith before me or some other magistrate having cognizance of the case of said offense so committed, to answer said complaint and be further dealt with according to law.*

Given under my hand **and seal** *this* **27ᵗʰ** *day of* **July** *A.D. 19* **31.**

_____

(Signed by J.H. Wilhermsdorfer) County Judge.

PEACE BOND.

STATE OF NEBRASKA   )
)   ss.
County of Sioux,   )

Be it remembered that before me, the undersigned, J.H. Wilhermsdorfer County Judge of said County, personally appeared Charles M. Russell, and L.C. Larson, and acknowledged themselves indebted to the State of Nebraska, in the sum of Five Hundred Dollars, to be levied of their lands and tenements, goods and chattels, if default be made in the condition following;

WHEREAS Charles M. Russell, has been arrested on the complaint of Henry Sweezy, alleging that he the said Henry Sweezy has just cause to fear and does fear that said Henry Sweezy with intent to do great bodily harm Charles M. Russell has offered to give bond to keep the peace, in such amount as may be fixed by me, said magistrate, and for a period of time to be fixed by me;

Now, therefore, the condition of this obligation is such that if the said Charles M. Russell, shall keep the peace and be of good behavior generally for the period of one year then this recognizance to be void, otherwise to be and remain in full force and effect.

(signed by Charles M. Russell and L.C. Larson)

Taken and acknowledged before me this 28th day of July, 1931.

_____

(Signed by J. H. Wilhermsdorfer)
County Judge.

State of Nebraska,
Sioux County   ss
On this 28th day of July, 1931, personally appeared before me Charles M. Russell, principal and L.C. Larson, surety, and acknowledged that their signatures to the above bond to keep the peace to be their voluntary act and added for the purposes set out therein.

_____

(Signed by J. H. Wilhermsdorfer)
County Judge

APPENDIX D

CHARLES M. RUSSELL

ARREST #2

ADDITIONAL LEGAL DOCUMENTS

1932

WHEREAS, before me **J.H.Wilhermsdorfer,County Judge** *within and for said County of* **Sioux** — — *complaint has been made in writing, signed and sworn to by* **C.S.Williams, County Sheriff,** — — *and filed according to law, that* **Charles M,Russell,** — — *of said county, on or about the* **20th,** *day of* **January,** — — *A. D.* 1932*., in the County of* **Sioux** — — *, in the State of Nebraska.* then and there being,did then and there wilfully, unlawfully and feloniously enter the dwelling house of Jennie Cutler armed with a dangerous weapon, to wit; a revolver with the intent to rob and steal, and did then and there threaten to disfigure, main and kill Hugh Hiatt and GlennCutler, and then and there ordered the said Hugh Hiatt to relinquish and hand over to the said Charles M. Russell certain personal property , to wit; a 25-35 caliber Winchester rifle, then and there being situate in said dwelling house, and the property of the said Glenn Cutler contrary to the form of Statutes in such cases made and provided, and against the peace and dignity of the people of the State of Nebraska,

DRW: Error: Should be * "maim"

These are, therefore, to command you to forthwith to take the said **Charles M.Russell,** — — *if he be found in your county; or if he shall have fled, that you pursue after the said* **Charles M.Russell,** — *into any other county within the state, and take and safely keep the said* **Charles M.Russell,** — *so that you bring his body forthwith before me or some other magistrate having cognizance of the case of said offense so committed, to answer said complaint and be further dealt with according to law.*

Given under my hand **and seal** *this* **22nd** *day of* **January,** *A. D.* 1932.

County Judge.

TRANSCRIPT OF PROCEEDINGS HAD BEFORE ME J.H.WILHERMSDORFER,
COUNTY JUDGE,SIOUX COUNTY,NEBRASKA,

Wherein;
The State of Nebraska,is Plaintiff,)
        and   )   TRANSCRIPT.
Charles M.Russell,is Defendant.)

- -

January 20th 1932, Complaint in writing and upon oath was made before
me in form following,

          IN THE COUNTY COURT OF SIOUX COUNTY,NEBRASKA,

THE STATE OF NEBRASKA,   )
       VS.   )   Complaint for Feloniously Entering
)   Building - Section 28-539
CHARLES M.RUSSELL,   )

State of Nebraska,   )
) ss.
County of Sioux   )

      The complaint and information of C.S.WIlliams, County Sheriff of
the County aforesaid, made in the name of the State of Nebraska,before
me, the County Judge,within and for said County this 20th day of January
A.D. 1932. who being duly sworn, on his oath,says that Charles M.Russell
on the 20th day of January A.D. 1932, in the County aforesaid,then and
there being, did then and there wilfully, unlawfully and feloniously
enter the dwelling house of Jannie Cuttler armed with a dangerous weapon
, to wit; a revolver, with the intent to rob and steal , and did then and
there threaten to disfigure, main and kill Hugh Hiatt and Glenn Cuttler,
and then and there ordered the said Hugh Hiatt,to relinquish and hand
over to the said Charles M.Russell,certain personal property,to wit;
a 25-35 caliber Winchester rifle, then and there being situate in said
dwelling house, and the property of the said Glenn Cuttler contrary to
the form of Statutes in such cases made and provided, and against the
peace and dignity of the people of the State of Nebraska.

                                      C.S.Williams
                                       County Sheriff.

Subscribed in my presence,and sworn to before me, this 20th day of
January 1932.
      (seal)

                                     J.H.Wilhermsdorfer
                                       County Judge.

January 20th,1932, I, Issued warrant for the said Charles M.Russell,
and placed same in the hands of C.S.Williams. Sheriff,

                                     J.H.Wilhermsdorfer
                                       County Judge.

January 25th 1932. Warrant returned and filed endorsed as follows,

STATE OF NEBRASKA)
) ss.
Sioux County,   )

Received this warrant 22nd Jan 1932, and pusuant to the command thereof
I have arrested the within named Charles M.Russell, and now have his
body before the Court.

             Fees,   Dated this 25th day of January, 1932.
Arrest,- - - - - - - - $ 1.00
Milage 70 miles,- - -   10.50   C.S.Williams.
Attendance, - - - - -   1.00   Sheriff of Sioux County.
           total, $12.50

DRW: Error: Should be "maim"

WARRANT

THE STATE OF NEBRASKA
vs.

Charles M. Russell.

and filed this

_____ day of *January* 19 32.

[signature]
County Judge

278 — Printed and for sale by Omaha Printing Co., Omaha

STATE OF NEBRASKA,
Scott County *ss.*

Received this warrant 22 nd *Jan.* 19 32

and pursuant to the command thereof I have

arrested the within named

Charles M Russell

and now have his body before the Court.

Dated this 25 day of *Jan* 19 32

C. S. Williams
Sheriff of *Scott* County

FEES

Arrest		$1.00
Mileage 70	Miles $	10 50
Attendance	$	1 00
	Total $	12 50

IL BOND

THE STATE OF NEBRASKA,
vs.
Charles M. Russell,

January 27th, A.D. 1932.

Willermsdorf
County Judge.

STATE OF NEBRASKA,
County of **Sioux** } ss. I, **Frank Russell**,

who have signed the foregoing bail bond as surety, being first duly sworn, on oath depose and say that I am the owner of the following described real estate, situated in the County of **Sioux** and State of Nebraska, to wit: **W½.NW¼,Sec28,SE¼ NW¼.SE¼ NW¼.E½ SW¼SW¼ SW¼,SE¼, Sec 32,N½ SW¼,NW¼ SE¼, Sec33,All of 29,N½ NW¼SW¼ NW¼ Sec32,NE¼ E½ W½N½ SE¼Sec630,Twp31, Range 54.**
which is of the value of $ **7000.00.** above all incumbrances and exemptions; that I am the owner of personal property of the value of $ **2500.00.** above all incumbrances and exemptions; and that I am not surety in any other case pending except the following:

TITLE OF CAUSE	COURT	AMOUNT OF BOND
		$
		$

Subscribed and sworn to before me this
27th day of **January,** 19**32**

Willermsdorf
County Judge.

Frank S Russell
SURETY SIGN HERE

STATE OF NEBRASKA,
County of **Sioux** } ss. I, **Dan Jordan,**

who have signed the foregoing bail bond as surety, being first duly sworn, on oath depose and say that I am the owner of the following described real estate, situated in the County of **Sioux** and State of Nebraska, to wit: **All of Sections 15, 8, twp, 34, Range 55, and all of Sections 28, 29, E½Sec 30,all of Section 20,E½ of sec 21,Twp 33,Range 55,**
which is of the value of $ **25000.00,** above all incumbrances and exemptions; that I am the owner of personal property of the value of $ **------** above all incumbrances and exemptions; and that I am not surety in any other case pending except the following:

TITLE OF CAUSE	COURT	AMOUNT OF BOND
S		$
		$

Subscribed and sworn to before me this
27th day of **January,** 19**32**

Willermsdorf
County Judge.

Dan Jordan
SURETY SIGN HERE

STATE OF NEBRASKA,
County of _____ } ss. I, _____

who have signed the foregoing bail bond as surety, being first duly sworn, on oath depose and say that I am the owner of the following described real estate, situated in the County of _____ and State of Nebraska, to wit: _____

which is of the value of $ _____ above all incumbrances and exemptions; that I am the owner of personal property of the value of $ _____ above all incumbrances and exemptions; and that I am not surety in any other case pending except the following:

TITLE OF CAUSE	COURT	AMOUNT OF BOND
		$
		$

Subscribed and sworn to before me this
_____ day of _____ 19 _____

SURETY SIGN HERE

308

STATE OF NEBRASKA

vs.

Charles M. Russell,

Defendant.

BAIL BOND

BE IT REMEMBERED that on the 27th, day of January 1932.

Charles M. Russell, as Principal,

and Frank Russell, and Dan Jordan, as Sureties,

of the County of Sioux, and State of Nebraska, personally appeared before

me, J.H. Wilhermsdorfer, County Judge

in and for said County of Sioux, and acknowledged themselves jointly and severally indebted to the State of Nebraska, in the penal sum of Seven Thousand Five Hundred and No/100, - - - - - - - DOLLARS, to be levied of their goods and chattels, lands and tenements, if default is made in the condition following:

THE CONDITION OF THIS RECOGNIZANCE is such that if the said

Charles M. Russell,

shall personally appear before the District Court in and for said Sioux County, State of Nebraska, forthwith, if now in session, and if not in session, then on the first day of the next jury term thereof, and from time to time and from term to term as may be ordered by the said Court until the final determination of the aforesaid cause wherein the said

Charles M. Russell,

is charged with the crime of Feloniously entering building, Section 28-539, and not depart the Court without leave, then this recognizance to be void, otherwise to remain in full force and effect.

IN WITNESS WHEREOF, we have hereunto set our hands at Harrison Nebraska, this 27th, day of January, 1932.

C. M. Russell

Frank S Russell

Dan Jordan

Taken, acknowledged and subscribed to before me and sureties approved by me this 27th, day of January, A. D. 19 32.

J H Wilhermsdorf

County Judge.

309

(3)

STATE OF Nebraska,)
) ss.
County of Sioux,) I, Frank S.Russell, who have signed the foregoing bail bond as surety, being first duly sworn, on oath depose and say that I am the owner of the following described real estate, situated in the County of Sioux,and State of Nebraska,to-wit;W½NW¼, Sec 28,SE¼SW¼,NW¼,E½SW¼, SE¼,32, N½SW¼,NW¼SE¼,-33,All of 29,N½NW¼, SW¼NW¼,*32NE¼,E½NW¼,W½ SW¼- 30,Twp, 31,Range 54,which is of the value of $7000.00.above all incumbrances and exemptions;that I am the owner of personal property of the value of $2500.00. above all incumbrances and exemptions; that I am not surety in any other case pending.

Subscribed and sworn to before me this
27th day of January 1932.
J.H.Wilhermsdorfer,
County Judge, (seal)

Frank S.Russell

STATE OF NEBRASKA)
) ss.
County of Sioux) I, Dan Jordan, who have signed the foregoing bail bond as surety,being first duly sworn, on oath depose and say that I am the owner of the following described real estate situated in the County of Sioux,and State of Nebraska,to-wit; all of sections 15, 8, Twp,34, Range 55, and all of sections 28, 29, E½, Sec,30,all of Section 20,E½ of Sec,21, Twp,33, Range 55, which is of the value of $25000.00. above all incumbrance and exemptions; that I am the owner of personal property$-----, above all incumbrances and exemptions; and that I am not surety in any other case pending.

Subscribed and sworn to before me this
27th day of January 1932.
J.H.Wilhermsdorfer,
County Judge. (seal)

Dan Jordan

- -

CERTIFICATE OF TRANSCRIPT

STATE OF NEBRASKA.
County of Sioux

IN THE COUNTY COURT OF

Sioux County,

I, J.H.Wilhermsdorfer, County Judge, in and for said County, do hereby certify that I have compared the foregoing copy of docket entries in the case wherein the State of Nebraska prosecutes Charles M.Russell, with the original record thereof now remaining in said Court, and the papers hereto attached and marked exhibit No,1. to exhibit No, 2, are all of the original files in said case and the same have all been compared,

with the original record thereof, now remaining in said court; that the same is a correct transcript thereof, and of the whole of said original record; that said court has no clerk authorized to sign certificates in his own name, and that I have the legal custody and control of said original record; that said court is a court of record, has a seal, and that said seal is hereto affixed; and that the foregoing attestation is in due form, according to the laws of the State of Nebraska.

IN WITNESS WHEREOF, I have hereunto set my hand

and affixed the seal of said court this

day of January, A.D. 1932.

X H Wilhermsdorff
County Judge.

CERTIFICATE OF TRANSCRIPT

District ~~COUNTY~~ COURT

....

County, Nebraska

~~IN THE MATTER OF~~

State of Nebraska

vs

Charles M. Russell

COPY OF

STATE OF NEBRASKA
County of Sioux } ss

Filed in the office of the Clerk of the

District Court of said County this 2

day of March A.D., 1932

[signature]

Clerk District Court

APPENDIX E

CHARLES M. RUSSELL

ARREST #3

ADDITIONAL LEGAL DOCUMENTS

1937

No. **209** Doc. **1** Page **216**

State Complaint

**Sioux** Court

THE STATE OF NEBRASKA

_vs._

**Charles M. Russell**

Filed this **25**th _day of_

**October** _A.D. 19_ **37** .

(Signed by J.H. Wilhermsdorfer)

(Criminal)

TRANSCRIPT OF PROCEEDINGS HAD BEFORE ME, J.H. WILHERMSDORFER,
COUNTY JUDGE, SIOUX COUNTY, NEBRASKA.

Wherein;

The State of Nebraska, is Plaintiff,	)	
	)	
and	)	TRANSCRIPT.
	)	
Charles M. Russell, is Defendant	)	

. . . .

December 23rd, 1937, Complaint in writing and upon oath was made before me in form following:

State of Nebraska	)	IN THE COUNTY COURT OF SIOUX COUNTY, NEBRASKA
Plaintiff	)	
vs	)	COMPLAINT FOR PEACE WARRANT
	)	
Charles M. Russell	)	
Defendant	)	

State of Nebraska, Sioux County, ss: The complaint and information of J.B. Bravard of the County of Sioux, State of Nebraska, made in the name of the State of Nebraska before J.H. Wilhermsdorfer, Judge of the County court of Sioux county, Nebraska, this 23rd day of December, 1937, who being duly sworn on his oath says that he has just cause to fear and does fear that Charles M. Russell, defendant, of said county, will unlawfully, willfully and maliciously in and upon the said J.B. Bravard, make an assault him, and the said J.B. Bravard, will unlawfully shoot, beat, strike and wound, with intent to do great bodily harm, contrary to the statute in such cases made and provided and against the peace and dignity of the State of Nebraska.

_____J.B. Bravard_____

Subscribed in my presence and sworn to before me this 23rd day of December, 1937.

    (SEAL)   _____J.H. Wilhermsdorfer_____
County Judge

December 23rd, 1937, I issued warrant for the said Charles M. Russell and placed same in the hands of C.S. Williams, Sheriff.

_____J.H. Wilhermsdorfer_____
County Judge

December 23rd, 1937, Warrant returned and filed endorsed as follows:

State of Nebraska	)	
	)	ss.
County of Sioux	)	12-23-37

IN THE COUNTY COURT OF SIOUX COUNTY, NEBRASKA

State of Nebraska)
      Plaintiff)   COMPLAINT FOR PEACE WARRANT
         vs)
)
Charles M. Russell)
      Defendant)

State of Nebraska, Sioux County, ss: The complaint and information of J.B. Bravard of the County of Sioux, State of Nebraska, made in the name of the State of Nebraska before J.H. Wilhermsdorfer, judge of the county Court of Sioux county, Nebraska, this 23rd day of December, 1937, who being duly sworn on his oath says that he has just cause to fear and does fear that Charles M. Russell, defendant, of said County, will unlawfully, willfully and maliciously in and upon the said J.B. Bravard, make an assault him, and the said J. B. Bravard, will unlawfully shoot, beat, strike and wound, with intent to do great bodily harm contrary to the statute in such cases made and provided and against the peace and dignity of the State of Nebraska.

_____
(signed by J.B. Bravard)

    Subscribed in my presence and sworn to before me this 23rd day of December, 1937.

_____
County Judge (signed by J.H.Wilhermsdorfer)

12-23-37

COUNTY COURT,

Sioux County,

- -

Doc. ___1___ No. __212__ Page ___219___

- -

THE STATE OF NEBRASKA

Vs.

___Charles M. Russell___

_____

Crime __Complaint for Peace Warrant__

_____

Filed _____December 23rd_____ 19 37

___J.H. Wilhermsdorfer___
County Judge

In the County Court of Sioux County, Nebraska.

The State of Nebraska,

vs.

Charles M. Russell,

Justification of Sureties.

Filed January, 3rd, 1938.

_____

(signed by J.H. Wilhermsdorfer) County Judge.

In the County Court of Sioux County, Nebraska.

The State of Nebraska,

vs.

Charles M. Russell.

Filed January, 3rd, 1938.

_____

(signed by J.H. Wilhermsdorfer) County Judge.

PEACE BOND.

****

1-3-38

IN THE COUNTY COURT OF SIOUX COUNTY, NEBRASKA

State of Nebraska

       Plaintiff

      Vs

                          PEACE BOND

Charles M. Russell

       Defendant

State of Nebraska, County of Sioux, SS: Be it remembered that on the 3rd day of January,

1938, Charles M. Russell as principal and _____Van W. Westler_____ and

_____Frank S. Russell_____ of Sioux County and State of Nebraska, aforesaid

appeared personally before the undersigned J.H. Wilhermsdorfer, County Judge in and

for the County of Sioux and State of Nebraska and jointly and severally acknowledged

themselves to be indebted to the State of Nebraska in the sum of One Thousand Dollars

($1000.00) to be made and levied on their respective goods, chattels, lands and

tenements, to be void however, if the said Charles M. Russell shall personally be and

appear before the District Court of Sioux County, Nebraska, on the first day of the next

term thereof or forthwith if it be term time of said District Court and in the meantime be

of good behavior generally and especially toward J.B. Bravard and shall further deliver to

the Sheriff of Sioux County all the fire arms owned by him or in his possession or under

his control to be kept in the vault of the Sheriff of Sioux County pending the final

outcome of the final disposition of this action, and to do and receive what shall be

enjoined by said court upon him and shall not depart from said court without leave.

      Witness our hands this 3rd day of January, 1938.

                                 ———————— ——————————

                                 Principal (signed by Charles M. Russell)

Witness:

————————————————

(signed by W.E. Mumby)   Surety (signed by Van W. Westler)

                                 Surety (signed by Frank S. Russell)

CERTIFICATE OF TRANSCRIPT

STATE OF NEBRASKA,

ss:

Sioux County

IN THE COUNTY COURT OF **SIOUX COUNTY, NEBRASKA.**

I, **J.H. Wilhermsdorfer,** County Judge, in and for said County,

do hereby certify that I have compared the foregoing copy of **Docket entries in the**

case wherein The State of Nebraska prosecute Charles W. Russell with the original

record thereof now remaining in said Court, and that the papers hereto attached

and marked exhibit No. 1. to Exhibit No. 5. inclusive are all of the original files in

said case and the same has all been compared,

with the original record thereof, now remaining in said court; that the same is a correct
transcript thereof, and of the whole of said original record; that said court has no clerk
authorized to sign certificates in his own name, and that I have the legal custody and
control of said original record; that said court is a court of record, has a seal, and that said
seal in hereto affixed; and that the foregoing attestation is in due form, according to the
laws of the State of Nebraska.

IN WITNESS WHEREOF, I have hereunto set my hand

and affixed the seal of said court this

17th day of **January** A.D. **1938**

_____
(signed by J.H. Wilhermsdorfer)
County Judge.

INDEX

Note: The following have not been listed in the Index due to extensive use throughout the book:

Sheriff Sid Williams, Sr.
Sioux County
Nebraska

BRING 'EM BACK ALIVE SID
   10, 97, 98, 116, 169, 205,
   252, 268

18th Amendment 115, 116
3M Company 97
45 Colt 6-shooter 60
6-shooter 60, 133
77 ranch 71

A

Aberey, N.J. 28
Aberg 93
Abrogast, John 138, 139
Ackley, Barton 217
Acton, Smokey 217
Affidavit, Homestead 273
Africa 45, 46
Agate 219, 225, 228, 229
Agate Ranch 57
Agate Springs Ranch 192
Ak-Sar-Ben 4, 85, 86, 87, 89, 90,
   91, 93, 94, 96, 236
Alabama 230
Alberta 91
Allen, Bob 143, 144
Alliance, NE 57, 93, 142, 159, 195,
   218, 221, 222, 223, 228, 229,
   246, 247, 249
Almanza, Felencio 142
Alsace-Lorraine 182
Altig, Theresa 200
Altig, William H. 200
Alton, IL 199
American Fur Co. 192
Anderson, Dave 53, 59, 60, 256
Anderson, David 10, 59, 60
Anderson, John 200
Anderson, Paul 225
Anderson, Samuel 38
Andrews 181, 182, 214, 216
Andrews, Charles H. 193
Anglo-Saxon 47
Anti-Saloon League 115
Apache 61
Arabia 46

Arapahoe 61
Ardmore 3, 10, 16, 51, 53, 59, 60,
   61, 64, 65, 67, 75, 81, 99, 103,
   110, 111, 113, 127, 128, 177,
   197, 255, 256
Ardmore bridge 60, 255
Ardmore Ranch 3, 57, 64
Ardmore, S.D. 19, 20, 34, 273
Arizona 67, 251, 253, 254, 256
Arkansas 67, 81, 109, 191, 250
Arnold, Mr. 95
Arnold, Richard 215, 217
Arrest Warrant, Charles Russell,
   No. 1, 1931 208, 209
Arrest Warrant, Charles Russell,
   No. 2, 1932 210
Arrest Warrant, Charles Russell,
   No. 3, 1937 212
Arrest Warrant, Glen Hilliard,
   1927 125
Atkinson 71
Atlantic Ocean 45
AU7 Ranch 61
Aunt Ethel 51
Aunt Eva 13, 14, 110, 111

B

Bail Bond, Frank/Charles Russell
   307, 309, 310
Bailey, Frank 220
Baker, F.S. 120, 121
Baldwin, Ernest 235
Baldwin, Harry 207
Balkans 46
Balwin, Nina 243
Bannon, Frank 262
Bannon, Nellie 121
Bannon, Wm. 174
Bar T 58
Barkus, Lynn 244
Barkus, Monk 248
Barnes filling station 214
Barnes, Sarah 264
Barnett, Jack 230
Barrett, F.A. 220
Bartell, Gordon 190

Bartholdi 295
Bastrop County, Texas 109
Batie, J. Russell 74
Battle of Lightning Creek 60, 61,
   62
Battle of The Little Big Horn 13
Battle of Wounded Knee 61
Bayard 97, 169, 250
Bearbower, Clarence 230
Beauvais, Terra 192
Beaver, Willy & Floyd 197
Becker, Lester 29
Becker, Shanah 29
Beers, Ralph 249
Beeson, Ralph 170
Behr, Frank 129
Beldon, L.E. 192
Bell, John 185
Bell, Mrs. 251
Belmont Park 96
Belmont Stakes 85
Belmont, NE 179
Berkshire County 41
Bern 13, 51, 53, 58, 59, 64, 110
Bertholdi 290
Beverley, NE 237
Bigelow 219
Bigelow, Del 105, 235, 236
Billings 85
Bismark, ND 244
Bixler, Meredith 9
Black Air 92
Black Hills 10, 58, 61, 97, 109, 197,
   228
Black Kettle 62
Blair, Gerald 250
Blair, NE 175
Blake, Arthur 215, 217
Blessing, Frank 67
Blessing, Hattie 67, 69
Blevens, Lee 126, 141, 155, 214,
   261, 264, 265
Blevins, Lee 126, 141, 155, 214,
   264
Bonsall, Mary 121
Boston, MA. 15

Bostrum, Ruby 219, 220
Boulder, CO 142
Bourbon, Jack 250
Bourret 4, 64, 93, 105, 151
Bourret Ranch 4, 57, 64
Bourret, Jack 93
Bourret, James 64
Bourret, John 64
Bourret, Will 64
Bowdarc Record 192
Bowen 192
Bowman, Willis 150
Box Butte County 57, 145, 159,
   180, 192, 223, 252, 263
Boyd, E.H. 179, 180
Braden, Newton 226
Brakeman, E. 88
Brakeman, Everett 86, 91
Brand Inspection Document 106
Brandon, Newton 225
Bravard, J.B. 204, 207, 212
Breeders Cup 96
Brennan, Major John R. 62
Bretthauer, Adam 246, 258
Brewster, B.E. 193
Bricelyn, MN 242
Bridgeport, NE 126
Briggs, Glen 228
Britain 46
British 46
British islands 47
Britt, Paul 234
Broderick, C.P. 120, 121
Broderick, Mary E. 136, 193, 198
Broderick, Tom 62, 152
Bronson, Edgar Beecher 192
Brooks, James 38
Brooks, James L. 39
Brooks, Sarah 37
Brookville, NY 98
Brothwell, Fred 218, 220, 221
Brothwell, Harry 219, 220, 221
Brown Co., NE 192
Brown, A.M. (Editor, Harrison Sun)
   117, 140
Brown, Judge C.O. 167, 168, 173,
   174
Brown, Wilson 96
Brownsville 51
Brozoska, Raymond 147
Brule 61
Bryan, Governor 163
Buckingham, L.A. 120
Buffalo Bill 110, 193
Buffington, John 258
Bulfert, Bob 96
Bulgaria 46

Burchfield, Thomas 37
Burke, SD 228
Burkey 42
Burkey, Clarence L. 36, 41
Burns, Henry 168
Bushmen of East Africa 46
Bushnell 230
Butler, Jim 223
Butte 81, 85, 145, 159, 180, 192,
   223, 252, 263
Butte, Montana 1908 81, 82, 83, 84

C

C.H. Unitt Hardware 237
C.S. Williams Photo, 1874 17
C.S. Williams Photo, 1898 18
C.S. Williams Photo, 1904 19
C.S. Williams Photo, 1905 20
Cain, Kenneth 246, 258
Calgary 91
Campbell 45
Campbell & Co. 190
Campbell, A. 287, 288
Campbell, Alex 13
Campbell, Alexander 13
Campbell, Mark 13, 287, 288
Campbell, Martha 3, 13, 28, 40, 44,
   287, 288
Canada 4, 91, 113, 168
Canton 226
Capone, Al 116, 117, 162
Captain Billy 3, 13, 14, 36
Cardenas, Manuel 182, 183, 185
Caressing 96
Carlson, Guy 229
Carroll, H.M. 290, 295
Carter, Edward 235
Carter, Gordon 217
Carter, Judge, E.F. 190
Case, Lyman 124, 142, 145, 289
Casper, WY 175, 216, 228, 251
Cedar County 14, 15, 16, 28, 40, 51
Celtic 46
Central Asia 46
Chadron 16, 51, 52, 57, 59, 110,
   113, 118, 127, 128, 155, 159,
   162, 167, 170, 171, 178, 183,
   184, 185, 186, 190, 192, 215,
   228, 241, 249, 255, 256, 263,
   264
Chadron Chronicle 179
Chandler, Buck 228
Charge Forced Entry, Charles M.
   Russell 305
Cheney, Merle 190
Cherokee, OK 217
Cherry Co. 192

Cheyenne 61, 109, 122, 123, 168,
   171, 192, 193, 229, 241, 254
Cheyenne Co. 57, 192
Chicago 75, 110, 114, 158, 168
"Chick" Coffee Ranch 122
Chief Horney Frog 62
Chief Smith 62
Childs, L.M. 121, 193, 198, 256
Childs, Mert 109
Chilson, Jess 246
Chinaman Jim 81
Chippewa 61
Chisholm Trail, Texas 203
Chrismen, Sam 190
Christian, J.H. 234
Churchill Downs 96
Circle Bar Ranch 3, 10, 53, 57, 58,
   59, 60, 128, 255, 256
Civil War 3, 6, 13, 14, 16, 51, 59,
   115, 202
Civil War pension 14, 16
Clark, Deputy State Sheriff 114,
   144, 158, 226, 242
Clark, E.E. 223, 225
Clark, Ed 103
Clark, Zada 238
Clarksville 14
Clearwater, NE 167
Cloi Beth 93
Coffee 267
Coffee Park 52
Coffee, Charles 192
Coffee, Chick 122
Coffee, Guy 124
Coffee, J.T. 237
Coffee, John T. 106
Coffee, Mary 245
Coffee, Rex 228
Coffee, Virginia 9
Coffeeville 67
Coleman, Mr. 162
Coleville, Dan 192
Colorado 123, 124, 162, 240, 246
Columbus 85
Commissioner Proceedings 176
Commissioner Proceedings, Partial
   List 176
Congress 28, 53, 115
Contrearas, Ereberit 182, 183, 185,
   186
Cook, Captain James H. 109, 171
Cook, Harold 228
Cook, James 110
Cortez, Francisco 174
Cotton, Clyde 229
Cottonwood 248, 249
Cottonwood Creek 192

Council Bluffs, IO 171, 172
County Commissioners 109, 118,
    251, 256
County Courthouse 118, 132
County of Cedar 28, 291, 293, 294
County of Winona 29, 289, 292
Courthouse, New, 1930 189
Courthouse, New, Officials 198
Courthouse, Original Sioux County,
    1888-1930 189
Courthouse, Original Sioux County,
    1929 140
Covington, Nebraska 110
Cowell, Bob 127
Cox, W.M. 163
Crawford 13, 36, 37, 39, 40, 41, 43,
    51, 57, 127, 147, 168, 174,
    175, 179, 180, 182, 183, 190,
    191, 222, 239, 240, 244, 246,
    248, 249, 250, 255, 262, 263,
    287, 288
Crawford County 13, 15, 37, 39,
    41, 43, 287, 288
Cree 61
Crites, E.D. 185, 190, 264
Crites, E.E. 220
Crites, Fred 127
Crook Co. 62
Crookston 217
Crowell, I.W. 238
Culbertson 237
Cullers, A.C. 248, 249
Cunfield, Ira 289
Cunningham, Fred 129, 134, 152,
    153, 154, 155, 156, 157, 158,
    161, 200
Cunningham, H. B. 145
Cunningham, Leon 247, 248
Cunningham, Mrs. Fred 157
Curly 228
Custard 287, 288
Custer 13, 60
Custer Co. 258
Custer's Defeat 17
Custiss 13
Cutler, Glenn 211, 244, 305, 306
Cutler, Jennie 305, 306
Cutlers 204, 206

D

Dakota Reservations 59
Dakota Territory 109, 110, 113,
    290, 295
Dalbey, Cal 99
Dallam, Carl 200
Daniells, Judge 62

Darling Girl 92, 98
Dather, Nathan 190
Davis, A.C. 120, 121, 136, 147, 190,
    193, 198, 234, 235, 236, 257
Davis, Dan 169
Davis, George 241
Davis, Harry L. 163
Davis, Horace M. 158
Davis, J.W. 105
Davis, M.F. 150
Davis, Special Agent 159
Davison, Fred 70
Davison, LaVerne 205
Dawes Co. 57, 162, 179, 185, 192,
    249, 265
Day, Pat 96
Deadwood 97
DeBano, William 149, 151, 232,
    234
DeBock, Leo 105
DeGehring, Albert 225
Dehaven, Richard 132
DeJarvis 178
DeKay, Leslie 205
Delahunty, Mary 192
Denver 182, 223, 238, 240, 241
Derby, Harry E. 120
Derrick, W.W. 74
Desormeaux, Kent 96
Destruction of Twenty Three Moon-
    shine Stills 140
Detroit 64
Devel Co. 57
Dewitt, Harold 223
Dick Daring 93, 94
Dieckman, John 103, 105, 114, 121
Diehl & Sons 179
Dilling, George 233, 234
Dineen ranch 138
Dinsmore, Wm. 295
Disposal of Illegal Booze 140
Distaff 96
Donald W. 4, 86, 87, 88, 89, 92, 93,
    94, 204
Douglas, Malcolm 251
Douglas, WY 62, 111, 114, 170
Dout, Clarence 207
Downey, Ethel 7, 128
Downey, Frank 99, 103, 225, 256
Downey, Mrs. Frank 225
Doyle, Mary 132
Dr. Coogle 98
Dr. Fager 97
Dryer Ranch 4, 65, 113
Dryer, Orville 65
Duck Creek Camp 1905 63

Duncan, J.B. 114, 137, 145, 146,
    150, 156, 160, 199, 215, 218,
    232, 234, 262
Dunlap, Chester 222, 223
Dunlap, J.H., 105
Dunlap, Jack 103, 161
Dunlap, Leo 225
Dunlap, Oliver 222, 223
Dunn, Henry 241
Dunn, Vernon 105
Dyer, L.L. (Lorne) 263, 264

E

E. G. Meier Garage 237
Earp, Wyatt 98
East Africa 45, 46
Edgemont 13, 51, 58, 59, 62, 64,
    91, 103, 110, 111, 128, 200,
    222, 225, 256, 267
Edgemont Pool-Wagon 63
Edgemont, S.D. 57
Edmond, OK 86
Edmonton 91
Ehrdardt, Earl 200
Ellicott, Earle 235
Elmore, MN 243
Emery, Elizabeth 121, 193, 198,
    236
Emery, Roy S. 234
Emmons & Brewster 192
Emmons, E.J. 218
Engebretsen, Alda 52
Engebretsen, Morris 52
England 46, 47
English 47
Eric Scherven Ranch 223
Eschenbrenner, Officer 250
Ethel 59
Ethel, Aunt 51
Ethiopia 45
Europe 46, 71
Evanston 243
Eversaul, Charles 190
Ewing, Jack 228

F

Fairfield Township 37, 41, 43
Fairfield Twp, PA 36
Fairmont, MN 242
Falkenberg, Louis 62
Fall River Co., S.D. 15, 57
Fall River County 10, 62, 65, 99,
    177, 225, 256
Fallowfield Twp. 36, 39
Family Group Sheet 32

Family Photograph-Granddad,
   Donald R., LaVerne, Ila Mae
   87
Fanning, Harry 220
Fanning, Wm. 220, 221
Farrington, Clarence 135, 137
Farwell, Liz 99
Farwell, R.I. (Liz) 99
Farwell, Ray 256
Fears, Milton 145
Federle, Ferd, Mrs. 217
Federle, John 144
Federle, Mary Lou 144
Federle, Max 151
Fellers, Rena 192
Fellows, General 41
Fiddler, W.E. 192
Fields, Charley 93
Fields, Clinton 258
Fields, Dee 258
Fisher, A.C. 220
Fisher, Allen G. 159, 184
Fisher, C.A. 185
Fisher, Charles 220, 249
Fitzgerald, Bill 99
Five Wives 69
Fjordbak 170
Florence, NE 169
Florida 36, 85, 98
Floyd 59
Floyd (Stuffy) 7, 111
Fonner Park 96
Forge, George 244
Forrester, Jacob 178
Forsling, O.E. 114, 131, 132, 144,
   149, 151, 156, 163
Fort Laramie 192
Fort Pierre 192
Fort Robinson 57, 71, 192, 262
Fox, Orval, O.L. 235, 236, 249
Foxwell, John 192
France 46
Franks, Ethel 248, 249
Frederick, Charles 172, 173
Freeman, Herman 230
Fremont 243
Fremont Elkhorn 51, 192
French 36, 46, 71, 205, 250
French Creek 36
Frenchman Creek 237
Fresno, CA 253
Fricke, Henry 199
Frost, MN 243
Frye, Howard E. 224
Ft. Donelson 14
Ft. Randall 51, 59

Ft. Robinson 181, 182, 183, 184,
   185, 186, 193
Fullin, Jas 151, 193
Furbeck, Russell 144

G

Galloway, Reuben, Mrs. 255
Garden County 57, 225
Garrotsburg 14
Gayman, Daily 138, 146
Gelston, E.D. & Co. 28
Geneva, PA 39
Gering, NE 137, 193, 229
Gerlach, Geo. L. 188
Gerlach, Jesse 188, 234
Germany 46
Gerry, E.B. 292
Getchell, John W. 200
Gilbert, B.C. 177
Gillette 246, 261
Gillette, Jerome 264
Glade, Albert T. 201
Glarchin, Eva 290
Glarehen, Bill 295
Glen 57, 110, 126, 168, 171, 183,
   191, 207, 216, 220, 246, 247,
   261, 262, 263, 264
Godenes, Modesto 160
Golden Glow 92
Golden, CO 215
Goldsmith, E.L. & Co. 193
Gompert 150
Gonsalez, Salvadore 160
Goshen Co., WY 57
Grade School, Harrison 196
Gragg, Forrest 230, 232, 233, 234
Graham, Dr. 192
Graham, Mrs. Catherine 192
Graham, Reverend Billy 14
Grand Island 95, 96, 103, 111, 180,
   223
Grand Junction, CO 202
Gray Bear 62
Great Falls 85, 94
Great Geneva Swamp 36
Great Plains Area 61
Great Sand Hills 192
Greeley 123, 124
Green, Earl 218
Greenwood 288
Greenwood Township 13, 36, 37,
   39, 40, 287
Grimm, Curt 126, 127
Grimm, Curtis 126, 141
Grimm, Ed 127
Grimm, Florence 126, 141

Griswold, E.H. 193
Grote & Bates 105
Grunke, E.C. 175
Guell, Manuel 145
Guilar, Fermin 135

H

Hahn, Everett 168
Hall, F.M. 121, 185, 234, 235, 236
Hall, Matt 147
Hallock 91
Hamaker, Dave 188
Hammond, Ted 247
Hancock, Ralph 228
Haney, Harry 141, 144, 177
Hanks, D.C. Jr. 190
Hanson, Charles M. 62
Hanson, V.L. 183, 236
Hanson, W.H. 167
Harkin, Gertrude 131
Harkins, Daniel 40
Harris 237, 238
Harris, Capt. Israel 41
Harris, Caroline M. 200
Harrison 51, 52, 57, 62, 75, 81, 85,
   98, 103, 111, 141, 146, 182,
   205, 223, 243
Harrison Chevrolet Dealer 113
Harrison House Hotel 114
Harrison Nebraska Museum 9
Harrison State Bank 188
Hartington, NE 256
Hartman, Rudie 253
Hassed, Major 182
Hassed, Sheriff 173, 219, 223, 225
Hastings, NE 229
Hat Creek 59, 172, 173, 192, 193,
   255
Havel, Lewis 158
Havlik, Charles 147, 190
Hay Springs 57, 61, 197
Hearkins 37
Heckert, Harry 114, 118
Hedges, Max 267
Helena 85, 94
Hemingford 57, 142, 180, 194, 195,
   248, 263
Henry, Charlie 179, 180, 193
Henry, Gayle 65, 269
Henry, Jacob 65
Henry, Jake 192
Henry, Josie 65
Henry, NE 224
Herren, Dick 205
Herrington, James 44
Herz, Crumby 99

Hiatt, Hugh 211, 305, 306
Hickey, I.D. 198
Hickey, L.D. 105
Hickey, Lewis H. 199
High School, Sioux County 196
Highway #20 71
Highway #71 64
Hildebrand, Ralph 204
Hilder, Albert 244
Hill 267, 241, 256, 266
Hill, George 190, 256
Hill, George W. 109, 118
Hilliard, Glen A. 122, 124
Hilliard, Glen, Arrest Warrant, 1927 125
Hitchcock, Co. 237
Hoevet, Ed 127, 130, 134
Hoffman, Henry 120, 234, 235, 236
Holt Co. 175, 192
Holt, L.C. 182
Homestead 57, 274, 276, 277, 279, 284
Homestead Application, 1892 54, 275
Homestead Proof Testimony of Claimant, 1896 55
Homestead Proof, Final Affidavit 282
Homestead Proof, Testimony of Witness 280, 281
Homestead, No. I, 1896 56
Hoos, Judy 9
Hootch, Judge 127
Hoover, Curtiss 158
Hopkins, Harry L. 73
Horn 249
Horney Frog, Chief 62
Hornsby 229
Horseshoe, ID 251
Hot Springs 58, 67, 81, 85, 92, 93, 99, 111, 128, 167, 178, 255
Hot Springs, S.D. 57
Hotel de Williams 137
Houk, Mrs. Wm. 236
Housh, O.D. 129
Houx, Rose 234
Howard, Marcie 241
Howard, Mark 52
Howard, Ross 99
Howell, C.R. 230
Hoy, D.A. 234
Hoyt, W. L. 124, 243
Hrasek, Frank 250
Hungary 46
Hunt, Dave 267
Hunter Company Derby 99
Huston, Mr. 183

Hutchinson, Earl 234
Hutchinson, Verne 253
Hutton, Harold 109, 110
Hyannis, NE 195, 258

I

Ila Mae 10, 115, 123, 149, 256
Illinois 9, 14, 16, 214
Illinois State Archives 14
Illinois State Archives, Civil War Service, 1862 20
Illinois Volunteers 14
Indian Agent 62
Indian Creek 53, 59, 65, 71, 78, 113, 128, 223, 225
Indian Creek (Woodruff Ranch) 57, 66
Indian Reservations in Dakota Territory 109
Indian Scare of 1890-91 3, 58, 61
Innovation 99
Iowa 240
Iran 46
Iraq 46
Ireland 67
Irish 47
Israel, Capt., Harris Co. 41
It'Sallinthechase 96

J

Jackson Twp. 290
Jackson, Stanley 141
Jaclyn, Carrie H. 290
James, George 190
Jamison, Charles C. 193
Jeffers, Orville 128, 129
Jefferson, President Thomas 41
Jeffrey, Harold 238, 239
Jeffreys, Harold 145
Jensen, Dorothy 240, 241
Jensen, Jens 240
Jensen, Marion 238, 240, 241, 242, 243
Jimerson, John 235
Johnson County 7
Johnson, Carl 230
Johnson, Pearl 67, 69
Johnson, Ralph 215, 217
Johnston, Ray 135, 137
Jolsten, B. 219, 223
Jones 214
Jones Law 115
Jones, Ed 64
Jones, Sheriff 159, 180
Jordan Ranch 131
Jordan, Allen 131, 132, 134, 136

Jordan, Blanche 131
Jordan, Bob 132
Jordan, Buck 219, 223
Jordan, Dan 5, 114, 131, 132, 133, 134, 136, 307, 308, 309
Jordan, Della 131
Jordan, Dick 131
Jordan, Dorothy 131
Jordan, Gerty 131, 174
Jordan, Grandma 131
Jordan, Mary 131
Jordan, Neil 234, 235, 236
Jordan, Rita 132
Jordan, Sadie 132
Jordan, Sarah 131
Jordan, Shirley 132
Joslyn, Cary H. 290

K

Kalamazoo, MI 240
Kansas 64, 67, 228
Kansas City 64, 228
Kaufman, Conrad 160
Kearney, NE 242
Keel, Morris 269
Kentucky 14, 85, 96, 97
Kentucky Derby 85
Kenya 45
Kephart, Harold 226
Kerl, Mr. 91
Keyapaha Co. 192
King, Joe 228
Kiowas 61
Kissack, W.T. 120
Klamath Falls, OR 228
Klein, Dan 192
Knight, Sherman 86, 91
Knori, George 217
Knori, Gus 158
Knori, Manie 161, 162, 214, 215, 220
Knori, Raleigh 177
Knori, Sammie 177
Koch 269
Koch Mercantile 216, 217
Koch Mercantile store 215
Koch, Bob 269
Koch, Gladys 269
Koch, Henry 163
Koch, Luther 269
Koch, Martin 194, 223
Konrath, Jacob 178
Konrath, John 178
Konrath, Joseph 121
Konraths 113
Kreman 264, 265

Kreman, Henry 192, 263
Kroening, Herman 56
Kubista, Joe 163

L

La Bonte Hotel 170
La Vonne 67
Labbo, William 230
Lacy 253
Lacy, F.J. 241
Lacy, Goodsin, Mrs. 255
Lacy, Jack 92, 204
Lacy, Jim 231
Lacy, John 174, 183
Lacy, John Jr. 257
Lacy, W.J. 200
Laettner, Denise 149
Laettner, Donald 149
Laettner, Ed 149
Laettner, Ila Mae 149
Laettner, John 149
Lake Erie 13
Lake Ranch 192, 247
Lamar, CO 223
Lamar, NE 168
LaMay, Joe 226, 227, 258
Lamb, H.C. 234
Lambert, Elvon 190
Lance Creek 62
Lansing, KS 228
Laramie Co., WY 57
Larsen, L.C. 220, 301

Last Big Win, 1937 90
Latimer, IA 240
Lau, Mr. 188
Lawler, Thelma 236, 244
Lawmaster, D.H. 151
Lawton, OK 215
Leathers, Edward 200
Lee, Bob 95
Lee, O.C. 242, 243
Leeling, Lawrence 139
Leeling, Wendell 131
LeLaCheur, Wm. 226
Lewis, J.C. 120, 193, 198, 234, 235
Lightning Creek 3, 60, 61, 62
Lincoln 85, 93, 96, 127, 153, 167,
    175, 190, 197, 203, 217, 219,
    221, 246, 247, 249, 261
Little Bighorn River, MT 17
Livestock Sales Document, 1934
    104
LO Pool-Wagon 63
Loafer 90
Lockard, Roy 180
Locker, Russel 220

Lockwood, Edmund 193
Lopes, G.W. 287, 288
Lorrain Cross 182
Lost Springs, WY 219
Loton, Ken 58
Lowe, Colonel W.W. 14
Lowry Hotel 207, 228
Lowry, Alex 169, 175
Lowsier 113
Lushbough, Mr. 197
Lusk 62, 71, 127, 132, 168, 172,
    173, 174, 200, 218, 219, 222,
    223, 225, 243, 248, 255, 256
Lusk Herald 62
Luth, V.C. 234
Lux, Carl 192
Lyon, Anna 193
Lyon, Anna A. 198
Lyon, E.B. 176
Lyon, E.D. 121, 193

M

Macumber, John A. 264
Mader family 58, 64
Mahlman, Ernest 190
Majors, Clarence 230
Mallet Bros. 192
Mandan, ND 244
Manitoba 91
Mannington, W. VA 215
Manville, WY 170
Map, Indian Creek (Woodruff
    Ranch) 66
Marking, John 181, 200, 216, 228,
    244, 250, 258
Marquis, Floyd 229
Marshall County, Iowa 202
Marsteller, V. 217, 241
Martin, John 105
Martinez, Joe 161
Mason, Fred 120, 226
Massachusetts 36, 41
Massengale, Harvey 219, 220, 221
Mathers, Sheriff Lee 62
Matthews Farm 138
Maude, S. 81, 82, 84
McCarron, Chris 96
McCarthy, Jerry 258
McClure, John 234
McCook, NE 237, 238
McCoy, James 215, 216, 217
McFaden, John 44
McGinley, A.J. 193
McGuire, Pete 215
McIntosh, Clay 190
McKim, Clyde M. 200
McKim, Mona Mae 200

McKnight, William L. 97
McKruzir, Hanson E. 293
McNeff, Deputy Sheriff 127
McNeil, Dr. 225
McQueen, Albert 147, 155, 156
Mead, Hal 185
Meade Township 41
Meadville 36
Meier, E. 216, 237, 253
Meiers, Ed 113, 253
Meiers, Pete 132
Melgate, Henry 105
Mendoza, Ed 229, 230
Meng, George 234
Merriman, NE 197
Mesamed, Meark 28
Messing, John 56, 280
Methodist Cemetery, Geneva, PA
    39
Meyer, E. 248, 249, 263
Meyer, E.L. 123, 126, 134, 136,
    159, 167, 168, 177, 190, 193,
    215, 217, 218, 220, 221, 228,
    229, 246, 247, 249
Meyer, F.W. 190
Meyer, George 135, 137
Meyer, Judge 223, 262, 264, 265
Mickaelsen, Howard 177
Mickaelsen, Richard 177
Middle East 46
Middleton, Doc 5, 10, 109, 110,
    111, 112
Milburn, Guy 200
Miller, Sheriff 62
Minatare 85, 98
Minnesota 13, 14, 16, 28, 29, 51,
    59, 61, 73, 242, 256, 287, 288,
    289, 292
Minnick, E.B. 142, 145
Minter, W.B. 173
Miss Evalyn (Eva) Moore 59
Mississippi 219
Missoula, MT 251
Missouri 51, 59, 64, 67, 192, 226
Missouri River 51
Missouri Valley 51, 192
Mitchell 85, 93, 137, 150, 155, 201,
    216, 217, 240, 241, 246, 256
Mitchell, E.C. 256
Mitchell, Jack 216
Mitchell, NE 201
Mockenhaupt, Henry 158
Mockenhaupt, M.H. 231
Monjarez, Jesus 200
Monroe Canyon 177
Montana 81, 85, 94, 131
Montgomery, Art 225

Montrose 144, 256
Moody, Albert 239, 242
Moody, Wm., Sheriff 162
Moore, Dora 59
Moore, Evalyn (Eva) 59
Moore, Lawrence 239
Moran, Bugs 116
Moreno, Justo 95
Morison Lumber Company 236
Morison, Joe 236
Morrill Co. 57, 169
Morrill, NE 114, 122, 138, 246
Morris, Harry 234, 235, 236, 257
Morris, Joe 192
Morris, Sadie 192
Morrison Lumber Co. 204
Mortensen 258
Mothersead & York 190
Mounts, Rick 9, 116, 207
Moxley 126
Mullenix, Grady 149
Mullenix, Stephanie 149
Mumby, County Attorney 216, 221
Mumby, Keith 202
Mumby, W.E. 113, 129, 130, 134,
    147, 155, 160, 170, 174, 180,
    181, 185, 193, 199, 202, 214,
    217, 220, 234, 235, 236, 237,
    241, 246, 247, 249, 254, 263,
    264, 321

Mumby, W.E., (County Attorney)
    140, 198, 213, 232
Murphy, Dr. 172

N

Nakatani, Corey 96
Nash, C.A. 145, 149
National Archives 14, 16
National Geographic Society 45
National Services Administration
    14
Nebraska Penitentiary 153
Nerud, John 4, 85, 97, 98
New York 85, 96, 98
Newcastle 61, 62, 93, 142, 243
Newell, Jess 155, 236
Newman, Art 178
Newman, William L. 114
Nicholson, Wm. S. 200
Niobrara County 57, 61, 65
Nisland, ND 182
No Conflict-Homestead Certificate
    1896 283
Node 65, 71
Node, P.O. 57
Nolan, Walt 177

Norfolk, NE 178, 217, 227, 255
Norman, Mr. 174
North Dakota 126
North Platte, NE 197
Northeastern Nebraska 14
Northern Europe 46
Northfield, MN 240
Northwestern Railway Co. 184
Norton, KS 141

O

O- Ranch 53
O'Brien, S.L. 127
O'Connell, Emma 134
O'Connell, Michael J. 134
O'Neil, NE 171
O1O Ranch 192
Odd Fellows Building 146
Oelrich, SD 177
Officer 96
Ogallala 61
Okfuskee Co., OK 205
Oklahoma 9, 96, 205, 217
Omaha 74, 77, 85, 86, 91, 93, 94,
    95, 96, 97, 103, 114, 127, 169,
    170, 175, 177, 183, 184, 185,
    186, 236, 299, 300
Omaha City Park 85
Open Range Roundup, Ardmore 63
Orella, NE 57, 159, 162, 169, 174
Osback, Axel 194
Oshkosh, NE 159
Ostrander, John 56
Overland Trail 109
Oxford Hotel 215, 218

P

Pace, L.P. 149
Paducah 14
Palisade, CO 256
Paris, KY 97
Parker, AZ 256
Parley, John 258
Parmely, Arthur J. 200
Parmely, Sylvia M. 200
Parsons, Frank 141, 179, 180, 190
Parsons, John 179, 180
Patterson, Mike 96
Pauley, John 246
Paulson, Ernest 222
Pedersen, E.M. 223
Pedley, Norris 241
Penitentiary, State 203
Pennington, W.M. 193
Pennsylvania 13, 16, 36, 37, 41, 43,
    287, 288

Perkins 199
Petty, Sheriff 225
Pfeister, Dick 256
Pfost, J.F. 193
Phipps, Rodney 132
Phoenix 67, 254
Pholen, Red 267
Pierre, SD 177
Pine Ridge 10, 51, 62
Pine Ridge Indian Reservation 10,
    62
Pipestone, MN 240
Plumb, Henry 225
Pontius, E.F. 120, 200
Porter 264
Porter, Bob 177
Porter, Forest 143
Porter, J.E. 180, 262
Powers, Robert 43, 44
Preston, Billy 126
Price, Donald 251, 253, 254
Price, Ferd 237, 238
Price, Two-Gun 252
Priest, Dr. 181, 185
Priest, Dr. W.H. 131
Prince, Attorney 180
Prohibition Liquor Laws 115, 116,
    117
Publication, Proof of Homestead
    1896 278
Pullen, Ernest 103
Pullen, Fred 190

Q

Quinn, Agnes 67, 70
Quintard, Rolland 179

R

Rambo, Patricia 67
Ramsey, George W. 291, 293, 294
Ramsey, Lizzie E. 294
Rapid City, SD 85, 86, 92, 97, 167,
    182
Rautz, William 247
Rawlins 249
Raymond, L.L. 126, 138, 146,155
Reckling, Dr. 255
Red Cloud 192, 238
Red Willow Co. 237
Reed, F.J. 150
Regina 91
Remington Park 96
Republican Nominee, Sheriff, 1926
    119
Republican Nominee, Sheriff, 1930
    148

331

Resolution 256
Resolution, May 16, 1938 257
Revolutionary War 36, 41
Revolver Holster, 1900 112
Rich, C.M. 232, 234, 236
Richardson, Tom 225
Richardson, Wiley 169, 175, 188, 194
Richer, Wm. T. 99
Ridenour, Sheriff 225
Riggins 247
Riley, Howard 180
Riley, James 109
Riley, Raymond 105
Ring, Lee 105
Rising, Marvin 261, 263, 264, 265
Ritchie, Ernest 232
Riverton, WY 249
Robertson, Omer 184, 185
Robinson 224
Robinson, George 225
Robinson, J.S. 223
Rochelle, J.B. 243
Rock Co. 192
Rock Springs 254
Rockefeller, John D. Jr. 159
Rockport, MO 226
Rogers, James 167
Romania 46
Root, Charles 217, 218
Rosebud Reservation 61
Roseville 14
Ross, Norman 244
Rowland, W.F. 228
Royal Highlanders 200
Ruffing, Mike 247
Rushville 57, 126
Russell Ranch 8
Russell, Belle 202
Russell, C.M. 10
Russell, Charles M. 8, 10, 169, 202, 203, 204, 206, 207, 252, 262, 268, 297, 299, 300, 301,302, 306, 307, 308, 309, 310, 311, 312, 313, 315, 316, 317, 318, 319, 320, 321, 322
Russell, Charles M., Arrest No. 1-1931 208, 209
Russell, Charles M., Arrest No. 2-1932 210
Russell, Charles M., Complaint-Forced Entry 211
Russell, Charles M., Menacing Threats 212
Russell, Charles M., Peace Bond 213
Russell, Frank 202

Russell, Frank S. 213, 307, 308, 309, 310
Russell, Harvey Jr. 202
Russell, Mae 202
Rustling Silk, 1908 81, 82, 83

S

Sage, Rosa 192, 201
Salt Lake City 254
Sandoz, G.E. 171
Sankey, Happy 267
Santa Anita Derby 85
Saratoga 29, 289, 292
Saskatchewan 91
Saskatoon 91
Satterle, Ed 193
Schaefer, Nick 105
Schamahorn, J.A. 193
Scherven, Erik 221, 222, 223
Schnell, George 215
Schneringer, Raymond 261, 263, 264, 265
Schnurr & Mumby 130
Schnurr, A.L. 105, 121, 126, 128, 129, 130, 134, 136, 142, 147, 162, 168, 170, 180, 181, 182, 183, 184, 185, 190, 193, 195, 198, 256
Schnurr, Al, County prosecutor 113
Schnurr, Clarence 113
Schnurr, Ralph 130
Schraeder, George 247
Schultz, William 169, 175
Schutt, Lawrence 180
Scotch 47
Scotland 45
Scott, Albert 226
Scottsbluff 52, 137, 138, 146, 150, 154, 155, 156, 157, 190, 193, 223, 224, 229, 230, 240, 241, 243, 246, 263, 265
Scroggins, Jos L. 295
Scroll 93
Seaman 114
Seaman, S.R. 118
Seely, Sarah 13, 36, 39
Seley, S.H. 287, 288
Senior Citizens Center 132
Serres Brothers 192
Serres, Jimmy 65
Shafer, George 193
Shalina 91
Sheep Creek 61, 139
Shepherd Cattle Company 105
Sheridan Co. 57, 192
Sherrill, Lou 161, 246

Shinbur, Elver 234, 235
Short, Leroy 129
Sid Jr. 7, 58, 205
Sidney 59
Sidney F. 82
Sidney, NE 109, 128
Sidney-Black Hills Trail 109
Siebken, Mr. 103
Simend, Col. Benjamin 41
Sine, L.C. 214
Sioux 58, 61, 62
Sioux City 144
Sioux Co., NE 15, 57
Sioux County Fair & Rodeo 85
Sioux County Historical Society 9, 193
Sioux County Sheriff 9, 91, 114, 116, 117, 268
Sioux Falls, SD 167, 242
Sioux Indians 10, 109
Sioux War of 1862 13
Six Shooter 3, 60
Six Shooter, 44-40 Caliber 203
Skaggs 264
Skavdahl, Harold 258
Skavdahl, Oscar 236
Slattery, Bill 207
Slattery, Daniel 162, 169, 220
Slattery, Don 207
Slattery, Marie 220
Slingerland, Charles 193
Sloan, Elizabeth 200
Sloan, Enos 200
Smith, Bela 178
Smith, James 230
Smith, Red 97
Smith, Wilbur 105
Smithland 28
Snell, Conrad 163
South Dakota 3, 4, 10, 13, 16, 51, 53, 58, 59, 61, 62, 64, 65, 67, 73, 85, 86, 91, 97, 99, 103, 128, 131, 167, 177, 197, 225, 240, 255, 256, 263, 267, 268
South Dakota (Dryer) Ranch 57
Sowbelly Canyon 52, 189
Sowbelly Creek 52, 248
Spain 96
Spanish American War 149
Spearfish, SD 251
Spokane, WA 251
Spoon Buttes 122
Spring Hill 36
Spring Round Up, 1905 63
Springfield 59, 67, 242
St. Charles, MN 13, 15, 17, 256
Stafford, Gloria 114

Standard Oil Company 219
Standard Service Station 132, 205
Stanek, Joe 114, 139, 143, 144, 146, 149, 178, 181, 183, 185, 258
Stanek, Joe, Deputy Sheriff 140, 143, 156, 158, 175, 193, 198
State Department of Trade & Commerce 188
State Deputy Sheriff Ed Clark 114
State Fair Park 96
Staudenmaier, Alois 203
Staudenmaier, Linda 203
Staudenmier, Charlie 203
Steele, Andrew Thomas 200
Steele, Ila Mae 200
Stewart, Short 92
Stock Growers National Bank 122, 123
Stockgrowers Association 159
Stoneking, Earl 248, 249, 258
Stoop, Charlie 113
Story Brothers 105
Story, George 243
Story, Oscar 222
Stover, Glen 159
Strappy 93
Sturdivant ranch 122
Sturdivant, Adaline, Addie, Addy (Rogers) 7, 122, 123, 124, 131
Sturdivant, Charles 123, 131
Sturdivant, Frank 123, 131
Sturdivant, J.H. 61
Sturdivant, Joseph H. 61, 122, 200, 203
Sturdivant, LaVerne 68, 70, 123, 124, 131
Sturdivant, LaVerne L. 122
Sumartore 267
Summit 51, 132, 192
Summit Theatre 132
Susie Mae 92
Sutton, John, Jr. 38
Swanson, George 190
Swanson, Peter 191
Sweet Memorium 93
Sweetheart 92, 98
Sweezey, Henry 204, 207, 208, 299, 300
Swinbank, J. C., County Agent 74, 75

T

Take Me Out 96
Tangen, John 193

Tanner & Davis 169, 175
Tanzania 45
Tayler, Johnathan 37
Taylor, Charles 235
Taylor, John 38
Telander, Charles 150
Tennessee 14
Tetse Creek 52, 189
Tewell, James 235
Tewell, Judge 126
Texas 95, 109, 139, 203
Thatcher, Joseph 38
Thermopolis, WY 175
Thomas 265
Thomas, B.F. 51, 59, 193
Thomas, B.F. and Sarah (Hamlin) 67
Thomas, C.E. 234
Thomas, Lily 69
Thomas, Lily 51, 59, 67, 193
Thomas, Lloyd 263
Thomas, Minnie 51
Thomas, Sam 105
Thompson, Carl 230
Thompson, H.H. 238
Toft, Roy 244
Torrington 122, 124, 139, 150, 157, 167, 194, 218, 223
Townsend, Clint 200
Transcript, Certificate of 311, 312
Transcript, Complaint-Forced Entry 306
Treat, John 43, 44
Trenton 237
Tristate Map, Sid Williams Country 57
Trophy 90
Troy 29, 289, 292
Tucker, John 172
Turkey 46

U

Umphenour, Charles 193
Union Stock Yards, Omaha 74, 77
United States 13, 41, 61, 71, 75, 85, 98, 115, 154, 162, 183, 184, 185
Unitt Hardware 237
Unitt, P.H. 242
University of Nebraska 130
Unzueta, Francisco 181, 182, 183, 184, 185, 186
Utah 51

V

Valentine 61, 183, 217, 218

Van Cleef, Harvey 129, 134, 138, 145, 151
Van Tassell, WY 57, 103, 170, 238
Vaughan, Mrs. 214
Vaughan, William 214
Velazquez, Jorge 96
Verity, C.E. 193
Vernon, Smokey 217
Viele Drug Store 163
Viele, F.D. 241
Vikings 46
Vincent, Charles 249, 250
Vivian, Penny 71, 103
Volstead Act 115

W

W.J. Lacy & Son Garage 200
Wagner, Albert 151, 159
Wagner, Marion 151, 159
Wagner, Ray 151, 159, 162
Wales 45, 46
Walker, W. 163, 234
Wallace, Bob 5, 10, 113
Wallace, Carroll 113
Wallace, Harold 226
Wallace, Jerald 113
Wallace, M.R. 258
Wallace, Merritt 113
Wallace, Quentin 113
Wallace, Robert 113
Waln, Kenny 229
Walter Johnson 81
Wamper Place 222
Wancapona, NE 28
Warbonnet Creek 192, 193
Warbonnet Ranch 192, 193
Warneke Ranch 201
Warren Co., IL 14, 15
Warren, S.W. 215
Warren, Walt 93
Washington 16, 28, 36, 41, 44, 53, 265
Washington, D.C. 16, 28
Washington, George 41, 44
Washington, President George 41
Wasserburger 267
Wasserburger, Barbara 131
Wasserburger, C.R. 216
Wasserburger, Chris 256
Wasserburger, George 205, 206
Wasserburger, Harry 144, 226
Wasserburger, Jacob 234, 235, 257
Wasserburger, Mary Lou 144
Wasserburger, Nillie 144
Watford City, ND 244
Wathen, Henry 230

Watts, John 200
Waverly 14
Webberville Property, Michigan 4, 64
Webberville, Michigan 64
Weber, Anna 168, 171, 207
Webster Co. 238
Wehn, W. 277, 279
Welch 45, 47
Wellington RR 220
Wells, Mrs. C.L. 182, 183
Wertz, O.H. 176
Western Niobrara County 61
Westler, Van 176
Westler, Van W. 176, 213
Westler, Wilbur M. 202
Weston County 62
Westward Migration Route-Our Williams Family 15
Wheatland, WY 225
White Eagle Service Station 147, 197
White Eagle Station 147, 214
White River 192, 202, 206, 214
Whiteaker, Mrs. E.E. 176, 239
Whitney & Murphy 192
Wickersham, Doris 9
Wickersham, George 179, 180, 250
Wiedenfeldt, Peter 53, 56, 281
Wilhermsdorfer, County Judge 126, 127, 128, 129, 131, 133, 134, 137, 138, 141, 142, 144, 145, 146, 149, 150, 154, 156, 159, 167, 168, 174, 175, 177, 179, 184, 190, 193, 215, 217, 223, 247, 248, 256, 262, 299, 300, 301, 315, 316, 317, 318, 319, 320, 321, 322
Wilhermsdorfer, J.H. 198
Wilkenson, Dennis 171
Wilkins, Edwin 193, 222, 223
William the Conquerer 46, 47
William, Porter 387
Williams & Dunlap 105
Williams "Captain Billy" 13
Williams Cemetery 36
Williams, Abraham 41
Williams, Alex 28
Williams, Alexander 32, 58
Williams, Arthur 40, 44
Williams, Bern 53, 64, 110
Williams, Bernie 10, 13, 16, 128
Williams, Billy 36, 95
Williams, C. Sid, Jr. 62
Williams, C.P. 3, 13, 110
Williams, Captain Chauncey 13
Williams, Charles S. III 7

Williams, Charles Sidney, Jr. 61, 67
Williams, Chauncey 13, 28, 32
Williams, Darius 40, 44
Williams, Dean 36, 42, 71, 95, 111, 113, 127
Williams, Don 9
Williams, Don D. 7
Williams, Donald R. 61
Williams, Elizabeth 32
Williams, Ethel 67, 69
Williams, Eva 13, 110, 111
Williams, Florence 67
Williams, Floyd (Stuffy) 7, 67, 71, 95, 103, 111, 113, 127, 128, 256
Williams, Frank 28
Williams, Franklin 32
Williams, George Washington 40, 44
Williams, Grandmother 16, 59
Williams, Hannah 39
Williams, Harrison 32
Williams, Harry 5, 28, 67, 110, 111
Williams, Harry (?) 32, 112
Williams, Ila Mae 10, 115, 123, 149, 256
Williams, J. Effie 32
Williams, James F. 39, 44
Williams, Jeff 7
Williams, John 39, 44
Williams, John Penn 39
Williams, Joseph 40, 44
Williams, Judy 7
Williams, LaVerne (Sturdivant) 70, 256
Williams, LaVonne 67, 70
Williams, Lewis 14, 16, 28, 29, 32, 59, 120, 193, 234, 235, 287, 288, 289
Williams, Lewis, Inventory of Effects, 1865 27
Williams, Lewis, Record of Death & Interment, 1865 26
Williams, Lily (Thomas) 69
Williams, Linda 67
Williams, Lizzie 28
Williams, Lydia 40, 44
Williams, Mark 28
Williams, Martha 6, 28, 29, 67, 110, 285, 287, 288, 289, 290, 291, 292, 293, 294, 295
Williams, Martha (Campbell) 33, 34
Williams, Martha V. 59, 128
Williams, Martha, Application for Reimbursement, 1923 30, 31
Williams, Mary 32

Williams, Miles 32
Williams, Mrs. 225
Williams, Nellie 16, 32, 51, 121
Williams, O.B. 32, 256
Williams, O.B. (Bern) 51
Williams, Oliver Emmett 14
Williams, P.C. 28
Williams, Patricia 67
Williams, Pearl 64
Williams, Pearl (Johnson) 69
Williams, Perry 13, 14, 16, 29, 36, 44, 51, 59, 287, 288, 289, 291, 292, 293, 294
Williams, Perry C. 29, 36, 40, 289, 291, 292, 293, 294
Williams, Perry, Civil War Service Record 22, 23, 24, 25
Williams, Peter 40, 44
Williams, Rob 4, 95, 96
Williams, Robert 3, 36, 38, 39, 41, 42, 43, 44
Williams, Robert "Robbie" 95
Williams, Royal 256
Williams, Russell 28, 32, 35, 51, 58, 67, 189, 256
Williams, Samuel 39
Williams, Sarah 37, 39, 40, 44
Williams, Seabra 36, 41, 43, 44
Williams, Sheila 96
Williams, Sid Jr. 7, 53, 58, 62, 71, 81, 85, 111, 113, 127, 128, 129, 131, 132, 133, 138, 146, 174, 179, 181, 205, 236, 256, 261
Williams, Sidney Jr. 67, 103, 113, 115, 132, 257
Williams, Steve 7
Williams, William 13, 36, 37, 38, 39, 43, 44
Williams, Wm. Jr. 38
Williamstown, MA 15, 36, 41
Wilson, A.D. 234
Wilson, Cecil 220, 221
Wilson, John L. 234
Wilson, Press L. 234, 235
Winners Circle 88
Winnipeg 91
Winona County 29, 289
Wisconsin 10, 73, 99
Witt, Art 261
Witt, Dick 159, 202, 207, 261, 262, 263, 264, 265
Witt, Elaine 204
Witt, Henrietta 261
Witt, L.A. 105
Wolcoth 242, 243
Womens Christian Temperance Union 115

Wood, J.W. 171
Wood, Mr. 188
Woodrough, Federal Judge 155,
    183, 184, 185
Woodruff 4, 16, 64, 65, 67, 71, 113,
    143, 269
Woodruff Ranch 4, 64, 65, 67, 71
Woodruff, Carrie 65
Woodruff, W.B., Mrs. 176
Woodruff, Walt, Place 143
Woodruff, Walter 65
Woods, Jay 263
Worland, WY 223
World War I 71, 72

World War II 265
Worley, O. N. 167
Worthington, MN 242
Wounded Knee 58, 59, 60, 61, 110
Wright, George 159
Wyant, Wilton 171, 172
Wynot 14, 40
Wyoming 3, 4, 7, 53, 61, 62, 65, 71,
    78, 97, 109, 111, 122, 137,
    145, 150, 162, 167, 168, 170,
    175, 188, 191, 197, 219, 222,
    223, 225, 226, 241, 243, 249,
    250, 253, 268
Wyoming Ranch 57, 65

Y

Yankton 59
Ybarra, Mike 177
Yohe, Guy 207
York, W.A. 185
Yxta, Joe 229, 230

Z

Zigler, J.C. 291
Zimmerman, Charles 5, 172, 173
Zimmerman, Irvin 172, 185
Zimmerman, John 85
Zimmerman, W.H. 192

BIBLIOGRAPHY

The Harrison Sun Newspaper archives helped immensely in the writing of this book. The remaining list of books, magazines and newspapers were only of marginal benefit. However, they did improve my perspective of the post Civil War – pre-World War II period; the time of your grandfather's life.

BOOKS

Andrist, Ralph K. – The Long Death, The Last Days of the Plains Indians; Collier Books; Collier Macmillan Publishers; London.

Bronson, Edgar Beecher – Cowboy Life in the Western Plains: The Reminiscences of a Ranchman; University of Nebraska Press; 1962.

Cook, Harold J. – Tales of the 04 Ranch, 1887-1909; University of Nebraska Press; Lincoln.

Cook, James H. – Fifty Years on the Old Frontier, 1923; Yale University Press.

Cook, James H. – Fifty Years on the Old Frontier, 1957; University of Oklahoma Press.

Granges, Robert T., Jr. – Fort Robinson: Outpost on the Plains, 1958; Nebraska History; Volume 39, Number 3.

Harrison Ladies Community Club, a Compilation-Sioux County Memoirs of Its Pioneers, 1967; Printed by the Harrison Sun News; Harrison, Nebraska.

Mattes, Merrill J. – Scottsbluff National Monument, National Park Service Historical Handbook #28, 1958; For sale U.S. Government Printing Office, Washington, D.C., 20402

Roberts, R.J. – The History of Agate Springs; Nebraska State Historical Society; Reprint from Nebraska History; Volume 47, Number 3; September, 1966.

Sanders, Peggy – Images of America, Fall River County and Hot Springs-Views From the Past, 1881-1955; Arcadia Publishing, an Imprint of Tempus Publishing Inc.; Chicago, Illinois.

Sioux County History Book Committee – A Compilation Sioux County History, First 100 Years, 1886-1986; Curtis Media Corporation; 1986.

Spring, Agnes Wright – The Cheyenne and Black Hills Stage and Express Routes; University of Nebraska Press; Lincoln.

The Historical Committee of the Robbers Roost Historical Society – Pioneering on the Cheyenne River; The Lusk Herald; Lusk, Wyoming, 1947 and 1956.

MAGAZINES

Bartels, Alan J. – "On the Hunt for Doc Middleton"; Nebraska Life; May/June 2011; Nebraska Life Publishing; Norfolk, Nebraska.

Heller, Bill – "Maintaining a Sharp Edge"; Thoroughbred Times; The Weekly Newsmagazine of Thoroughbred Racing; January 12, 2002; Published at Irvine, California.

NEWSPAPERS

Ardmore Record; Ardmore, South Dakota; In private files.

Crawford Clipper; Crawford, Nebraska.

Dawes County Journal; Chadron, Nebraska.

Edgemont Tribune; Edgemont, South Dakota.

Lusk Herald; Lusk, Wyoming.

Omaha Daily Herald; Omaha, Nebraska.